European Family Law Volume III

European Family Law Volume III

Family Law in a European Perspective

Edited by

Jens M. Scherpe

University Senior Lecturer, University of Cambridge, and Fellow of Gonville and Caius College, Cambridge, UK

Cheltenham, UK • Northampton, MA, USA

Published by
Edward Elgar Publishing Limited
The Lypiatts
15 Lansdown Road
Cheltenham
Glos GL50 2JA
UK

Edward Elgar Publishing, Inc.
William Pratt House
9 Dewey Court
Northampton
Massachusetts 01060
USA

A catalogue record for this book
is available from the British Library

Library of Congress Control Number: 2015943242

This book is available electronically in the **Elgar**online
Law subject collection
DOI 10.4337/9781785363054

ISBN 978 1 78536 304 7 (cased)
ISBN 978 1 78536 298 9 (4 volume set)
ISBN 978 1 78536 305 4 (eBook)

Typeset by Columns Design XML Ltd, Reading

Printed and bound in Great Britain by Clays Ltd, St Ives plc

Contents

Contributors

Masha Antokolskaia, University of Amsterdam, The Netherlands

Paul Beaumont, University of Aberdeen, Scotland, United Kingdom

Ian Curry-Sumner, Voorts Legal Services, Dordrecht, The Netherlands

Claire Fenton-Glynn, University of Cambridge, England, United Kingdom

Josep Ferrer-Riba, Universitat Pompeu Fabra, Barcelona, Catalonia, Spain

Rob George, University College London, England, United Kingdom

Jonathan Herring, University of Oxford, England, United Kingdom

Joanna Miles, University of Cambridge, England, United Kingdom

Jens M. Scherpe, University of Cambridge, England, United Kingdom

Caroline Sörgjerd, Familjens jurist, Stockholm, Sweden

Katarina Trimmings, University of Aberdeen, Scotland, United Kingdom

Preface and acknowledgements

This book set on European Family Law was a massive undertaking, with 35 chapters by 37 contributors and was fraught with many practical difficulties, including joyful family events and also differing interpretations of the term 'final deadline'. Therefore it took much longer than expected, and I am very, very grateful to the publisher (and especially the Commissioning Editor John-Paul McDonald and Deputy Managing Editor Jane Bayliss as well as Sally Philip and Gillian Pickering) and the contributors for their patience and understanding. This applies especially to those colleagues who contributed the national reports in Volume II of the series and who therefore not only had to put up with my rigid ideas regarding the basic structure of horizontal, vertical and individual family law and the equally rigid ideas about the contents of these reports, but in many cases also had to update their chapters (even several times) when the finalisation of the book took longer than expected.

I would like to thank the Newton Trust for the support in the form of a Small Research Grant, which enabled me to get some editorial assistance. This was undertaken by Charlotte Leslie, and I am very grateful for her support as well, and also to Rosie Šnajdr and Elizabeth Aitken who helped securing the grant in the first place and with administering it.

Many people have contributed to this book in its various stages, particularly in the beginning when discussing its structure with me, which jurisdictions and topics to pick and which colleagues to approach to write them; and towards the end, with additional editorial assistance and when discussing my contributions and especially Volume IV with me. So I would like to thank (in no particular order) Anne Röthel, Claire Nielsen, Joanna Miles, Albertina Albors-Llorens, Claire Fenton-Glynn, Ruth Lamont, Brian Sloan, Walter Pintens, Joshua Baker and Peter Dunne – this book set would not be the same without you and your support, and perhaps it would not exist at all.

Finally, I would like to thank my nuclear (!) family: First, my two daughters, Helma and Lilo, who were both born during the period in which this book set was written and thus did not really contribute to the book set apart from being most delightful distractions, but undoubtedly saw a little less of me than they could have because of it – please do not hold this against me when you are old enough to do so, and no, it certainly does not entitle you to a pony. And second, my wonderful wife, Ann-Christin, who very often had bear the brunt of my frustration with the lack of progress and of course with my foul moods when my own writing did not come together as I had hoped – you could have a pony if you really wanted one (although I would of course try to talk you out of it), but I am very grateful that you do not. Thank you so much for everything.

Jens M. Scherpe, St. Nicholas' Day 2015.

European family law – Introduction to the book set

Jens M. Scherpe

The central aim of this book set is to inform the reader about the emerging European family law. As this area is in a surprising state of flux, some of the details provided might be out of date by the time the books are read. But since the aim of the set is not to provide detailed knowledge but rather to focus on underlying principles and highlight certain developments, in the view of the authors this does not detract from its value. This set is intended to serve as a resource for anyone interested in family law in general and in European family law in particular, and does not purport to provide comprehensive answers to all the complex questions raised in this area of law. In many ways, therefore, it is meant to provide a starting point for research, which is indeed why all of the contributions not only contain a wealth of references in the footnotes but also a short list of suggested further reading in the respective topic at the end.

In many ways, putting together a book set on European family law was a daunting task. Not only is the definition of what a 'family' is increasingly undergoing changes in many jurisdictions, even what should be considered 'family *law*' is highly debated. If one adds 'European' into that mix, yet more questions arise. What is 'European' in this context? Does this comprise the entire continent, that is, should it go beyond the Member States of the European Union? To that the answer, at least for the purposes of this book set, is a clear 'yes'. As readers will have noted, the book set is called 'European Family Law' rather than 'European Union Family Law', and thus its scope extends beyond the borders of the European Union, and national reports on Russia, Switzerland and Turkey have been included in Volume II.

Many of my colleagues, particularly those involved in the teaching and research of European Union law, have suggested to me that this project was a complete absurdity, as there was no such thing as a 'European family law'. I was told that as there was no body, no institution that actually had the power, legislative or otherwise, to create (or worse, impose) a 'European family law', there could be no such thing. In addition, I was told by several colleagues on many occasions that family law is and should remain a purely national matter, as it is too deeply rooted in the social and legal traditions of the respective jurisdictions and is not susceptible at all to harmonisation or unification – or even meaningful comparison. While these views of course made a point (at least to some extent), I nevertheless disagreed. But perhaps the disagreement arose only from a misunderstanding of what 'European family law' actually is. If my colleagues were referring to a comprehensive European Family Law Code, then of course they were right. But the absence of such a code does not mean that there is presently no European family law at all. On the contrary, as this book set shows, there is without any doubt an emerging European family law, comprising principles shared across jurisdictions, and there are institutions and organisations shaping this law. This European family law is not comprehensive; it is selective, covering some areas but not others – but it is certainly there and it continues to grow. And it is this European family law that this book set is about.

The **first volume** looks at the 'impact of institutions and organisations' on the emerging European family law and thus at what in Volume IV will be termed 'institutional European family law'. First and foremost, these institutions are the *European Union* and the *Court of Justice of the European Union* (Chapter 1 by Geert De Baere and Kathleen Gutman) and the *European Court of Human Rights* (Chapter 2 by Dagmar Coester-Waltjen). While the European Union has no direct competence to regulate national family laws, many legal acts of the European Union and decisions of the Court of Justice of the European Union establish 'minimum standards' for Member States in the area of their family law. The same is true of the growing body of case law of the European Court of Human Rights. The decisions of this court are of course only binding on the parties before it, but they nevertheless have a massive impact on all Contracting States, thus establishing minimum standards for often very specific areas of family law. In an increasingly 'globalised' world where families move between countries more and more, there is also increasing pressure on private international law, not only at the national level but also upon the *private international law instruments* of the *European Union* (Chapter 7 by Dieter Martiny) and the *Hague Conference* (Chapter 5 by Hannah Baker and Maja Groff). The impact of many such instruments, not only on the private international laws of the respective states but also on substantive family law, cannot be underestimated. The same undoubtedly is true of the work of the *Council of Europe* (Chapter 3 by Nigel Lowe) and the *International Commission on*

Civil Status (Chapter 4 by Walter Pintens). The academic initiative of the *Commission on European Family Law (CEFL)* which, based on in-depth comparative studies, is drafting 'Principles of European Family Law', is also becoming influential (Chapter 6 by Katharina Boele-Woelki) and these Principles are increasingly taken into account when law reform is debated. Finally, the Christian faith is often seen as a 'basis' or at least a unifying factor of Europe and thus potentially, by extension, for European family law. Hence the impact of *religion* (even though, strictly speaking, religion is neither an institution nor an organisation) is considered in Volume 1 as well.

As mentioned at the beginning of this introduction, there is considerable debate on what 'family' or 'family law' is. That is why the overarching theme for the national reports presented in the **second volume** is that of 'the changing concept of "family" and challenges for domestic family law'. These short national reports[1] by necessity can only skim the surface of the respective national family laws, and they of course are not meant to provide a comprehensive description or analysis of these laws; rather they are supposed to give a snapshot of the development of family law in a changing world, divided into horizontal (legal relationships between adults), vertical (legal relationships between adults and children) and individual (name and gender identity) family law. In doing so, the existing differences between the jurisdictions become apparent as also do the similarities in development. So while the 'cultural restraints' argument – that national family laws are too embedded in their own legal culture to be susceptible to harmonisation – might hold true to a certain extent, certain common or emerging trends can be identified. Thus, as will be elaborated upon in Volume IV, an 'organically grown' European Family Law appears to be emerging, of course furthered by the developments described in Volume I.

In the **third volume** certain selected issues are looked at in a European perspective: *marriage* (Chapter 1 by Caroline Sörgjerd), *divorce* (Chapter 2 by Masha Antokolskaia), *unmarried cohabitation* (Chapter 3 by Joanna

---

[1] On the Benelux Countries (Frederik Swennen), England and Wales (Gillian Douglas), France (Laurence Francoz Terminal), Germany (Dieter Martiny), Greece (Eleni Zervogianni), Hungary (Orsolya Szeibert), Ireland (Brian Sloan), Italy (Maria G. Cubeddu-Wiedemann), the Nordic Countries (Tone Sverdrup), Russia (Olga Khazova), Scotland (Kenneth McK Norrie), Slovakia (Gabriela Kubíčková), Slovenia (Barbara Novak), Spain and Catalonia (Albert Lamarca Marquès), Switzerland (Ingeborg Schwenzer and Tomie Keller) and Turkey (Esin Örücü).

Miles), *same-sex relationships* (Chapter 4 by Ian Curry-Sumner), *financial consequences of divorce* (Chapter 5 by Jens M. Scherpe), the *child's welfare* (Chapter 6 by Rob George), *parentage and surrogacy* (Chapter 7 by Katarina Trimmings and Paul Beaumont), *parental responsibility* (Chapter 8 by Josep Ferrer-Riba), *adoption* (Chapter 9 by Claire Fenton-Glynn), and *family law and older people* (Chapter 10 by Jonathan Herring). These chapters cut across the topics and reports presented in the first and second volume of the book set, and show whether (and why) there is a European family law (or there are aspects of it) in the respective area, and, if so, to what extent.

The **fourth volume**, entitled 'The Present and the Future of European Family Law' and written by the editor of the first three volumes, contains a comparative summary and analysis, building on the other chapters of the book set. In doing so, a distinction is drawn between 'institutional' and 'organic' European family law. The former is perceived as the result of the institutional impact mainly discussed in Volume I but is of course of great significance for both Volume II and, especially, Volume III as well. The 'organic European family law' is the less well-defined, less tangible part of European family law that emerges gradually and that is the result of national law reform rather than imposition – but it is of course often brought about or even necessitated by decisions of the European Courts and by other institutional influences. The aim of the final volume is to draw together the information and analysis of the first three volumes (and other sources), to highlight developments and trends, and to provide an outlook on the future development of European family law.

Table of cases

European Court of Justice

NATIONAL

Austria

France

Table of legislation

Introduction to European family law volume III: Family law in a European perspective

Jens M. Scherpe

In this third volume of the 'European Family Law' book set several core topics of family law are examined from a European and comparative perspective. The specific topics were chosen as between them they cover the topics most debated in family law in the last and presumably also this century. They cover areas where the national family laws have reacted or will need to react to the challenges of societal changes, medical advances and institutional pressures including decisions of the European Courts (on which see relevant contributions in Volume I).

Five of the contributions in this volume cover the relationships between adults. The nature and concept of *marriage* has changed considerably over the years, particularly since the middle of the last century and towards its end; marriage has – at least nominally – become a partnership of equals. This, for example has become apparent in the *financial consequences of divorce* and indeed also in the changes the law of *divorce* itself has seen in the last 70 years. By now all European jurisdictions allow for divorce, and in no jurisdictions can divorce only be based on fault grounds. At the same time in many jurisdictions there exists an increasing legal recognition of *unmarried cohabitation*, often necessitated by the dramatic increase in couples living in such relationships and of children born outside of marriage. In many jurisdictions (although admittedly predominantly in Western Europe) *same-sex relationships* have gained legal recognition, often initially as registered partnerships; though increasingly marriage has been opened up to same-sex couples as well. The landscape of adult relationships has undergone a profound transformation in many jurisdictions, not only because of the changes that the law of marriage has undergone but also because family laws are moving away from being purely marriage-centric.

1

A similar paradigm-shift can also be seen in child law, with which the following four contributions are concerned, which has changed radically from being parent-centred towards being child-centred. The relationship between parents and their children has thus seen a shift towards the *child's welfare*, which provides the central yardstick for all decisions and the framing of legal rules concerning children. Concepts of *parental responsibility* are gradually replacing those of parental power, parental custody and parental authority. *Adoption* is no longer seen as a 'service' for childless couples but as a means to secure the best possible upbringing of particular children, by which permanent legal separation from birth parents is only a last resort. *Parentage* itself is not the concept that it once was, as artificial reproductive techniques including *surrogacy* allow the detaching of genetic from gestational and social parenthood. Not even the old adage *mater semper certa est* is valid in all circumstances anymore. All of these developments, combined with the increased recognition of adult relationships and indeed parenthood in family relationships outside the institution of marriage, have posed and continue to pose significant challenges for 'traditional' family law and particularly for child law. This has led to reforms in many jurisdictions and continues to exert pressure on legislatures to adapt their laws to the realities of modern family life and new technologies.

In many ways this third volume therefore is complementary to the first two volumes of this book set, as its contributions cut across the topics and reports presented in the first and second volumes.[1] Yet the contributions also stand by themselves and do not require the previous two volumes be read or be to hand. Each of the contributions identifies common themes, developments and trends and sometimes also a convergence of family laws. Therefore the contributions in this volume show that there are indeed both 'institutional'[2] and 'organic'[3] elements and principles of European Family Law.

---

[1] It is necessary to note that the authors of this volume for organisational reasons unfortunately did not have access to the contributions of the second volume, although ideally that would have been the case. The contributions of the second and the third volume therefore are only brought together in the fourth and final volume on *The Present and Future of European Family Law*.

[2] I.e. deriving directly or indirectly from the institutions discussed in volume one of the book set.

[3] I.e. having 'grown' domestically, although often with external influences by institutions or developments in other jurisdictions.

1.   Marriage in a European perspective

Caroline Sörgjerd

1.   INTRODUCTION

Is there a European 'concept' of marriage? In this chapter common developments relating to marriage in Europe are identified. More precisely, certain common interests or core values, which have been found worth protecting through legislation based on marriage over time and in different European countries, are identified and analysed.[1] Sweden, which is internationally known for its 'progressive' laws relating to marriage and cohabitation models,[2] is used as an example and a platform for international comparisons with France, Spain, Germany and The Netherlands. The idea is not to map different regulations based on marriage in Europe and compare them in detail. This has already been done by other legal scholars.[3] Instead an ideological line of development will be illustrated, which became visible in Sweden in the 1920s and gradually in many other European countries since then.

The European perspective on marriage also includes an analysis of relevant jurisprudence by the European Court of Human Rights (the Strasbourg Court), based on the European Convention of Human Rights (the ECHR) and dealing with civil status issues. The Strasbourg Court is a significant actor in the human rights arena in Europe with considerable impact on legal development in a wide range of European jurisdictions.

The Strasbourg Court is not the only body dealing with human rights in Europe. Another actor which has become increasingly preoccupied with such issues is the European Union (EU). There is a link between the free movement of persons within the EU and the principle of equality, in the sense that a person's civil status needs to be portable across EU borders in order to safeguard that the principle of free movement of persons works efficiently.[4] Protecting human rights has also become an *independent* goal of the EU, disconnected from the principle of free movement. The EU has adopted a human rights catalogue of its own – the EU Charter[5] – and acceded to the ECHR, which further underlines the weight placed on human rights issues at EU level. However, for

---

[1]   Documents issued before 1 February 2013 have been taken into account. Documents issued thereafter have only been considered selectively.

[2]   A Agell, *The Swedish Legislation on Marriage and Cohabitation, A Journey without A Destination*, (Scandinavian Studies in Law 1980) 12. See also D Bradley, *Family Law and Political Culture, Modern Legal Studies, Scandinavian Laws in Comparative Perspective* (Sweet & Maxwell 1996) 9.

[3]   Comparative research has been carried out by the Commission on European Family Law (CEFL). The CEFL was founded 1 September 2001 and its main objective is providing theoretical and practical research in relation to the harmonisation of family law in Europe, inter alia by formulating sets of 'Principles of European Family Law'. See http://www.ceflonline.net/ (accessed 8 July 2015) and the contribution by Boele-Woelki, chapter 6 of Vol I of this book set.

[4]   K Boele-Woelki, 'The Legal Recognition of Same-Sex Relationships within the European Union' (2007–2008) 82 *Tulane Law Review* 1978.

[5]   Charter of Fundamental Rights of the European Union (2000/C364/01).

matters of delimitation the EU perspective will not be further dealt with in this chapter.[6] Another issue which will not be dealt with is whether harmonisation and unification of laws in Europe is a desirable goal.[7]

2. COMMON EUROPEAN DEVELOPMENTS: THREE THEMES RELATING TO MARRIAGE

2.1 Theme 1: Equality – Legal Parity between Husband and Wife

2.1.1 The Swedish Marriage Code of 1920 as an early example

Creating equality between men and women is a high priority in most European countries in the 21st century. [In Sweden, this development started particularly early. A historical landmark was reached in 1920 through the adoption of the new Marriage Code.[8] Through the Marriage Code of 1920 the hierarchy of marriage formally ended, in the sense that married women were emancipated from their husbands' legal guardianship. Equality was a key concept, expressed in the preparatory work to the 1920 Code: 'The spouses shall, as far as possible, be placed side by side, as equally free and independent persons, without any legally established right for one to decide over the other or alone in joint family matters.'[9]

In line with this ideology husband and wife were treated as two equals in all respects under the law. This meant that married women became

---

[6] See for instance C Sörgjerd, *Reconstructing Marriage – The Legal Status of Relationships in a Changing Society* (Intersentia 2012) 275–93.

[7] See for instance M Antokolskaia, *Harmonisation of Family Law in Europe: A Historical Perspective, A Tale of Two Millennia* (Intersentia 2006); M Jänterä-Jareborg, 'En harmoniserad familjerätt för Europa? Internationellt privaträttsliga och rättsjämförande perspektiv', (2009) 122(3) Tidsskrift for Rettsvitenskap 323–53; K Boele-Woelki (ed.), *Perspectives for the Unification and Harmonisation of Family Law in Europe* (Intersentia 2003); K Boele-Woelki and T Sverdrup (eds), *European Challenges in Contemporary Family Law* (Intersentia 2003); E Örücü, 'The Principles of European Family Law put to the Test: Diversity in Harmony or Harmony in Diversity?', in E Örücü and J Mair (eds), *Juxtaposing Legal Systems and the Principles of European Family Law on Divorce and Maintenance* (Intersentia 2007) 233–54.

[8] The 1920 Code replaced its predecessor the 1734 Code. The Marriage Codes of 1734 and 1920 have been analysed in detail by C Sörgjerd in *Reconstructing Marriage – the Legal Status of Relationships in a Changing Society* (n 6) 23–90.

[9] NJA II 1921, p 6. Author's translation.

entitled to administer their property and to act as legal guardians of their children.(A new marital property regime was introduced – the deferred community of property regime.[10] The regime gave each spouse a latent claim for half of the total net value of the marital property, but the claim could only be realised upon dissolution of the marriage.) The deferred community of property regime, which still applies in Sweden, is wide in scope and encompasses property owned prior to the marriage as well as property acquired during the marriage. It ensures the financially weaker party an equal share of the financially stronger party's wealth, if the marriage ends. In the 1920s and 1930s, when women were still mainly housewives without an income of their own, one could say that the regime improved their position in the rare case of divorce. During marriage, spouses are entitled to the same standard of living.

A new outlook on divorce was expressed in the Marriage Code of 1920.[11] The general idea was that it was no longer found desirable to deter couples from divorcing through upholding strict rules on divorce and compulsory church mediation. In other words, divorce changed from being looked upon as a sanction or a punishment for failing with the marriage to a remedy when the marriage had irretrievably broken down.[12] When the spouses were in agreement, divorce was made available after a one year period of legal separation, on the ground of long and constant discord. The word of the spouses was sufficient as evidence that the discord still remained after the legal separation.[13]

In respect of unilateral divorce applications, a so-called divorce catalogue was introduced in the Marriage Code of 1920, providing seven alternative grounds for divorce. Thus divorce was available if a spouse:

---

[10]   On matrimonial property see Scherpe, chapter 5 in this volume.

[11]   In fact, the new rules on divorce had already been introduced in 1915, through a separate enactment which was then transferred into the 1920 Code. See The Law Commission Report of 1913, Lagberedningens förslag till revision av giftermålsbalken och vissa delar av ärvdabalken I. Förslag till lag om äktenskaps ingående och upplösning m.m. 1913 and NJA II 1921, no 1, Den nya giftermålsbalken I.

[12]   M Antokolskaia, 'The Search for a Common Core of Divorce Law: State Intervention v. Spouses' Autonomy', in M Martin-Casals and J Ribot (eds), *The Role of Self-determination in the Modernisation of Family Law in Europe*, (Girona: Documenta Universitaria 2006) 34.

[13]   Sörgjerd, *Reconstructing Marriage – the Legal Status of Relationships in a Changing Society*, (n 6) 80.

(1)   had remarried in breach of the law (bigamy);
(2)   had sexual intercourse or fornication with somebody other than the spouse;
(3)   had infected the other spouse with a venereal decease;
(4)   had attempted to take the other spouse's life, or had committed aggravated assault on the other spouse or the children;
(5)   had been convicted for certain felonies;
(6)   abused alcohol; or
(7)   was mentally ill.

The new outlook on divorce and the extensive 'divorce catalogue' might give the impression that divorce was common in Sweden in the 1920s. However, this was not the case. Divorce remained rare in the 1920s and 1930s, although a slight increase can be noted. In 1925, 1,748 divorce decrees were issued and in 1935 the figure amounted to 2,718 divorces. During this time period the number of marriages concluded increased from 37,419 in 1925 to 51,306 in 1935. Moreover, the Swedish population increased slightly.[14] It follows that most marriages in the 1920s and 1930s were still in practice concluded for life.

How then was the Marriage Code with its new outlook on divorce received in society? In fact, the Marriage Code of 1920, the emancipation of women and the emphasis on equality did not have any immediate impact on the everyday lives of the Swedish people in general. Only 4 per cent of all married women carried out paid work in Sweden in the 1920s.[15] In the 1920s and 1930s, the 'traditional' division of duties between husband and wife continued to apply in most families. This meant that wives in general remained in charge of the home and the children, whereas husbands worked outside the home and were responsible for earning the family living. In other words, equality was primarily a theoretical issue in Sweden at this time. The intention behind the 1920 Marriage Code was not to challenge gender-roles within the family. In fact, a traditional division of duties, according to which the woman cared for the home and the children and the husband was the breadwinner, was thought to best serve the family's interests.[16] In the rare case of divorce, spousal maintenance was normally awarded. This was important since it

---

[14]   In 1925 the Swedish population amounted to 6,053,562 persons and in 1935 the figure was 6,250,506. Committee Report, (SOU 2007:17) p 203, with reference to the National Central Bureau of Statistics.

[15]   Committee Report (SOU 1964:35) p 17. In 1940, this figure was 9% and in 1960 it was 23%.

[16]   NJA II 1921, 8 and 23.

was regarded as degrading for a divorced woman to be forced to work outside the home.[17]

Nevertheless, the ideological significance of the Marriage Code of 1920 should not be underestimated. Through the Marriage Code of 1920 women obtained majority and legal capacity and it was emphasised in the law that different contributions during marriage – household work and gainful employment – were regarded as *equally* valuable. The 1920 Marriage Code can be seen as having laid the legal and ideological foundation for the legal development to come in the late 1960s and 1970s, when the principle of equality gained ground in society and influenced people's behaviour in the family.

2.1.2 Comparative observations: Germany, Spain, The Netherlands and France

The Swedish Marriage Code of 1920, together with the equivalent acts in Norway and Denmark, was generally regarded as progressive and pioneering in the field of equality between men and women.[18] How does the Swedish legal development relating to marriage compare to the legal developments in four other 'progressive' European jurisdictions, namely The Netherlands, Germany, France and Spain?[19] When did these countries implement the idea of equality between husband and wife into their domestic regulations governing marriage?[20]

(Germany was the first out of these four countries to adopt durable rules which granted married women full legal capacity and administration

---

[17] The Swedish Law Commission Report of 1913, 448.

[18] The Swedish Marriage Code of 1920 was the result of a Nordic (Danish, Swedish and Norwegian) legal cooperation. This cooperation is described by Sörgjerd, in *Reconstructing Marriage – The Legal Status of Relationships in a Changing Society* (n 6) 57–61. See also Bradley, *Family Law and Political Culture* (n 2) and Antokolskaia, *Harmonisation of Family Law in Europe: A Historical Perspective, A Tale of Two Millennia* (n 7).

[19] In all these countries, rules recognising the legal status of same-sex couples have been introduced. In this respect, the countries can be regarded as 'progressive' and suitable for comparison. The Netherlands, Spain and France have adopted gender-neutral marriage acts. In Germany, same-sex couples have access to a form of registered partnership 'life partnership'. This development, however, has mostly taken place during the 21st century. Spain, for instance, has been said to have obstructed 'modernisation' of for instance divorce laws during the 20th century, see Antokolskaia, Chapter 2 in this volume.

[20] A more detailed analysis is presented in Sörgjerd, *Reconstructing Marriage – The Legal Status of Relationships in a Changing Society* (n 6) 84–90, based on the reports drafted by the Commission on European Family Law.

rights in respect of their property. This was achieved through an enactment in 1953.[21] In 1958, a new marital property regime entered into force in Germany, that is, the <u>community of accrued gains</u>, introduced through the German Equality Law of 1957 and replacing the previous regime based on the principle of separation of property. One cannot generally say that one matrimonial property regime favours equality more than another, but unlike its predecessor, the new regime contained a provision which stated that the wife's household work was equally valuable as the husband's gainful employment, more precisely it was established that household work was also a means of contribution.[22] Moreover, the new regime created more equality between husband and wife by making property accrued during marriage subject to equal division upon dissolution. This signals that both types of contributions to the family's well-being count: work in the home *and* gainful employment. From this point of view it appears fair that the homemaker receives compensation for her (or his) contribution to the marriage upon dissolution.

As mentioned above the Swedish Marriage Code of 1920 contained a similar provision which underlined the equal value of household work and gainful employment. It can be noted, however, that according to the wording of the German Civil Code, household work was exclusively assigned to the wife until 1976.[23] According to the Swedish Marriage Code of 1920, it was not explicitly stated that household work was assigned to the wife; it was just emphasised that it was equally important as gainful employment.[24] In practice, however, as pointed out above, a traditional division of duties applied in Sweden as well so at that time the difference was purely linguistic and symbolic.

Similarly, in The Netherlands the incapacity of married women was abolished in the 1950s, more precisely in 1957. Through this law reform women became authorised to administer their property as well as the spouses' 'community property'. Nevertheless, a provision stating that the

---

[21] The German Constitution of 1949, article 117.

[22] This provision was kept until 1976. K Boele-Woelki, B Braat and I Curry-Sumner (eds), *European Family Law in Action, Volume IV: Property Relations between Spouses* (Intersentia 2009) 62, question 2. German Report written by D Martiny and N Dethloff, available 8 July 2015 at http://www.ceflonline.net/.

[23] Boele-Woelki, Braat and Curry-Sumner (eds), *European Family Law in Action, Volume IV: Property Relations between Spouses*, (n 22) 62, question 2. German Report written by Martiny and Dethloff.

[24] The Marriage Code of 1920, chapter 5, s 2.

husband was the head of the marriage was kept in the Dutch Civil Code until 1970.[25] The community of property regime which is still the default regime in The Netherlands, in principle comprises all assets, whether acquired before or during the marriage, as a gift or through inheritance.[26]

(In Spain, women did not obtain full legal capacity until 1981.)It took time to create legal parity between husband and wife in Spain due to the period of the Dictatorship of General Franco, which lasted between 1939 and 1975. During the Franco regime, traditional gender roles were promoted through the law, in a strictly Catholic religious climate. The emancipation of women was considered contrary to the political goals and values of the regime.[27] The 1981 reform aimed at creating equality between husband and wife. The previous system according to which the husband alone administrated the spouses' property was substituted by joint administration by the spouses. Moreover household work was explicitly mentioned in the law as a form of contribution to household expenses. The community of acquisitions was the default system but the couple could opt for another system through a contract before or during marriage. The community of acquisitions (also community of acquests), which still applies as the default system in the federal law of Spain today,

(¹ DEF.

---

[25] *European Family Law in Action, Volume IV: Property Relations between Spouses* (n 22) 67, question 2. Dutch Report written by K Boele-Woelki, F Schonewille and W Schrama, available 8 July 2015 at http://www.ceflonline.net/.

[26] *European Family Law in Action, Volume IV: Property Relations between Spouses* (n 22) 312, question 20. Dutch Report written by Boele-Woelki, Schonewille and Schrama. Spouses or spouses-to-be can opt for another regime through an agreement, prior to or during marriage; on this see K Boele-Woelki, and B Braat, 'Marital Agreements and Private Autonomy in the Netherlands', in J Scherpe (ed.), *Marital Agreements and Private Autonomy in Comparative Perspective* (Hart Publishing 2012) 229–55. A spouse can also claim compensation in certain situations. New, more extensive rules on compensation entered into force 1 January 2012. See also European Commission and European Notarial Network: http://www.coupleseurope.eu/en/netherlands/topics/2-is-there-a-statutory-matrimonial-property-regime-and-if-so-what-does-it-provide, accessed 8 July 2015.

→ [27] For a short time prior to this regime, namely during the Second Spanish Republic (1931–1939) the principle of equality between husband and wife was expressed in the Constitution: 'marriage is based upon equality of rights for both sexes …'. See K Boele-Woelki, B Braat and I Curry-Sumner (eds) *European Family Law in Action, Volume I: Grounds for Divorce* (Intersentia 2003) 51, question 2. Spanish Report written by M Martín-Casals, J Ribot and J Solé, 5, and available 8 July 2015 at http://www.ceflonline.net/. The Constitution was formally effective until 1939 but after the outbreak of the Civil War in 1936 it did not apply in practice.

means that property obtained by each of the spouses while the system is in effect is common and to be divided equally upon dissolution.[28] ⌉

⌊In France, husband and wife were granted full equal rights of participation in matters concerning their joint property through the Reform Act of 1985.[29]⌋ Prior to this, in 1965, a comprehensive reform concerning the spouses' property relations had been carried out in France, introducing the participation in acquisitions regime. This reform, however, did not aim primarily at creating equality between spouses and the husband remained the 'head of the community' with sole authority to administer the marital property. ⌈Through the reform Act of 1985, however, the husband's superior position was abolished and husband and wife were placed on par in the law, as equally entitled to dispose of their personal property and their common assets.[30]⌋

The overall impression is that creating equality between husband and wife has been (and remains) a central political goal in many European countries during the 20th and 21st centuries. In Sweden, as well as in Denmark and Norway, enactments on this theme were implemented into the domestic laws governing marriage at an early point in time.[31] The early Swedish focus in the law on achieving equality between husband and wife and making divorce more accessible can explain why Sweden was ready to launch new 'progressive' enactments relating to marriage already in the 1970s. At this point in time most other European countries were still preoccupied with achieving full equality between husband and wife, or had recently introduced such rules. As will be further developed

---

[28] European Commission and European Notarial Network: http://www.coupleseurope.eu/en/spain/topics/2-is-there-a-statutory-matrimonial-property-regime-and-if-so-what-does-it-provide, accessed 8 July 2015.

[29] Boele-Woelki, Braat and Curry-Sumner (eds) *European Family Law in Action, Volume IV: Property Relations between Spouses* (n 22) 60, question 2. French Report written by F Ferrand and B Braat. Important steps toward this goal were taken during the first half of the 20th century. In 1907 the married woman was granted the right to administrate earnings gained through a profession of her own and in 1938 and 1942 she officially obtained legal capacity to conclude agreements without her husband's consent.

[30] Boele-Woelki, Braat and Curry-Sumner (eds), *European Family Law in Action, Volume IV: Property Relations between Spouses* (n 22) 60, question 2. French Report written by Ferrand and Braat. Some dispositions of for instance the joint home require both spouses' participation. Available 8 July 2015 at http://www.coupleseurope.eu/en/france/topics/2-is-there-a-statutory-matrimonial-property-regime-and-if-so-what-does-it-provide.

[31] Sörgjerd, *Reconstructing Marriage – The Legal Status of Relationships in a Changing Society* (n 6) 57–61.

below the Swedish enactments of the 1970s enhanced the private dimension of marriage, by increasing the autonomy of individuals and reducing the level of participation of the public and the authorities in their 'private sphere'.

2.2 Theme 2: Privacy – Reducing the Official Participation in Matters Relating to Marriage

2.2.1 The Swedish Enactments of the 1970s and the Marriage Code of 1987

The Swedish Marriage Code of 1920 remained in force for more than 60 years, until it was replaced by the Marriage Code of 1987. However, significant enactments were adopted in the 1970s, dealing with conclusion and dissolution of marriage as well as spousal maintenance claims after divorce. The enactments of the 1970s, which were transferred into the 1987 Code, marked a new approach to marriage and divorce.

These enactments were facilitated by changes that had taken place in the Swedish society. By 1970, the Swedish welfare state had been established, providing services such as health care, child care and old-age care, as well as a basic social security system. These changes enabled women to work outside the home and helped to do away with the opposition to women's gainful employment.[32] In fact, women were now expressly encouraged to work outside the home and it had become common and socially accepted for men to take part in household work.[33] Through an enactment in 1978 it was explicitly stated in the Marriage Code that domestic work and taking care of children were duties for both spouses.[34] In other words equal participation of both spouses in matters concerning their family was being 'marketed' by politicians as a desirable goal.

---

[32] See section 2.1.1 above.

[33] The Social Democratic Party played a significant role in the process of transferring the legal concept of equality to the everyday family life of people in general. Toward the end of the 1920s, in a time of high unemployment figures and an alarmingly low birth rate, the launching of the 'folk home' as a basis for establishing a Swedish welfare state was timely by the Social Democratic Party leader Per Albin Hansson. The Social Democratic Party won the general election in 1932 and remained in power continually for the next 40 years. Sörgjerd, *Reconstructing Marriage – The Legal Status of Relationships in a Changing Society* (n 6) 92–97.

[34] Government Bill (Prop 1978/79:12) pp 215 f and 180 f. This provision was transferred into the Marriage Code of 1987, chapter 1, s 2.

Through rules adopted in 1973, it became easier to conclude as well as to dissolve a marriage. The impediments to marriage were minimised and divorce was turned into a personal right of each spouse, available more or less 'on demand'. In the Government Bill of 1973 it was stated that: '[N]ew rules on dissolution of marriage are founded on the basic idea that conclusion as well as continuation of marriage should be based on the parties' free will to live together, subject to marriage regulation. This means that a spouse's wish to dissolve the marriage should always be respected.'[35]

Under Swedish divorce law, adopted in 1973 and still applicable today, divorce can be granted directly upon the joint application of the spouses. Ancillary effects, such as maintenance claims and property division issues, if disputed, can be dealt with in separate proceedings which do not delay the divorce decree. Fault has no relevance whatsoever for the outcome of divorce proceedings.[36] In respect of unilateral divorce claims, a six-month period of reconsideration is required before divorce is granted. A reconsideration-period of six months is also required if there are children in the family under the age of 16.[37]

In 1978, new rules on spousal maintenance after divorce were adopted, which gave statutory support to principles established in case law. The basic idea behind the enactments of 1973 and 1978 was that all legal effects of marriage should end when the marriage ended. The spouses were treated as two equals under the law and they should strive at being financially independent after divorce. This restrictive view on spousal maintenance *after* divorce was thought to encourage each spouse to be self-sufficient also *during* marriage. It was possible to introduce restrictive rules on spousal maintenance after divorce in Sweden, largely because of the role of the welfare state, with special support given to single parent households, a state subsidised preschool system and various

---

[35] Government Bill (Prop 1973:32) p 74. Author's translation.

[36] Prior to the introduction of no-fault divorce, disloyal behaviour, adultery for instance, could have an impact on ancillary matters such as child custody disputes. Government Bill (Prop 1973:32) p 86.

[37] A reconsideration period also applies if both spouses request one. When six months have expired, either spouse can demand that the divorce be finalised. If no such claim has been made a year after the divorce application was filed, the case is dismissed. The Marriage Code of 1987, chapter 5. Moreover, the generous property division rules can compensate a financially weaker spouse upon dissolution of the marriage. Property owned prior to the marriage is included, as well as property acquired through inheritance or as a result of a will, unless otherwise stated by the donor.

other financial subsidies. Without this system divorced women in general would be more reliant on spousal maintenance after divorce.[38]

The Swedish family law enactments of the 1970s were based on a new official outlook on marriage and civil status issues. Through the enactments, dealing with conclusion and dissolution of marriage as well as spousal maintenance, certain core values relating to marriage changed. In short, the private dimension of marriage was strengthened. The new idea was to trust the individual spouse's own ability to make rational decisions about the marriage and to minimise the level of official interference through legislation which expressed moral values concerning lifestyle and cohabitation choices. The spouses were to be treated as two independent individuals with autonomous rights and duties. This new outlook can be seen as somewhat of a contrast to the previous view on marriage as primarily a mutual, lifelong family project and the couple as an entity rather than two individuals. In the legal literature, this new Swedish policy has been discussed in terms of 'neutrality'.[39]

2.2.2 The Swedish Neutrality Policy
In 1969, in the Government Guidelines to the Family Law Committee which drafted the Swedish enactments of the 1970s, the new policy in respect of family law legislation was formulated accordingly:

> New legislation should ... be neutral as far as possible with regard to various forms of cohabitation and divergent moral concepts. Marriage has had and should have a central place within family law, but we ought to endeavour to ensure that family law legislation does not include any regulations, which create unnecessary difficulty or inconvenience for those who have children and establish a family without getting married.[40]

The idea behind the Swedish enactments of the 1970s was that adult individuals should be trusted to make rational decisions concerning their relationship without unnecessary morally-based 'intervention' by the authorities. Consequently, married couples should not be treated more favourably in the law than unmarried couples, or vice versa, through

---

[38] Sörgjerd, *Reconstructing Marriage – The Legal Status of Relationships in a Changing Society* (n 6) 130–2.

[39] Sörgjerd, *Reconstructing Marriage – The Legal Status of Relationships in a Changing Society* (n 6) 97–9 and 116–19.

[40] Guidelines by the Chief of the Legal Department to the Commission on Family Law, 15 August 1969, Riksdagsberättelsen 1970, Ju 52, p 81. See Committee Report (SOU 1972:41), p 58. As translated by J Graversen, *Family Law as a Reflection of Family Ideology* (1990) 79.

tax-related or other benefits.[41] The Swedish enactments of the 1970s reflect these basic values.[42] Divorce on demand was introduced and cohabitation without marriage was regulated in a special act – The 1973 Act on the Joint Dwelling of an Unmarried Couple.[43] The practical impact of the neutrality policy on the Swedish legal development in the field of family law is a debated issue in the legal literature. Some find the neutrality policy to be exaggerated and tone down its impact on Swedish family law legislation, whereas others view it as the starting point for legally recognising and regulating additional cohabitation forms.[44]

Neutrality in the sense described above is not just a Swedish phenomenon. Enactments which have enhanced the private features of marriage, by increasing the spouses' individual and joint autonomy, have been adopted in many other European countries as well and cohabitation forms other than marriage have been subject to legislative measures.[45] In my opinion, what makes Sweden different in this respect is that the ambition labelled 'neutrality' was explicitly mentioned in the Government Guidelines in 1969, as an underlying goal behind the enactments of the 1970s. This indicates a sincere political interest in strengthening the private features of the marriage regulation, which was expressed at a comparatively early point in time. One could say that the 'value-neutral' approach in the 1970s to different cohabitation forms and lifestyles paved the way

---

[41]   At this time, changes were made in the taxation law so that spouses were treated as two separate individuals with their own taxable incomes. According to the old taxation rules, spouses' taxable incomes had been treated as one entity, which could disfavour spouses with a high income and even compel them to divorce and then live together outside of marriage for tax related reasons. Government Bill (Prop 1973:32) pp 83 f. See also J Sundberg, 'Marriage or No Marriage in Swedish Law' (1971) 20 *International and Comparative Law Quarterly* 230 f.

[42]   See section 2.2.1 above.

[43]   Lag om ogifta samboendes gemensamma bostad, which entered into force 1 January, 1974. The 1970s were innovative and radical times in Sweden. In 1972, the idea of abolishing all ceremonial features of marriage and replacing it with a registration procedure was discussed in a Committee Report. All that would be required for the marriage to be legally valid would be notification of a public official with legal capacity to administer and register such agreements. Committee Report (SOU 1972:41). However, this idea was dismissed already in the committee report.

[44]   This debate is accounted for by Sörgjerd, *Reconstructing Marriage – The Legal Status of Relationships in a Changing Society* (n 6) 116–19.

[45]   This development has been described by Antokolskaia, 'The Search for a Common Core of Divorce Law: State Intervention v. Spouses' Autonomy' (n 12) 33–58.

for adopting more detailed rules on cohabitation without marriage in the 1980s and for the legal recognition of same-sex couples in the 1990s and early 2000s.[46] In other words in Sweden the policy to remain neutral to cohabitation models functioned as a bridge between two political interests, namely 'privacy' and 'pluralism', and linked these two themes together.

2.2.3 Comparative observations

In many European jurisdictions, new family law enactments have been introduced, which have reduced the level of official participation in the couple's private sphere. This development is particularly noticeable in the field of divorce law. One could say that there is a common 'trend' toward making divorce more accessible to the individual.

The Swedish rules governing divorce, adopted in the 1970s, still stand out as 'progressive' in a contemporary European context. But others are following suit. In 2005, Spain also adopted liberal (in the sense of divorce friendly) rules which resemble the Swedish divorce legislation.[47] The Spanish divorce rules do not require that spouses live apart prior to the divorce application and no grounds for divorce are stipulated. As under the Swedish divorce law, the petition for divorce as such, by one or both spouses, is sufficient for obtaining a court decision granting the divorce. A difference compared to the Swedish rules is that no period of (re)consideration is required under Spanish law. On the other hand, Spanish law requires that all ancillary matters are resolved before the

---

[46]   Although same-sex couples were not subject to legislative measures in the 1970s, it was stated in a Law Commission Report that '... cohabitation between two persons of the same sex is a perfectly acceptable form of family life from society's point of view'. Swedish Law Commission Report (LU 1973:20) p 116. Author's translation.

[47]   European   Judicial   Network: http://ec.europa.eu/civiljustice/divorce/ divorce_spa_en.htm, accessed 8 July 2015. Prior to 2005, according to rules enacted in 1981, legal separation for one or three years was obligatory prior to divorce under Spanish divorce law. Boele-Woelki, Braat and Curry-Sumner (eds), *European Family Law in Action, Volume I: Grounds for Divorce* (n 27), question 11, p 185. Spanish Report written by M Martín-Casals, available 8 July 2015 at http://www.ceflonline.net/. The only exception to this rule was if one spouse had tried to kill the other spouse or his or her children. Divorce upon the request of one of the spouses was possible on certain grounds and legal separation was an alternative way out of a marriage, according to the 1932 Constitution. Spanish report, question 2, pp 50 f.

divorce decree can be issued and this can be time-consuming.[48] Swedish law prescribes a period of reconsideration in certain situations, but if the spouses are in agreement to divorce and do not have young children, divorce can be issued immediately, even if ancillary matters are disputed.

(Divorce upon the unilateral request of a spouse has also existed in Finland since 1987 (after a six-month period of reconsideration).[49] Denmark and Norway, however, have not (yet) followed the Swedish and Finnish examples in this respect. Instead divorce normally requires a one-year period of separation (six months in Denmark if the spouses mutually consent to the divorce).[50] In certain situations, however, divorce can be granted directly, without a period of separation.[51])

(In France, for instance, divorce based on mutual consent was established in statutory law in 1975, as one ground for divorce among several others. A main objective of the reform was to liberalise divorce.[52]) However, there were restrictions. A basic prerequisite for obtaining divorce based on mutual consent was that the marriage had lasted at least six months prior to the application for divorce and that the spouses could present an agreement concerning all ancillary matters.[53] The spouses had to appear twice in front of the judge; first, in order to discuss the details of their contract concerning ancillary matters and second, to finalise it.[54]

Through the French Divorce Act of 2004, which entered into force on 1 January 2005, divorce based on mutual consent was facilitated.[55] As a result, marriages of short duration can also be dissolved based on mutual

---

[48] European Judicial Network: http://ec.europa.eu/civiljustice/divorce/divorce_spa_en.htm, accessed 8 July 2015. See also J Ferrer Riba, 'Same-Sex Marriage, Express Divorce and Related Developments in Spanish Marriage Law', *International Survey of Family Law* (Jordan Publishing, 2006) 142.

[49] See Antokolskaia, 'The Search for a Common Core of Divorce Law: State Intervention v. Spouses' Autonomy' (n 12) 52. According to Antokolskaia, divorce based on mutual consent has also existed in Russia since 1995.

[50] The Norwegian Marriage Act, chapter 4 and the Danish Marriage Act, chapter 4.

[51] For instance in respect of serious acts of violence.

[52] C Butruille-Cardew,, 'The 2004 French Divorce Law and International Prospects' [2006] *International Family Law Journal* 144.

[53] Boele-Woelki, Braat and Curry-Sumner (eds), *European Family Law in Action, Volume I: Grounds for Divorce* (n 27), question 29, p 313. French Report written by Ferrand.

[54] Boele-Woelki, Braat and Curry-Sumner (eds), *European Family Law in Action, Volume I: Grounds for Divorce* (n 27), question 29, p 313 f. French Report written by Ferrand.

[55] Law N° 2004-439, 26 May 2004.

consent and no period of separation is required.[56] Another novelty is that the spouses only have to appear once in front of the judge.[57] However, in order to obtain divorce based on mutual consent they still have to present a contract with arrangements concerning all ancillary matters.[58] Another factor which delays divorce in France is that the spouses need to be represented by a lawyer. They cannot file for divorce jointly on their own.[59]

The French Divorce Act of 2004 stipulates three other grounds for divorce (beside mutual consent): (1) acceptance of the principle of marital breakdown (when the couple agrees to divorce but disagrees on ancillary issues); (2) breakdown of communal life; and (3) fault.[60] Divorce based on the breakdown of the marriage may always be granted after a two-year separation of the couple, without any further inquiries. This is a liberalisation compared to the 1975 Act, which prescribed six years of separation.[61] It can be noted that the same principle applies in Sweden; if the spouses have lived apart for two years prior to the divorce application no additional reconsideration period is required.[62] According to French law, divorce based on mutual consent is always an option and divorce proceedings initiated on a different ground can be changed subsequently by the couple to a proceeding based on their mutual consent.[63] This indicates that it is generally regarded as preferable if the spouses both consent to the divorce and reach agreements on ancillary matters on their own, with minimal intervention by the authorities.

---

[56] Butruille-Cardew, 'The 2004 French Divorce Law and International Prospects' (n 52).

[57] A possibility for the judge to make an interim order in case of domestic violence was also introduced, valid for four months.

[58] Boele-Woelki, Braat and Curry-Sumner (eds), *European Family Law in Action, Volume I: Grounds for Divorce* (n 27), question 29, p 313. French Report written by Ferrand. The contract is presented to the Notary if the spouses have real estate. Otherwise, the spouses themselves can draw up the agreement without participation of the Notary.

[59] However, if they apply for divorce based on mutual consent, they can be represented by the same lawyer.

[60] Butruille-Cardew, 'The 2004 French Divorce Law and International Prospects' (n 52). Divorce based on acceptance of marital breakdown was first introduced in 1975.

[61] Butruille-Cardew, 'The 2004 French Divorce Law and International Prospects' (n 52) 145.

[62] The Swedish Marriage Code of 1987, chapter 5, section 4.

[63] This possibility was introduced in 1975 and established in article 246 of the Code Civil.

Neither Dutch nor German law recognises divorce based on mutual consent as an autonomous (direct) ground for divorce. Instead 'irretrievable breakdown' of the marriage is the sole ground for divorce in these two jurisdictions. In the Netherlands, divorce based on the irretrievable breakdown of the marriage was introduced as the sole ground for divorce in 1971.[64] The spouses' word that the marriage has permanently broken down is sufficient as evidence in this respect and no further investigation is made by the judge.[65] Under German law 'hardship clauses' can be used to prove the breakdown of the marriage. A period of separation is required prior to the divorce, one year in respect of mutual applications for divorce and three years in respect of unilateral applications. If the spouses apply jointly for divorce, the presumption is that the marriage has broken down permanently.[66] Under German law, representation of a lawyer is compulsory and under Dutch law the application for divorce must be signed and delivered by a procurator litis. This is a difference compared to Swedish law, according to which the spouses need not consult a lawyer. In fact under Swedish law spouses are encouraged not to hire lawyers. Special forms containing the relevant questions and information are available at the websites of the district courts which one or both spouses can fill out and send in. Divorce is an administrative procedure and the spouses do not appear in front of a judge or an authority.[67]

This small survey shows that there are still differences in respect of how accessible and speedy divorce is in practice. Different time periods of separation are required and few countries have gone as far as introducing divorce as a unilateral right – 'on demand'. A common core in the legal development relating to marriage in Europe since the 1960s and 1970s is to gradually increase the autonomy of the spouses and thus in a sense *privatise* marriage, by allowing divorce based on mutual

---

[64] Boele-Woelki, Braat and Curry-Sumner (eds), *European Family Law in Action, Volume I: Grounds for Divorce* (n 27) questions 2 and 4, pp 44 and 89. Dutch Report written by K Boele-Woelki, O Cherednychenko and L Coenraad, and available 8 July 2015 at http://www.ceflonline.net/.

[65] Boele-Woelki, Braat and Curry-Sumner (eds), *European Family Law in Action, Volume I: Grounds for Divorce* (n 27), question 4, p 89. Dutch Report written by Boele-Woelki, Cherednychenko and Coenraad.

[66] Boele-Woelki, Braat and Curry-Sumner (eds), *European Family Law in Action, Volume I: Grounds for Divorce* (n 27), question 4, pp 80 f. German Report written by D Martiny.

[67] Boele-Woelki, Braat and Curry-Sumner (eds), *European Family Law in Action, Volume I: Grounds for Divorce* (n 27), question 9, p 154. Swedish report written by: M Jänterä-Jareborg.

consent or based on the irretrievable breakdown of the marriage. Many national legislators have abandoned the idea of counteracting divorce through divorce regulation and emphasise the value of individual autonomy.⌉

⌈The general trend in Europe in the 21st century is to abolish or diminish the impact of fault in divorce proceedings.[68]⌋In France, Germany and The Netherlands, fault can still be taken into consideration in connection with divorce, although only to a limited extent. In France, fault has been retained as a direct ground for divorce, but since the 2004 Act, the general idea in France is that financial consequences of divorce should not depend on the question of who is to blame for the breakdown of the marriage. Thus fault grounds are applied restrictively.[69] In German divorce proceedings, fault plays but a marginal role. The element of fault could, however, in exceptional cases prevent divorce from being granted at that specific time, if divorce would result in exceptional hardship for a spouse.[70] In Dutch divorce proceedings the applicant can submit evidence to the judge, by proving personal facts and circumstances which have led to the permanent deterioration of the marriage; for instance, adulterous behaviour of a spouse. Divorce can no longer be rejected because the petitioning spouse is to blame for the deterioration of the marriage, but it appears that fault can be taken into account in connection with spousal maintenance claims.[71]

⌈From a Swedish perspective, which is also the generally prevailing view in many European countries, excluding fault from divorce proceedings can be seen as a means to protect the privacy and integrity of the individuals concerned.⌋More precisely, excluding fault makes divorce more accessible, at least indirectly, in the sense that fault grounds risk deterring a 'guilty' spouse from going through with a divorce, out of fear of appearing immoral or indecent. Moreover, establishing which spouse is to blame for the breakdown of the marriage risks creating conflicts between the spouses and this can be detrimental to the well-being of their

---

[68]   See Masha Antokolskaia, chapter 2 in this volume.

[69]   Nevertheless, the judge has certain discretion in this respect. Butruille-Cardew, 'The 2004 French Divorce Law and International Prospects' (n 52).

[70]   Boele-Woelki, Braat and Curry-Sumner (eds), *European Family Law in Action, Volume I: Grounds for Divorce* (n 27), question 12, pp 188–90. German Report written by Martiny. The circumstances, however, would have to be very exceptional.

[71]   Boele-Woelki, Braat and Curry-Sumner (eds), *European Family Law in Action, Volume I: Grounds for Divorce* (n 27), question 11, pp 177 f and 193. Dutch Report written by Boele-Woelki, Cherednychenko and Coenraad.

children. In other words fault generally aggravates rather than solves problems, to the detriment of children.[72] Medical and psychological research supports the view that severe conflicts between parents are more harmful to children than the parents' divorce as such.[73] In fact, the detrimental effects on children of conflicts between parents was a reason why France considered abolishing fault as a direct ground for divorce in connection with the 2004 reform. In the end, however, fault was retained as a ground for divorce in France but applied restrictively.[74] This can be seen as a first step toward abolishing fault all together.

2.3 Theme 3: Pluralism – Regulating and Recognising New Cohabitation Models

2.3.1 The Swedish Acts on Cohabitation without Marriage: 1973, 1987 and 2003[75]

(Sexual relationships outside of marriage have become socially accepted in many European countries and numerous couples have children without being married) In Sweden more than 50 percent of all children are born to unmarried mothers, most of who presumably live with the child's father.[76] A special act governs such informal cohabitee relationships – The Cohabitees Act of 2003. The act is highly relevant since a third of all

---

[72] This was a widely agreed conception in Germany in the 1970s. See Antokolskaia, 'The Search for a Common Core of Divorce Law: State Intervention v. Spouses' Autonomy', (n 12) 49.

[73] In fact, this research shows that experiencing divorce as a child does not necessarily correlate to poor mental health as an adult. T Ängarne-Lindberg, *Grown-Up Children of Divorce – Experiences and Health*, Linköping University Medical Dissertations No 1173, 2010. See also M Gähler, 'Self-Reported Psychological Well-being among Adult Children of Divorce in Sweden', (1998) 41(3) *Acta Sociologica* 209–25. See also Antokolskaia, 'The Search for a Common Core of Divorce Law: State Intervention v. Spouses' Autonomy' (n 12), 47–52.

[74] Butruille-Cardew, 'The 2004 French Divorce Law and International Prospects' (n 52).

[75] See also E Ryrstedt, 'The Swedish Cohabitees Act', in J Scherpe and N Yassari (eds), The Legal Status of Cohabitants (Mohr Siebeck 2005) 415–38.

[76] The latest figures available are from 2009 and compiled by Statistics Sweden (available 8 July 2015 at http://www.scb.se/statistik/_publikationer/ BE0101_2009A01_BR_08_BE0110TAB.pdf). Most likely, many of these unwed mothers are living with the child's father. No statistics are available in this respect.

couples living together in Sweden are estimated to be unmarried 'co-habitees', in sense of the Cohabitees Act:[77] 'two persons living together in a relationship, on a permanent basis, sharing a household'.[78]

(Already in 1936, in a Swedish Committee Report, sexual relationships outside of marriage were discussed in a tolerant tone, provided that it was a question of long-term loving relationships and not casual sexual encounters.[79] This early approval of (long-term) sexual relationships outside of marriage most likely paved the way for the value-neutral approach to cohabitation forms expressed in 1969 and for adopting a special act on cohabitation without marriage in 1973.)

In 1973, the Act on the Joint dwelling of an Unmarried Couple was adopted.[80] The 1973 Act was limited in scope, only providing the cohabitee with the greatest need with the possibility of taking over a tenancy contract or a condominium, against compensation. The 1973 Act applied by default, just like its successors, that is, without a special procedure establishing the consent of the couple to being subject to legal rules. The Act became applicable upon the application of either party when the relationship ended. The 1973 Act, although limited in scope, can be seen as a starting point for adopting more comprehensive rules on cohabitation without marriage in the 1980s.

The Cohabitees Joint Homes Act of 1987 widened the scope of the 1973 Act, with property division rules which were based on the property division rules applicable to spouses and laid down in the Marriage Code.[81] However, the property which could be subject to division after a cohabitee relationship was much more limited in scope than upon divorce, as only the net value of the cohabiting couple's joint home and household goods, acquired for the purpose of their joint use, could be subject to division. A corresponding 'cohabitees act' applicable to same-sex couples was adopted in 1987 – The Homosexual Cohabitees Act – which applied by reference to the act applicable to couples of opposite sex.[82] (In 2003 a 'gender-neutral' cohabitees act was adopted,

---

[77]   Government Bill (Prop 2002/03:80) Ny sambolag, p 24. In 1985, this figure was 20%.

[78]   In Swedish: 'två personer som stadigvarande bor tillsammans i ett parförhållande och har gemensamt hushåll' (author's translation). The Cohabitees Act, s 1.

[79]   Committee Report (SOU 1936:59) p 76.

[80]   The Act on the Joint Dwelling of an Unmarried Couple (Lag om ogifta samboendes gemensamma bostad) which entered into force on 1 January 1974.

[81]   Lag (1987:232) om sambors gemensamma hem.

[82]   Lag (1987:813) om homosexuella sambor.

primarily for the symbolic purpose of including same-sex and different-sex cohabitees in the same enactment, but the legislator also seized the opportunity to clarify a few issues at the same time.[83] The scope of the 2003 Act largely remains the same as that in the 1987 Act.)

Marriage is no longer the only cohabitation model available. Once marriage had been emphasised as primarily a private matter between individuals (in the 1970s), which the state or the public should refrain from intervening in, legally recognising and regulating other cohabitation models rather than marriage was close at hand.[84] First unmarried couples living together were the target of legislative measures and thereafter same-sex couples. From this point of view, the Swedish cohabitee enactments can be seen as expressions of legal pluralism.

2.3.2 Legal recognition of same-sex relationships[85]

(More than two-thirds of the member states of the EU have adopted or are preparing statutory registration schemes which include same-sex couples.[86]) Globally, in December 2012, marriage is available to same-sex couples in 11 countries: Argentina, Belgium, Canada, Denmark, Iceland, The Netherlands, Norway, Portugal, South Africa, Spain and Sweden.[87]

---

[83] Sambolag (2003:376).

[84] Then again, applying rules by default, which are based on the marriage regulation, to unmarried couples can also be seen as increasing the level of official participation in the private sphere. See Sörgjerd, *Reconstructing Marriage – The Legal Status of Relationships in a Changing Society* (n 6) 139–44.

[85] See also Ian Curry-Sumner, chapter 4 in this volume; K Boele-Woelki and A Fuchs (eds), Legal Recognition of Same-Sex Relationships in Europe (Intersentia 2012) and J Basedow et al (eds), Die Rechtsstellung gleichgeschlechtlicher Lebensgemeinschaften (Mohr Siebeck 2000).

[86] Updated information about the legal status of same-sex couples in the world can be found at: CBC News: http://www.cbc.ca/world/story/2009/05/26/f-same-sex-timeline.html (accessed 8 July 2015). The figure, two-thirds, was calculated by K Boele-Woelki, in 'The Legal Recognition of Same-Sex Relationships Within the European Union' [2007–2008] *Tulane Law Review*,1960 f. See also M Saez, 'Same sex marriage, same sex cohabitation, and same sex families around the world: Why is "same" so different?', General Report for the XVIII International Congress of the International Academy of Comparative Law, Washington, 2010 and Report by ILGA Europe, April, 2011 (available 8 July 2015 at http://ec.europa.eu/justice/newsroom/civil/opinion/files/110510/organisations/ilga_en.pdf).

[87] See map at CBC News: http://www.cbc.ca/world/story/2009/05/26/f-same-sex-timeline.html (n 86). Moreover, as shown on the map, same-sex marriage is legal in certain jurisdictions, for instance in some states in the United States, in Mexico City and in the province of Alagoas in Brazil.

On 12 February 2013, a bill on same-sex marriage was approved by the French lower house of parliament. It was subsequently approved by the senate and the new law was passed. In May 2013, the first same-sex marriage took place in France.[88] A step toward legalising same-sex marriage was also taken in England and Wales in February 2013, when a bill on same-sex marriage passed the first vote in the parliament. It passed the second vote in July 2013 and the new Marriage Act was adopted. (The number of countries that have introduced marriage or another formalised institution available to same-sex couples is rapidly increasing in Europe.)

(This development is supported by the development at EU level, where facilitating the free movement of persons, same-sex couples included, is a prioritised issue, for instance in the field of family reunification.[89] The rapid legal development in recognising the rights of same-sex couples can also be linked to the strong impact of the general human rights discourse in Europe. (Laws which safeguard the rights of same-sex couples and homosexual individuals in society are often justified with reference to human rights principles such as equal treatment and non-discrimination, which it is necessary to protect in a democratic society.[90])

---

[88] http://www.guardian.co.uk/world/2013/feb/12/french-gay-marriage-bill (accessed 8 July 2015). See also Ian Curry-Sumner, chapter 4 in this volume.

[89] The work of the European Union Agency for Fundamental Rights can be mentioned. It has an advisory function toward the EU institutions and the member states, performing research and providing expert advice on the topic of fundamental rights. Furthermore, The Green Paper on the right to family reunification of third-country nationals living in the European Union can be noted (Directive 2003/86/EC), Brussels, 15.11.2011 COM(2011) 735 final. The Green Paper, inter alia, aims at facilitating the free circulation of documents in the EU. The aim is to initiate a discussion among interested member states on how to facilitate recognition of documents concerning for instance EU citizens' civil status within the EU. This Green Paper might contribute to facilitating the free movement of EU citizens within the EU, but still without forcing member states to recognise a same-sex marriage or registered partnership as equal to marriage. See http://eur-lex.europa.eu/LexUriServ/LexUriServ.do?uri=COM:2011:0735:FIN:EN:PDF, accessed 11 October 2012. For an analysis of case law of the European Union dealing with same-sex couples, see Sörgjerd, *Reconstructing Marriage – The Legal Status of Relationships in a Changing Society* (n 6) 285–90. See also H Toner, *Partnership Rights, Free Movement and EU Law* (Modern Studies in European Law, Hart Publishing 2003).

[90] This is, for instance, pointed out by M Bonini-Baraldi, 'Variations on the Theme of Status, Contract and Sexuality: An Italian Perspective on the Circulation of Models', in K Boele-Woelki (ed.) *Perspectives for the Unification and Harmonization of Family Law in Europe* (Intersentia 2003) 321.

Same-sex couples' protection under the European Convention on Human Rights will be discussed below.[91]

[In Sweden, a Registered Partnership Act was adopted in 1994, based on equivalent Acts adopted in Denmark in 1989 and Norway in 1993.[92]] In the Swedish preparatory work to the Registered Partnership Act, the human rights discourse was present. An ideologically coloured political rhetoric was used which strongly resembles a human rights document, with references to human equality:

> Our standpoint has an ideological foundation, based as it is on human equality, both as between individuals and under the law. We acknowledge homosexual love as equal in value to heterosexual love ... We wish to accommodate the desire of homosexual couples for a valuable setting for their relations, as a way of manifesting their love.[93]

(Through the Swedish Registered Partnership Act, most legal effects of marriage were made applicable to same-sex couples. Initially, however, some legal effects of marriage were explicitly exempted from the scope of the Swedish Act.)These exceptions dealt with rules on legal parenthood, gender-based provisions and international treaties. However, these differences between same-sex and different sex couples were criticised and challenged, on a political level and by spokespersons for gay rights. (As a result in 2003, rules on adoption – second-parent adoption as well as adoption of children from abroad – were made applicable to same-sex couples and in 2005 lesbian couples were granted access to medically assisted procreation.[94])

Also Iceland and Finland followed the Danish, Norwegian and Swedish examples, in 1996 and 2001 respectively, by adopting similar

---

[91]   See section 3.3.3 below.

[92]   Denmark: Act on Registered Partnership (No 372, 7 June 1989). The Act entered into force 1 October 1989. Norway: Act on Registered Partnership (No 40, 30 April 1993). The Act entered into force 1 August 1993. Sweden: The Registered Partnership Act (1994:1117, 23 June 1994) The Act entered into force 1 January 1995. On this see P Dopffel and J Scherpe, 'Gleichgeschlechtliche Lebensgemeinschaften im Recht der nordischen Länder', in Basedow et al (eds), *Die Rechtsstellung gleichgeschlechtlicher Lebensgemeinschaften* (n 85) 7–49 and I Lund-Andersen, 'The Nordic Countries: Same Direction – Different Speeds', in Boele Woelki and Fuchs (eds), *Legal Recognition of Same-Sex Relationships in Europe* (n. 85) 3–17.

[93]   Committee Report (SOU 1993:98) Part A, p 21.

[94]   A similar legal development has taken place in the other Scandinavian countries, except in Finland. Finland is the only Scandinavian country that does not allow adoption by same-sex couples and which has not introduced a

registered partnership acts and together forming what has been referred to as a 'Scandinavian model' of registered partnership.[95] Other 'registration models' exist elsewhere in Europe, such as the French 'pacte civil de solidarité' (PACS), which is much more limited in legal effect than the Nordic model and applicable to different-sex and same-sex couples. However, as mentioned in section 2.3.2 above, France now also allows same-sex marriages. There is also, for instance, the Dutch model of registered partnership, which has been kept after the introduction of a gender-neutral marriage concept. The Dutch registered partnership is open to same-sex and different-sex couples, and in practice functions as a 'light version' of marriage, which is easier to dissolve than a regular marriage.[96] In 2009 the Swedish Registered Partnership Act was replaced by a gender-neutral marriage enactment.[97] At the time of writing all Nordic countries except Finland have opened up marriage to same-sex couples.[98]

However, there is no consensus in Europe – and even less so globally – that same-sex couples should be tolerated, let alone legally recognised. Homosexuality remains controversial in, for instance, Bulgaria, Estonia and Romania, where it has recently been specified in the law that

---

gender-neutral marriage concept. See for instance M Jänterä-Jareborg, 'Parenthood for Same-Sex Couples', in *Liber Memorialis Petar Sarcevic, Universalism, Tradition and the Individual* (Sellier European Law Publishers 2006) 75–91.

[95] M Jänterä-Jareborg, 'Registered Partnerships in Private International Law: The Scandinavian Approach', in Boele-Woelki and Fuchs (eds) *Legal Recognition of Same-Sex Couples in Europe* (n 85) 149 and M Jänterä-Jareborg and C Sörgjerd, 'The Experiences with Registered Partnership in Scandinavia', FamPra.ch 3/2004, Stämpfli Verlag AG, 577–79. The Icelandic Act on Registered Partnership (No 87, 12 June 1996) entered into force 27 June 1996 and the Finnish Act on Registered Partnerships (950/2001) entered into force 1 March 2002.

[96] For an account of different enactments for same-sex couples, see Boele-Woelki and Fuchs (eds), *Legal Recognition of Same-Sex Relationships in Europe* (n 85). The Dutch institutions – registered partnership and marriage – are analysed by Sörgjerd in *Reconstructing Marriage – The Legal Status of Relationships in a Changing Society* (n 6) 243–48.

[97] In October 2009, the Bishops of the Church of Sweden voted in favour of officiating legally valid marriages between couples of the same sex. Thus, in Sweden, couples of the same sex, like couples of opposite sex, can choose between a legally valid civil or religious church ceremony.

[98] Sörgjerd, *Reconstructing Marriage – The Legal Status of Relationships in a Changing Society* (n 6) 268–74.

marriage is reserved for different-sex couples.[99] (Moreover, in October 2012, the Ukraine parliament voted in favour of a proposal which will prohibit the spreading of what is referred to as 'homosexual propaganda'.[100] On a global level, homosexual sexual acts between consenting adults are criminalised in some 70 or 80 countries and capital punishment appears to be prescribed in seven of these countries.[101])

The overall impression is that improving the legal status of same-sex couples is a topical issue in a great number of European jurisdictions, whereas it largely remains controversial globally. (The political interest in adopting special rules for same-sex couples is in line with the general idea that individuals should be free to live according to their own wishes, without official interference through legislation which is based on moral values concerning the 'right' way to live.) However, as will be further illustrated below, there is still no consensus in Europe as regards the legal status of same-sex relationships.

3. MARRIAGE AND THE ECHR – INTERPRETATIONS BY THE STRASBOURG COURT

3.1 Background

(Achieving equality between husband and wife and different cohabitation models in society has been and still is a driving force to legislation in many European countries during the 20th and 21st centuries) Now I will link this development to the human rights discourse in Europe, more precisely to the relevant provisions of the European Convention of Human Rights, as interpreted by the Strasbourg Court.

(In the late 1940s, in the aftermath of World War II, protecting individuals' human rights vis-à-vis the state became urgent in Europe)

---

[99] See The European Union Agency for Fundamental Rights (FRA) (available 8 July 2015 at http://www.fra.europa.eu/fraWebsite/attachments/FRA-LGBT-report-update2010.pdf) 8.

[100] Press release by The Swedish Federation for Lesbian, Gay, Bisexual and Transgender Rights (RFSL) (available 8 July 2015 at http://www.rfsl.se/?p=324&aid=12373).

[101] The death penalty currently appears to be prescribed for homosexual sexual acts in the following countries: Iran, Saudi Arabia, Yemen, United Arab Emirates, Mauritania, Afghanistan and Pakistan, as well as in some parts of Sudan and Nigeria. In Uganda according to the Anti-Homosexuality Act 2014 homosexual sexual acts can be punished with life imprisonment; an earlier draft had included the possibility of death penalty.

Given the horrible crimes against humanity carried out during the war, it was clear that nations could not be fully trusted to treat their citizens in accordance with basic human values.[102] There was a general fear in the West over the spread of communism and it was deemed necessary to counteract the installation of a new totalitarian regime.[103] This concern resulted in the formation of different international bodies dealing with human rights issues from a public international law perspective.

In the global arena, the United Nations was founded in 1945 and its General Assembly proclaimed the United Nation's Universal Declaration of Human Rights in 1948.[104] At European level, the Council of Europe was founded in 1949, but the drafting of the European Convention on Human Rights had already begun 1948. The Convention was opened for signature in 1950 and the year 1952 can be regarded as the year of completion, that is, when the First Protocol to the main Convention was concluded. At the same time, the Strasbourg Court was established for the purpose of ensuring that member states complied with the articles laid down in the Convention.[105] Since then the ECHR has been amended by seven additional Protocols.[106])

States that have chosen to accede to the ECHR – and to some or all of its additional Protocols – are obligated according to international law to respect the fundamental human rights of the Convention, not only in respect of the country's own citizens, but also in respect of foreign nationals abiding on its territory and belonging to its jurisdiction.[107] Individuals have the right to file complaints with the Strasbourg Court that a state has failed to guarantee them the enjoyment of the rights laid down in the Convention, provided that all domestic remedies have been exhausted and that formalities such as applicable time-limits have been followed.[108]

---

[102]   I Cameron, *An Introduction to the European Convention on Human Rights* (6th edn, Iustus 2011) 25.

[103]   E Bates, *The Evolution of the European Convention on Human Rights, From its Inception to the Creation of a Permanent Court of Human Rights* (Oxford University Press 2010) 5.

[104]   The UN will not be further analysed here.

[105]   Bates, *The Evolution of the European Convention on Human Rights* (n 103) 23 f.

[106]   Protocol numbers: 1, 4, 6, 7, 11, 12 and 13. Most aspects of the additional protocols have been inserted in Protocol 11. A varying number of states have chosen to accede to each additional Protocol.

[107]   ECHR, article 1.

[108]   Bates, *The Evolution of the European Convention on Human Rights* (n 103) 2.

When studying the legal development relating to marriage in Europe, three articles in the ECHR are of special interest: article 8 (the right to respect for one's private and family life), article 12 (the right to marry and found a family) and article 14 (the prohibition against discrimination).

3.2 Article 8: The Right to Protection of One's Private Life and Family Life

N.B.

1. Everyone has the right to respect for his private and family life, his home and his correspondence.
2. There shall be no interference by a public authority with the exercise of this right except such as is in accordance with the law and is necessary in a democratic society in the interests of national security, public safety or the economic well-being of the country, for the prevention of disorder or crime, for the protection of health or morals, or for the protection of the rights and freedoms of others.

3.2.1 General remarks

The right to one's privacy has been a recurring theme in legal development in Europe since the 1960s and 1970s. In Sweden, this was expressed in terms of 'neutrality' in the late 1960s, the idea being that individuals should as far as possible be trusted to make rational decisions concerning their relationships without unnecessary morally-based 'intervention' by the authorities. Making divorce easier to obtain is in line with this policy. Also, legally recognising same-sex couples through special enactments reflects a general intention to leave lifestyle choices up to the individuals concerned. The same basic message can be found in article 8 of the ECHR – the protection of a person's privacy.

Article 8 of the ECHR covers many aspects of privacy. It protects a person's private and family life, as well as a person's home and correspondence.[109] In this chapter, however, only cases dealing with civil status issues will be dealt with. The idea is to investigate to what extent the line of development, which is visible at national level in Europe and accounted for above, is visible also at European level, that is, the development away from marriage as the only legally relevant cohabitation model, in favour of a more pluralistic view on who constitutes a 'family'.

---

[109] Article 8 includes issues such as personal integrity against the press and confidential data. See Cameron, *An Introduction to the European Convention on Human Rights* (n 102) 116–18.

3.2.2   Two levels of protection within the 'privacy sphere'

Who is recognised as family and enjoys protection of their 'family life' under article 8? (The protection of a couple's 'family life' is more extensive than the protection of a couple's 'private life', the former including, inter alia, a right for those who qualify as family under the article to live together and an obligation for the national legislator to protect the family in its domestic family law.[110])

There is no doubt that spouses of different sex are included, provided that it is not a marriage of convenience, entered into solely for immigration purposes.[111](In 1986, in the case of *Johnston and Others v Ireland*, the Strasbourg Court ruled that *unmarried* cohabiting couples also enjoy protection of their 'family life' under article 8.)In that case, an Irish man was unable to marry the woman he had been living with for 15 years because he was already married to another woman and divorce was not permitted according to Irish law at that time. According to the Strasbourg Court, the unmarried couple constituted a family for the purposes of article 8 and was entitled to protection, notwithstanding the fact that their relationship existed outside of marriage. This meant, for instance, that they were entitled to the same social benefits as a married couple, but as specifically stated in the judgment: 'Article 8 cannot be interpreted as imposing an obligation to establish a special regime for a particular category of unmarried couples.'[112] Furthermore, in the *Johnston*-case, the Strasbourg Court underlined that article 8 did not include a right to divorce.[113]

---

[110]   See *Abdulaziz v UK*, App No 921480, (ECHR, 28 May 1985). See also R Wintemute, 'Strasbourg to the Rescue? Same-Sex Partners and Parents under the European Convention' in R Wintemute and M Andenæs (eds), *Legal Recognition of Same-Sex Partnerships: A Study of National, European and International Law* (Oxford, Hart Publishing, 2004) 715. It can be noted that article 8 does not guarantee rights of immigration.

[111]   See Toner, *Partnership Rights, Free Movement and EU Law* (n 89) 80.

[112]   *Johnston and Others v Ireland*, App No 9697/82 (ECHR, 18 December 1986) para 68.

[113]   *Johnston and Others v Ireland*, App No 9697/82 (ECHR, 18 December 1986) paras 52–54. Divorce is a sensitive issue in Roman Catholic influenced States like Ireland, Malta and Poland, because marriage constitutes a non-soluble sacrament according to the Catholic faith. A discord can be noted between, on the one hand, 'progressive' member states such as the Nordic States and the Netherlands and, on the other hand, the more 'conservative' member states, such as Malta, Ireland and Poland. This discord is particularly visible in respect of issues relating to divorce, sexual equality, transsexualism and homosexuality. The 'conservative' member states take a cautious approach in such matters, which are

(When determining if a couple enjoys protection of their 'family life' under article 8, the Strasbourg Court has taken into account factors such as how stable the relationship is and the parties' intention with the relationship. Relationships that have lasted for a long time are more likely to qualify as family life than short-term relationships, as are relationships where the couple has joint finances or joint children.[114] De facto cohabitation is another important but not necessary factor when determining if a couple enjoys protection of their 'family life' under article 8.[115])

(In 2010, in the case of *Schalk and Kopf v Austria,* the Strasbourg Court for the first time stated that same-sex couples enjoy protection of their 'family life' according to article 8 of the ECHR.[116]) Prior to these judgments, a same sex couple had only been granted protection of their 'private life' – not their 'family life'. (However, the Court established that same-sex couples do not have a right to marry.) This case will be further analysed in section 3.3.3. The Strasbourg Court has improved the legal position of homosexual individuals while exercising their rights under the Convention. For instance, bans on homosexual conduct in national legislation have been found contrary to article 8 – the right to respect for one's private life.[117]

In summary, the relationship forms qualifying as 'family' under article 8 have gradually been extended through a dynamic interpretation model of the Strasbourg Court. (Marriage between a man and a woman is no longer the only cohabitation form protected under article 8 of the ECHR)

---

sensitive from the point of view of traditional (Catholic) values, whereas the most 'progressive' states have facilitated divorce and opened up marriage to same-sex couples. (See Cameron, *An Introduction to the European Convention on Human Rights* (n 102) 115.) For a thorough account for the legal development in Spain, another 'Catholic' region, see, Sörgjerd, *Reconstructing Marriage – The Legal Status of Relationships in a Changing Society* (n 6) 249–67.

[114]   Toner, *Partnership Rights, Free Movement and EU Law* (n 89) 81. See also I Curry-Sumner, *The Charter of Fundamental Rights of the European Union and Sexual Orientation*, in P Lødrup and E Modvar, *Family Life and Human Rights* (Gyldendal 2004) 876 and Wintemute, 'Strasbourg to the Rescue? Same-Sex Partners and Parents under the European Convention' (n 110) 721–3.

[115]   Toner, *Partnership Rights, Free Movement and EU Law* (n 89) 81, with reference to relevant case law on this topic.

[116]   *Schalk and Kopf v Austria* App No 30141/04 (ECHR, 24 June 2010).

[117]   *Dudgeon v UK* App No 7525/76 (ECHR, 22 October 1981); *Norris v Ireland* App No 10581/83 (ECHR, 26 October 1988); *Modinos v Cyprus* App No 15070/89 (ECHR, 22 April 1993) and *A.D.T. v UK* App No 35765/97 (ECHR, 31 July 2000).

Like in many European jurisdictions, unmarried couples and same-sex couples have been granted a certain level of protection of their relationships. However, as will be shown below, access to marriage under article 12 is still applied restrictively.

3.3   Article 12: The Right to Marry and Found a Family

N.B.

Men and women of marriageable age have the right to marry and to found a family, according to the national laws governing the exercise of this right.

3.3.1   General remarks

(The right to marry and found a family in article 12 is closely connected to the right to family life in article 8.)Articles 8 and 12 both protect the family as something of a corner stone in society. [In short, article 8 prohibits interference with an existing relationship or family unit, whereas article 12 governs the right to form family ties through marriage.[118] However, the right to marry according to article 12 is interpreted more narrowly than the right to one's private life and family life under article 8. A restrictive understanding of the right to marry and found a family is stipulated in the wording of article 12; the right to marry and found a family only applies 'according to the national laws governing the exercise of this right'.

What does the reference to 'national laws' mean in article 12? In the legal literature it has been pointed out that the right to marry cannot be a matter for domestic laws alone to decide; (the Convention is a public international law document adopted for the purpose of providing a certain basic level of protection regardless of what domestic laws stipulate.[119])If a member state could place whichever restrictions it pleased on this right, it would be pointless to include the right in the Convention in the first place.[120] (This means that a member state may restrict the right to marry through its domestic law – the states have a margin of appreciation – but the aim with the restriction must be

---

[118]   R White and C Ovey, *The European Convention on Human Rights* (5th edn, Oxford University Press 2010) 334.

[119]   H Danelius, *Mänskliga rättigheter i europeisk praxis* (4th Edition, Norstedts Juridik 2012) 503. White and Ovey, *The European Convention on Human Rights* (n 118) 353.

→ [120]   Cameron, *An Introduction to the European Convention on Human Rights* (n 102) 137.

legitimate and proportionate in relation to the goal sought to achieve.[121]) As a result, the details in the marriage regulation vary among the member states, for instance in respect of impediments to marriage and marriageable age. An example of a legitimate and proportionate restriction is to prevent incest or polygamy.[122]

Generally the states' margin of appreciation is wide in respect of matters relating to public morality, since there is no European consensus on what 'good' morality is.[123] In certain family law matters – irrespective of their sensitive character – the Strasbourg Court has gradually become more dynamic and thereby, in a sense, forced 'progressive' values on the more 'conservative' member states.[124] There is a limit to the state's margin of appreciation even in sensitive issues such as marriage and divorce; otherwise the right would mean nothing. For example in 1987, (in the case of *F v Switzerland*, the Court found that banning an adulterous party from remarrying for three years, pursuant to a specific provision in the Swiss Civil Code which applied at that time, for the purpose of protecting the institution of marriage, constituted a breach of article 12.[125])The Court found that the Swiss provision undermined the very essence of the right to marry.[126]

[The judgment in *F v. Switzerland* is in line with the legal development in many European jurisdictions, toward reducing moral input in the marriage regulation, in order to facilitate divorce and enhance marriage as an institution based on equality and individual freedom] Punishing the

---

[121] White and Ovey, *The European Convention on Human Rights* (n 118) 353.

[122] Ibid. In *B and L v UK* App No 36536/02 (ECHR, 13 September 2005, noted by Scherpe [2006] *Cambridge Law Journal* 32–5) rules prohibiting marriage between a daughter-in-law and her father-in-law, were considered to be a violation of article 12. The prohibition aimed to protect the integrity of the family unit.

[123] Danelius, *Mänskliga rättigheter i europeisk praxis* (n 119) 52.

[124] Iain Cameron points out that the 'progressive' Northern states can be accused of going too far in this respect and thereby neglecting important traditional values in a country. Cameron, *An Introduction to the European Convention on Human Rights* (n 102) 116.

[125] European Court of Human Rights: *F v Switzerland* App No 11329/85 (ECHR, 18 December 1987). See also the case of *Airey v Ireland* App No 6289/73, (ECHR, 9 October 1979). The case concerned judicial separation.

[126] Cameron, *An Introduction to the European Convention on Human Rights* (n 102) 138. For an analysis of what the essence of marriage is, see Sörgjerd, *Reconstructing Marriage – The Legal Status of Relationships in a Changing Society* (n 6).

spouse who is 'to blame' for the breakdown of the marriage by obstructing that spouse from concluding a new marriage, was a type of moral intervention by the public into the individual's private sphere, which was not found acceptable from a human rights perspective.

3.3.2 Transsexual and transgender persons and the right to marry

When the ECHR was adopted in 1950, the right to marry only applied to couples of opposite biological sex. The Strasbourg Court cannot adopt new rights but it can interpret existing rights in a dynamic fashion which widens the meaning of the concepts.[127] Recognising a transsexual persons' right to marry someone of their opposite (assigned) sex is an example of this dynamic interpretation model.

[In 2002, in the case of *Christine Goodwin v the United Kingdom*, the Strasbourg Court for the first time found that denying transsexual persons who had undergone gender-reassignment surgery the right to marry someone of the opposite sex constituted a breach of article 12 of the ECHR. In previous decisions on the same topic – *Rees* (1986), *Cossey* (1990) and *Sheffield and Horsham* (1998) – the Strasbourg Court allowed the national governments a wide margin of appreciation and no violation of the Convention was found.[128] Since the *Goodwin*-case, however, the member states' margin of appreciation is much narrower when dealing with transsexual persons' rights under the Convention. The member states are generally free to regulate the details concerning a change of legal gender without violating the Convention (article 8), but they cannot infringe transsexual persons' right to marry someone of their opposite assigned sex according to article 12.[129])

In the *Goodwin* case, the Strasbourg Court stated that it 'attaches less importance to the lack of evidence of a common European approach to the resolution of the legal and practical problems posed, than to the clear and uncontested evidence of a continuing international trend in favour not only of increased social acceptance of transsexuals but of legal recognition of the new sexual identity of post-operative transsexuals.'[130]

---

[127] Cameron, *An Introduction to the European Convention on Human Rights* (n 102) 74. Sometimes the line between widening an existing right and adopting a new one appears thin.

[128] *Rees v The United Kingdom* App No 9532/81 (ECHR, 17 October 1986); *Cossey v UK* App No 10843/84 (ECHR, 27 September 1990) and *Sheffield and Horsham v UK* App No 22885/93; 23390/94 (ECHR, 30 July 1998).

[129] Danelius, *Mänskliga rättigheter i europeisk praxis* (n 119) 502.

[130] *Christine Goodwin v UK* App No 28957/95 (ECHR, 11 July, 2002) para 85.

In other words clear and uncontested evidence of a European trend to recognise the rights of transsexual persons was not necessary for the outcome in the *Goodwin* case, which in fact contradicted the prevailing laws of most European countries. As will be discussed below, it would be possible, at least in theory, to apply the same line of argument to same-sex couples, that is, to open up marriage to same-sex couples as a result of a 'continuing international trend' to recognise the rights of homosexuals in society.[131]

3.3.3 The legal status of same-sex couples: toward a European consensus?[132]

Given the fact that transsexual persons have been granted the right to marry pursuant to article 12, without full consensus in the member states, perhaps also same-sex marriage will be recognised in the future, through a similar dynamic interpretation method.[133] In the *Goodwin* case the Court stressed that the Convention is a living instrument which needs to be adjusted to present-day conditions.[134]

In 2010, in the *Schalk and Kopf*-case the Strasbourg Court ruled that same-sex couples enjoy protection of their *family life* under article 8 and not just of their *private life*. In that case, two men who were living together in a stable relationship in Austria applied for permission to marry each other in Austria. Austrian law did not allow same-sex marriage and no formalised union for same-sex couples had been adopted at the time. (The Austrian Registered Partnership Act was adopted in

---

[131]   See section 3.3.3 below.

[132]   See Ian Curry-Sumner, chapter 4 in this volume. See also J Scherpe, 'From "Odious Crime" to Family Life – Same-sex Couples and the ECHR', in A-L Verbeke, JM Scherpe, C Declerck, T Helms and P Senaeve (eds), Confronting the Frontiers of Family and Succession Law – Liber amicorum Walter Pintens (Intersentia 2012) 1225–40 and J Scherpe, 'The Legal Recognition of Same-Sex Couples in Europe and the Role of the European Court of Human Rights' (2013) 10 Equal Rights Review 83–96 (available in print and 8 July 2015 at http://www.equalrightstrust.org/ertdocumentbank/ERR10_sp1.pdf).

[133]   On the other hand, the outcome of the Goodwin case can be interpreted as underlining the idea of marriage as a heterosexual union. See Sörgjerd, *Reconstructing Marriage – The Legal Status of Relationships in a Changing Society* (n 6) 299–300.

[134]   *Christine Goodwin v UK* App No 28957/95 (ECHR, 11 July 2002) paras 74-75. See also for instance *EB v France* App No 43546/02 (ECHR, 22 January 2008) para 92.

2010.)[135] When the couple's request was denied by Austrian authorities, they turned to the Strasbourg Court and claimed that they had been victims of unlawful discrimination based on their sexual orientation, more precisely because they as a same-sex couple could not marry or otherwise have their relationship formally recognised by Austrian law.[136] The Strasbourg Court recognised that many member states had introduced rules providing same-sex couples with access to a formalised institution. However, the Court pointed out, the substantial rules differed considerably from one country to another in respect of legal effects.[137] Thus there was still no *consensus* in Europe on the issue of legal recognition of same-sex couples.

The merit of the *Schalk and Kopf*-case, from the perspective of same-sex couples and their spokespersons, is that same-sex couples qualify as enjoying 'family life' under article 8 and not just 'private life'. The Court underlined that the verdict does not mean that national Governments are obligated to introduce a special legal institution for same-sex couples, but they are compelled to treat unmarried same-sex and different-sex couples equally in respect of social and other benefits. This was illustrated in another case – The case of *P.B. and J.S. v Austria,* also decided in the summer of 2010.

⟦In the *P.B and J.S* case, the Strasbourg Court for the first time ruled that a same-sex couple's 'family life' had in fact been violated.⟧ The case concerned a homosexual man's demands for access to his partner's sickness and accident insurance. Treating unmarried couples of the same sex differently than unmarried cohabiting couples of the opposite sex constituted a breach of article 14 in conjunction with article 8.

These two cases – *Schalk and Kopf* and *P.B. and J.S.* – can be seen as examples of the Court's dynamic interpretation method.[138] They can be interpreted as the Court taking one step toward obliging member states to introduce a formalised institution for same-sex couples, in order to

---

[135]   The Registered Partnership Act, Federal Law Gazette (Bundesgesetzblatt) Vol I, No 135/2009. The Act entered into force 1 January 2010.

[136]   *Schalk and Kopf v Austria* App No 30141/04 (ECHR, 24 June 2010) para 3.

[137]   *Schalk and Kopf v Austria* App No 30141/04 (ECHR, 24 June 2010) para 31.

[138]   See also *Valliantos and others v Greece* App Nos. 29381/09 and 32684/09 (ECHR, 7 November 2013), where the Court ruled that excluding same-sex couples in Greece from registering a civil union, an option available to heterosexual unmarried couples, violated rights protected by article 14 in conjunction with article 8 of the Convention.

safeguard the protection of their family life.[139] However, as it turns out, the Court is not ready to go that far, at least not yet. (In 2012, in the case of <u>Gas and Dubois v France,</u> the Strasbourg Court ruled that excluding same-sex couples from access to marriage was not discriminatory; that is, article 14 in conjunction with article 8 of the ECHR had not been violated.[140])

In the Gas and Dubois case, two women had entered into a 'PACS' in 2002. In the year 2000, the couple had had a child by means of assisted procreation in Belgium, using an anonymous sperm donor. They raised the child together and in 2006 the birth mother's partner applied to adopt the child (with the birth mother's consent). The French tribunals rejected the application by virtue of the French civil code, which stipulates that only spouses can achieve joint parenthood through adoption. Same-sex marriage is about to be legalised in France in 2013, most likely along with rules on adoption by same-sex couples, but at the time of the *Gas and Dubois* case same-sex couples could neither marry nor adopt under French law. The Strasbourg Court ruled that there had been no discrimination because of the couple's sexual orientation in the present case, since unmarried same-sex couples were treated equally to unmarried different-sex couples and there is no obligation to grant same-sex couples access to marriage or to a legal institution with equivalent legal effects, as established in the Schalk and Kopf case.

In summary, the Strasbourg Court does not appear to be on the verge of compelling member states to grant same-sex couples access to marriage. Same-sex marriage remains a sensitive issue in Europe and article 12 leaves a wide margin of appreciation to the member states. On the other hand, the legal development relating to same-sex couples has been extremely rapid in Europe during the past few decades, which speaks in favour of a rapid development and a dynamic interpretation also in the jurisprudence of the Strasbourg Court.

---

[139] Sörgjerd, *Reconstructing Marriage – The Legal Status of Relationships in a Changing Society* (n 6) 303–11.

[140] *Gas and Dubois v France* App No 25951/07, Judgment of 15 March 2012. The decision is in French but the facts of the case can be found at http://hudoc.echr.coe.int/sites/eng/pages/search.aspx#%7B%22dmdocnumber%22 %3A%5B%22882709%22%5D%2C%22display%22%3A%5B0%5D%7D. For an English summary see The Guardian, 'Can a homosexual person adopt his or her partner's child?' 2 April, 2012. http://www.guardian.co.uk/law/2012/apr/02/ can-gay-person-adopt-partners-child (both accessed 8 July 2015).

4. CONCLUDING REMARKS

Is there a European definition or common conception of marriage? As I see it, it is not possible to find one uncontested definition of marriage, not within a country and even less so across Europe. Marriage is a complex and dynamic institution. It is not just a legal contract, concluded by two persons for the purpose of settling their financial matters; it is also a product of its historical, cultural and religious functions in society.[141] (As the Strasbourg Court has put it: 'marriage has deep-rooted social and cultural connotations which may differ largely from one society to another'.[142])

What one can do, however, in order to increase our understanding of how marriage functions in 21st century Europe, is to identify common interests or core values which have been found worth protecting through legislation over time in different European countries. When doing so, a general line of development appears. This development first focuses on achieving equality – legal parity – between men and women and then moves on to reducing the level of official participation in the couple's private sphere, inter alia by making divorce more accessible. Adopting laws which recognise the rights of unmarried and same-sex couples, in favour of a more pluralistic outlook on civil status issues, constitutes a third 'stage' in this development: pluralism. The jurisprudence of the Strasbourg Court, based on the ECHR, has stimulated this development through dynamic interpretations. As a result, the member states' margin of appreciation has gradually diminished in selected fields, whereas the Strasbourg Court has remained more cautious in other matters, which are considered to be best left to national authorities to determine.

The three themes – *equality, privacy and pluralism* – are important keys to understanding how marriage functions in Europe in the 21st century. Marriage is a legal institution based on equality between the couple. It is also based on the idea of respect for the individual's privacy and couples are trusted to make rational decisions about their relationship without unnecessary interference by the authorities. The emphasis on party and individual autonomy has resulted in, for instance, law reforms aiming at reducing the impact of fault in divorce proceedings and the introduction of divorce based on mutual consent or even 'on demand'.

---

[141] See Sörgjerd, *Reconstructing Marriage – The Legal Status of Relationships in a Changing Society* (n 6).

[142] *Schalk and Kopf v Austria* App No 30141/04 (ECHR, 24 June 2010) para 62, with reference to a case from 2005 – *B and L v UK*, para 36. See section 3.4.2 above.

The focus on *equality* and *privacy* has helped pave the way for the third theme – *pluralism*. If everyone is truly equal under the law and if lifestyle choices belong to the individual's 'private sphere', people's differences in this respect must be accepted, respected and even, to some extent, protected through legislation. This has opened up the legal recognition of same-sex couples in the domestic laws of several European countries. Special enactments have been introduced, which vary in substance and form but share a common ambition, namely to improve the legal status of same-sex couples and counteract discrimination. The human rights discourse in Europe has fuelled this development, by emphasising equality and non-discrimination. In some countries the institutions created with same-sex couples in mind are also open to unmarried couples of the opposite sex.[143]

What will happen to the institution of marriage if the development towards more privacy, autonomy and pluralism continues? Will the institution of marriage still serve a relevant purpose from a legal point of view in the future, or will marriage become superfluous and be abolished? As I see it, privacy as an isolated phenomenon, can perhaps be a 'threat' to the institution of marriage. There are ways to privately celebrate and solemnise a relationship and of honouring a couple's commitment to each other without involving the authorities through a legally binding ceremony. However, in my opinion, marriage still serves a relevant purpose and should not be abolished as a legal institution. Marriage comes with a package of legal rules, which are based on the idea of creating equality between the spouses and specially designed to recognise different kinds of contributions to the mutual 'family project' as equally valuable. Couples cannot be fully trusted to regulate their financial situation through agreements in an equal and fair manner; a certain level of official participation is needed.

Moreover, if privacy can be a threat to marriage, then pluralism can be the remedy. The experience with the Swedish gender neutral marriage reform of 2009 illustrates this. The Swedish 2009 enactment was not about same-sex couples acquiring the legal effects of marriage. The Registered Partnership Act of 1994 already provided same-sex partners with access to the same legal rules as those acquired through marriage. The Swedish reform of 2009 was about the symbolic value of calling a union 'marriage' instead of 'registered partnership'. It became clear, from a Swedish perspective, that marriage is not just a package of legal rules

---

[143] This is the case in respect of, for instance the French PACS and the Dutch Registered Partnership.

but also a kind of trademark, which signals durability and long-term commitment and this was attractive to same-sex couples.[144] Since 2009, in Sweden, marriage also signals equal treatment and non-discrimination.

Against this background one could say that if marriage was heading toward complete 'privatisation' and thereby by extension risked becoming superfluous as a legal institution, then same-sex couples recharged the symbolic value of marriage as a civil status and thereby saved it. This line of reasoning can be applied to many European jurisdictions, where same-sex couples have been legally recognised. Modernising marriage is a way to keep it á jour with contemporary values. It is likely that marriage will continue to be an important cohabitation model and civil status in Europe, as long as it does not stagnate but continues to prove flexible and adaptable to changing values in society.

RECOMMENDATIONS FOR FURTHER READING

M Antokolskaia, *Harmonisation of Family Law in Europe: A Historical Perspective, A Tale of Two Millennia* (Intersentia 2006).

K Boele-Woelki (ed.), *Perspectives for the Unification and Harmonisation of Family Law in Europe* (Intersentia 2003).

K Boele-Woelki, *The Legal Recognition of Same-Sex Relationships Within the European Union* (2007–2008) 82 *Tulane Law Review* 1949–1981.

K Boele-Woelki and A Fuchs (eds), *Legal Recognition of Same-Sex Relationships in Europe* (Intersentia 2012).

D Bradley, *Family Law and Political Culture* (Modern Legal Studies, Scandinavian Laws in Comparative Perspective, Sweet & Maxwell 1996).

MA Glendon, *The Transformation of Family Law, State, Law and Family in the United States and Western Europe* (University of Chicago Press 1989).

M Jänterä-Jareborg, *Family Law in the European Judicial Space – Concerns Regarding Nation-State's Autonomy and Legal Coherence, National Law and Europeanization* (Suomalainen Lakimieshydistys 2009) 29–61.

J Scherpe and N Yassari (eds), *Die Rechtsstellung nichtehelicher Lebensgemeinschaften/The Legal Status of Cohabitants* (Mohr Siebeck 2005).

C Sörgjerd, *Reconstructing Marriage, The Legal Status of Relationships in a Changing Society* (Intersentia 2012).

Publications by the Commission on European Family Law, especially European Family Law in Action, Volumes 1, 2 and 4, see http://ceflonline.net/.

---

[144] Sörgjerd, *Reconstructing Marriage – The Legal Status of Relationships in a Changing Society* (n 6).

2. Divorce law in a European perspective

Masha Antokolskaia

1. INTRODUCTION

Even a simple glance at how divorce grounds are formally labelled in various European jurisdictions reveals quite some diversity. This picture is confirmed by the account of divorce laws in Europe provided in the 2003 Commission on European Family Law (CEFL) National Reports.[1] This chapter gives an overview of recent developments in divorce laws in Europe, with the main focus being on analysing divorce grounds from both a formal and a functional perspective. In addition, some insight is given into the issue of administrative divorce, which is currently attracting growing interest from various legislatures.

This chapter is divided into three parts following this introduction. Part 2 discusses possible reasons for the current diversity of divorce laws in Europe, along with a brief historical introduction and a deliberation on the impact of European human rights instruments on divorce law in Europe. Part 3 provides a close-up analysis, in two sections, of recent developments in divorce law. The first of these two sections examines several jurisdictions (England and Wales, France, Germany, Italy, Ireland and Malta) and their interpretations of 'irretrievable breakdown of marriage', while the second section focuses on several other jurisdictions (Sweden, Russia, Norway, Spain and Portugal) and a model law (the CEFL Principles on Divorce) that moves beyond the concept of irretrievable breakdown. Part 4 discusses and scrutinises the grounds for divorce currently co-existing in Europe, while Part 5 examines an impending challenge to the law of divorce procedure in the form of the administrative divorce.

---

[1] http://ceflonline.net/country-reports-by-jurisdiction/ (accessed 9 July 2015) and K Boele-Woelki, B Braat and I Curry Sumner (eds), *European Family Law in Action – Volume I: Grounds for Divorce* (Intersentia 2003), 2.2.1.1. For a synopsis, see D Martiny, 'Divorce and Maintenance between Former Spouses – Initial Results of the Commission on European Family Law', in K Boele-Woelki, (ed.), *Perspectives for the Unification and Harmonisation of Family Law in Europe* (Intersentia 2003) 534.

2. EXPLAINING DIVERSITY

2.1 Historical Introduction: Compromises between Conservative and Progressive Camps

An explanation for the current diversity of divorce laws in Europe could be sought in the political differences between European countries. Ever since the French Revolution, as I suggested in 'A Harmonisation of Family Law in Europe: A Tale of Two Millennia',[2] [Europe has been split into a progressive camp inspired by the ideology of the Enlightenment and a conservative camp aspiring to preserve or restore traditional family forms and values.] Divorce law has historically been one of the major battlefields between those two camps, and the divorce laws that have emerged are the results of compromises between them. Throughout the 19th and much of the 20th century, conservatives in Western Europe successfully managed, save for a few exceptions, to obstruct any far-reaching liberalisation of divorce laws (and in Italy, Spain, Portugal, Ireland and Malta even obstructed its very introduction). Nonetheless a creeping liberalisation of divorce slowly accrued under pressure from the progressive camp. Indeed, from the 1960s onwards, the lead was taken by advocates of liberalisation (and, in countries not allowing divorce, by parties in favour of its introduction or reintroduction). Although the political and ideological sensitivities of divorce still made compromise between the conservative and progressive camps an indispensable pre-condition of almost every divorce law reform, the proponents of liberalisation were by then in a far better position to determine the outcome of these compromises. The drive towards modernisation of divorce laws swiftly gained momentum. The transformation of divorce law also underwent a major qualitative change as previous divorce law liberalisation had, for the most part, amounted to a 'steady accumulation of specific grounds',[3] largely accomplished by adding 'new specific matrimonial offences and conditions' to existing ones.[4] Nevertheless, as the following overview shows, recent divorce reforms in the majority of European jurisdictions have still required a compromise between the conservative and progressive camps.

---

[2] M Antokolskaia, *Harmonisation of Family Law in Europe: A Historical Perspective. A Tale of Two Millennia* (Intersentia 2006).

[3] R Phillips, *Putting Asunder: A History of Divorce in Western Society* (Cambridge University Press 1988) 563.

[4] Ibid.

The close-up in Part 3 shows how differences in the balance of political power in European states have led to rather different outcomes in the field of divorce law.

2.2 Limited Impact of European Human Rights Instruments

Another reason for the current diversity of divorce laws in Europe is that the impact of international human law instruments in this field is much more limited than perhaps could be expected. In contrast to the position in the United States,[5] the right to dissolve a marriage in Europe never attained the status of an individual human right protected under the European Convention on Human Rights (ECHR).[6] The explanation for this lies mainly in the political sensitivity of divorce, as clearly illustrated in the 1986 case of *Johnston and others v Ireland*,[7] which has so far been the only attempt to invoke ECHR protection of the right to divorce. In this case, an Irishman (who had obtained a judicial separation from his first wife many years previously) together with his second partner challenged the Irish law that – at that time – did not permit full divorce and remarriage. The European Court of Human Rights (ECtHR) refused to apply a dynamic interpretation of article 12 and instead accepted Ireland's defence, whereby it was claimed, referring to the *travaux préparatoires* of the Convention, that the Convention text's omission of the right to dissolve a marriage was deliberate.[8] Surprisingly, the ECtHR – contrary to its own practice – did not elaborate on the existence of European 'common ground' regarding divorce. This was remarkable, considering that at that time only two contracting states (Ireland and Malta) did not allow full divorce, while the vast majority of the states shared a consensus on this matter. Instead, the Court stated, without any further substantiation, that 'having regard to the diversity of the practices followed and the situations obtaining in the Contracting States, the notion's requirements will vary considerably from case to case. Accordingly, this is an area in which the Contracting Parties enjoy a wide margin of appreciation in determining the steps to be taken to ensure

---

[5]   M-A Glendon, *The Transformation of Family Law* (University of Chicago Press 1989) 190.

[6]   D van Grunderbeeck, *Beginselen van personen- en familierecht. Een mensenrechtelijke benadering* (Intersentia 2003) 261 ff.

[7]   *Johnston and others v Ireland* (1986) EHRM 112, App No 9697/82 (18 December 1986).

[8]   Ibid 52–3.

compliance with the Convention'.[9] Lastly, in spite of the persuasive dissenting opinion by Judge De Meyer,[10] the Court refused to recognise the right to dissolve marriage as a right protected under the ECHR. It could be questioned how the same Court that forbade different treatment of illegitimate children in the *Marckx* case[11] could come to such a decision in the Irish divorce case. The explanation would seem to be that on 26 June 1986, some four days before the final deliberation in the *Johnston* case, the overwhelming majority of the Irish electorate had just rejected divorce in a first referendum. The unavailability of divorce in Ireland had therefore acquired the highest political legitimacy.[12] There was little chance that the Irish government would simply acquiesce in the event of a contradictory decision on the part of the Court. It is quite plausible, therefore, that 'the Court carefully backed down in the *Johnston* case in order to preserve its own authority'.[13] The end result is that the protection provided by the Convention on this particular subject was established at the level of a very low common denominator indeed. As no similar case has since been brought before the Court, the *Johnston* case has never been overruled.

What is much harder to understand is why, 15 years later, the right to dissolve a marriage was not incorporated in the European Union (EU) Charter of Human Rights. This is quite remarkable, given that by the time the Charter was being drafted, even Ireland had introduced divorce and the only outliers were Malta and the Vatican City State. Although it is impossible to know whether this was a deliberate omission or just an oversight, it means in practice that, even today, divorce does not have the status of an individual human right, and the right to dissolve a marriage is not protected either by the ECHR or under EU law.

---

[9] Ibid 55.

[10] Ibid, see dissenting opinion of Judge De Meyer 35–40.

[11] *Marckx v Belgium* App No 6833/74 (13 June 1979), A31.

[12] Paul Mahoney stressed that 'the Court (and the Commission) should be careful not to allow that machinery to be used so as to enable disappointed opponents of some policy to obtain a victory in Strasbourg that they have been unable to obtain in the elective and democratic forum in their own country'. P Mahoney, 'Marvellous Richness of Diversity or Invidious Cultural Relativism?' (1998) 19 HRLJ 1, 3.

[13] N Johnson, 'Recent Developments: The Breadth of Family Law Review under the European Convention on Human Rights' (1995) 36 *Harvard International Law Journal* 513.

3. SUBSTANTIVE DIVORCE LAWS IN EUROPE: A CLOSE-UP

3.1 Many Faces of Irretrievable Breakdown

3.1.1 England: the reform that failed

3.1.1.1 1969 Reform: fault grounds called irretrievable breakdown The main problem in divorce law in England and Wales on the eve of the 1969 reform was that while the law on the statute books did not provide for divorce by mutual consent, consensual divorce by collusion was flourishing in fact. Although the pre-reform law allowed only for fault divorce, couples could in fact get a divorce 'as easily as a motor licence and rather more easily than a passport'.[14] The only condition was that the husband was prepared to behave 'like a gentleman'[15] by playing guilty in divorce proceedings initiated by the wife.[16] The problem of mass divorce by collusion was acknowledged both by conservatives and their progressive opponents. However, the ways they proposed to resolve the problem were very much at odds with one another. These conflicting approaches made compromise rather difficult and largely determined the contradictory nature of the 1969 divorce reform. The reform was preceded by two important reports: one, *Putting Asunder*,[17] was drawn up by a group of experts appointed by the Archbishop of Canterbury, while the other, *Reform of the Grounds of Divorce: the Field of Choice*,[18] was issued by the Law Commission. Both the Law Commission and the Archbishop of Canterbury's group shared the view that matrimonial offence as a ground for divorce should be replaced by the ground of the irretrievable breakdown of the marriage. The groups held very different views, however, on how an irretrievable breakdown should be established. The Archbishop's group insisted that the spouses' mutual consent alone may not constitute sufficient proof of breakdown. Therefore, *Putting Asunder* initially proposed a full inquiry into the breakdown of marriage in every

---

[14] H Herbert, 'Holy Deadlock' (1934), cited in S Cretney, 'Divorce Reform in England: Humbug and Hypocrisy or a Smooth Transition?', in M Freeman (ed.), *Divorce: Where Next?* (Dartmouth, 1996) 41.

[15] Ibid.

[16] See S Jenkinson 'The Co-Respondent's Role in Divorce Reform After 1923', in R Probert and C Barton (eds), *Fifty Years in Family Law. Essays for Stephen Cretney* (Intersentia 2012) 201–2.

[17] Phillips, *Putting Asunder: A History of Divorce in Western Society* (n 3).

[18] Law Commission, *Reform of the Grounds of Divorce: the Field of Choice* (Law Commission, 1966).

divorce case.[19] The Law Commission considered a full inquiry 'procedurally impracticable', and initially proposed deriving evidence of an irretrievable breakdown from the existence of a stated period of separation and the absence of evidence to the contrary.[20] The compromise reached between the two groups' approaches formed the basis of the Divorce Reform Act 1969.[21]

According to this Act, irretrievable breakdown should be established without a full inquiry, but only upon proof of the existence of specific, listed circumstances, referred to in the statutes as 'facts'.[22] Three of these facts were essentially fault grounds: that the respondent has committed adultery and that shared life was intolerable; that the respondent has behaved in such a way that the petitioner cannot reasonably be expected to live with the respondent; and the respondent's desertion for at least two years. These circumstances closely resembled 'the same old matrimonial faults'[23] of adultery, desertion and cruelty, the latter now being comprised in the behaviour fact.[24] In addition, two new no-fault facts were added: two years of living apart followed by application for divorce by mutual consent, or five years of living apart followed by unilateral application contested by the other spouse. Interestingly, the 1969 Act allowed parties to divorce and remarry before all the practical consequences of their divorce had been settled.[25] The ancillary matters could be dealt with later, in separate proceedings. The 1969 compromise resulted in legislation that, as well as being rather conservative by European standards, was also fairly contradictory. Despite proclaiming irretrievable breakdown of marriage as the sole ground for divorce, it effectively retained the old fault grounds, while also introducing the possibility of a no-fault divorce. Moreover, the new legislation proved to be rather inefficient in achieving one of the main objectives of the reform as it left too much scope for divorce by collusion, which was precisely what it had been intended to end.

---

[19] Ibid, 46.
[20] Law Commission, *The Field of Choice* (n 18) 53.
[21] This Act came into force on 1 January 1971 and was consolidated in 1973 into the Matrimonial Causes Act, which is still in force.
[22] B H Lee, *Divorce Reform in England* (Peter Owen 1974) 73.
[23] L Stone, *Road to Divorce. England 1530–1987* (Oxford University Press 1990) 307.
[24] Ibid.
[25] Although there was a statutory requirement to consider, but not settle, issues relating to children.

Another important change came, without much political debate, by way of delegated legislation. In 1973, the United Kingdom government, unable to cope with the growing number of divorce petitions,[26] introduced a 'special procedure'[27] for a range of non-contested cases.[28] (In 1977 this procedure was extended to all non-contested cases.[29] Since, in reality, almost all divorce petitions were non-contested, the special procedure became in practice the ordinary divorce procedure.[30] The special procedure allowed divorce to be granted without a court hearing or legal aid.[31] State control of divorce thus became very much a fiction.) Under the special procedure, the time between petition and decree in a non-contested divorce case based on one of the fault grounds amounted to less than four months.[32] By contrast, divorce by mutual consent required two years of separation. It is no wonder that most consenting couples opted for a shorter and cheaper fault divorce by collusion, rather than having to wait two years.[33] The emerging gap between law on the statute books and law in action once more accentuated the 'unsatisfactory nature of the compromise between offence-based facts and the breakdown principle'.[34]

3.1.1.2 The stillborn 1996 Family Law Act   Dissatisfaction with this situation started to increase in the 1980s.[35] However, while advocates of liberalisation viewed existing divorce as too difficult, conservatives

---

[26]   B Hale, 'The Family Law Act 1996 – the Death of Marriage?', in C Bridge (ed.), *Family Law Towards the Millennium: Essays for P M Bromley*, (Butterworths 1997) 6.

[27]   For a description of the special procedure, see Cretney, 'Divorce Reform in England: Humbug and Hypocrisy or a Smooth Transition?' (n 14) 56, n 19.

[28]   Namely for certain cases where no minor children of the family were involved. S Cretney, *Family Law in the Twentieth Century. A History* (Oxford University Press 2003) 382.

[29]   Ibid, 382.

[30]   Ibid.

[31]   Ibid.

[32]   *Fourth Annual Report of the Advisory Board in Family Law*, 2000/2001, para 3.5.

[33]   The Law Commission referred to 73% of divorce petitions being based on fault facts. Law Commission, *The Ground for Divorce* (1990), para 2.3.

[34]   Cretney, 'Divorce Reform in England: Humbug and Hypocrisy or a Smooth Transition?' (n 14) 42.

[35]   For an overview, see Cretney, *Family Law in the Twentieth Century* (n 28) 385 ff.

claimed it was too easy.[36] In 1988 the Law Commission published *Facing the Future*,[37] a discussion paper on the grounds for divorce. This attacked the existing divorce law for being incoherent, hypocritical and too restrictive.[38] At the same time, the conservatives attacked the existing legislation from the completely opposite angle, with their main concerns being that the special procedure had introduced 'divorce by post'[39] and had made divorce 'too easy'.[40] The forthcoming legislation was once again doomed to become a compromise. After years of proposals and amendments, the infamous stillborn 1996 Family Law Act was adopted.[41] This new Act allowed divorce after a one-year period of reflection in the case of non-contested divorces in which no minor children were involved. A defendant in a contested divorce case could ask for an additional six-month period of reflection. If a couple had children under the age of 16, the period of reflection was automatically extended by six months,[42] even if the planned divorce was by mutual consent.[43] But this was not all; in effect, getting divorced could take considerably longer than before

---

[36] As the Law Commission summarised in its 1990 report, the disagreement was so great that there was not even consensus about what it meant to make divorce 'easier'. For the advocates of liberalisation, easy divorce meant a 'short or painless' one, whereas for the conservative it could mean something different. Law Commission, *The Ground for Divorce* (1990), para 3.46.

[37] Law Commission, *Facing the Future* (1988).

[38] The Commission pointed out that it 'increased confusion for litigants', 'encouraged collusion' and that 'the ensuring hostility makes divorce more painful, not only for parties, but also for the children'. Law Commission, *Facing the Future* (1988), paras 3.48–3.50.

[39] Hale, 'The Family Law Act 1996 – the Death of Marriage?', (n 26) 6.

[40] S Cretney, J Masson and R Bailey-Harris, *Principles of Family Law* (7th edn, Sweet and Maxwell 2002) 297. Lady Hale complained that, 'oddly enough, this summary [*Facing the Future*] did not emphasise one of the most serious criticisms of the present law: that it allows a couple to be divorced, and therefore to remarry, before all the practical consequences of their separation from one another have been decided'. Hale, 'The Family Law Act 1996 – the Death of Marriage?' (n 26) 6.

[41] Received Royal Ascent on 4 July 1996.

[42] Family Law Act 1996, s 7.

[43] This amendment was upheld by the House of Commons despite strong opposition on the part of child protection organisations. Hale, 'The Family Law Act 1996 – the Death of Marriage?' (n 26) 15.

because all matters, including any ancillary matters, had to be adjudicated within the same proceedings.[44] All in all, the conservatives had almost managed to turn the 'divorce clock back'[45] as the newly proposed no-fault divorce made obtaining a divorce more lengthy and difficult than the existing fault-based divorce available under the special procedure. By 1996, however, there was no going back. Partly in response to the disappointment arising from the piloting of the new procedure,[46] the government withdrew its support for the Act, and in 2001 asked Parliament to repeal it.[47] The compromise embodied in the Act proved unworkable. The very nature of this compromise was designed to satisfy both the progressive-minded camp by seeking to introduce no-fault divorce and the marriage-saving aspirations of the conservatives.[48] By trying simultaneously to pursue 'conflicting policy objectives',[49] the new law 'created a rich possibility of potentially unworkable contradictions'.[50] In the end everything turned full circle as England and Wales had to fall back on the provisions of the 1969 Act (consolidated in 1973 into the Matrimonial Causes Act), and since then no government has dared burn its fingers on divorce law.

3.1.2   France: lingering divorce à la carte

3.1.2.1   1975 Reform: introduction of divorce à la carte   On the eve of the 1975 reform the French legal situation largely resembled its English and Welsh counterpart. While the law on the statute books allowed only

---

[44]   The requirement to settle ancillary matters and therefore 'to take responsibility for themselves' was rightly labelled by David Bradley as 'true conservatism'. D Bradley, 'Comparative Law, Family Law and Common Law: Regulation of Sexual Morality in Finland' (2003) 2 *Journal of Law and Society* 138.

[45]   E Hasson, 'Divorce Reform in England, the Case of the Family Law Act 1996', in M Antokolskaia (ed.), *Herziening van het echtscheidingsrecht. Administratieve echtscheiding, mediation, voortgezet ouderschap* (SWP 2006) 285.

[46]   Lord Chancellor's Department, No 159/99, cited in Hasson, 'Divorce Reform in England, the Case of the Family Law Act 1996' (n 45) 290.

[47]   On 16 January 2001 the government announced it would repeal Part II of the Act. Lord Chancellor's Department, *Divorce Law Reform – Government Proposes to Repeal Part II of the Family Law Act 1996,* Press Notice 20/01. Part III, governing legal aid for mediation in family matters, came into force in 1997, only to be repealed in 1999 and replaced by the Access to Justice Act.

[48]   Hasson, 'Divorce Reform in England, the Case of the Family Law Act 1996' (n 45) 285–6.

[49]   Cretney, *Family Law in the Twentieth Century* (n 28) 389.

[50]   J Dewar, 'The Normal Chaos of Family Law' (1998) 4 *Modern Law Review* 477–8.

fault-based divorce, consensual divorce by collusion was estimated in practice to account for one-quarter of the total number of cases.[51]) Although both the proponents of liberalisation and their conservative opponents called for reform,[52] they did not agree on its direction. Thus, as in England and Wales, the pending divorce reform was doomed to become a compromise. However, the French legislature was prepared, more so than in England and Wales, to allow divorce by mutual consent. In the end, the French divorce law of 1975,[53] drafted by the eminent scholar Jean Carbonnier, came to accommodate a mixed system of fault and no-fault grounds (*'divorce à la carte'*).[54] This system was seen as reflecting the plurality of the concepts of marriage held in the pluralistic French society.[55] Thus, the new legislation provided for a wide range of different routes to divorce, including a fault-based divorce sanction, two forms of consensual divorce, and a unilateral divorce remedy on the ground of irretrievable breakdown, which was possible after six years of separation.[56] The fault grounds were preserved out of regard for the still popular view of divorce in terms of culpability.[57] This, however, was not without consequences. According to Commaille, both doctrine and case law after the reform amply demonstrated that 'the notion of fault has permeated other types of divorce proceedings'.[58]

3.1.2.2   2004 Reform: fault survived, divorce à la carte retained   Several weaknesses had become apparent during the almost 30 years of application of the 1975 Act.[59] One of the points of concern was that a spouse wanting to end a marriage, but having neither the consent of the other spouse nor the ability to instigate a fault procedure, 'remained a prisoner

---

[51]   J Foyer, 'The Reform of Family Law in France', in A Chloros (ed.), *The Reform of Family Law in Europe* (Kluwer 1978) 106.

[52]   The majority of respondents supported the divorce reform, according to an opinion poll conducted in the early 1970s. C Dadomo 'The Current Reform of French Law of Divorce' [2004] *International Family Law* 220.

[53]   The Act of 11 July 1975 entered into force on 1 January 1976.

[54]   J Carbonnier, *Droit civil: La famille, l'enfant, le couple* (21st edn, Press Universitaires de France 2002) 541.

[55]   G Cornu, *Droit Civil, La famille* (8th edn, Montchrestien 2003) No 312.

[56]   A Bénabent, *Droit civil: La Famille* (10th edn, Litec 2001) No 228.

[57]   J Carbonnier, 'La question du divorce: mémoire à consulter' D (1975) Chron. 118.

[58]   J Commaille, 'Towards a New Definition of Divorce', in I Trost (ed.), *Family in Change* (International Library 1980) 106.

[59]   Dadomo 'The Current Reform of French Law of Divorce' (n 52) 222.

of the conjugal bond'[60] for at least another six years. Another disturbing factor was that the ever-popular fault-based divorce appeared to 'aggravate conflict and destabilise [the] family environment' and to be 'traumatic for everyone'.[61] Moreover, there was general dissatisfaction with the length, complexity and costs of divorce proceedings.[62] In the late 1990s, therefore, the left-wing government formed after the elections of 1997 started preparations for reform. The government commissioned several reports and studies, the most important of which were the report by the sociologist Irène Théry[63] and the report by the law professor Françoise Dekeuwer-Défossez.[64] However, both reports proposed retaining fault-based divorce,[65] while one of the major aims of the reform agenda was the desire to abolish it. The other major issues were liberalisation of divorce on the ground of irretrievable breakdown, and the deformalisation of divorce by consent. It soon became clear, however, that even the proponents of modernising family law were divided into two groups.[66] The first group sought to introduce administrative divorce,[67] while also preserving the plurality of divorce grounds including the ground of fault,[68] whereas the second group advocated eliminating fault-based divorce altogether.[69] The idea of administrative divorce

---

[60]   A Bénabent, *Droit civil: La Famille* (2001) No 230.

[61]   H Fulchiron, S Ferré-André and A Gouttenoire, 'A Pause in the Reform of French Family Law', in A Bainham (ed.), *The International Survey of Family Law* (Jordan Publishing 2004) 186.

[62]   Dadomo, 'The Current Reform of French Law of Divorce' (n 52) 218.

[63]   I Théry, *Couple, filiation et parenté aujourd'hui: le droit face aux mutations de la famille et de la vie privée: rapport remis au Ministre de l'emploi et de la solidarité et au Garde des sceaux Ministre de la justice* (Odile Jacob 1998).

[64]   F Dekeuwer-Défossez, *Rénover, le droit de la famille: Propositions pour un droit adapté aux réalités et aux aspiration de notre temps: Rapport au Garde des Sceaux, Ministre de la justice* (La Documentation française, 1999).

[65]   *Report* Théry (1998) 113–15; *Report Dekeuwer-Défossez* (1999) 85.

[66]   B Bastard, 'Administrative Divorce in France: A Controversy over a Reform that Never Reached the Statute Book', in M MacLean (ed.), *Making Law for Families* (Hart Publishing 2000) 79.

[67]   One of the most influential proponents of administrative divorce has been Irène Théry. Her first proposal dated from 1993 (I Théry, *Le Démariage* (Odile Jacob 1993)) was later incorporated into the *Report Théry*.

[68]   Bastard, 'Administrative Divorce in France: A Controversy Over a Reform that Never Reached the Statute Book' (n 66) 79.

[69]   See, for instance, the articles in the *Gazette du Palais* by the family judge Danièle Ganancia ('Pour un divorce du XXI siècle' (1997) 16 and 33–9) and the law professor Alain Bénabent ('Plaidoyer pour quelques réformes du divorce'

met serious opposition[70] and, despite the benevolent interest of the Minister of Justice,[71] was ultimately dropped.[72] The attempt to eradicate fault took the shape of two private bills introduced during 2001, one[73] in the *Assemblée nationale* and the other[74] in the *Sénat*. However, the political momentum for introducing no-fault divorce in France was lost in June 2002, when President Chirac was re-elected and the former left-wing government lost its majority in Parliament. In the wake of this change both private bills became redundant, and in October 2002 the government announced plans for a new reform.[75] The resultant Act of 26 May 2004 is, however, merely a modified version of the existing divorce *à la carte*.[76]

The new Act maintains the plurality of the grounds of divorce: the new article 229 in the *Code Civil* provides for divorce (1) by mutual consent; (2) upon mutual acceptance of the breakdown of the marriage; (3) upon the irretrievable breakdown of the conjugal bond; or (4) upon fault.[77] The main change lies in the modifications of these particular grounds.

Divorce by mutual consent (articles 230 and 232 of the Civil Code) has been significantly simplified and deformalised.[78] Spouses who agree on

---

(1997) 225–28.) Bénabent has even proposed introducing a modest form of unilateral divorce on demand. A Bénabent. *Droit civil: La Famille* (2001) No 100.

[70] The *Report Dekeuwer-Défossez* recommended caution in this matter. One of the most fervent opponents of administrative divorce, Jacqueline Rubellin-Devichi, argued that it would reduce marriage to mere cohabitation and jeopardise a weaker party. J Rubellin-Devichi, 'How Matters Stand Now in Relation to French Law Reform' 'La permanence des spécifiés nationales de droit de la famille' in A Bainham (ed.), *The International Survey of Family Law* (Jordan Publishing 2000) 155.

[71] Bastard, 'Administrative Divorce in France: A Controversy Over a Reform that Never Reached the Statute Book' (n 66) 76–7.

[72] Ibid 72 ff.

[73] Introduced by a Socialist MP. *Proposition de loi relative à la réforme du divorce*, No 3189, 26 June 2001.

[74] Introduced by Senator Nicolas About. *Proposition de loi visant à remplacer la procédure de divorce pour faute par une procédure de divorce pour cause objective*, No 12, 10 October 2001.

[75] Dadomo, 'The Current Reform of French Law of Divorce' (n 52) 223.

[76] The Act 2004-439 of 16 May 2004 came into force on 1 January 2005.

[77] '*Le divorce peut être prononcé en cas: (-) soit de consentement mutuel; (-) soit d'acceptation du principe de la rupture du mariage; (-) soit d'altération définitive du lien conjugal, (-) soit de faute*'.

[78] A Bénabent, *La réforme du divorce article par article* (Defrénois 2004) 38–9.

the divorce and ancillary matters may now obtain a divorce decree at a single hearing, provided the court approves their agreement on ancillary matters.[79] The second hearing is necessary only if the judge finds the agreement on ancillary matters to provide insufficient protection of the interests of the children or one of the spouses.[80]

Divorce upon mutual acceptance implies one spouse applying for a divorce following acceptance by both spouses that their marriage has irretrievably broken down (articles 233–234 of the Civil Code). In this way, divorce by acceptance is turned into a 'true and realistic divorce by mutual consent, in which parties' agreement relates only to recognition of the breakdown, not to the consequences'.[81] Divorce on this ground can be requested by both spouses or by only one of them.[82] The procedure has also been simplified, and once acceptance has been given, it can no longer be withdrawn.[83]

Divorce upon unilateral request on the basis of the irretrievable breakdown of marriage requires only a two-year *de facto* separation (articles 237–238 of the Civil Code). The reform of this ground is claimed to be the most essential departure from the previous law. It was accompanied by serious controversy as, in some quarters, unilateral divorce was still equated with repudiation.[84] Not only has the period of separation been shortened from six to two years, but also, and more importantly, the two-year separation now constitutes an irrefutable presumption of the irretrievable breakdown of the marriage.[85] This innovation has been interpreted as a general recognition of the right to divorce in French law.[86]

Divorce based on fault has been retained because of the firm belief that it still 'meets the needs of the majority of French people'.[87] It involves an application by the 'innocent' spouse invoking 'a serious or renewed violation of the duties and obligations of marriage that made continuance

---

[79]   French Civil Code, articles 230 and 232.

[80]   The new article 232(2) of the French Civil Code.

[81]   Fulchiron, Ferré-André and Gouttenoire, 'A Pause in the Reform of French Family Law' (n 61) 185.

[82]   The new article 233 of the French Civil Code.

[83]   The new article 233(2) of the French Civil Code.

[84]   C Mahé, 'De Franse wetgever op weg naar afschaffing van "schuldscheiding"' (2002) 1 FJR 21–2

[85]   H Fulchiron, 'The New French Divorce Law', in A Bainham (ed.), *The International Survey of Family Law* (Jordan Publishing 2005) 246.

[86]   Ibid.

[87]   Fulchiron, Ferré-André and Gouttenoire, 'A Pause in the Reform of French Family Law' (n 61) 184.

of married life unbearable' (article 242 of the Civil Code). The general definition of fault has remained the same, while the last specific fault ground (conviction for certain crimes) has disappeared.[88] The invocation of fault as a ground for divorce no longer has any influence on distributing the financial burden of divorce.[89]

(The new French legislation was praised for its well-balanced and pacifying character.[90] The Minister of Justice described the reform as 'organised around three large axes: a law based on pluralism and respect of choice, a law of divorce more simple and more caring for the future, and a protective divorce law founded in responsibility'.[91])

3.1.3 Germany: objective proof of the breakdown

The German 1976 divorce reform had an easier start than its counterparts in England, Wales and France as, alongside the ground of fault, the 1938 *Ehegesetz* (Marriage Act) already provided for divorce on the ground of the irretrievable breakdown. However, it too wrestled with the problem of divorce by collusion as a no-fault divorce required three years of separation, while a fault divorce could be obtained without delay. Around 95 per cent of divorce actions were consequently brought on the ground of matrimonial offence, with only 5 per cent of divorcing spouses choosing the no-fault route.[92] Such a wide gap between law on the statute books and law in action made reform all but inevitable. The most important debates consequently concerned the questions of what should constitute sufficient proof of the breakdown, and especially whether mutual consent alone should be regarded as such proof.

As in England and Wales and France, the new German legislation was doomed to become a compromise,[93] however, with irretrievable break-down becoming the sole ground for divorce. The general principle was

---

88   A Bénabent *La réforme du divorce article par article* (n 78) 49.
89   H Fulchiron, 'The New French Divorce Law' (n 85) 247.
90   Ibid.
91   'La réforme qui vous est présentée s'ordonne autour de trois grands axes: un droit du divorce pluraliste et respectueux des choix, un droit du divorce plus simple et soucieux de l'avenir, un droit du divorce protecteur, fondé sur la responsabilité'. Presentation by the Minister of Justice, Dominique Perben, in the *Sénat* on 2 January 2004 (available 9 July 2015 at http://www.senat.fr/seances/ s200401/s20040107/s20040107001.html#int26).
92   D Giesen, 'The Reform of Family Law in Germany' (1978) 4 *Family Law Quarterly* 120.
93   'To the surprise of many people, the reform was finally achieved by a series of 'ingenious' compromises in a vexed parliamentary situation. By these compromises, the legislature remarkably succeeded in avoiding clear and definite

that a marriage may be dissolved by divorce if it has broken down. A marriage has broken down if the conjugal community of the spouses no longer exists and the spouses cannot be expected to restore it (§ 1565 of the German Civil Code (BGB)). That would of course have enabled spouses to obtain a consensual divorce without delay. However, owing to a last-minute concession to the Christian Democrats, who dominated the *Bundesrat*[94] and who considered unqualified divorce by mutual consent to be incompatible with the idea of protecting marriage, the opportunities for consensual divorce were restricted.[95] If spouses have not been living apart for at least one year, the marriage may be dissolved only in exceptional circumstances. In other words, where the petitioner attests that continuing the marriage would cause him or her unreasonable hardship resulting from causes that can be attributed to the other spouse (§ 1565(2) of the BGB).[96] According to § 1566 of the BGB, a marriage is irrebuttably presumed to have broken down if the spouses have lived apart for a year and both spouses petition for divorce or if the respondent consents to divorce. If the spouses have been living apart for three years, this constitutes an irrefutable presumption of breakdown, even in the case of a unilateral application.[97] These two presumptions exemplify the legislature's preference for the objective mode of proof of breakdown. The accessibility of divorce by consent is additionally restricted by the requirement that the spouses should agree on ancillary matters.[98]

State control over divorce was also upheld by maintaining a hardship clause, which enables a court to deny a divorce even if breakdown is proven. In the case of a unilateral application for divorce, the respondent spouse can try to prevent the divorce by proving that it would lead to exceptional hardship for him or her.[99]

---

positions on many problems. It thus followed the time-honoured pattern of evading politically sensitive issues by adopting meaningless rules which serve to neutralize rival claims'. W Müller-Freienfels, 'The Marriage Law Reform of 1976 in the Federal Republic of Germany' (1979) 28 *International and Comparative Law Quarterly* 186.

[94]　M-A Glendon, *The Transformation of Family Law* (University of Chicago Press 1989) 179–80.

[95]　Ibid.

[96]　N Dethloff, *Familienrecht* (30th edn, Beck 2012) 78.

[97]　Para 1566 III of the BGB. See D Martiny, 'Family Law', in I Zekoll and M Reimann (eds), *Introduction to German Law* (2nd edn, Kluwer 2005) 259.

[98]　Code of Civil Procedure, § 630. See D Martiny CEFL National Report for Germany: *Grounds for Divorce* (2003) 16 (available 9 July 2015 at http://ceflonline.net/wp-content/uploads/Germany-Divorce.pdf).

[99]　See N Dethloff, *Familienrecht* (n 96) 179.

3.1.4 Italy: divorzisti defeat anti-divorzisti

(The first[100] divorce law in Italy was promulgated in 1970[101] after years of bitter confrontation between *divorzisti* and *anti-divorzisti*.[102])Four year later, the new legislation was unsuccessfully challenged during the referendum on the abrogation of law.[103]

The dual system of marriage celebration, introduced in Italy by the 1929 Concordat, resulted in some peculiarities in Italian divorce law.(In the case of civil marriage, divorce dissolved the matrimonial bond, whereas in the case of religious marriage it terminated only the civil effects of marriage.[104])Although the law provided for both fault and no-fault divorce, it was initially strongly dominated by fault.[105] (The importance of fault decreased significantly in 1975, when all fault grounds for judicial separation were abolished[106] and the sole ground for separation became the facts leading to the conclusion that the 'continuation of cohabitation [is] intolerable or [will] prejudice severely the upbringing of the children'.[107]) In 1987, the divorce law was slightly liberalised by the introduction of divorce by joint application and the reduction from five to three years in the period of separation required for a consensual divorce.[108] However, even after that, Italian divorce law has remained relatively restrictive by European standards, as a two-stage process and a long period of separation are still normally required before a separation can be converted into divorce.[109]

---

[100] Divorce was briefly introduced in Italy by Napoleon, but this was largely a dead letter and was subsequently repealed. G Sgritta and P Tufari, 'Italy', in P Chester (ed.), *Divorce in Europe* (Nijhoff 1977) 255.

[101] Law No 898, of 1 December 1970, came into force on 18 December 1970.

[102] M Rheinstein, *Marriage Stability, Divorce, and the Law* (University of Chicago Press 1972) 189.

[103] V Pocar and P Ronfani, 'Family Law in Italy: Legislative Innovations and Social Change' (1978) 4 *Law and Society Review* 612.

[104] V Librando, 'The Reform of Family Law in Italy', in A Chloros (ed.), *The Reform of Family Law in Europe* (Kluwer 1978) 167.

[105] Phillips, *Putting Asunder* (n 3) 574.

[106] Ibid.

[107] Italian Civil Code, article 151. Pocar and Ronfani, 'Family Law in Italy: Legislative Innovations and Social Change' (n 103) 634.

[108] S Patti, CEFL National Report for Italy: *Grounds for Divorce* (2003) 4 (available 9 July 2015 at http://ceflonline.net/wp-content/uploads/Italy-Divorce.pdf).

[109] Phillips, *Putting Asunder* (n 3) 576.

3.1.5   Ireland: a thorny way to divorce

(Ireland introduced a constitutional ban on divorce in 1937, some 15 years
after it gained independence from the British Empire. The indissolubility
of marriage was perceived as part of national Irish, Catholic identity.[110])
In Ireland, therefore, the introduction of divorce required not only a
change in the Constitution – which was only possible through a referendum – but also a change in the national self-image. On the eve of the first
attempt to introduce divorce, 75,000 of the total population of 3.5
million[111] were 'trapped in broken marriages',[112] while 22.9 per cent of
all Irish children were born out of wedlock.[113]

The pro-divorce camp lost the first referendum on ending the constitutional ban in 1986, with the proposed amendment being rejected by a
majority of nearly two to one.[114] In 1995, however, a second referendum
was held, and this time the proponents of divorce won by a close margin
of 0.6 per cent.[115] (As a result, Ireland introduced a divorce law in
1996.[116] In contrast to other European countries, however, Ireland lists
the grounds for divorce directly in its Constitution. This means that any
subsequent amendment of divorce legislation will require a further
referendum.[117])Although the new law provides for no-fault divorce on the
ground of the irretrievable breakdown of marriage, the conditions that
have to be met in order to obtain a divorce on this ground make the
dissolution of marriage extremely difficult. Article 41.3.2° of the Irish

---

[110]   See M Dillon, *Debating Divorce. Moral Conflict in Ireland* (University
Press of Kentucky 1993) 14–15 and 21–4; C James, 'Cead Mile Failte. Ireland
Welcomes Divorce: The 1995 Irish Divorce Referendum and the Family
(Divorce) Act of 1996' (1997) 8 *Duke Journal of Comparative and International
Law* 175.

[111]   According to the Central Statistics Office of Ireland data for 1991.

[112]   S Fette, 'Learning From Our Mistakes: The Aftermath of the American
Divorce Revolution as a Lesson to the Republic of Ireland' (1997) 7 *Indiana
International and Comparative Law Review* 391.

[113]   According to the Central Statistics Office of Ireland data for 1985.

[114]   A total of 935,843 votes were cast against the amendment, with 538,279
in favour of it. A Shatter, *Family Law in the Republic of Ireland* (3rd edn,
Wolfhound Press 1986) 250.

[115]   This time, 50.3% voted in favour of ending the constitutional ban, while
49.7% voted against it. C Price, 'Finding Fault with Irish Divorce Law' (1997)
19 *Loyola of Los Angeles International and Comparative Law Review* 669.

[116]   The Divorce Act was passed on 27 November 1996 and came into force
on 27 February 1997.

[117]   J Burley and F Regan, 'Divorce in Ireland: The Fear, the Floodgates and
the Reality' (2002) 16(2) *International Journal of Law, Policy and the Family*
202, 218.

Constitution states that a court can grant a divorce only if the following three preconditions are simultaneously met: (1) the spouses have lived apart for a period of at least four years during the previous five years; (2) there is no prospect of reconciliation; and (3) the court is satisfied with the provisions made for the spouse, children and any other dependents.[118] Irish law therefore combines the objective criterion for marital breakdown (namely, a long period of separation) with the subjective criterion that the court must be convinced that there is no prospect of reconciliation. This makes obtaining a divorce in Ireland twice as difficult as in countries with either a subjective or an objective criterion. On the one hand, Irish law demands a long period of separation, irrespective of the circumstances of the case. On the other hand, even after this period has expired, the court can still deny a divorce petition if it is not convinced that reconciliation is impossible.[119] In this way, a divorce petition can be dismissed even in the face of both spouses' explicit wish to end their marriage.[120]

3.1.6　Malta: the last bastion falls

In 2011 Malta became the last European country, with the exception of the Vatican City State, to introduce full divorce with the possibility of remarriage. After the majority of the Maltese population voted in favour of divorce in the referendum held in May 2011,[121] the divorce law[122] was promulgated and came into force on 1 October 2011. Malta's divorce legislation very much resembles that of Ireland. Article 66B of the Civil Code of Malta states, for example, that divorce shall not be granted except upon a demand made jointly by the two spouses or by one of them against the other spouse. Additionally, the Court must be satisfied that by the date the divorce proceedings commence the spouses will have lived apart for a period of, or periods amounting to, at least four years in the immediately preceding five years, or at least four years must have lapsed since the date of legal separation, while there must also be no reasonable

---

[118]　Geoffrey Shannon, CEFL National Report for Republic of Ireland: *Grounds for Divorce* (2003) 1 (available 9 July 2015 at http://ceflonline.net/wp-content/uploads/Ireland-Divorce.pdf).

[119]　N Everitt, 'Some Remarks on the Recent Developments of Divorce Law in the Republic of Ireland and England' (2001) I Familia 204.

[120]　M Walls and D Bergin, *The Law of Divorce in Ireland* (Jordans 1997) 14.

[121]　'Malta to legalise divorce after bitter referendum', *The Independent*, 30 May 2011.

[122]　Act XIV of 2011 amending the Civil Code.

prospect of reconciliation between the spouses, and the spouses and all their children must receive adequate maintenance.

3.2 Beyond Irretrievable Breakdown

3.2.1 Sweden: divorce on demand re-enters European scene

Even before the Swedish legislature took a radical step to liberalise divorce law in 1973, Swedish divorce law was already one of the most permissive in Europe. Although the 1915 reform had retained fault grounds, no-fault divorce for both contested and non-contested cases had been available in Swedish law from the start of the 20th century.[123]

When 'new radicalism'[124] came to dominate the Swedish political scene in the late 1960s, the government proclaimed that 'Legislation should not under any circumstances force a person to continue to live under a marriage from which he wishes to free himself'.[125] It was believed that consistent application of the contractarian model of marriage required marriage to be entered into as a contract and to be able to be dissolved like a contract.[126] Introducing the divorce on demand that was available under classical Roman law and briefly reintroduced in Europe by Russian post-revolutionary law[127] made Sweden the forerunner of the liberalisation of divorce law in Europe. The 1973 Act[128] reduced the State's involvement to a minimum, with the autonomous decision of the spouse(s) becoming the ground for divorce. If both spouses agree on the divorce and no minor children are involved, the

---

[123] See section 11.2.1. of Part III.
[124] L Gyllensten, 'Swedish Radicalism in the 1960s: An Experiment in Political and Cultural Debate', in D Hancock and G Sjoberg (eds), *Politics in the Post-Welfare State: Responses to the New Individualism* (Columbia University Press 1972) 281.
[125] Abstract of protocol in justice department matters, 15 August 1969.
[126] J Sundberg, 'Marriage or No Marriage. The Directives for the Revision of Swedish Family Law' (1971) 20 *International and Comparative Law Quarterly* 234.
[127] One of the opponents of the reform noted that 'Perhaps it is a shocking idea that if one wants to understand the situation in the Sweden of tomorrow, one has to study Bolshevik Russia and the Rome of Antiquity'. J Sundberg, 'Marriage or no Marriage. The Directives for the Revision of Swedish Family Law' (1971) 20 ICLQ 233.
[128] This Act entered into force on 1 January 1974. In 1987 the rules on divorce were incorporated into the new Marriage Code. See M Jänterä-Jareborg, CEFL National Report for Sweden: *Grounds for Divorce* (2003) (available 9 July at http://ceflonline.net/wp-content/uploads/Sweden-Divorce.pdf).

divorce has to be granted immediately upon their demand.[129])Not even a short period of reflection is required, even though not everyone agreed with the 'rationale that adult independent spouses do not need any time for reflection'.[130] However, the desire to respect spouses' autonomy seems not to have been the only reason for introducing immediate divorce. Another, more pragmatic, reason was to be found in the increasing competition between the institution of marriage and the increasingly common non-marital cohabitation, which could of course be terminated without delay or intervention by the State.[131] If a divorce is requested by only one of the spouses, or if the spouses have minor children, the divorce automatically has to be granted if the request for divorce is renewed after a six-month period of reflection. No inquiry into the reasons for divorce has to be held,[132] and no defence against the divorce petition is possible. Hence, partly for ideological and partly for pragmatic reasons, Swedish law has openly abandoned the concept of the irretrievable breakdown of marriage and started, instead, to consider divorce in terms of entitlements and rights.[133]

3.2.2 Norway: divorce on demand after a period of separation

As in Sweden, no-fault grounds were introduced into Norwegian divorce law at the start of the 20th century. The 1909 Divorce Act allowed for dissolution of marriage on the ground of mutual consent after one year of judicial separation, while divorce on unilateral request was permitted upon the irretrievable breakdown of marriage or if a number of fault grounds existed.[134] In contrast to Sweden, however, Norway has retained the dual judicial-administrative divorce system. Following a Supreme Court judgment in 1952, judicial separation and divorce on the ground of the irretrievable breakdown of marriage have been granted without

---

[129] Jänterä-Jareborg, National Report (n 128) 3–4.
[130] A Lögdber, 'The Reform of Family Law in the Scandinavian Countries', in A Chloros (ed.), *The Reform of Family Law in Europe* (Kluwer 1978) 206.
[131] Ibid.
[132] Jänterä-Jareborg, National Report (n 128) 4.
[133] D Bradley, *Family Law and Political Culture Family Law and Political Culture*. Scandinavian Laws in Comparative Perspective (Sweet & Maxwell 1996) 71–72.
[134] T Sverdrup, CEFL National Report for Norway: *Grounds for Divorce* (2003) 2 (available 9 July 2015 at http://ceflonline.net/wp-content/uploads/Norway-Divorce.pdf).

inquiry.[135] The 1991 Marriage Act[136] went beyond irretrievable break-down of marriage and introduced the possibility of divorce on demand after a period of separation. Under § 20 of the Marriage Act, a spouse who believes that he or she cannot continue cohabitation may demand a judicial separation. After one year of judicial separation (§ 21 of the Marriage Act) or two years of *de facto* separation (§ 22 of the Marriage Act), a spouse is entitled to demand a divorce. Immediate divorce can be granted to a spouse who is, or is at risk of becoming, a victim of serious abuse (§ 23 of the Marriage Act). Under § 27 of the same Act, divorce can be granted either by a county governor in an administrative proced-ure or by a judge in a court procedure.

3.2.3 Russia: irretrievable breakdown or divorce on demand?

Prior to the new Family Code of 1995,[137] Russian divorce law was considerably more liberal than even Swedish pre-reform law. The main characteristics of the 1969 law were the availability of administrative divorce and the discrepancy between the formal ground for divorce (irretrievable breakdown) and actual practice. No proof of breakdown was required in the administrative procedure, while in a court procedure, however, irretrievable breakdown of the marriage still had to be proved.

[The new divorce law was intended to diminish the role of the state in divorce proceedings and to ensure better protection of spouses' privacy.] (While the irretrievable breakdown of the marriage still remained the formal divorce ground in a contested divorce, one of the assumptions behind the 1995 Code was that the spouses, rather than the judge, were in the best position to decide whether their marriage had come to an end.[138]) The Act explicitly states that spouses are not required to disclose the reasons for a non-contested divorce.[139] Non-contested divorce remains, however, a matter of both administrative and court jurisdiction. The new Code extends the administrative procedure to divorce cases in which spouses have disputes on ancillary matters. In such situations it is

---

[135] Norwegian Supreme Court Reports, 1952 812. Cited in T Sverdrup, National Report for Norway (n 134) 2.

[136] Act No 47 of 4 July 1991 relating to Marriage (The Marriage Act). For an English translation, see http://ceflonline.net/wp-content/uploads/Norway-Divorce-Legislation.pdf (accessed 9 July 2015).

[137] Russian Family Code of 8 December 1995, in force since 1 March 1996.

[138] M Antokolskaia, CEFL National Report for Russia: *Grounds for Divorce* (2003) 9 (available 9 July 2015 at http://ceflonline.net/wp-content/uploads/Russia-Divorce.pdf).

[139] Family Code of the Russian Federation, article 23(1).

possible first to obtain an administrative divorce, and then to go to court to litigate on the ancillary matters. Consenting spouses with minor children are also still required to go to court, but the reason for retaining court jurisdiction in these cases is solely to ensure that agreements concerning children do not escape judicial scrutiny. The role of the court in non-contested cases is no longer any different from that of the administrative body.[140] Neither the court nor the civil register is entitled to investigate the reasons for divorce or to refuse to grant a divorce. In fact, both simply rubber-stamp the spouses' decisions to end their marriage.

The rules governing contested divorce are somewhat ambiguous. On the one hand, article 22 of the Family Code states that 'the marriage has to be dissolved if it is proven that further cohabitation of the spouses is no longer feasible'. Thus, just as before, irretrievable breakdown of the marriage still has to be proven. On the other hand, however, article 22(2) states that 'the marriage has to be dissolved if attempts to reconcile the spouses have failed and one of the spouses continues to insist on divorce'. In attempting to achieve reconciliation, the court can do no more than postpone the divorce by up to three months. If, after three months, a petitioner renews his or her demand, the court is obliged to grant the divorce. Therefore it can be assumed that renewal of a divorce petition constitutes an irrefutable presumption of the breakdown of the marriage. With this interpretation it is clear that, behind the façade of irretrievable breakdown, the new Russian legislation actually introduced divorce on demand. This interpretation, however, has not been supported in case law.[141] In 1998, for example, the Supreme Court interpreted the Code of Civil Procedure in a way that required the petitioner in a contested case to state the reasons for divorce in the petition.[142] If the petitioner in a contested divorce case fails to state the reason for requesting a divorce in the petition, the court can order a stay in proceedings until the petitioner fulfils this requirement. As this stay has no time limit, it is a relatively effective means of forcing a spouse to disclose the reasons for wanting a divorce. The court investigation into the reasons for divorce is, however, a rather pointless endeavour. Whatever reasons the petitioner may give in the petition, they cannot influence the outcome of the case as the Family Code leaves the court no scope to

---

[140] Antokolskaia, National Report for Russia (n 138) 7.

[141] A Netchaeva, *Semeinoe pravo* (Jurist 1998) 107; L Pchelintzeva, *Semeinoe pravo* (Norma-Infra 1999) 154–6.

[142] Directive No 15 of 5 November 1998 entitled 'On the Application of the Legislation by Dissolving Divorce Cases' item 7.

attach any consequences to its views on these reasons. If a petitioner renews the demand after three months, the court has no option in law but to grant a divorce order.[143] Therefore, the grounds for divorce under current Russian law can on paper be summarised as divorce by mutual consent in the event of a consensual divorce and divorce following irretrievable breakdown in the event of unilateral request, but in fact the ground is really divorce on demand.

3.2.4   Spain embraces divorce on demand

Developments in Spanish divorce law in the 20th century have displayed spectacular swings. While the Republican government managed to adopt a liberal divorce law in 1932,[144] this was subsequently suspended by the fascist Franco government in 1938,[145] and a year later[146] abrogated with retroactive effect.[147] As in Portugal, the Spanish dictatorship survived World War II and lasted until the death of Franco in 1975. Divorce was not reintroduced until 1981,[148] and even then, although it included no-fault grounds, was rather restrictive.[149] In 2005, however, the Socialist government of Rodríguez Zapatero made Spanish divorce law one of the most liberal in Europe by openly introducing divorce on demand.[150] Under the new Act,[151] divorce can be obtained by mutual consent from three months after the date of the marriage, providing the spouses reach agreement on ancillary matters such as care of the children and visitation arrangements, visitation arrangements for grandparents (if necessary), use of the family home, child maintenance, liquidation of the marital property regime (if necessary) and spousal maintenance (if necessary). Divorce is also possible upon the unilateral request of one of the spouses

---

[143]   Antokolskaia, National Report for Russia (n 138) 7–10.
[144]   Divorce Act of 2 March 1932. Divorce by mutual consent, for example, was permitted after two years of *de facto* separation if both spouses applied for divorce, and after three years of *de facto* separation if only one of them did. D Langner, *Eheschließung und Ehescheidung nach spanischem Recht* (Peter Lang 1984) 9.
[145]   Decree of 2 March 1938.
[146]   Act of 23 September 1939.
[147]   Phillips, *Putting Asunder* (n 3) 541.
[148]   Act No 30 of 7 July 1981.
[149]   D Langner, *Eheschließung und Ehescheidung nach spanischem Recht* (n 144) 102.
[150]   Act 15/2005 of 8 July 2005. On the new Spanish divorce law, see G García Cantero, 'Family Law Reform in Differing Directions', in A Bainham (ed.), *The International Survey of Family Law* (Jordan Publishing 2006) 433–6.
[151]   Spanish Civil Code, articles 81 and 86.

from three months after the date of the marriage, or immediately in the event of a risk to a spouse or child. Spouses do not need to specify divorce grounds or reach agreement on ancillary matters in the case of a unilaterally requested divorce. The petitioner is expected, however, to make reasonable proposals for resolving any ancillary matters.

3.2.5   CEFL Principles on Divorce: a model for Europe?

Although the Commission on European Family (CEFL) Principles of European Family Law regarding Divorce[152] are not legislation, but only a non-binding model, they represent an important step in the development of divorce law in Europe and so must be considered in this overview. The CEFL Principles on Divorce, which were published in 2004 by the CEFL,[153] were elaborated by an independent group of scholars, informally representing 22 jurisdictions in Europe. The Principles are meant to represent the best of the European rules on divorce,[154] and can therefore serve as a source of inspiration for national legislatures contemplating divorce law reform.[155]

The CEFL made several principal choices with regard to the grounds for divorce. First, the Principles go beyond the ground of the irretrievable breakdown of marriage, thus reflecting the far-reaching watering-down of the concept of the irretrievable breakdown as discussed above. The CEFL also chose two separate grounds, consensual and unilateral divorce.

Mutual consent was explicitly made a ground for the divorce of spouses who both wish to dissolve their marriage.[156] This choice was based on the finding that mutual consent *de facto* constitutes a ground for divorce in many European jurisdictions. Although consent is a formal

---

[152]   K Boele-Woelki et al, *Principles of European Family Law regarding Divorce and Maintenance between Former Spouses* (Intersentia 2004).

[153]   See http://ceflonline.net/. Established in 2001 as an academic initiative in order to elaborate *The Principles of European Family Law*, which could provide a model for voluntary bottom-up harmonisation of family law in Europe.

[154]   See M Antokolskaia, 'The "Better Law" Approach and the Harmonisation of Family Law', in K Boele-Woelki, (ed.), *Perspectives for the Unification and Harmonisation of Family Law in Europe* (Intersentia 2003) 159–83.

[155]   K Boele-Woelki, 'Comparative Research-based Drafting of Principles of European Family Law', in M Faure et al (eds), *Towards a European Ius Commune in Legal Education and Research* (Intersentia 2002) 182.

[156]   Principle 1:4.

ground for divorce in only a minority of European countries,[157] the great majority of jurisdictions provide for divorce upon mutual consent under various headings. The CEFL, however, opted for a very liberal 'minority' model of divorce by mutual consent. (According to Principles 1:4 to 1:7, no period of separation and no agreement on ancillary matters[158] are required for such a divorce.) Divorce can be granted immediately, without any period of reflection, if no minor children are involved and the spouses reach agreement on ancillary matters.[159] In adopting immediate divorce the CEFL drew on the Swedish model of divorce, which has so far not been followed by any other European country.

[In the case of non-consensual divorce, the CEFL opted for a one-year factual separation as a divorce ground.[160] The advantage of this solution was stated to be that it provided for a simple objective test, without any need to inquire into matrimonial fault or the breakdown of the marriage.[161]) However, this 'better law' solution may be objected to both by countries with more restrictive legislation and requiring longer periods of separation and by countries with more permissive legislation and where spouses do not have to wait for one year.

To complete the picture of permissive divorce rules contained in the CEFL Principles, it should be noted that the CEFL opted for only limited linkage between divorce as such and the adjudication of ancillary matters. Both in consensual and non-consensual divorce, the authority competent to grant a divorce is obliged to decide only on ancillary matters relating to minor children.[162]

It is still too early to speculate whether the Principles will be much used as a model, although there is at least one positive example to

---

[157]   See comment to Principle 1:4. K Boele-Woelki et al, *Principles of European Family Law regarding Divorce and Maintenance between Former Spouses* (n 152) 30.

[158]   Such agreement is strongly encouraged by making the possibility of immediate divorce, without a period of reflection, conditional upon its conclusion. Principles 1:5 (1) and (2).

[159]   Principle 1:5 (2).

[160]   Principle 1:8.

[161]   Commentary on Principle 1:8. K Boele-Woelki, et al, *Principles of European Family Law regarding Divorce and Maintenance between Former Spouses* (n 152) 55.

[162]   Principles 1:2 and 1:10.

date:[163] the 2008 Portuguese Divorce Act, discussed below, was modelled on the Principles.[164]

3.2.6 Portugal follows CEFL principles

Divorce in Portugal had a turbulent history throughout the 20th century. Although the country introduced liberal divorce legislation after the 1910 revolution,[165] the Concordat signed in 1940 by the Salazar regime made divorce impossible for Catholics, who form the vast majority of the Portuguese population.[166] The possibility of divorce was reintroduced in 1975 after the end of the Salazar regime,[167] with provision for no-fault divorce, including divorce by mutual consent, being introduced the following year.[168] In 1995, Portugal became one of the few European countries to allow administrative divorce.[169] In 2008 divorce law was reformed in line with the CEFL Principles.[170] Administrative divorce in the Civil Registry Office became possible in the case of divorce by mutual consent, providing the parties reached agreement on ancillary matters.[171] If no such agreement is reached, the parties have to seek recourse to the court. A court can grant unilateral divorce in the event of separation for one year, mental illness of one of the spouses for more than one year that seriously impedes communal life, desertion for more

---

[163] Another example of the Principles being used in discussions on the reform of national divorce law is the Scottish legislature, which has used the Principles 'as course for arguing for the amendment of the current law on divorce'. K Boele-Woelki, 'The Principles of European Family Law: Aims and Prospects' (2005) 1(2) *Utrecht Law Review* 160, 167 (available 9 July at www.utrechtlawreview.org).

[164] G de Oliveira, 'Recent Developments in Portuguese Family Law' [2009] 15 FamRZ, 1559–61; K Boele-Woelki, 'Zwischen Konvergenz und Divergenz: Die CEFL Prinzipien zum Europäischen Familienrecht' [2009] RabelsZ, 241–67.

[165] S Sottomayor, 'The Introduction and Impact of Joint Custody in Portugal' [1999] 13 IJLPF 247–9.

[166] G de Oliveira, CEFL National Report for Portugal: *Grounds for Divorce* (2003) 2 (available 9 July 2015 at http://ceflonline.net/wp-content/uploads/Portugal-Divorce.pdf).

[167] S Sottomayor, 'The Introduction and Impact of Joint Custody in Portugal' (n 165) 249.

[168] Decrees No 261 of 27 May 1975 and No. 56 of 13 May 1976. S Sottomayor, 'The Introduction and Impact of Joint Custody in Portugal' (n 165) 249–50.

[169] Decree No 131 of 6 June 1995. Guilherme de Oliveira, National Report (2003) (n 166) 3.

[170] See n 157.

[171] Civil Code of Portugal, article 1775.

than one year or any other facts that indicate an irretrievable breakdown
of the marriage.[172])

4. SCRUTINISING GROUNDS FOR DIVORCE: A CONFUSING ENDEAVOUR

4.1 Coexistence of Different Generations of Divorce Laws and Functional Disequivalence

The preceding overview shows that at least five different types of divorce
grounds can be distinguished in this respect: fault, irretrievable breakdown of marriage, consent, requirement for a period of separation, and
divorce on demand. Looking beyond the formal labels shows a picture
that – paraphrasing Zweigert and Kötz[173] – could be referred to as
'functional disequivalence'.(Confusingly enough, virtually every type of
divorce can be hidden under the label of 'irretrievable breakdown', from
fault-based (in England and Wales, Scotland, Greece and, to a certain
extent, also Poland, for example) to divorce by consent (Netherlands) and
divorce on demand (Russia).)

These grounds have entered or re-entered the European stage at various
moments in history and under the influence of various circumstances and
ideas, and so could be characterised as different generations of divorce
law.[174](The fault divorce (in other words, divorce as a sanction) came into
play during the Protestant Reformation under the influence of Reformed
theology, while irretrievable breakdown of the marriage (in other words,
divorce as a remedy of failure) and mutual consent (in other words,
divorce as an autonomous decision by the spouses themselves) developed
on the eve of and during the French Revolution under the influence of the
Enlightenment, and divorce on demand (in other words, divorce as an
individual right) appeared after the Russian Revolution of 1917 as a
result of the radical secularisation and de-ideologisation of marriage.)
These grounds are products of different epochs, and all are simultaneously present in contemporary Europe. Moreover, they also exist in

---

[172] Civil Code of Portugal, article 1781,
[173] Zweigert and Kötz use the concept of 'functional equivalence'. K
Zweigert and H Kötz, *An Introduction to Comparative Law* (3rd edn, Clarendon
Press 1998) 34 ff.
[174] See Roderick Phillips for a slightly different periodisation. Phillips,
Putting Asunder (n 3) 571.

many jurisdictions alongside or in combination with one another.[175] Thus, French divorce law accommodates fault grounds alongside mutual consent and irretrievable breakdown, while German law sees a period of separation with or without mutual consent as proof of the irretrievable breakdown of a marriage.

4.2 Fault Grounds: Fault Unwilling to Leave the Stage

The 'no-fault revolution' of the 1960s and 1970s created an expectation that fault would disappear from divorce law before too long. Around the turn of millennium, however, attempts to eradicate fault failed in major jurisdictions such as France and England and Wales. Moreover, two Eastern European countries, Latvia[176] and Lithuania,[177] recently re-introduced fault grounds into their divorce laws.

Yet, since fault is no longer the *only* ground for divorce in any European country, it has ceased to be the main issue in the divorce debate. For as long as many countries allowed divorce *exclusively* on the ground of fault, this analysis had its merits: in that situation the 'innocent' spouse had no option other than an infringing, accusational procedure, while the 'guilty' spouse had no option except to buy or coerce the cooperation of the 'innocent' party. The situation nowadays, however, is completely different as no European country retains fault as the sole ground for divorce.[178] Invoking fault is now only one of the many options available, albeit the one often providing the fastest route to a divorce. Moreover, since courts no longer investigate the alleged fault in any depth, fault grounds can often provide an easier and faster route to divorce for consenting spouses. In England and Wales, for instance, an undefended fault divorce under the 'special procedure' allows consenting spouses to dissolve their marriage more quickly than by mutual consent as the latter requires a two-year separation.[179] Thus, although the

---

[175] For more details, see M Antokolskaia, 'Convergence and Divergence of Divorce Laws in Europe' (2006) 18(3) *Child and Family Law Quarterly* 307.

[176] Introduced in 1993 by the restored Latvian Civil Code of 1937 (articles 71–72 and 74).

[177] Introduced by article 3.60 of the 2000 Civil Code of Lithuania (in force since 1 July 2001). See Š Kaserauskas, 'Moving in the Same Direction? Presentation of Family Law Reforms in Lithuania' in A Bainham (ed.), *The International Survey of Family Law* (Jordan Publishing 2004) 330–1.

[178] D Martiny, 'Divorce and Maintenance between Former Spouses – Initial Results of the Commission on European Family Law' (n 1) 534.

[179] Cretney, 'Divorce Reform in England: Humbug and Hypocrisy or a Smooth Transition?' (n 14) 56 n 19.

retention of fault grounds still has (an often symbolic) meaning, it no longer says much about the permissiveness of a particular country's divorce law, and the abolition of such grounds does not automatically mean that divorce will become any easier.

4.3 Irretrievable Breakdown of Marriage: An Unnecessary Legal Concept?

Irretrievable breakdown can be proven in three different ways. These are by (1) a subjective criterion alone: if the court is convinced that the marriage cannot be saved (as applies in Bulgaria, the Netherlands, Poland and Hungary, for example); (2) an objective criterion alone: a stated period of separation with or without a spouse's consent; or (3) a combination of subjective and objective criteria.

In the jurisdictions that prescribe a subjective criterion alone, the court inquiry is largely a dead letter in non-contested cases; however, in contested cases it may be quite intrusive, especially in countries such as Poland, where allocation of fault is required.[180]

In the jurisdictions using an objective criterion, a stated period of judicial or *de facto* separation amounts to an irrefutable presumption of the irretrievable breakdown of a marriage. The accessibility of divorce essentially depends on the length of the separation. These periods vary quite significantly (for unilateral divorce, they amount to six years in Austria, for example while a period of five years is required in England and Wales, four years in Switzerland and Greece, three years in Italy and Germany, two years in France, and one year in Denmark, Norway and Iceland). As these periods are rather lengthy in most jurisdictions, this form of divorce is less attractive if a shorter route is available.

In jurisdictions such as Ireland and Malta, which combine subjective (convincing the court or other competent authority) and objective (four-year period of separation) criteria, it is twice as difficult to prove the breakdown as, even after the stated period of separation has expired, the court can refuse a divorce if it is not convinced that the marriage has irretrievably broken down.

---

[180] A Maczynski and T Sokolowski, CEFL National Report for Poland: *Grounds for Divorce* (2003) 10 (available 9 July 2015 at http://ceflonline.net/wp-content/uploads/Poland-Divorce.pdf).

4.4 Mutual Consent

(In some jurisdictions (for example, Austria, the Czech Republic, Germany, the Netherlands, England and Wales, and Scotland), divorce by consent is labelled as irretrievable breakdown, and constitutes an irrefutable presumption of the same. In other countries (Belgium, Bulgaria, France, Greece and Portugal, for example), consent is characterised as a separate ground.)In all these cases, the court or other competent authority grants divorce automatically and without inquiry into the reasons for it. However, most jurisdictions still consider divorce by consent to be a somehow dangerous diminution of the state's control over the dissolution of marriage. The multiple restrictions on the right to divorce by consent often make it a slower and less attractive form of divorce. (Only Dutch (for spouses without minor children) and Russian law allow for divorce on the ground of simple consent without any further restrictions.) In other European jurisdictions, consensual divorce is restrained by various additional requirements. In some jurisdictions, for instance, the marriage must have been of a certain duration (one year in the Czech Republic and Greece), while other countries allow consensual divorce only after a certain period of separation (two years in England and Wales and Scotland, for example, and six months in Austria, Denmark, the Czech Republic and Iceland). In most European countries (Austria, Belgium, Bulgaria, Greece, Germany, Hungary, Denmark, Portugal and Spain) an agreement to divorce is not sufficient in itself as the spouses also have to reach agreement on ancillary matters. This list of restrictions reveals that most countries in Europe are still reluctant to recognise a simple, autonomous decision by spouses to end their marriage as a sufficient ground for divorce. In one way or another, the state continues to seek to protect spouses from their own 'ill-considered' decisions.[181]

4.5 Divorce on Demand

(Divorce on demand, where either spouse can obtain a divorce without any inquiry and irrespective of the consent or objections of the other spouse, is explicitly recognised in Sweden, Norway, Finland and Spain, and indirectly in Russia.)This is beyond doubt the easiest form of divorce and one that fully respects the decisions of a spouse and accepts that the state should not keep a marriage intact against the will of either one or

---

[181] D Martiny 'Divorce and Maintenance between Former Spouses – Initial Results of the Commission on European Family Law' (n 1) 536. Martiny also notes that 'consent seems to be a dangerous kind of marriage dissolution'. Ibid.

both of the parties. The only form of state intervention in this kind of divorce is a short waiting or reconciliation period of three months in Spain and Russia, and six months in Finland and Sweden (although in Sweden, this applies only in cases of contested divorces or divorces involving minor children).

Many countries allow not just one but multiple grounds for divorce. In these countries, consenting spouses have the opportunity of 'ground shopping'. Empirical data suggest that spouses, assisted by their lawyers, are always able to choose the shortest route to divorce, just as water will always find its way to the lowest point.[182]

5. ADMINISTRATIVE DIVORCE: A CHALLENGE TO DIVORCE PROCEDURE LAW

The differences in divorce procedures between one jurisdiction and another are even greater than those between divorce grounds. This overview examines only one challenge to procedural divorce law: the admission or non-admission of the administrative divorce.

Two contrasting opinions are discernible in the debate surrounding the current renewal of interest in administrative divorce in Europe. The first of these sees administrative divorce as representing the summit of the dejuridification of divorce,[183] whereas the second views a preference for administrative or judicial divorce as only 'a matter of taste or tradition'.[184] Any association of administrative divorce with deregulation, however, reflects an erroneous understanding of this form of divorce as a single homogeneous phenomenon.[185] A closer look reveals an important difference between the two historical traditions of administrative divorce

---

[182] In England and Wales, for example, 68.6% of divorces are granted on fault grounds (N Lowe, CEFL National Report for England and Wales: *Grounds for Divorce* (2003) 6 (available 9 July 2015 at http://ceflonline.net/wp-content/uploads/England-Divorce.pdf)) as this has proven to be the shortest route to a divorce.

[183] H Andrup, B Buchhofer and K Ziegert, 'Formal Marriage Under the Crossfire of Social Change', in J Eekelaar and S Katz (eds), *Marriage and Cohabitation in Contemporary Society* (Butterworths 1980) 38.

[184] T Schmidt, 'The Scandinavian Law of Procedure in Matrimonial Causes' in Eekelaar and Katz (eds), *The Resolution of Family Conflicts* (Butterworths 1984) 97.

[185] Andrup, Buchhofer and Ziegert, 'Formal Marriage Under the Crossfire of Social Change' (n 183) 38.

coexisting in present-day Europe. The first tradition stems from 18th-century Scandinavia and allows an administrative authority that is competent to grant administrative divorce quasi-judicial discretionary powers to scrutinise divorce grounds and agreements on ancillary matters. This type of administrative divorce does not necessarily go hand-in-hand with dejuridification, however. The second tradition emerged in Russia after the revolution of 1917. Here, the competent authority lacks any power to scrutinise divorce grounds and agreements on ancillary matters. This type of administrative procedure can truly be regarded as dejuridification and deregulation as the state authority's role extends no further than rubber-stamping.

The difference between these two types of divorce is rooted in history. When the Scandinavian kings started granting administrative divorces after the Reformation, their sole aim was to mitigate the restrictive Protestant grounds for judicial divorce.[186] This led to the emergence of the dual administrative-judicial system of divorce in the Nordic countries. Seeking to diminish state intervention was not an issue at that time, and so the powers to scrutinise the grounds for divorce and the agreements on ancillary matters available to the Royal Administration were no less than the corresponding powers of the courts. Over the course of the 19th century, the granting of administrative divorce was liberalised[187] and the competence to grant such a divorce was transferred to the local authorities, without any reduction in their power to check agreements. Although the further liberalisation of divorce law in Scandinavia ruled out the authorities' use of administrative and judicial powers to scrutinise the

---

[186] From the early 18th century, the Swedish (J Sellin, *Marriage and Divorce Legislation in Sweden* (University of Pennsylvania 1922) 36), Danish and Norwegian kings started granting full administrative divorce on a wider range of grounds than those provided for by judicial divorce. Initially, dispensation was granted only in cases of grave hardship. From about 1770 onwards, however, the number of grounds for dispensation started increasing. Dispensation even became possible on the ground of incompatibility. Since 1790, dispensation has been possible in Denmark in the event of a legal separation for three years. T Schmidt, 'The Scandinavian Law of Procedure in Matrimonial Causes' (n 184) 74.

[187] There were no fixed grounds for administrative divorce by Royal dispensation. Therefore it could be granted 'for any cause deemed sufficient by the King,' although certain grounds were specifically listed in the Decree. J Sellin, *Marriage and Divorce Legislation in Sweden* (n 186) 36. Divorce by Royal dispensation could be granted even when no fault was involved, for instance in a case of a 'difference of temperament and opinion, which ... turned into disgust and hatred' between the spouses (ibid 36–7).

grounds for divorce by mutual consent,[188] the administrative authorities' powers to scrutinise the agreements on ancillary matters remained intact. (The Eastern European tradition of administrative divorce was born under completely different circumstances during the radical reforms of Russian family law in the 1920s.) In 1917 an administrative procedure without inquiry was established for divorce by mutual consent, and in 1926 the administrative procedure without inquiry was extended to all divorce cases.[189] The main aim in introducing administrative divorce in Russia was indeed dejuridification and a desire to reduce state control over divorce. From the outset, therefore, the competent authority was not granted powers to scrutinise either the grounds for divorce or any agreements on ancillary matters.[190] During the Soviet period, administrative divorce was exported to all the now-former Soviet Republics, most of which have retained administrative divorce even after gaining or regaining their independence. (These differing historical roots and heritages account for much of the current heterogeneity of administrative divorce in Europe.)

(Divorce 'Scandinavian-style' still exists in Norway,[191] Denmark[192] and Iceland. When Portugal introduced administrative divorce in 1995, it also implicitly chose the Scandinavian model by granting the competent authority the power to scrutinise agreements on ancillary matters,[193] and this choice was upheld in 2008. The Russian model meanwhile is

---

[188]   Mutual consent on divorce is a pre-condition for administrative divorce in all Scandinavian countries allowing administrative divorce, with the exception of Norway and Denmark. T Sverdrup, National Report for Norway (n 134) 5; I Lund-Andersen and L Krabbe, CEFL National Report for Denmark: *Grounds for Divorce* (2003) 6 (available 9 July 2015 at http://ceflonline.net/wp-content/uploads/Denmark-Divorce.pdf).

[189]   Family Code of 1926, article 19.

[190]   There was a general consensus that spouses could not be kept in a marriage, even if only one of them wanted out of it. The state declined to decide upon the dissolution of marriage, leaving the floor to the autonomous decisions of the spouses themselves. Marriage was dissolved upon the demand of one or both of the spouses; the registration of divorce was, therefore, merely a formality', D Genkin et al, *Istoria sovetskogo grazhdanskogo prava 1917–1947* (Juridicheskaia Literatura 1949) 441.

[191]   Norwegian Marriage Act of 4 July 1991, s 27.

[192]   Danish Contraction and Dissolution of Marriage Act of 9 March 1999, s 42.

[193]   G de Oliveira, CEFL National Report for Portugal: *Grounds for Divorce* (n 166) 3.

currently applied in four countries: Russia,[194] Estonia,[195] Moldova[196] and Ukraine.[197])

(Proposals *de lege ferenda,* aimed at introducing administrative divorce, were recently made in France,[198] while the concept of administrative divorce has also attracted attention in Germany[199] and England and Wales.[200] In the Netherlands, a private member's bill aimed at introducing administrative divorce was rejected by the First Chamber[201] in 2004,[202] but the current government's coalition agreement states an intention to legislate on the subject.)

Alongside the growing interest in and a certain proliferation of administrative divorce, an opposite, yet equally strong trend is discernible.(Two Western European counties (Sweden and Finland) ended a long-standing tradition of a two-tier system and opted instead, in the early 20th century, for a unitary system of judicial divorce,[203] while three Eastern European countries (Lithuania,[204] Latvia[205] and Belarus)[206] abolished administrative divorce at the end of the 20th century after the collapse of the Soviet Union.)

---

[194]   Russian Family Code of 8 December 1995, article 19.

[195]   Estonian Family Act of 12 October 1994, article 27.

[196]   Family Code of Moldova of 26 October 2000, article 35.

[197]   Family Code of Ukraine of 10 January 2002, articles 105(1) and 106–107.

[198]   See B Bastard, 'Administrative Divorce in France: A Controversy Over a Reform that Never Reached the Statute Book' (n 66) 72–91.

[199]   I Schwenzer, 'Registerscheidung', in P Gottwald e.a. (ed.), *Festschrift für Dieter Henrich* (Gieseking 2000) 533–44.

[200]   Family Justice Review, *Final Report* (MOJ 2011). See also J Herring, 'Divorce, Internet Hubs and Stephen Cretney', in R Probert and C Barton (eds), *Fifty Years in Family Law. Essays for Stephen Cretney* (Intersentia 2012) 187–200.

[201]   The Dutch Senate.

[202]   See M Antokolskaia (ed.), *Herziening van het echtscheidingsrecht. Administratieve echtscheiding, mediation, voortgezet ouderschap* (SWP 2006).

[203]   Sweden and Finland abolished administrative divorce in 1915 and 1921 respectively. T Schmidt, 'The Scandinavian Law of Procedure in Matrimonial Causes' (n 184).

[204]   Š Kaserauskas, 'Moving in the Same Direction? Presentation of Family Law Reforms in Lithuania' (n 177) 329.

[205]   Latvian Civil Code of 1937, reintroduced on 1 September 1993. See J Vebers, 'Family Law in Latvia: From Establishment of the Independent State of Latvia in 1918 to Restoration of Independence in 1993', in A Bainham (ed.), *The International Survey of Family Law* (Martinus Nijhoff Publishers 1997) 214.

[206]   Belarusian Code of Marriage and Family of 3 June 1999.

(In all European countries that allow administrative divorce, the administrative procedure currently exists alongside the judicial procedure.[207] In 2007, however, Denmark promulgated a law[208] whereby the existing two-tier system gave way to a system in which each divorce case will start with an administrative authority and will be referred to a court only if, for example, the parties fail to reach the required agreements on ancillary matters.[209]

The scope of application of administrative divorce 'Scandinavian-style' is also rather dissimilar to the administrative divorce 'Russian-style'. The differences in the preconditions for administrative divorce are readily explicable, given the dissimilarity between the administrative authorities' competence to scrutinise agreements on ancillary matters. In Western European countries, where the opportunity to scrutinise such agreements exists, administrative divorce is, as a rule, also available to couples with minor children. Agreement on ancillary matters is also a precondition for administrative divorce in all Western European countries except Norway.[210] The competent authorities scrutinise these agreements in order to protect the interests of the children and the weaker spouse. Thus, in Denmark, spouses have to reach agreement on the obligation to pay maintenance after divorce, on the transfer of tenancy of the matrimonial home and, if necessary, on how pensions will be divided and compensation for overpayment in the event of a prenuptial contract.[211] Since the introduction in 2003 of automatic continuation of joint custody after divorce, the previously required agreement on child custody no longer constitutes a prerequisite for an administrative divorce.[212] The lawyers of the *Statsforvaltning* – the authority competent to grant an administrative divorce – are entitled to determine whether an agreement contains conditions that are unconscionable for one of spouses.[213] In Portugal, spouses must present an agreement or a judicial decision on parental

---

[207]   Administrative divorce was the only way of dissolving a marriage in Russia from 1926 to 1944.

[208]   Act No 525 of 24 June 2005, which entered into force on 1 January 2007.

[209]   C Gyldenløve Jeppesen de Boer, 'Administratieve echtscheiding in Denemarken' [2005] FJR 233–4.

[210]   Tone Sverdrup, National Report for Norway (n 134) 9–10.

[211]   Gyldenløve Jeppesen de Boer, 'Administratieve echtscheiding in Denemarken' (n 209) 232–3.

[212]   I Lund-Andersen and C Gyldenløve Jeppesen de Boer, CEFL National Report for Denmark: *Parental Responsibilities* (2006) 14–15 (available 9 July 2015 at http://ceflonline.net/wp-content/uploads/Denmark-Parental-Responsibilities.pdf).

[213]   Lund-Andersen and Krabbe, National Report for Denmark (n 188) 8.

responsibilities (if there are minor children), as well as agreements on maintenance for a spouse who requires it, on the future of the family home and on division of matrimonial property.[214] The agreements on the matrimonial home and spousal maintenance are scrutinised by the Director of the Civil Registry,[215] who is entitled to ask the parties to alter any provisions the Director considers unreasonable.[216] If the Director has any doubts with regard to the agreement on child custody, the agreement will be sent to the Attorney General. If the latter considers the custody agreement not to be in the best interests of the child and the parents refuse to alter the relevant provisions, the divorce case must be referred to court.[217] Icelandic law also makes agreement on ancillary matters – subject to the scrutiny of a county governor – a prerequisite for administrative divorce.[218] Although Norwegian law does not make admissibility of administrative divorce dependent on any agreements on ancillary matters,[219] spouses must attend a mandatory mediation session if they have children under the age of 16.[220]

The situation in Eastern Europe is rather different. The Department of Registration of Civil Acts, which is the competent authority for administrative divorce in all Eastern European countries, is neither authorised nor *de facto* capable of scrutinising agreements made by spouses. Therefore, administrative divorce is not available to couples with minor children in any of those countries. In Russia and Ukraine, access to administrative divorce is no longer conditional upon agreement on ancillary matters, while Moldova and Estonia require spouses only to declare that they have no disputes with regard to ancillary matters.[221] Although such a declaration was previously the common rule throughout the Soviet Union, the

---

[214]   Portuguese Family Code, article 1775 No 2 and article 14 Nos. 1 and 2 of Decree Law No 172/2001 of 13 October 2001. de Oliveira, National Report for Portugal (n 166) 12.

[215]   de Oliveira, National Report for Portugal (n 166) 13.

[216]   Portuguese Civil Code, article 1776 No. 2. de Oliveira, National Report for Portugal (n 166) 13.

[217]   Decree Law No. 172/2001 of 13 October 2001, article 14, Nos. 2, 4, 5, 6 and 7. de Oliveira, National Report for Portugal (n 166).

[218]   Marriage Act of Iceland of 30 April 1993, articles 41–44. See also B Björgvinsson, 'General Principles and Recent Developments in Icelandic Family Law', in Andrew Bainham (ed.), *The International Survey of Family Law* (Martinus Nijhoff Publishers 1995) 223.

[219]   Tone Sverdrup, National Report for Norway (n 134) 9–10.

[220]   Tone Sverdrup, National Report for Norway (n 134) 9.

[221]   Estonian Family Act of 12 October 1994, article 28(4) and article 36(4) of the Family Code of Moldova of 26 October 2000.

Russian legislature deliberately dropped this requirement in the 1995 Family Code. Ukraine took over this innovation in 2002, with the new approach being based on the idea that spouses should first be allowed to obtain an administrative divorce without delay, and only after that be required to go to court, if necessary, to settle any ancillary matters.[222]

The above synopsis leads to the conclusion that administrative divorce does not as such say much about the 'costs' of divorce. In several European jurisdictions, judicial divorce procedures have become easier than some administrative 'Scandinavian-style' divorces.[223] The most permissive divorce law in Europe – that of Sweden – is judicial, not administrative. In England and Wales, the 'special procedure', according to Cretney, 'almost amounts to administrative divorce'.[224] By contrast, administrative divorce by consent can only be obtained in Denmark after six months of separation, while administrative divorce without consent requires a one-year period of separation,[225] providing the spouses have also reached the required agreements on ancillary matters.

The above seems to support the statement that a choice for administrative or judicial divorce is only 'a matter of taste or tradition'. Automatically regarding administrative divorce as a paradigm of permissiveness and deregulation could be seen as being based on the same kind of clichés as associating no-fault divorce with easily accessible divorce. However, just like fault divorce, administrative divorce retains strong ideological and political connotations. Thus, in France, administrative dissolution of marriage without solemnity and state control has been mocked as 'degrading marital status to the state of concubinage', with the very ideological connotation of administrative divorce making it unacceptable.[226] In England and Wales, where a liberal 'Russian-style' online form of administrative divorce has been proposed,[227] Jonathan Herring has claimed that administrative divorce would undermine 'the solemnity, acknowledgment of public interest and respect for the parties' emotions

---

[222] See Antokolskaia, National Report for Russia (n 138) 12–13.

[223] T Schmidt, 'The Scandinavian Law of Procedure in Matrimonial Causes' (n 184) 97.

[224] Cretney 'Divorce Reform in England: Humbug and Hypocrisy or a Smooth Transition?' (n 14) 56 n 19.

[225] Lund-Andersen and Krabbe, National Report for Denmark (n 188) 7.

[226] J Rubellin-Devichi, 'How Matters Stand Now in Relation to French Law Reform' (n 70) 155. The same author associated administrative divorce with the Soviet Union. *Le Point,* 13 December 1997, cited in B Bastard, 'Administrative Divorce in France: A Controversy over a Reform that Never Reached the Statute Book' (n 66) 81.

[227] Family Justice Review, *Final Report* (MOJ 2011).

and encouragement of investment in marriage'.[228] In the Netherlands, where administrative divorce 'Scandinavian-style', which was proposed and rejected in 2004, would have been *less* permissive than the existing judicial divorce, the Christian-Democrat Minister of Justice opposed it by stating that 'even if the judge at the end of the [divorce] procedure is a mere formality, he should nonetheless remain in place' in order to highlight the special role of the state in the dissolution of marriage.[229]

In conclusion it can be said that a preference for administrative or judicial divorce as such may indeed be regarded as 'a matter of taste or tradition', but that the choice to adopt either a Scandinavian or Russian-style model of administrative divorce is essentially a political one.

6. CONCLUSION

The preceding overview of current divorce law in Europe reveals a picture of considerable diversity. Despite far-reaching modernisation during the 'no-fault revolution' of the 1960s and 1970s, divorce law still varies considerably from country to country. This difference is evident not only from the perspective of the formal grounds for divorce, but also from a functional point of view. The differences between current divorce laws in Europe no longer lie along the axes of fault/no-fault. Irretrievable breakdown of marriage becomes more and more an empty shell and yet more jurisdictions are choosing to leave it behind them. (If we look beyond the labels, we can distinguish four more or less functional grounds for divorce: (1) fault-based grounds; (2) irretrievable breakdown in the narrow sense of the term; (3) divorce by consent; and (4) divorce on demand.)What really counts is not how a divorce ground is formally labelled, but rather what divorce costs in terms of time, money and intrusion into the spouses' private lives. The extent to which these costs differ becomes all too evident if we compare Irish and Maltese law, where spouses have to wait four years for a consensual divorce and (at least as far as the statute books are concerned) state the reasons for divorce, with the immediate divorce on demand that is available in Sweden. Growing interest in administrative divorce adds increased diversity in the field of divorce procedure. This shows how small the common

---

[228]   J Herring, 'Divorce, Internet Hubs and Stephen Cretney', in R Probert and C Barton (eds), *Fifty Years in Family Law: Essays for Stephen Cretney* (Intersentia 2012) 200.
[229]   Second Chamber of Parliament, Proceedings II, 2002–2003, No 34 2575.

core of divorce law is in Europe at present, both in terms of the divorce procedure, the divorce grounds, and the costs of divorce.

This diversity of divorce laws can be attributable to the ideological sensitivity of divorce, which makes compromise between conservative and progressive camps a precondition of most divorce law reforms. Differences in the balance of political power between progressive and conservative camps are largely responsible for the great variety of compromises and, consequently, dissimilar outcomes in the field of divorce law. The same political sensitivities explain why international human rights instruments have so far had very little impact on divorce law. Indeed, the most recent reforms of divorce law in England and Wales and France show that these political sensitivities are far from fading away, while the debate surrounding the introduction of administrative divorce shows that any preference for a Scandinavian or Russian-style administrative procedure remains subject to the same political sensitivities. There are good reasons, therefore, to expect the diversity of divorce laws in Europe to persist in the future.

RECOMMENDATIONS FOR FURTHER READING

A Agell, 'The Underlying Principles of Consensual Divorce', in K Boele-Woelki (ed.), *Common Core and Better Law in European Family Law* (Intersentia 2005) 59–69.

M Antokolskaia, *Harmonisation of Family Law in Europe: A Historical Perspective. A Tale of Two Millennia* (Intersentia 2006) 313–67; 494–5.

M Antokolskaia, 'Convergence and Divergence of Divorce Laws in Europe' (2006) 22(4) CFLQ 397–422.

K Boele-Woelki et al. (eds), *Principles of European Family Law Regarding Divorce and Maintenance Between Former Spouses* (Intersentia 2004) 7–65.

K Boele-Woelki, B Braat and I Curry-Sumner (eds), *European Family Law in Action, Volume I: Grounds for Divorce* (Intersentia 2003).

D Bradley, *Family Law and Political Culture Family Law and Political Culture. Scandinavian Laws in Comparative Perspective* (Sweet & Maxwell 1996).

CEFL national reports, accessed at http://ceflonline.net/divorce-maintenance-reports-by-jurisdiction/

S Cretney, 'Breaking the Shackles of Culture and Religion in the Field of Divorce?', in K Boele-Woelki (ed.), *Common Core and Better Law in European Family Law* (Intersentia 2005) 3–14.

D Martiny, 'Divorce and Maintenance between Former Spouses – Initial Results of the Commission on European Family Law', in K Boele-Woelki, (ed.), *Perspectives for the Unification and Harmonisation of Family Law in Europe* (Intersentia 2003) 529–551.

R Phillips, *Putting Asunder: A History of Divorce in Western Society* (1988).

M Roth, 'Future Divorce Law – Two Types of Divorce', in K Boele-Woelki (ed.), *Common Core and Better Law in European Family Law* (Intersentia 2005) 41–57.

B Verschraegen, 'Divorce', in A Chloros et al (eds), *International Encyclopedia of Comparative Law, Persons and Family*, Volume 4 (Brill 2004/2007), ch 5.

3. Unmarried cohabitation in a European perspective

Joanna Miles*

1. INTRODUCTION: 'UNMARRIED COHABITATION' AND LEGAL ISSUES TO BE ADDRESSED

Such is the current diversity of legally recognised family forms across Europe and beyond that it is necessary before embarking on any survey of this area to define the scope of the inquiry. Contemporary debates regarding family law and policy in the regulation of relationships between adults are dominated by two distinct but connected issues: (i) the

---

  * I have aimed to describe the law in this chapter as it was in January 2013, though have incorporated reference to the subsequent Spanish Constitutional Court decision on Navarra's cohabitation law; readers should otherwise be alert to the possibility of changes in the jurisdictions discussed since that date.

treatment of same-sex couples; and (ii) the treatment of couples who have not formalised their relationship.

The nature of the debate in relation to (ii) is complicated by the fact that a number of jurisdictions now allow at least some couples to formalise their relationships in institutions other than 'marriage': the advent of various schemes of registered partnership or other civil union (to use relatively neutral terminology) has resulted in a proliferation of formalised family forms and so an increasingly complex set of options for family regulation. (This growth of new legal institutions has in large part been driven by issue (i): a concern to respond to the legal predicament of same-sex couples who are in most jurisdictions (for the time being at least) unable to formalise their relationship through marriage, traditionally defined.)

Meanwhile, others are concerned about the situation of opposite-sex couples (in particular) who have not married and so of individuals who are not subject to, and protected by, the regime of legal duties and rights attendant on that institution. The question arises whether such de facto relationships ought also to attract some of those legal consequences of marriage, perhaps simply by virtue of the fact of the relationship (though possibly subject to additional criteria for eligibility, such as minimum duration requirements or the presence of children, not being within the prohibited degrees, not being married to a third party).

In some jurisdictions, debates regarding (i) and (ii) have become combined with the result that both problems are purportedly 'solved' by the creation of a single new legal regime, for example a scheme of registered partnership open to both opposite- and same-sex couples[1] or the subjection of both opposite- and same-sex cohabitants to the same set of default rights and remedies.[2] Whilst such developments may broadly be welcomed for the additional legal protection that they undoubtedly bring to many, neither can be regarded as a satisfactory solution for both (i) and (ii). The introduction of new means of formalising a relationship may provide same-sex couples with an option (to formalise) hitherto denied them; but the extension of any such new scheme to opposite-sex couples at a stroke downgrades the relative standing of the scheme compared to marriage: where opposite-sex couples now have a choice of two institutions, one of which they enjoy to the exclusion of same-sex

---

[1]   Notably the French *pacte civil de solidarité*, discussed below.

[2]   See for example Sweden's Cohabitants Act 2003 and the interpretation of various English statutes protecting the unmarried couple to extend to same-sex relationships: e.g. *Fitzpatrick v Sterling Housing Association* [2001] 1 AC 27; *Ghaidan v Godin-Mendoza* [2004] UKHL 30.

couples, same-sex couples are confined to one institution which they must share with the opposite-sex couples. Meanwhile, many of those in opposite-sex (and now same-sex) relationships who were unable to secure their partner's agreement to marry are equally unable to secure his or her agreement to register, and so they remain unprotected by law. On the other hand, the extension by default of more rights and duties to *de facto* relationships provides a better solution to that latter difficulty, but does nothing to address the complaint of same-sex couples that they still have no formalised institution for which they can enrol.

The fundamental problem of same-sex relationship recognition is better addressed first by enabling same-sex couples to formalise their relationship, whether through some new form of registered partnership which confers rights and duties functionally equivalent to those enjoyed by spouses or through an enlarged institution of marriage. That is not this chapter's concern: readers should refer to Ian Curry-Sumner's contribution to this volume (Chapter 4). This chapter assumes that such a step has been taken, and instead inquires principally about the situation of those couples – opposite-sex and same-sex – who have not formalised their relationship in marriage or a marriage-equivalent institution. My purpose is to explore the range of options made available to those whom I shall call 'cohabitants' or 'cohabiting couples'; the reader should assume that this expression covers both opposite- and same-sex relationships. Finally, the reader should note that this chapter is concerned solely with 'couple' or 'conjugal' relationships[3] and not with purely platonic relationships, such as those of adult siblings who live together.[4]

I need next to define the scope of my inquiry in terms of the range of legal issues encountered by such couples which I intend to address. Relationship status is potentially significant in a hugely diverse range of legal situations which may broadly be categorised as (a) <u>vertical</u>: the relationship between the couple, or individual members of the couple,

---

[3]   In examining the law of each jurisdiction, it is important to note whether cohabitation will be recognised only between couples who could validly marry: e.g. they are not already married or in an equivalent registered relationship, they are not within the prohibited degrees, and so on.

[4]   See, for example, the situation considered in *Burden v UK* (App No 13378/05, ECHR) (2008) 47 EHRR 38; and the availability of Belgian law's *cohabitation légale* to related pairs, discussed below. A number of Australian states make provision for the registration and default recognition of personal/domestic relationships in certain circumstances: see, for example, Relationships Act 2003 (Tasmania); see also the Adult Interdependent Relationships Act 2002 (Alberta, Canada).

and the state – e.g. in relation to taxation, social security, immigration and nationality rights; (b) horizontal/external: the relationship between the couple, or individual members of the couple, and a third private individual – e.g. the employer of one partner, the medical team treating one partner, the purchaser of property used by the couple as a home; and (c) horizontal/internal: the legal incidents of the relationship between the cohabitants themselves. This last category of legal problem will be my principal focus, in particular the question of whether cohabitants have access to any sort of special property or financial rights and remedies against each other at the point of relationship breakdown, over and above those afforded to them by the general law, by virtue of their status as a cohabiting couple. Limitations of space preclude any detailed attention to obligations arising during the currency of the relationship or upon the death of one partner, but the analytical models suggested in this chapter may be used to compare jurisdictions' treatment of cohabitants in those areas too. Nor shall I consider issues relating to the relationship between the cohabitants and any children of their family since that is better viewed as an aspect of child law (and the relationship of parent/child) rather than an aspect of the legal regulation of the inter-adult relationship: readers should refer to chapters by Trimmings and Beaumont (Chapter 7) and by Ferrer-Riba (Chapter 8) in this volume.

The scope of the problem now defined, I shall first briefly examine the demographic and socio-legal research data which form the backdrop to the legal issues addressed and then go on to consider what, if any, law directly addressing the situation of cohabiting couples or impetus for development of national laws in this area derives from pan-European legal norms and institutions. I shall then turn to the means by which different jurisdictions go about providing rights and remedies to cohabitants on separation, noting that legal responses to this issue must engage with two different sets of choices: the choice between 'opt-in' and default (or 'opt-out') schemes; and the choice between assimilating the legal treatment of cohabitants with the situation of spouses, or providing some different (less generous) level of protection to the partner making the relevant claim. The nature and extent of legal recognition varies considerably across Europe, and in several European jurisdictions the legal protection of cohabitants who have not formalised their relationship in any way (by opting in to a scheme, assuming that even that option is offered) remains minimal or non-existent. Indeed, in concluding the chapter I suggest that, whilst the full range of legal responses is represented across the continent, Europe as a whole may still be regarded as a strongly marriage-centric (or certainly formalisation-centric) set of jurisdictions, such that, for the time being, prospects of greater recognition of *de facto* (that is, unregistered) cohabiting couples at a pan-European level – and certainly at a supra-national level – seem remote.

2. DEMOGRAPHIC DATA AND FINDINGS FROM SOCIO-LEGAL RESEARCH

(Pan-European data published by Eurostat reveal a clear set of related trends developing since the 1970s: marriage rates across Europe are dropping, numbers of divorces increasing and levels of non-marital fertility rising.[5])Since the experiences of cohabitants can be difficult to capture in official statistics owing to the informal nature of the relationship, extra-marital birth rates provide a very rough proxy for the prevalence of at least some types of cohabitation in any given jurisdiction. National household surveys are able to identify cohabiting relationships, and some recent surveys have sought specifically to identify births to co-residential parents in order to examine changes in parents' relationships in the run-up to and following the child's birth.[6]

Eurostat reports that there has been an overall reduction of 34 per cent in the number of marriages contracted within the EU-27 countries between 1970 and 2009, and the crude divorce rate has doubled over the same period (though this is partly a reflection of increased liberalisation in divorce laws across Europe in that time).[7] Not surprisingly, the decline in the popularity and stability of marriage has been mirrored by a large growth in the number and proportion of births to unmarried mothers, many of them in co-residential relationships with their child's father. In 1990, 17.4 per cent of births were extra-marital; in 2010, 37.4 per cent of children were born to unmarried parents.[8]

---

[5] Eurostat, *Europe in figures: Eurostat yearbook 2012* (Publications Office of the EU 2012), 2.4–2.5 (available 10 July 2015 at http://http://ec.europa.eu/eurostat).

[6] E.g. B Perelli-Harris et al, 'Changes in Union Status during the Transition to Parenthood in Eleven European Countries, 1970s to early 2000s' (2012) 66 *Population Studies* 167.

[7] Ibid, at 124 and tables 2.4.1 and 2.4.2.

[8] Ibid, at 125 and table 2.4.3.

While the general direction of travel across Europe is largely similar,[9] the speed of travel and so magnitude of change varies between jurisdictions. Marriage rates vary between 7.9 per 1,000 inhabitants (in Cyprus) and 3.2 (in Bulgaria and Slovenia); divorce rates between 0.7 per 1,000 inhabitants (in Ireland) and 3.0 (in Lithuania and Belgium); and extra-marital births between just 6.9 per cent of live births (in Greece) and more than half in five jurisdictions (including Sweden and France).[10] But while the prevalence of cohabitation varies substantially between jurisdictions, all European jurisdictions are facing similar demographic changes which in turn necessarily prompt the legislator to consider how, if at all, to accommodate the rise in unmarried cohabitation within a family law hitherto dominated by the law of marriage.

Smaller scale national socio-legal research (principally in relation to opposite-sex cohabitation) provides important insights into these large scale data, highlighting the heterogeneity of relationships that may be found within the category 'cohabitation' and the divergence of at least some types of cohabitation from marriage. Public attitude surveying casts light on the views of the general public and specific sectors of the public (for example, cohabitants themselves) on what cohabitation does and should mean in terms of its legal consequences. It is important that such research be undertaken in each jurisdiction: differences in the nature and social meaning of cohabitation and in parties' expectations of what legal obligations it does and should entail may arise from the different cultural, religious and economic (as well as legal) contexts in which cohabitation is practised.[11] Evidence about the nature of cohabitation in a given jurisdiction – about its diversity or not, about its similarity or not to marriage – is potentially important for the policymaker considering what, if any, additional legal regulation to offer, or to impose by default, on this group. Certain types of regulation may be more appropriate for some types of cohabiting couples than others. The data may suggest that legal rights and remedies should not be made available generally to 'cohabiting

---

[9]   Though note the different trajectories of uniform formation and child-bearing found by Perelli-Harris et al (ibid) in the eleven jurisdictions they examined. Only in Sweden and Iceland did the percentage of live births outside marriage drop between 2000 and 2010 (and then only very slightly and from a very high position): Eurostat (2012), table 2.4.3.

[10]   Ibid, at 124–5 and tables above.

[11]   This point is also noted by Wendy Schrama, 'General Lessons for Europe Based on a Comparison of the Legal Status of Non-Marital Cohabitants in the Netherlands and Germany', in K Boele-Woelki (ed.) *Common Core and Better Law in European Family Law* (Intersentia 2005).

couples', but rather be targeted in some way, or that some element of choice should be built into the legal scheme (whether by making legal regulation dependent on the exercise of positive choice, or by providing some means for couples to opt out of regulation otherwise imposed by default).

England and Wales provides a leading example of the type of research that can be undertaken in order better to understand the characteristics of cohabiting relationships and what people think about them.[12] In analysing their findings, researchers have divided cohabitants into different (not mutually exclusive) categories: (i) those cohabiting short-term, perhaps early in life and largely for convenience, rather than in consequence of a long-term commitment; (ii) those cohabiting by way of trial-marriage, contemplating but having not yet made a long-term commitment analogous to marriage; (iii) those cohabiting with a new partner following the dissolution of a marriage to another person, deliberating choosing not to make the specific commitment of marriage again; (iv) those who choose cohabitation in preference to marriage but who regard their relationship in many respects, including its long-term commitment, as analogous to it. Children might be born into any of these relationships, though it is unlikely that that would occur (as a deliberate step) in category (i), and relationships in (i) are likely also to be the shortest. Research into different couples' money management techniques has also revealed diversity, some cohabitants operating as independent individuals, others (especially those with children) operating in partnership as spouses do.[13] This heterogeneity amongst cohabiting relationships – some of which are akin to marriage, others of which are quite different from marriage (some deliberately so) – itself means that policymakers must consider carefully whether, and if so how, to regulate cohabitation in law.

---

[12]   In particular, the work of Anne Barlow and colleagues, including Barlow et al, *Cohabitation, Marriage and the Law* (Hart Publishing 2005), Barlow et al 'Cohabitation and the Law: Myths, Money and the Media' in Park et al (eds) *British Social Attitudes: the 24th Report* (Sage 2008); C Smart and P Stevens, *Cohabitation Breakdown* (Family Policy Studies Centre 2000); K Kiernan, 'The Rise of Cohabitation and Childbearing Outside Marriage in Western Europe' (2001) 15 *International Journal of Law, Policy and the Family* 1. The UK research is extensively cited in Law Commission, *Cohabitation: The Financial Consequences of Relationship Breakdown*, Law Com CP 179 (TSO, 2006), Part 5 and the following Report Law Com No 307, Part 2.

[13]   See chapters by C Vogler and C Burgoyne and S Sonnenberg in J Miles and R Probert (eds) *Sharing Lives, Dividing Assets* (Hart Publishing 2009).

3. NO SUBSTANTIAL PAN-EUROPEAN LAW OF UNMARRIED COHABITATION

National legislators' responses to unmarried cohabitation are very largely a matter for them, relatively unconstrained by legal norms emanating from pan-European law, whether international (under the European Convention on Human Rights) or supra-national (European Union (EU) law). As Masha Antokolskaia has observed, given the political sensitivity of unmarried cohabitation in many jurisdictions, Europe has thus far taken a 'lowest common denominator' approach, deferring to national judgements of what is appropriate for each state.[14]

3.1 Unmarried Cohabitants and the European Convention on Human Rights

The European Court of Human Rights has had relatively little to say about the legal treatment of unmarried cohabitants in terms of the relationship between the adults (as opposed to the legal status of children born to such couples and their relationship with each of their parents). (Certainly, both opposite- and same-sex couples, with or without children, are now recognised as enjoying 'family life' which must be respected under Article 8.[15])However, whilst that shields such relationships from state interference, the Court has declined to find that the state owes significant positive obligations towards such relationships. It has also very largely dismissed applications brought under Article 14 in conjunction with Article 8 complaining that such couples are treated differently from spouses, for example in being denied financial remedies following the parties' separation[16] or the death of one partner,[17] or in relation to the calculation of welfare benefits and taxation.[18] For example, in the context of remedies on death, while the Commission in _Saucedo Gomez v Spain_[19]

---

[14] M Antokolskaia, *Harmonisation of Family Law in Europe: A Historical Perspective* (Intersentia 2006) 15.9.

[15] *Johnston v Ireland* (1987) ECHR A-112; *Saucedo Gomez v Spain* (App No 37784/97) 26 January 1999, unreported; *Schalk and Kopf v Austria* (App No 30141/04) (2011) 53 EHRR 20.

[16] *Johnston v Ireland* (1987) ECHR A-112.

[17] *Saucedo Gomez v Spain* (App No 37784/97) 26 January 1999.

[18] E.g. *Courten v UK* (App No 4479/06) 4 November 2008, unreported; *MW v UK* (App No 11313/02, ECHR) 23 June 2009, unreported; *Shackell v UK* (App No45851/99, ECHR) 27 April 2000, unreported.

[19] (App No 37784/97) 26 January 1999.

appeared prepared to hold that a surviving cohabitant might be regarded as being in an analogous position to a surviving spouse,[20] the state was held to be justified in distinguishing between marriage and cohabitation in order to promote the traditional concept of family – that is, that based on marriage.

The advent of registered partnership schemes for same-sex couples has led the Court to extend its reasoning to support states in maintaining clear-cut rules distinguishing between couples who have and have not made public, legally binding commitments towards each other, whether enshrined in marriage or some other formalised relationship.[21] However, whilst the interpretation and application of the Convention's guarantees are evolving as a 'living instrument' in response to legal developments in states within the Council of Europe, those states remain at liberty to prefer formalised over informal relationships, at least where the couple in question had the option to formalise their relationship.[22]

3.2   Unmarried Cohabitants and European Union Law[23]

As McGlynn's account of the law demonstrates,[24] EU Law currently affects the situation of unmarried cohabitants in only a relatively narrow range of areas, principally: free movement of workers and their family members; asylum and immigration; and benefits for partners in the context of employment law. It has no direct impact in the horizontal/ internal areas of domestic law which form the principal focus of this chapter.[25] The European Charter of Rights and Fundamental Freedoms

---

[20]   Even this view is not always adopted: e.g. *Burden v UK* (App No 13378/05), (2008) 47 EHRR 38, [65].

[21]   *Burden v UK* (App No 13378/05) (2008) 47 EHRR 38.

[22]   Which will not be the case for same-sex couples in all jurisdictions; the Court in *Schalk and Kopf v Austria* (App No 30141/04) (2011) 53 EHRR 20 expressed no view on whether Austria would have been in breach of the Convention had it not introduced its registered partnership scheme before the case came before the Court.

[23]   The account of the law and discussion of it in this section relies heavily on the work of Clare McGlynn, and on my discussions with Dr Ruth Lamont, University of Liverpool and Prof Catherine Barnard, University of Cambridge, to both of whom I am very much indebted.

[24]   C McGlynn, *Families and the European Union: Law, Politics and Pluralism* (Cambridge University Press 2006), ch 5.

[25]   Orders characterised as being for maintenance following the end of a cohabiting relationship would fall within the Maintenance Regulation for private international law purposes: Council Regulation (EC) No 4/2009 on jurisdiction,

has so far had little impact even within the areas of EU competence just identified, and the EU maintains a largely traditional, heterosexual, marriage-centric approach to family life, subservient to national laws.

The fullest recognition of cohabiting couples in EU law relates to free movement, but cohabitants' recognition is substantially inferior to that afforded to workers' spouses. (Whereas marriage generates automatic rights of movement and residence for the worker's spouse[26] (as does registered partnership, though only if the host state recognises such relationships as equivalent to marriage and subject to any conditions laid down by that state's laws),[27] the Free Movement Directive of 2004 requires Member States only – in accordance with its national legislation – to 'facilitate' the free movement of unmarried partners of the worker, and then only in the case of a 'durable relationship, duly attested': the rights created by the Directive do not apply.[28])However, the limited nature of cohabitants' rights (qua cohabitant) may have little impact in practice, owing to the availability of other grounds – not based on the cohabiting relationship – which permit that individual to move and/or acquire a right of residence, for example: the expansive nature of the concept of 'worker',[29] rights flowing from parenthood of a child with

---

applicable law, recognition and enforcement of decisions and cooperation in matters relating to maintenance obligations. Early ambitions to include the property consequences of cohabitants' separation within the current work on private international law implications of matrimonial property laws have come to nothing: see EU Commission Green Paper on Conflict of Laws in matters concerning matrimonial property regimes, 17 July 2006, COM (2006) 400 final (SEC (2006) 952), which included questions regarding the property consequences of registered partnership and unregistered cohabitation, as well as marriage.

[26] Affirmed in *Metock* Case C-127/08 and *Sahin* C-551/07. The concept of 'spouse' in EU law has long been understood to depend on formal legal marriage: *Netherlands v Reed* Case 59/85.

[27] Directive 2004/58, articles 2 and 3(1).

[28] Directive 2004/58, article 3(2)(b). The only exception is that if the state allows the unmarried partners of its own nationals to enter, non-discrimination on grounds of nationality requires that it extend the same right to partners of Community nationals: *Netherlands v Reed* Case 59/85.

[29] Directive 2004/38/EC (the Citizens' Rights Directive), notably articles 7(3) and 14(4)(b).

rights of residence,[30] and rights conferred by the Citizens' Rights Directive.[31]

The ready availability of these alternative bases for the rights perhaps explains why there has been so little litigation around cohabitants' rights specifically. Indeed, the CJEU has not yet engaged with any argument to the effect that the different treatment of cohabitants and spouses in this arena constitutes discrimination under Article 21 of the EU Charter of Rights, and so EU law has not (yet) augmented the limited jurisprudence of the European Court of Human Rights in this field. Several authors note that the European Parliament has been progressive in its calls for the wider recognition of non-traditional family forms.[32] However, the political nature of negotiations in this arena (arguably at the expense of proper attention to what Charter and other enforceable EU legal principles – notably freedom of movement – might require)[33] is such that EU institutions as a whole and EU law seem likely for the time being to retain a predominantly conservative approach to the recognition of inter-adult relationships.[34]

Given the reserved approach of the ECHR and CJEU – but given also recognition that interpretation of both the Convention and EU law can develop in light of widespread social change[35] – the impetus for change at both international and supra-national level will need to come from the nation states. The remainder of this chapter therefore focuses on a comparative analysis of European jurisdictions' approaches, in particular to the legal rights and remedies of cohabitants on separation.

4. PAN-EUROPEAN DIVERSITY: COMPARING ACROSS TWO AXES OF LEGAL REGULATION

It is helpful in examining and comparing the responses of different jurisdictions to the situation of cohabitants on separation to categorise

---

[30] *Iida v City of Ulm* Case C-40/11; *European Parliament v Council of the EU* Case C-540/03; and, most controversially, *Ruiz Zambrano v Office national de l'emploi* Case C-34/09.

[31] Directive 2004/38.

[32] See McGlynn's discussion of the role of the Parliament in the development of Directive 2004/58: (n 24) 128; H Toner, *Partnership Rights, Free Movement and EU Law* (Hart Publishing 2004) 63–7; Antokolskaia (n 14) 15.9.2.

[33] See Toner (n 32) 64.

[34] McGlynn (n 24), ch 5 generally.

[35] In the EU context, see McGlynn's discussion (n 24) 123–4.

each jurisdiction's response in terms of two axes or, perhaps permitting a more nuanced analysis, two spectrums. This discussion assumes that a jurisdiction has elected to recognise cohabitants at all in law, rather than just leave them to use whatever rights and remedies might be afforded by the general law, but many European jurisdictions continue to adopt the latter approach.

The first axis or spectrum concerns the basis upon which rights and remedies are to be accessed, if granted at all: (1) 'opt-in': that is, only if the couple has by some positive act registered or otherwise formalised their relationship; or (2) by default and (possibly) subject to 'opt-out': that is, the rights and remedies apply to all cohabiting couples – or all couples whose relationship satisfies a set of objectively determined eligibility criteria – but couples who do not wish to be subject to the regime may opt out by agreement, though (at the farther end of this spectrum) not from legal provisions which are made mandatory on grounds of public policy.

The second axis or spectrum examines the substance of the rights and remedies thereby conferred in particular by reference to their similarity or not to those rights and remedies enjoyed by spouses on divorce: (A) the 'assimilationist' position, which puts cohabitants broadly in the same position as spouses; and (B) the 'differential' position, which gives cohabitants different – that is to say, inferior – rights and remedies to spouses.

One might additionally seek in comparing jurisdictions' responses to the economic consequences of cohabitation to engage in a more concrete examination of the substantive nature of the rights and remedies conferred: for example, whether the cohabitant enjoys a right to equal sharing of a given property pool, whether the cohabitant may claim maintenance and on what grounds, and so on. However, whilst that issue is also of considerable interest,[36] the substantive details of the rights and remedies is likely to reflect something about each jurisdiction's general approach to financial rights and remedies on relationship breakdown, specifically on divorce: for example, a jurisdiction which operates community of property between spouses is unlikely to adopt a discretionary system of equitable redistribution between cohabitants, and vice versa – these two systems are quite alien to each other. Fuller comparative understanding of each jurisdiction's law on cohabitation in those terms

---

[36] I explore it briefly in parts 3.2 and 3.3 of J Miles, 'Financial Relief between Cohabitants on Separation', in K Boele-Woelki and T Sverdrup (eds), *European Challenges in Contemporary Family Law* (Intersentia 2008).

would therefore require us first to examine its matrimonial laws. But whatever the situation of a given jurisdiction may be in the senses discussed in the last paragraph, the policymaker addressing the law of cohabitation in any jurisdiction is likely to take as a starting point the legal position of spouses and work from that. Hence my decision to focus here on the extent to which that policymaker has elected to treat cohabitants similarly to spouses, both in requiring them to opt-in in order to access rights (just as spouses must take the positive step of marrying) or not, and in affording to them rights and remedies which match those of spouses (whatever those rights and remedies might entail) or not.[37]

The position of any given jurisdiction in terms of those two spectrums will reflect that jurisdiction's response to a set of competing concerns which policymakers must address: protection for the institution of marriage, protection of private autonomy/choice, and protection of the economically vulnerable.[38] Different understandings of what each of those means and how each concern manifests in each jurisdiction, together with different conclusions regarding the priority of those concerns and so the appropriate balance to be struck between them, produce very different outcomes in terms of the legal regulation of cohabitation, reflecting differences in dominant political ideology regarding the family and its regulation by the state.[39] Some jurisdictions have specific constitutional protection for marriage, though, as the recent example of Ireland shows, that is not necessarily an insuperable obstacle to legislating for cohabitants, at least in a way which confers on them less extensive rights than spouses.[40] Others – such as some of the Balkan states – have

---

[37] The substantive content of the rights and remedies is likely also to be closely related to local socio-economic conditions and wider legal entitlements: for example, the nature of the housing market and availability of affordable rental accommodation; rates of female, especially maternal, labour market attachment; generosity or otherwise of social security provision and subsidised childcare: what works in a strong welfare state may not be at all workable in a jurisdiction with far less state support for individuals or families.

[38] See also Antokolskaia's discussion (n 14).

[39] See D Bradley, 'Regulation of Unmarried Cohabitation in West-European Jurisdictions: Determinants of Legal Policy' (2001) 15 *International Journal of Law, Policy and the Family* 22.

[40] See article 41 of the Constitution of Ireland (Bunreacht Na hÉireann) and the new Irish Civil Partnership and Certain Rights and Obligations of Cohabitants Act 2010, the enactment of which was preceded by careful attention to the constitutionality of such legislation: see for example the Options Paper Presented by the Working Group on Domestic Partnership (2006), 4.02 (available 10 July 2015 at http://www.justice.ie/en/JELR/OptionsPaper.pdf/Files/OptionsPaper.pdf).

constitutional protection for cohabitants as well.[41] Moreover, it has been noted by various authors that religious, socially conservative, liberal and some feminist agendas can unite in (very differently grounded) opposition to cohabitation law reform, so the politics of this area are not straightforward. The following sections sketch out the basic arguments likely to be in play in relation to each spectrum.

4.1   Opt-in or Default/Opt-out?

The debate between opt-in and default/opt-out regimes brings into play all of the competing concerns listed above, raising a series of questions to which a jurisdiction will need to supply answers.[42]

First, what might be the impact of reform on the institution of marriage? On the one hand, creating an opt-in regime might be thought to undermine the institution of marriage by providing couples otherwise eligible to marry with an alternative, 'lighter' option and so an incentive to contract that relationship rather than marry. Equally, creating a default or opt-out regime might be thought to have that same effect by imposing rights and duties on couples without requiring them first to register their relationship, again giving couples reason not to take that formal step. But, on the other hand, such arguments might be entirely misplaced: it must be asked how exactly the creation of legal protection for another class of relationship can damage 'the institution' of marriage, in either normative or practical terms.

Secondly, what might be the impact of reform on individual autonomy? An opt-in regime might be thought better able to protect individual autonomy than a default scheme, by ensuring (as marriage does) that only those individuals who specifically assent to being subject to legal obligations are brought within the scheme. This might also better reflect the diversity that may exist in terms of cohabitants' level of commitment. Certainly a default regime that permitted no opt-out would appear to ignore autonomy in cohabiting relationships, effectively confining individuals to a choice about whether to cohabit at all. But an opt-in scheme might be thought to protect autonomy at the expense of denying protection to vulnerable individuals who are unable to persuade their partner to formalise their relationship, or are simply unaware of the need

---

[41]   See for example article 61 of the Croatian Constitution, article 40(2) of the Macedonian Constitution.

[42]   The arguments explored in this section draw significantly on the work of the Law Commission for England and Wales in Part 5 of its extensive consultation paper (n 12) (2006).

to formalise their relationship in order to secure legal protection. Consideration needs to be given to whether a default regime with opt-out facility might offer a better compromise between the desire to protect autonomy and acknowledge the diversity of cohabiting relationships and the desire to protect the economically vulnerable by securing protection of the latter unless the couple (as a couple) choose to remove themselves from the scheme.

Third, what might be the impact on these arguments of the choice of eligibility criteria? It might be thought that the force of arguments in favour of default regimes, particularly if no opt-out facility is to be provided, depend in part on the eligibility criteria deployed to determine which couples would fall within the scheme by default. Eligibility cast too widely might catch too many couples for whom the resulting rights and remedies might be thought unsuited (though that of course depends on what form and content those rights and remedies would take) and so put a large number of couples to the cost of having to opt out. A jurisdiction might wish, if it is to protect any cohabitants by default, to reserve that protection for cohabitants with children, leaving cohabitants who do not have children either excluded from the scheme, required to opt in, or included only following the passage of a number of years. Such eligibility requirements (whether registration, presence of children, minimum duration) may be intended to serve various functions: a normative function of identifying particular relationships deemed deserving of access to the scheme in consequence of demonstrated commitment (perhaps equivalent to parties having expressly opted in); a more practical function of seeking to capture those relationships which, given the passage of time or the birth of children, might typically be expected to have developed the sort of financial interdependency which financial remedies are required to resolve, and to exclude shorter, more casual relationships; or, more practically still, simply to reduce the number of cases which might arise and demand the resources of the legal system to resolve.

While these arguments can be conducted purely at the level of principle, local empirical evidence about couples' relationships, behaviours, attitudes and beliefs about the law may usefully support or refute factual premises on which they rely. As noted above, it is particularly important that local evidence is relied upon wherever possible, as conditions in one jurisdiction may be very different from another as a result of longstanding religious and cultural traditions, socio-economic conditions, and so on.

Arguments based on protection of the institution of marriage may be thought to depend for their force on whether there is a public interest in protecting marriage and in encouraging couples to marry rather than cohabit because marriage demonstrably achieves public goods such as greater relationship stability or better outcomes for children. But careful research needs to be undertaken to determine whether such benefits be demonstrated empirically.[43] Even if they can, such benefits may or may not be felt to constitute sufficient reason to deprive those who have not married of *any* protection. (This is closely related to the second axis of assimilation or different treatment). Indeed, another empirical question to be addressed is whether making available either an alternative formal institution or a default scheme of protection would negatively affect the marriage rate.[44]

Arguments based on the protection of autonomy depend for their force on evidence about the reality of choice, and in particular of informed choice, amongst those whose choices the argument seeks to respect. Evidence of widespread public misapprehension about the legal consequences of marriage and cohabitation – for example, a belief that both attract the same consequences – significantly undermine the claim that those who have not married are deliberately rejecting the legal consequences of that institution and so should not be subjected to them automatically.[45] Can it be demonstrated that public education campaigns would be effective in addressing such myths? Even if they could, that would not answer the predicament of the already vulnerable cohabitant in an 'uneven' relationship whose legally-aware partner refuses to marry,[46]

---

[43] For a UK study demonstrating substantial selection effects in operation (i.e. characteristics of couples other than their relationship status accounting for most of the differences observed between families based on marriage and on cohabitation), see C Crawford et al, 'Cohabitation, Marriage and Child Outcomes: An Empirical Analysis of the Relationship between Marital Status and Child Outcomes in the UK using the Millennium Cohort Study' (2012) 24 *Child and Family Law Quarterly* 176, based on an Institute for Fiscal Studies project on *Cohabitation, Marriage, Relationship Stability and Child Outcomes* (available 10 July 2015at http://www.ifs.org.uk/comms/comm120.pdf).

[44] Here it may be necessary to rely on data from another jurisdiction. For an analysis of cohabitation law reform's (lack of) impact on Australian marriage rates, see K Kiernan, A Barlow and R Merlo, 'Cohabitation Law Reform and its Impact on Marriage' (2006) 36 *Family Law* 1074.

[45] In the British context, see in particular A Barlow et al, 'Just a Piece of Paper? Marriage and Cohabitation', in A Park et al (eds) *British Social Attitudes: the 18th Report* (Sage 2001); in the Netherlands and Germany, see Schrama (n 11) 265.

[46] See A Barlow, C Burgoyne and J Smithson, *The Living Together Campaign – An Investigation of its Impact on Legally Aware Cohabitants* (MOJ

nor would it mean that couples who do not formalise their relationship in marriage or create a legal regime for themselves through contract (for example) positively reject the notion that they should be legally obligated to each other: their inaction may be more indicative of inertia, 'optimism bias' (that is, a touching assumption that their relationship will endure so that there is no need to cater for its demise), lack of responsiveness to legal imperatives, or other priorities, rather than a rejection of legal regulation.[47]

Arguments for default schemes to protect economically weaker parties may be thought to depend in part on evidence about the extent of the social problem which the creation of new private law obligations would be aimed to alleviate. Is a sufficient number of individuals materially disadvantaged at the end of cohabiting relationships in circumstances and to an extent which merits such legal intervention, or do the parties' rights under the general law, local labour market and housing market conditions, childcare and social security provision mean that former cohabitants can be expected to promptly achieve economic security without special private family law remedies? In many jurisdictions, a substantial driver of public policy may be a concern for the situation of children of the couple who may be disadvantaged directly or indirectly by the absence of financial remedies for the economically weaker parent with whom that child may mainly live following separation.[48]

2007), and A Barlow and J Smithson 'Legal Assumptions, Cohabitants' Talk and the Rocky Road to Reform' (2010) 22(3) *Child and Family Law Quarterly* 328.

[47] Some cohabitants would be resistant: see Barlow et al's identification of 'romantic' and 'ideologue' cohabitants who will, for very different reasons, resist the law's message (op cit); see also M Maclean and J Eekelaar, 'Marriage and the Moral Bases of Personal Relationship' (2004) 31 *Journal of Law and Society* 510; J Lewis, 'Perceptions of Risk in Intimate Relationships: The Implications for Social Provision' (2005) 35 *Journal of Social Policy* 39.

[48] See, in the English context, R Probert 'Trusts and the Modern Woman – Establishing an Interest in the Family Home' (2001) 13 *Child and Family Law Quarterly* 275, but contrast the examples found in empirical research: S Arthur et al, *Settling Up: Making Financial Arrangements after Divorce or Separation* (National Centre for Social Research 2002); R Tennant et al, *Separating from Cohabitation: Making Arrangements for Finances and Parenting* DCA Research Series 7/06, (DCA 2006); G Douglas et al, *A Failure of Trust: Resolving Property Disputes on Cohabitation Breakdown* (Cardiff 2007).

4.2 Assimilation or Different Treatment?

The second axis or spectrum requires a decision by each jurisdiction whether the legal scheme it has decided to create will simply assimilate the position of eligible cohabitants with that of spouses, treat them entirely differently (that is, by conferring rights which are less extensive than those enjoyed by spouses), or adopt some intermediate position, for example (by analogy with arguments made by Scherpe[49]) by adopting a starting point of assimilation but conferring on the courts discretion to treat a couple differently from spouses given the circumstances of the individual case, or by adopting for cohabitants some but not all of the different remedies or principles applicable between spouses.

As noted earlier, some jurisdictions' constitutional protection for the institution of marriage may be regarded as precluding assimilation but not rule out the adoption of a different regime for cohabitants. Other jurisdictions will engage in a similar normative debate about the desirability of equating cohabitants with spouses despite the lack of any constitutional constraint. Whether (and how far) assimilation is an appropriate step may also depend considerably on the nature of the financial and property rights and remedies enjoyed by spouses: what is suitable for spouses, in normative and functional terms, may not be considered suitable to the circumstances of cohabitants. This consideration has particular force where all or part of the regime which applies to spouses is fixed by legal rules from which no, or only very limited departure, is permitted (as is the case in most continental European jurisdictions).[50] By contrast, where the remedy is strongly discretionary or otherwise responsive to individual circumstances (as in England & Wales and Ireland), any court called upon to adjudicate between parties unable to settle their financial matters through negotiation will be able to adapt the remedy in light of the particular circumstances of each case.

Whether such discretion is thought necessary for cohabitants and whether the regime which applies to spouses is suitable (whether rule-based or discretionary) depends on the basis upon which the case for or against assimilation is to be made. Certain provision available between spouses might be deemed on normative grounds to be inapplicable to

---

[49] Writing in the context of legislative strategy in the conclusion to JM Scherpe and N Yassari (eds), *Die Rechtsstellung nichtehelicher Lebensgemeinschaften/The Legal Status of Cohabitants* (Mohr Siebeck 2005).

[50] See chapter 5 in this volume (Scherpe) and JM Scherpe, 'Marital Agreements and Private Autonomy in Comparative Perspective' in the book of the same title by JM Scherpe (ed.) (Hart Publishing 2012).

cohabitants. For example, a community of property or other sharing/
participation regime may be understood to be based on the partnership
created by the formal step of marriage, which mere informal cohabitation
cannot parallel; so too rights of support might be regarded as dependent
upon the express assumption of responsibility made expressly on marrying. Such arguments reflect both a concern to protect the institution of
marriage and the choices made by autonomous individuals to marry or
not and so to come within that specific regime or not. Alternatively,
however, it might be argued that property sharing or other spousal
remedies are ultimately justified not on the exercise of choice regarding
marriage but rather on protective grounds reflecting the dynamics of
financially interdependent relationships, and that those grounds have
equal force in the case of cohabitants who find themselves in functionally
identical circumstances at the end of their relationships. Or one might
adopt an intermediate position, regarding some spousal rights (such as
fixed entitlements to property sharing) as properly confined to the
partnership of marriage whilst considering that other remedies, particularly those which seek to respond directly to the actual economic
situation of the claimant arising from the relationship, find their justification in the practical situation of that individual regardless of the legal
form of the relationship.[51]

These latter arguments depend for their force in part on empirical
evidence about the functional equivalence, or not, of cohabitation and
marriage in any given jurisdiction.[52] So here again we have to be alert to
the diversity of cohabiting relationships, some – but not all – of which
may be functionally similar to marriage in ways which make the spousal
scheme suitable for them. To the extent that some cohabiting relationships are in functional terms sufficiently different from marriage that they
ought not to be subject to the same scheme of financial remedies, the
policymaker needs to choose from one of the following positions: (i)
whether no cohabitants' cases should be assimilated with those of
spouses and instead some wholly different scheme (or no scheme at all)
must be created; (ii) whether only certain cohabitants' cases should be
assimilated, for example, those who have opted into a functionally

---

[51]   For a very full exposition of the arguments in this sphere, see the sharp
contrast of view within the Supreme Court of Canada in *Nova Scotia v Walsh*
2002 SCC 83, [2002] 4 SCR 325 and *Quebec v A* 2013 SCC 5. See also
arguments from the academic literature rehearsed by the Law Commission for
England and Wales in its Consultation Paper (n 12), from 127.

[52]   See generally, R Probert, 'Cohabitation: Current Legal Solutions' (2009)
62(1) *Current Legal Problems* 316.

identical formal relationship or who have satisfied eligibility requirements designed broadly to filter out the functionally dissimilar relationships, or leaving it to the court to determine in each case whether to
assimilate or not; or (iii) whether the diversity can be adequately
accommodated by giving couples the right to opt out of the scheme, so
that they can determine for themselves whether they should be treated as
if married.

5. A COMPARATIVE OVERVIEW: GROUPING THE JURISDICTIONS

Combining the two axes of regulation identified above, the law of any
one jurisdiction may be (loosely) described in both senses as either
'opt-in assimilation', 'opt-in different', 'default/opt-out assimilation', or
'default/opt-out different'. The looseness of this four-part categorisation
reflects the fact that some jurisdictions will be, for example, more or less
assimilationist and/or afford more or less scope for parties to opt-out of
regulation imposed by default. Where appropriate, I also refer to the law
of non-European jurisdictions which exemplify particular categories. One
would ideally seek to position each jurisdiction precisely along the
relevant spectrum: for example, there is self-evidently considerable
difference between mandatory default schemes and those that afford
some degree of opt-out. I hope readers will forgive me for adopting the
looser structure of four designations: family law reform being a live issue
in many jurisdictions, the law may change shortly after publication such
that more fine-grained analysis of current laws may rapidly become
outdated. But the discussion which follows demonstrates how the two
spectrums may be deployed as analytical tools to be used in appraising
the current law and reform proposals in any jurisdiction at any given
time.

Whilst no European jurisdiction maintains the position that non-marital
cohabitation is illegal and cannot give rise to any legally enforceable
obligations, between them the European jurisdictions manifest the full
range of attitudes from Napoleonic dismissiveness (*'les concubins
ignorent la loi, la loi ignore donc les concubins'*, which leaves the parties
to fend for themselves using the general law) to fully fledged quasi-
marital status, at least for the purposes of financial consequences of
relationship breakdown.[53] Between these two poles, there is necessarily

---

[53] Notably, the various jurisdictions which operate within Spain between
them display a striking array of approaches, certainly prior to the Constitutional

considerable variety within the 'different treatment' jurisdictions in terms of just how different that treatment is: some laws may adopt parts, but not all, of matrimonial law, and so partially assimilate; others may deliberately steer a very different course which is intended to and does achieve very different outcomes; some laws may be very different on their face from matrimonial laws but produce quite similar outcomes in a lot of cases.

5.1   Opt-in Assimilation

The first category is somewhat anomalous in terms of the main focus of this chapter: those jurisdictions which treat as akin to spouses those who have opted into a scheme which is not designed to operate purely as a same-sex couple equivalent to marriage. Where a jurisdiction has created such an institution, effectively marriage in all (or very nearly all) but name, that institution is likely to have been intended to operate as a functional equivalent of marriage for same-sex couples but which, in pursuit of gender/sexuality equality/neutrality in the creation of new legal institutions or other local political considerations, has been made available to opposite-sex couples as well. This model is exemplified within Europe by the Dutch registered partnership[54] (which is distinctive from marriage as regards the more straightforward, administrative means of dissolving the relationship) and by some of the Spanish regional laws,[55] and beyond Europe by the New Zealand civil union[56] (dissoluble in the same way as marriage) and those Australian state/territory laws which create relationship registration schemes[57] (as in Dutch law, more readily

---

Court decision of 2013: see L Marquès, 'Regulating Cohabitation in Spain: The Unconstitutionality of Current Legislation' (2014) *International Family Law* 44–7; see also L Marquès, 'The Unconstitutionality of Cohabitation Regulation – Two Decisions of the Spanish Constitutional Court', in N Witzleb, R Ellger, P Mankowski, H Merkt and O Remine (eds), *Festschrift für Dieter Martiny zum 70. Geburtstag* (Mohr Siebeck 2014) 1141–61.

[54]   Registered Partnership Act. In force from 1 January 1998; for a comprehensive survey of the law and its genesis, see I Curry-Sumner, *All's Well that Ends Registered* (Intersentia, 2005), ch V.

[55]   Such as those in Galicia, the Balearic Islands, the Basque region and Valencia: see Marquès (n 53).

[56]   Civil Union Act 2004 (NZ).

[57]   For a useful survey of the various Australian state laws, see O Rundle, 'An Examination of the Relationship Registration Schemes in Australia' (2011) 25 *Australian Journal of Family Law* 121.

dissoluble), which give rise to financial remedies on separation on the same basis as spouses.

Since the parties have expressly opted in to the relationship, this model poses no problems in terms of respect for autonomy. To the extent that it affords couples an option other than marriage, it might be regarded as undermining the traditional institution of marriage. But to the extent that those who register their relationship are treated like spouses, the incentive to register rather than marry (for those who have a choice between the two, which same-sex couples do not in some of these jurisdictions) may be based largely on perceived cultural and social differences arising from the label 'marriage' and gendered roles typically associated with that institution; though, conversely, for so long as same-sex couples are denied access to marriage, that institution is likely to retain a 'gold standard' quality in relation to which registered partnership is or appears inferior at least to some. Once marriage is made available to all couples, it might be expected that that institution will be considerably more popular than an equivalent but alternative registered partnership. But it is interesting to note that the number of new Dutch registered partnerships per annum (whilst greatly out-numbered by new marriages for both opposite- and same-sex couples) has grown in recent years, with older individuals making up a higher proportion of new registered partnerships than of new marriages.[58]

Whilst the opt-in assimilation approach clearly caters for a particular group of couples who reject the institution of marriage whilst nevertheless wishing to enjoy its legal consequences, it does not alleviate the position of the economically vulnerable party whose partner will not formalise the relationship. It is important to note in this regard that Dutch law – unlike New Zealand, for example[59] – affords relatively few legal protections to informal cohabitants.

5.2 Opt-in Different

Of more interest for the purposes of this chapter are those jurisdictions which have created an entirely novel opt-in relationship for both opposite

---

[58] http://www.cbs.nl/en-GB/menu/themas/bevolking/publicaties/artikelen/archief/2011/2011-3331-wm.htm; and see tables which can be generated using the 'tables by theme' function in the 'Population' section at http://statline.cbs.nl/StatWeb/dome/default.aspx?LA=EN (both accessed 10 July 2015).

[59] See the inclusion of de facto relationships within the Property (Relationships) Act 1976, as amended, and the Family Proceedings Act 1980 (as amended).

and same-sex couples which deliberately does not seek to mirror marriage but provides a distinctive institution with less intensive legal consequences, in particular at the point of separation. As several commentators have observed, such developments have commonly been the product of political compromise, accommodating same-sex couples but only on unequal terms which seek to minimise the impact of their inclusion in family law.[60] The paramount European examples of this model are the French *pacte civil de solidarité* ('PACS')[61] and (even more distinctively, in terms of its wide eligibility criteria but limited private law consequences) the Belgian *cohabitation légale*.[62]

The Belgian *cohabitation légale* is unusual for being open to related pairs as well as to couples. However, although its legal consequences have been enlarged since its creation, notably in the areas of taxation and succession,[63] it confers very little by way of private law obligations between the parties. As Curry-Sumner notes, the significance of the duties that exist during the currency of the relationship (for example, to cohabit, to contribute to household expenses, and so on) are somewhat diluted by the ready dissolubility of the legal relationship (a common feature of most opt-in alternatives to marriage). And once dissolved, the former *cohabitation* confers no maintenance or property entitlement: there is only a limited presumption of joint ownership of assets which neither can prove to be their sole property; but it is likely that the former cohabitant remains liable to contribute towards the repayment of debts already incurred in relation to the relationship.[64]

---

[60] See for example Antokolskaia (n 14), 15.6; JM Scherpe, 'The Legal Status of Cohabitants – Requirements for Legal Recognition', in K Boele-Woelki (ed.), *Common Core and Better Law in European Family Law* (Intersentia 2005); and L Glennon, 'Displacing the "Conjugal Family" in Legal Policy – a Progressive Move?' (2005) 17 *Child and Family Law Quarterly* 141.

[61] French Civil Code, Art 515. See generally Curry-Sumner (n 54), ch IV; J Goddard, 'PACS Seven Years On – Is it Moving Towards Marriage?' (2007) *International Journal of Law, Policy and the Family* 310.

[62] Belgian Civil Code, articles 1475–1479 : see Curry-Sumner (n 54), ch III. Note also the laws of various autonomous Spanish regions for cohabiting couples (only), some of which provide for registration schemes either as the sole route to recognition, or as an alternative route to default recognition (though contrast Catalonia, whose scheme confined same-sex couples to the registration route): see Antokolskaia (n 14), 15.6.4.

[63] See J Sosson, 'Recent Evolutions (or Revolutions) in Belgian Family Law', in B Atkin (ed.), *International Survey of Family Law* (Jordan Publishing 2010) 53.

[64] See Curry-Sumner (n 54), 57–8.

The French PACS is confined to unrelated couples, but has proved increasingly popular as an alternative or precursor to marriage for opposite-sex couples, who dominate the annual registration figures (95 per cent of the 174,504 PACS registrations in 2009 are known to have involved opposite-sex couples,[65] a significant number of whom will go on to marry; there were 245,151 new marriages in 2009). Meanwhile, marriage rates overall are gradually declining, though not at a rate equivalent to the rise in PACS, which suggests that PACS is catering for a cohort who would not otherwise marry, at least not yet.[66]

It is notable that the rise in opposite-sex couple registrations has followed changes in the legal regime for *pacsés* (couples who have concluded a PACS) which bring them closer in some respects to the position of spouses (or by bringing spouses closer to the position of *pacsés*),[67] notably in relation to taxation.[68] However, as regards their private law relationship, in particular on separation, the position of pacsés is very different from that of spouses. Whilst they have a similar duty to contribute towards household expenses and associated debts during the relationship, no maintenance or compensation rights arise on separation (other than under the civil law), and the property consequences of their relationship will either be determined by the arrangement set out in their original *pacte* or, in the absence of such arrangement, be governed (after reforms which came into effect 2007) by separation of property, that is, the opposite default position from that applicable between spouses.[69]

Overall, it is remarkable how the PACS has drifted towards a greater assimilation with marriage in some areas of law whilst leaving dissolution of PACS and its economic consequences a matter entirely for the parties, with no requirement of judicial sanction, no default community

---

[65] Until 2007, French law barred the collection of statistics on PACS relating to couples' gender.

[66] F Prioux, M Mazuy and M Barbieri, *Recent Demographic Developments in France* (2010) 65 *Population – E* 363, 376ff, table 3 and table A.9. The website of the Institut National d'Etudes Démographique provides of wealth of empirical data on marriage, PACS and cohabitation http://www.ined.fr/en/resources (accessed 10 July 2015).

[67] As noted in the French report in B Atkin (ed.) *International Survey of Family Law* (Jordan Publishing 2012) 98.

[68] Prioux et al (n 66), 376.

[69] For PACS concluded pre-2007, the default position was one of *indivis par moitié*, i.e. a presumption – unless the parties provided otherwise – that property acquired by either party for valuable consideration following creation of the PACS was to be held jointly. The move to separation of property makes PACS more distinctive from marriage in this area.

of property and no mandatory maintenance/compensation.[70] This combination of assimilation in some areas of law, especially as regards taxation, but sharply different treatment in private law appears at least in part to be responsible for the increasing popularity of the PACS.[71]

Of course, in depending for their creation on the consent of both parties and in allowing for easy dissolution with minimal consequences, these French and Belgian opt-in relationships again fail to offer any protection on separation to those who either cannot persuade their partner to opt in at all or (in the case of the PACS) to do so on agreed terms more beneficial than the default position. And, like Dutch law, both French and Belgian law – true to the Napoleonic dictum – otherwise provide little or no recognition of informal cohabitation (*concubinage*) practised outside these formalised institutions.

5.3   Default/Opt-out Assimilation

A very different policy is evident in those jurisdictions which do afford legal consequences to *de facto* cohabitation, even to the extent of broadly assimilating their position with that of spouses, in some instances with mandatory effect. This fullest approach is evident within Europe in the Balkan jurisdictions and Ukraine,[72] and has become increasingly common beyond Europe, notably in New Zealand,[73] under recent changes to federal Australian law[74] and in some Canadian provinces.[75] New Zealand

---

[70]   Goddard (n 61), 315.

[71]   See also Antokolskaia's observations regarding the popularity of the Dutch cohabitation contract which attracts inheritance, tenancy, pension and tax law entitlements, but no financial rights or remedies on separation, compared with the relative lack of cohabitation contracts in Germany to which no such public law consequences attach: (n 14) 386–7.

[72]   2002 Family Code of Ukraine and parts of the Civil Code: see M Antokolskaia, 'Economic Consequences of Informal Heterosexual Cohabitation from a Comparative Perspective: Respect Parties' Autonomy or Protection of the Weaker Party?' in A-L Verbeke, JM Scherpe, C Declerck, T Helms and P Senaeve (eds), *Confronting the Frontiers of Family and Succession Law* (Intersentia 2012) 58.

[73]   Property (Relationships) Act 1976, Family Proceedings Act 1980, both as amended.

[74]   Family Law Act (Cth) 1975, as amended by the Family Law Amendment (De Facto Financial Matters and Other Measures) Act 2008; only Western Australia remains outside this legislation, though its own local legislation confers rights largely equivalent to those of spouses.

[75]   Though not required under the Canadian Charter of Rights and Fundamental Freedoms as a matter of non-discrimination: *Nova Scotia v Walsh* 2002

is the most striking jurisdiction internationally insofar as it affords *all* couples access to broadly the same legal regime, whether through marriage (opposite-sex only – though at the time of writing a same-sex marriage bill is before the NZ Parliament), civil union (any gender) or de facto relationships.[76]

The Balkan jurisdictions – including Bosnia-Herzegovina,[77] Croatia,[78] Macedonia,[79] Serbia[80] and Slovenia[81] – were amongst the first in Europe to legislate in recent times for unmarried cohabitation and they provide strong assimilation, at least in relation to the economic consequences of relationship breakdown.[82] All jurisdictions bring eligible cohabitants within the scope of matrimonial property law and maintenance obligations on separation; they enjoy the same contractual freedom as spouses

---

SCC 83, [2002] 4 SCR 325 and *Quebec v A* 2013 SCC 5. Whilst all provinces other than Quebec now include cohabitants in spousal support laws, only a few provinces include cohabitants in property division laws: Saskatchewan, Manitoba and (most recently) British Columbia, as to which see Family Law Act 2011 (BC), which came into force in March 2013.

[76] See Property (Relationships) Act 1976, ss 2E and 14A.

[77] Family Law Act, article 3, see Antokolskaia (n 72), at 56.

[78] Marriage and Family Relations Act; discussed by D Hrabar, 'Legal Status of Cohabitants in Croatia', in JM Scherpe and N Yassari (eds), *Die Rechtsstellung nichtehelicher Lebensgemeinschaften/The Legal Status of Cohabitants* (Mohr Siebeck 2005).

[79] Family Law Act 1992; D Mickovikj and A Ristov, 'The Legal Regulation of Nonmarital Cohabitation in Macedonian Family Law', in B Atkin (ed.), *International Survey of Family Law* (Jordan Publishing 2012).

[80] Family Law Act 2005; Oa Cvejić Jančić, 'Challenges of the Modern Family: Draft Civil Code of Serbia Relating to Family Law Relations' in B Atkin (ed.), *International Survey of Family Law* (Jordan Publishing 2012).

[81] Marriage and Family Relations Act 1976; M Geč-Korošec and S Kraljić, 'The Influence of Validly Established Cohabitation on Legal Relations between Cohabitants in Slovene Law', in A Bainham (ed.) *International Survey of Family Law* (Jordan Publishing 2001); V Rijavec and S Kraljić, 'Slowenien' in JM Scherpe and N Yassari (eds), *Die Rechtsstellung nichtehelicher Lebensgemeinschaften/The Legal Status of Cohabitants* (Mohr Siebeck 2005).

[82] They vary in the extent to which they include cohabitants within succession law and within personal laws, e.g. governing the parties' relations during the cohabitation: it has been remarked that Slovenia is the most assimilationist jurisdiction in this regard, with Croatia now following in its footsteps to a greater degree: see Antokolskaia (n 72), citing Scherpe.

in relation to property sharing but, like spouses, are mandatorily subjected to maintenance law.[83] With the exception of Croatia,[84] these
jurisdictions – unusually in Europe – currently protect only opposite-sex
cohabitants. Eligibility is otherwise based in some jurisdictions on the
parties having had children or satisfied a minimum duration requirement,[85] whilst others prescribe no minimum duration, instead simply
requiring that the parties be in a permanent relationship or shared life.[86]

It has been suggested, in relation to Croatia at least, that the motivation
for bringing cohabitants within the scope of these matrimonial laws was
not simply the influence of more liberal ideas about the family, but also a
concern for the vulnerable position of women in rural areas.[87] Given
what appears to be a strong protectionist concern, which had already
prompted courts to provide some protection for such women before
legislation was enacted, it is perhaps unsurprising that maintenance
provision should be made mandatory rather than subject to opt out.
Autonomy is protected to the extent that parties are free to determine
their own property relations, but whilst this puts them in no worse a
position overall than spouses, it necessarily limits (in this area of private
law at least) the extent to which cohabitation may be chosen as a
deliberately different type of relationship.

The recent decision of the Spanish Constitutional Court – in relation to
the default regime applicable in Navarra which assimilated cohabitants
with spouses after just one year of cohabitation without explicit opt-out
facility – adopts a very different attitude. In holding the law to be
unconstitutional on the ground that it violated the right to free development of personality, the Court clearly prioritised autonomy over concerns
for protection of the weaker party: in the view of the Court, any
regulation of cohabiting relationships must be based on their express,
voluntary agreement.[88]

---

[83]   Antokolskaia notes that an opt-out facility is being considered in the new
Draft Family Code for Slovenia: (n 72) 57; see also Barabara Novak, chapter 13
in Volume II of this book set.

[84]   A separate law on same-sex unions is currently under discussion in
Serbia: O Cvejić Jančić (n 80) 301.

[85]   E.g. in Croatia, a three year requirement is imposed for childless couples:
Hrabar (n 78) 402, 405–6; in Macedonia, which unusually does not confine
eligibility to those free to marry each other, has a one year requirement:
Mickovikj and Ristov (n 79).

[86]   E.g. Serbia: O Cvejić Jančić (n 80).

[87]   Hrabar (n 78).

[88]   Judgment of the Constitutional Court 93/2013: see L Marquès (n 53).

5.4 Default/Opt-out Different

The final grouping of jurisdictions within Europe which have legislated for cohabitants consists of those which confer legal consequences on cohabitation by default rather than via opt-in, but which offer only a lower level of protection than that enjoyed through marriage (and functionally equivalent civil or registered partnership law for same-sex couples). This approach – pioneered globally between the late 1970s and the mid-1980s by common law jurisdictions within Canada and Australia (many of which have since moved to an assimilationist position) – is evident in Europe in the common law/mixed jurisdictions of Ireland[89] and Scotland[90] (and is the recommended model for long-awaited reform in England & Wales[91]), and in a number of civil law jurisdictions including Sweden,[92] Norway,[93] certain of the autonomous Spanish regions and under Spanish federal law[94] and Hungary.[95]

---

[89] Civil Partnership and Certain Rights and Obligations of Cohabitants Act 2010, Part 15; see generally J Mee, 'Cohabitation Law Reform in Ireland' (2011) 24 *Child and Family Law Quarterly* 323.

[90] Family Law (Scotland) Act 2006; for discussion and early research findings on the operation of the new law, see F Wasoff, J Miles and E Mordaunt, *Legal Practitioners' Perspectives on the Cohabitation Provisions of the Family Law (Scotland) Act 2006* (CRFR, 2010), available 10 July 2015 at http://www.crfr.ac.uk/assets/Cohabitation-final-report.pdf.

[91] Law Commission for England and Wales (n 12) (2007).

[92] Cohabitants Act 2003; see E Ryrstedt, 'Legal Status of Cohabitants in Sweden' in JM Scherpe and N Yassari (eds), *Die Rechtsstellung nichtehelicher Lebensgemeinschaften/The Legal Status of Cohabitants* (Mohr Siebeck 2005), C Sörgjerd, 'Neutrality: the Death or the Revival of the Traditional Family?' in K Boele-Woelki (ed.), *Common Core and Better Law in European Family Law* (Intersentia 2005).

[93] Joint Household Act 1991; see E Ryrstedt 'Legal Status of Cohabitants in Norway' in JM Scherpe and N Yassari (eds), *Die Rechtsstellung nichtehelicher Lebensgemeinschaften/The Legal Status of Cohabitants* (Mohr Siebeck 2005), J Asland 'Legislation on Informal Cohabitation in Norway', in K Boele-Woelki (ed.), *Common Core and Better Law in European Family Law* (Intersentia 2005). See also the new Finnish legislation which creates specific family law remedies to reverse unjust enrichment, discussed by T Sverdrup, 'Statutory Regulation of Cohabiting Couples in the Nordic Countries', in K. Boele-Woelki et al (eds), *Family Law and Culture in Europe* (Intersentia 2014).

[94] See generally L Bueno Medina, 'The Spanish Relationships Legislation', in K Boele-Woelki (ed.), *Common Core and Better Law in European Family Law* (Intersentia 2005), and L Marquès (n 53); C Gonzalez Beilfuss, 'Die Rechtsstellung nichtehelicher Lebensgemeinschaften in Spanien und Portugal', in JM Scherpe and N Yassari (eds), *Die Rechtsstellung nichtehelicher*

These jurisdictions vary considerably in terms of eligibility criteria and the level of protection afforded to the economically weaker party. What protection is offered is conferred by default but generally subject to the right to opt out by agreement, even in relation to maintenance or compensation-based remedies (in those jurisdictions which offer them). In offering schemes of this nature, these jurisdictions might be thought to offer the best balance between concerns to protect the vulnerable (at least at some basic level), to protect autonomy and to maximise relationship diversity, both through the different provision for those within the scheme from that for spouses and through the preservation of an obligation-free area through the right to opt out.

In terms of eligibility requirements, while several of these jurisdictions prescribe no minimum duration requirement or require the presence of children, they generally require demonstration of a permanent/stable affective relationship in a joint household,[96] a relationship analogous to marriage,[97] and/or the sharing of a common household and an emotional and economic partnership,[98] and some adopt a checklist of factors to which to have regard in determining whether to characterise the relationship as one of cohabitants.[99] Hungary has, like several Australian states, also recently introduced the additional possibility of proving the cohabitation via registration.[100] Ireland stands out for its requirement that even couples with children satisfy a minimum duration requirement, albeit one shorter (at two years) than that applicable to couples without children

---

Lebensgemeinschaften/The Legal Status of Cohabitants (Mohr Siebeck 2005) 249–75; S Schlenker, 'Die Stellung gleichgeschlechtlicher Lebensgemeinschaften in Spanien und in spanischen Teilrechtsordnungen', in J Basedow, KJ Hopt, H Kötz and P Dopffel (eds), *Die Rechtsstellung gleichgeschlechtlicher Lebensgemeinschaften* (Mohr Siebeck 2000) 145–67; Antokolskaia (n 14) 15.6.4.

[95] Relevant provisions of the Civil Code, since 1977; see Hungary reports by O Szeibert in B Atkin (ed.) *International Survey of Family Law* (Jordan Publishing 2009 and 2012), and 'Unmarried Partnerships in Hungary' in K Boele-Woelki (ed.), *Common Core and Better Law in European Family Law* (Intersentia 2005).

[96] E.g. Cohabitants Act 2003 (Sweden), s 1.

[97] E.g. Family Law (Scotland) Act 2006, s 25.

[98] See Szeibert on Hungary (n 95) (2009), at 210.

[99] E.g. Civil Partnership and Certain Rights and Obligations of Cohabitants Act 2010 (Ireland), s 172.

[100] See Szeibert (n 95) (2009), at 206–7 on amendment of the Notarial Non-Litigious Proceedings Act No XLV 2008 by Act No XXIX 2009 on Registered Partnership and… Cohabitation. See also the laws of some autonomous Spanish regions, discussed by Antokolskaia (n 14) 15.6.4.

(five years).[101] Norway is more typical internationally in requiring a (two year) minimum duration for childless couples, but no minimum duration for those without; but atypical insofar as its law covers all domestic, non-marital homesharers, not just couples.

As noted above, the nature of the rights and remedies on offer at the point of separation varies considerably. Some of these jurisdictions offer only limited property sharing, with no maintenance rights: for example, Sweden – presumptively equal sharing of home and household goods on separation only; maintenance for Swedish spouses is of course rare in any event; Hungary – presumptively equal sharing under the Civil Code of 'common property', a concept of uncertain scope;[102] the introduction of both participation in acquests and maintenance rights have recently been proposed in Hungary.[103] Other jurisdictions offer need or compensation-based remedies rather than property sharing rights or remedies: for example, Ireland's new discretionary claim for financial relief based on financial dependency arising from the couple's relationship or its breakdown, which might be met by property adjustment, lump sum or periodical payments orders; Scotland's discretionary capital remedies based on economic advantage or disadvantage or the burden of caring for children – two of the five principles that apply to spouses on divorce in Scots law;[104] and various autonomous Spanish regions' compensation remedies or maintenance, especially for the primary carer of children. Least generously – and arguably better grouped with the next set of jurisdictions as it lacks provision specifically for 'cohabitants' per se – is Norway's coverage of cohabiting couples in its law for homesharers, which confers only a right to apply for occupation of the shared home and use of household goods, at market rates, following separation.

---

[101]   Civil Partnership and Certain Rights and Obligations of Cohabitants Act 2010, s 172(5). Contrast the new Finnish legislation which sets a minimum duration of five years only for those without children: see Sverdrup (n 93).

[102]   See Szeibert (n 95) for discussion, and the suggestion that in practice cohabitants' property rights may not be much different from those of spouses.

[103]   See Szeibert, on the draft Family Law Book in the new Civil Code (n 95) (2009), at 211–12 and (2012), at 121.

[104]   The Act also creates some presumptions in relation to joint ownership of certain property, but these are weak presumptions and do not in practice carry any significance.

5.5   No Specific Statutory Recognition

The borderline status of Norway brings us finally to the large group of European jurisdictions which provide no special family law remedies between cohabitants at the end of their relationships,[105] including (non-exhaustively) England & Wales, Germany, Switzerland, Austria, Denmark, Italy, Greece, Poland, the Czech Republic, Bulgaria,[106] the Baltic states and (save between 1926-44) Russia.[107] To these we might add France, Belgium and the Netherlands, insofar as cohabitants who have not opted into the relevant non-marital institution provided in those jurisdictions will be left unprotected by any special family law on relationship breakdown.

The absence of specific regulation by family law statute does not mean that cohabitants have no legal remedy at the end of their relationship. They will commonly be able to bring claims under the general law – of property, trusts, contract, unjust enrichment, even company law[108] – and the courts in many of these jurisdictions have generally sought to develop or adapt those principles in ways that help mitigate the economic difficulties that might be faced following separation from a cohabiting relationship. Arguments based on anti-discrimination and the functional similarity of cohabitants and spouses have overall had limited success, certainly as regards the relationship between the adult parties (as opposed to their relationship as parents of a common child). In Belgium, case law has occasionally sought to ameliorate cohabitants' position via discrimination arguments made under the European Convention on Human Rights, but such examples are said to have been isolated and have not formed the basis of any substantial development of the law relating to *de facto* cohabitation.[109] However, the Supreme Court in Spain has advocated case-by-case protection of the economically weaker cohabitant given their functional similarity to spouses, using the law of unjust enrichment and analogous application of spousal compensation provisions.[110]

---

[105]   Many of those jurisdictions recognise cohabitation in contexts other than private law remedies on separation.

[106]   Though a draft Family Code would introduce remedies for cohabitants.

[107]   See Antokolskaia (n 14) 374–7.

[108]   For example, in the case of Switzerland: see S Aeschlimann, 'Financial Compensation upon the Ending of Informal Relationships ...' in K Boele-Woelki (ed.), *Common Core and Better Law in European Family Law* (Intersentia 2005).

[109]   Sosson (n 63) 54, citing cases from the early 1980s.

[110]   See Bueno Medina (n 94) 308–9.

In many jurisdictions it must be acknowledged that inherent limitations of the general law remedies inhibit the effectiveness of such judicial initiatives. Contract-based solutions evidently share the limitation of opt-in schemes in that they depend upon the parties reaching agreement, and in this private law context that will involve one party agreeing to confer on the other party benefits that he or she would not otherwise be bound to supply. Property, trust and unjust enrichment-based solutions commonly depend on evidence of the parties' respective contributions towards the acquisition of property or more generally towards their shared life, and may be more or less accommodating and, if accommodating, more or less generous in their valuation of domestic (rather than financial) contributions.[111]

6. CONCLUSION: IS EUROPE STILL A MARRIAGE-CENTRIC CONTINENT?

So where will the future take us? Experience teaches this author that prediction in family law and policy is a dangerous game! Who could have predicted that Catholic Spain would be amongst the first European jurisdictions to legislate for same-sex marriage or that England and Wales would, as early as 2013, pass a gay marriage bill promoted by a Conservative-led government?[112] But for the time being, it seems appropriate still to describe Europe as a whole as a marriage-centric continent.

If one looked only at pan-European law – whether from the EU or from the European Court of Human Rights – it would be hard to contest that assessment. At the national level, debates around same-sex relationships, in particular around same-sex marriage, have a tendency to emphasise marriage (and other formalised relationships) and so to perpetuate the view that family regulation is principally achieved by allowing all couples the freedom to acquire that state-sanctioned status. Moreover, it is probably true that campaigning for same-sex relationship rights, whether executed via strategic litigation or via political lobbying, tends to be stronger than equivalent campaigning on behalf of economically vulnerable parties to non-marital relationships.

---

[111] Contrast, for example, I Lund-Andersen and E Ryrstedt's evaluations of Danish and Norwegian courts' respective efforts to develop the law of unjust enrichment for the domestic context, in JM Scherpe and N Yassari (eds), *Die Rechtsstellung nichtehelicher Lebensgemeinschaften/The Legal Status of Cohabitants* (Mohr Siebeck 2005).

[112] See the Marriage (Same Sex Couples) Act 2013.

If current demographic trends continue, jurisdictions may find it increasingly difficult to ignore the plight of cohabitants, but whether and how they respond seems destined to be dictated largely by local political considerations. However, for the time being, as Masha Antokolskaia has observed, 'legislation in favour of non-institutionalised heterosexual cohabitation still represents a minority phenomenon in Europe'.[113] Even a high rate of cohabitation and a progressive/liberal political tradition does not guarantee that the legislature will provide legal recognition, as the examples of Denmark and Finland – and beyond Europe, Québec – demonstrate. Convergence is difficult to spot. Indeed, given the considerable diversity that prevails across Europe in this area, not least amongst those jurisdictions which *do* provide financial and/or property rights and remedies between cohabitants on relationship breakdown, it will be some time before any inter- or supra-national legal imperative to legislate in this area is identified, such that either European Court will narrow the margin of appreciation currently afforded to national jurisdictions in this area of family law.

RECOMMENDED FURTHER READING

M Antokolskaia, *Harmonisation of Family Law in Europe: A Historical Perspective* (Intersentia 2006) ch 15, 'Non-marital cohabitation: from outlaw to functional alternative for marriage'.

M Antokolskaia, 'Economic Consequences of Informal Heterosexual Cohabitation from a Comparative Perspective: Respect Parties' Autonomy or Protection of the Weaker Party?' in A-L Verbeke, JM Scherpe, C Declerck, T Helms and P Senaeve (eds), *Confronting the Frontiers of Family and Succession Law* (Intersentia 2012).

J Asland et al, *Nordic Cohabitation Law* (Intersentia, 2015).

A Barlow et al, *Cohabitation, Marriage and the Law* (Hart Publishing 2005).

K Boele-Woelki (ed.), *Common Core and Better Law in European Family Law* (Intersentia 2005), Part III.

K Boele-Woelki, N Dethloff and W Gephart (eds), *Family Law and Culture in Europe* (Intersentia 2014), Part II.

K Kiernan, 'The Rise of Cohabitation and Childbearing outside Marriage in Western Europe' (2001) 15 *International Journal of Law, Policy and the Family* 1.

I Kroppenberg, D Schwab, Dieter Henrich, Peter Gottwald and Andreas Spickhoff (eds), *Rechtsregeln für nichteheliches Zusammenleben* (Beiträge zum europäischen Familienrecht, vol. 12; Gieseking 2009) – chapters on various jurisdictions (all in German, except for Sweden) and comparative chapter (in German).

C McGlynn, *Families and the European Union* (Cambridge University Press 2006) ch 5.

---

[113]   Antokolskaia (n 14) 372.

J Miles, 'Financial Relief between Cohabitants on Separation: Options for European Jurisdictions', in K Boele-Woelki and T Sverdrup (eds), *European Challenges in Contemporary Family Law* (Intersentia 2008).

B Perelli-Harris et al, 'Changes in Union Status during the Transition to Parenthood in Eleven European Countries, 1970s to Early 2000s' (2012) 66 *Population Studies* 167.

R Probert, *The Changing Legal Regulation of Cohabitation: From Fornicators to Family, 1600–2010* (Cambridge University Press 2012).

JM Scherpe and N Yassari (eds) *Die Rechtsstellung nichtehelicher Lebensgemein-schaften / The Legal Status of Cohabitants* (Mohr Siebeck 2005) – chapters in German and English on various jurisdictions and comparative chapter in German

Special issue on 'Family Law and Policy: Cohabitation and Marriage Promotion' (2004) 26(1) *Law and Policy*.

4. Same-sex relationships in a European perspective

Ian Curry-Sumner

1. INTRODUCTION

> Change is a funny thing. We are never quite sure what we are becoming or even why. Then one day we look at ourselves and wonder who we are and how we got that way.[1]

In 1990, who would ever have thought that there would come a time when a generation of new law students starting university would not even question the eligibility of same-sex couples to marry? And yet, that time has already arrived. The majority of students embarking upon a legal education at a Dutch university in September 2015 were four years old when Job Cohen, the Mayor of Amsterdam, celebrated the first-ever State endorsed same-sex marriage in Amsterdam, The Netherlands. For these students, the existence of same-sex marriage is oftentimes as much a

---

[1] Jodi Picoult, American author (1966-present).

given as the need to criminalise murderers or the need for a National Parliament. Yet, the road to this point in time has not been one without its trials and tribulations.

In this chapter, an attempt will be made to briefly outline the current state of the law with regard to the legal recognition of same-sex relationships in Europe (see section 2). This comparative synopsis will form the basis upon which a more theoretical framework will be discussed (see section 3). Such a theoretical framework will provide academics and legislatures alike with a template to discuss the issues related to these new phenomena in a structured and purposeful manner. Although this chapter is limited to the European context, where relevant, footnote references will be made to the legal situation outside of Europe. This chapter will also provide an overview of the developments that have taken place with regard to homosexuality and same-sex relationships at the European Court of Human Rights (see section 4). In doing so, this chapter hopes to provide a guide to this issue both from a substantive family law perspective, as well as a human rights perspective.

2. SUBSTANTIVE LAW COMPARISON

2.1 Introduction

26 years on since the first same-sex partnership registration ceremonies took place in Copenhagen, Denmark, the world has seen a remarkable and swift wave of legislative and judicial change with regard to the legal recognition of same-sex relationships. The debate has raged, is raging and will continue to rage on every continent of the planet. Currently, at least one country on every continent apart from Asia permits same-sex couples to register their relationship in a formal public ceremony, or celebrate their marriage.[2]

---

[2] SOUTH AMERICA: Brazil (civil unions since 2011 and same-sex marriage since 2013), Ecuador (same-sex civil unions since 2008), Uruguay (civil union since 2008 and same-sex marriage since 2013), Argentina (same-sex marriage since 2010) and in Chile presidential candidate Michelle Bachelet had promised to legalise same-sex marriage if elected President in November 2013. Colombia also allows for same-sex *de facto* unions, which provide couples with the same civil law rights as civil marriage. This is a result of a decision of the Constitutional Court in 2009 (Decision C-029 of 2009); NORTH AMERICA: Canada (same-sex marriage since 2005) and various states in the USA (California (2008/2013), Connecticut (2008), Delaware (2013), Hawaii (2013), Illinois (2014), Iowa (2009), Massachusetts (2004), Maryland (2013), Maine (2012),

Yet it should not be forgotten that this trend towards increased recognition must be placed against the status quo of many other countries in the world, where homosexuals risk imprisonment for their actions or even fear for their lives.[3] The recent Russian legislation prohibiting the 'promotion of homosexuality' provides an excellent example of the highly political, as well as global nature of this issue. These issues even led to some world leaders boycotting the Winter Olympic Games held in Sochi in 2014. This section will address the different relationship forms that have been used by legislatures across the European continent, namely same-sex marriage (see 2.2), registered relationship forms (see 2.3) and non-registered cohabitation (see 2.4).[4]

2.2 Same-sex Marriage

On 1 April 2001, The Netherlands became the first country in the world to open civil marriage to couples of the same-sex. This monumental occasion heralded the start of a slow trend towards increasing acceptance of same-sex marriage, not just in Europe, but around the globe. As of today, ten years after same-sex couples were allowed to start celebrating

---

Minnesota (2013), New Jersey (2013), New Hampshire (2010), New Mexico (2013), New York (2011), Oregon (2014), Pennsylvania (2014), Rhode Island (2013), Vermont (2009) and Washington (2012), as well as the District of Columbia (2009), the Federal Government (2013) and since 26th June 2015 nationwide; AFRICA: South Africa (same-sex marriage since 2006); OCEANIA: New Zealand (civil unions since 2004 and same-sex marriage since 2013) and various schemes in various states in Australia (Australian Capital Territory (2008), New South Wales (2010), Queensland (2012), Tasmania (2004), Victoria (2008)), as well as Pitcairn Islands (2015) ASIA: A proposal to introduce same-sex marriage was put forward in Nepal in 2011. In Vietnam, the Ministry of Justice requested that the National Assembly take action in the field of same-sex marriage before 2014. The Minister of Health proposed that same-sex marriage should be made legal with immediate effect. A proposal that has bi-partisan support in Thailand is currently before Parliament, but has been put on hold due to political turmoil. Furthermore, Israel and Mexico recognise same-sex marriages performed elsewhere, although have not provided for nation-wide legislation permitting same-sex marriages to be concluded in their juris-dictions themselves.

  [3]   In Iran, Mauritania, Saudi-Arabia, Sudan, United Arab Emirates, Yemen and Nigeria (12 northern provinces that apply Shari'a law) homosexuality is still punishable with the death penalty.

  [4]   See also J Scherpe, 'The Legal Recognition of Same-sex Couples in Europe and the Role of the European Court of Human Rights' (2013) 10 *Equal Rights Review* 83–96.

marriage ceremonies from Amsterdam to Zwolle, 14 countries in Europe currently allow for same-sex couples to get married (Belgium (2003), Denmark (2012), England & Wales (2014),[5] Finland (2017), France (2013), Greenland (2015), Iceland (2010), Ireland (entry into force to be announced), Luxembourg (2015), the Netherlands (2001), Norway (2009), Portugal (2010), Scotland (2014), Spain (2005) and Sweden (2009)).[6] Since 2014, foreign same-sex marriages are also recognized in Malta. Furthermore proposals are also under consideration in the Faroe Islands and Slovenia.[7] Although the German Bundesrat passed an initiative on 22 March 2013 which would have opened marriage to same-sex couples, this proposal is unlikely to continue any further at this moment in time.

Although in some jurisdictions the road towards opening same-sex or gender-neutral marriage was particularly straightforward,[8] in many jurisdictions, a long journey preceded the final jubilant celebrations. On 31 July 2009, for example, the Portuguese Constitutional Court rejected the argument that the Portuguese Constitution demanded the recognition of same-sex relationships (although at the same time the Court also stated that the Constitution did not oppose it).[9] Nonetheless, the Court left the issue to the legislature; a decision that has been echoed in many jurisdictions around the world (for example, The Netherlands and Vermont). In 2011, this author argued one could perhaps regard decisions of supreme courts and constitutional courts as a precursor to legislative

---

[5] As marriage is a devolved issue in the United Kingdom, the status of same-sex marriage is different in England & Wales, Scotland and Northern Ireland. Furthermore, two of the three British Crown Dependencies have also introduced forms of civil partnership (namely Jersey (2012) and the Isle of Man (2011)), as has one British Overseas Territory (Gibraltar (2014)).

[6] At the same time there are currently no fewer than 28 states that have constitutional bans on same-sex marriages. See I Curry-Sumner and ST Curry-Sumner, 'Is the Union Civil? Same-sex Marriages, Civil Unions, Domestic Partnerships and Reciprocal Benefits in the USA' (2008) 4(2) *Utrecht Law Review* 236–78, available 11 July 2015 at www.utrechtlawreview.org.

[7] See F Swennen and S Eggermont, 'Same-sex Couples in Central Europe: Hop, Step and Jump', in K Boele-Woelki and A Fuchs (eds), *Legal Recognition of Same-sex Relationships in Europe* (Intersentia 2012) 21.

[8] With respect to Iceland, see I Lund-Andersen, 'The Nordic Countries: Same Direction – Different Speeds', in K Boele-Woelki and A Fuchs (eds), *Legal Recognition of Same-sex Relationships in Europe* (Intersentia 2012) 9–12, §2.2.

[9] See further C Gonzalez-Beilfuss, 'All or Nothing: the Dilemma of Southern Jurisdictions', in Boele-Woelki and Fuchs (eds), *Legal Recognition of Same-sex Relationships in Europe* (Intersentia 2012) 42–4, §2.1.

change.[10] It was argued that the litmus test would be France, where the French Constitutional Court had held on 28 January 2011 that the ban on same-sex marriage in France was not unconstitutional.[11] In the essence the Constitutional Court passed the baton to the French National Assembly, stating that this was an issue for legislative action. After the election of François Hollande as President, a new bill was debated in the National assembly, ultimately resulting in the passage of legislation legalising same-sex marriage. The first same-sex marriage took place on in Montpellier on 29 May 2013. A similar constitutional case is, for example, expected to come before the Greek Supreme Court (*Areios Pagos*) after the Court of Appeals held on 14 April 2011 that a same-sex marriage concluded by the Mayor of Telos was non-existent.[12] This case has now also been sent to the European Court of Human Rights.[13] It is perhaps interesting to note that the European Parliament has also recently passed a resolution recognizing the right of same-sex couples to marry and have their relationship legally recognized.

At the same time, it is important to notice an opposing trend towards increasing prohibition of same-sex relationships. In 2011 constitutional bans on same-sex marriage were also proposed in four jurisdictions around the world (Chile, Hungary, Jamaica and Zambia). Currently at least 25 jurisdictions worldwide provide for the constitutional limitation of marriage to one man and one woman.[14] This

---

[10] I Curry-Sumner, 'A Patchwork of Partnerships: Comparative Overview of Registration Schemes in Europe', in Boele-Woelki and Fuchs (eds), *Legal Recognition of Same-Sex Couples in Europe* (Intersentia 2012) 71–82.

[11] Decision 2010-92. The same could also be said of the Italian Constitutional Court rejection in April 2010. See further Swennen and Eggermont (n 7) 25–6, §3.2 and Gonzalez-Beilfuss, (n 9) 52–3, §3.2.

[12] Jugdment 114/2008, *ChrID*, 2009, 617 et seq and Judgment 115/2009 *EfAD* 2009, 690 et seq. See further, AG Fessass, '18th Annual Congress of International Academy of Comparative Law, Washington DC. National Report: Greece', (2011) 19 *American University Journal of Gender, Social Policy and the Law* 187, at §V.

[13] In the meantime, a Greek Government official announced on 19 August 2011 that the Greek Government was to introduce legislation to introduce registered partnerships. This registration scheme was only open to different-sex couples, and has since led to a separate case before the European Court of Human Rights in *Vallianatos v Greece* App No 29381/09 and 32684/09 (ECHR, 7 November 2013).

[14] Cuba (1976), Burkina Faso (1991), Bulgaria (1991), Vietnam (1992), Paraguay (1992), Lithuania (1992), Cambodia (1993), Belarus (1994), Moldova (1994), Ukraine (1996), Poland (1997), Venezuela (1999), Rwanda (2003), Burundi (2005), Honduras (2005), Uganda (2005), Latvia (2005), Democratic

restrictive approach is also particularly noticeable in the Eastern European context.[15]

2.3 Registered Partnerships

In 1989, Denmark became the first country in the world to provide same-sex couples with a public registration service, enabling them to gain virtually all the rights and responsibilities of different-sex married couples.[16] This decision paved the way for the worldwide movement towards increasing recognition for same-sex relationships.[17] At present, no fewer than 21 European jurisdictions have introduced forms of formalised relationship registration.

The first wave of jurisdictions centered in the North, with Norway,[18] Sweden,[19] Greenland[20] and Iceland[21] becoming the second, third, fourth and fifth jurisdictions in the world to introduce forms of registered partnership. All four Nordic registered partnership schemes were very similar in form, being restricted to couples of the same-sex and creating an institution that with a few exceptions mirrored marriage. Although there were small internal differences (that is, differences between the domestic form of registered partnership and the domestic form of

---

Republic of Congo (2005), Serbia (2006), Montenegro (2007), Ecuador (2008), Bolivia (2009), Cayman Islands (2009), Dominican Republic (2010) and Kenya (2010).

[15] Constitutional bans on same-sex marriage are now applicable in ten European countries: Article 32, Belarus Constitution; Article 46 Bulgarian Constitution; Article L Hungarian Constitution; Article 110, Latvian Constitution; Article 38.3 Lithuanian Constitution; Article 48 Moldovan Constitution; Article 71 Montenegrin Constitution; Article 18 Polish Constitution; Article 62 Serbian Constitution; and Article 51 Ukrainian Constitution. As well as the recent amendments to the constitutions in Croatia (2013) and Slovenia (2014), and a proposal is currently pending in Macedonia (2015).

[16] For a detailed description of the historical background see P Dopffel and J Scherpe, 'Gleichgeschlechtliche Lebensgemeinschaften im Recht der nordischen Länder' (The Legal Status of Same-sex Couples in the Nordic Countries), in J Basedow et al (eds), *Die Rechtsstellung gleichgeschlechtlicher Lebensgemeinschaften* (Mohr Siebeck 2000) 7–49, as well as Lund Andersen (n 8).

[17] Lund-Andersen (n 8) 4, §2.1.

[18] Lov om registrer partnerskap nr. 40 av 30 April 1993.

[19] Lag om registrerat partnerskap, SFS 1994:1117.

[20] The registered partnership law was extended to Greenland on 26 April 1996 and is called *Inooqatigiittut nalunaarsorsimasut* in Greenlandic.

[21] Lög um staðfesta samvist, nr. 87 12 June 1996.

marriage[22]) and external differences (that is, differences between the various domestic forms of registered partnership[23]) these were minor compared to the general extension of marital rights to same-sex couples. One important difference that deserves mention here, however, concerned the rights of same-sex couples with respect to children. None of four Scandinavian jurisdictions extended the presumption of paternity to same-sex couples. As a result the woman married to the birth mother did not automatically become the legal parent of the child. Initially, adoption rights were also not extended to same-sex registered partners.[24] Nonetheless, as of 2011, stepchild adoption is now permitted in all five Nordic countries,[25] with joint adoption also being permitted in all jurisdictions apart from Finland.

The Netherlands was the next to follow suit in 1998 with the introduction of a form of registered partnership. However, the Dutch model was fundamentally different to the Scandinavian model, since the Dutch registered partnership scheme was also open to couples of different sex. As already stated here above, the Dutch Government had sought to combine the claims from the homosexual community to be granted the rights and benefits of marriage, with the claims from the heterosexual community for a purely secular state-recognised institution other than marriage.[26] However, along similar lines to the Scandinavian model, registered partnership granted partners virtually all the rights and benefits of marriage. The resulting institution of registered partnership is to this day a rather isolated institution in Europe with only a few other countries preferring to introduce a model open to both same-sex, as well as different-sex couples. The most recent addition to this category was Malta in 2013.

At the turn of the millennium, the calls for recognition of same-sex relationships in France and Belgium were also beginning to become more

---

[22]   For example in all four jurisdictions, registered partners were not permitted to register their partnership along similar lines to the State sanctioned church weddings. See further, Lund-Andersen (n 8) 13–14, §2.4.

[23]   In Denmark, for example, registered partners were initially not permitted to take each other's surname. See further Lund-Andersen (n 8) 3, §1.

[24]   Lund-Andersen, 'The Danish Registered Partnership Act', in Boele-Woelki and Fuchs (eds), *Legal Recognition of Same-Sex Couples in Europe* (Intersentia 2003) 17; M Savolainen, 'The Finnish and Swedish Partnership Acts – Similarities and Divergencies', in Boele-Woelki and Fuchs (eds), *Legal Recognition of Same-Sex Couples in Europe* (Intersentia 2003) 33–4.

[25]   In Denmark and Norway stepchild adoption is, however, not permitted if the child has been adopted from abroad.

[26]   See Swennen and Eggermont (n 7) 25–6, §3.2.

strident. Calls for the improvement of same-sex couple rights started as early as 1989 in France after two important decisions of the French Supreme Court.[27] In the first case, *Secher v Air France*, a male flight attendant sought a reduced-price plane ticket for his same-sex partner, as would have been available if his partner had been of different sex. The Court of Appeal in Paris held that expressions such as *conjoint en union libre, agent et sa concubine* and *vie maritale* could only be interpreted so as to cover the exclusive situation of one man and one woman living together as though they were husband and wife. The expressions were intended to be based upon marriage and as such could not be extended to same-sex couples.[28] In the second case, *Ladijka v Caisse primaire d'assurance maladie de Nantes*,[29] a woman was denied the benefit of her female partner's public health and maternity insurance cover, again coverage which would have been granted had her partner been of a different sex. The Court of Appeal in Rennes once again held that the concept of *vie maritale,* used in the applicable social security legislation, could only be applied to unmarried different-sex couples. The French Supreme Court affirmed both decisions.[30]

At the same time as the French Supreme Court's decisions, a perceptible movement was taking shape in France aimed at reforming conjugal life and eliminating the discrimination faced by non-married couples. Despite the generality of its stated aim, the primary goal was legal recognition of the union between two persons of the same sex.[31] Indeed, it was mainly groups concerned with defending the rights of homosexuals and those active in the ever continuing and increasing fight against AIDS who advocated law reform and rallied around the various parliamentary initiatives. Prior to the enactment of the infamous *pacte civil de solidarité*, at least five different versions were submitted to the French legislature for debate (each proposal was known by the abbreviation of

---

[27]   Fr. Cass., Soc. Ch. 11 July 1989, *Bull. Civ.*, Vol. 311, No. 514 and *Bull. Civ.*, Vol. 312, No. 515.

[28]   Cour d'Appel Paris, 1 Civ. Ch., 11 October 1995, on appeal from Conseil de prud'hommes de Paris, 14 November 1984, Case No. 8546.008/R (1986) *D* 380.

[29]   Cour d'Appel Rennes, 27 November 1985, on appeal from Commission de première instance de sécurité sociale de Nantes, 19 January 1984 (1986) *D* 380.

[30]   For discussion of the decisions, see annotated case by N Marcel Dorwling-Carter, *Gaz. Pal.* 1990, pp 216-28.

[31]   D Borrillo, 'The pacte civil de solidarité in France' in R Wintemute and M Andenæs (eds), *Legal Recognition of Same-sex Partnerships* (Hart Publishing 2001) 476.

the institution it aimed to create, namely the CPC (*contrat de partenariat civil*),[32] the CUC (*contrat d'union civile*),[33] the CUS (*contrat d'union sociale*),[34] the CUCS (*contrat d'union civile et sociale*)[35] and the PIC (*pacte d'intérêt commun*)[36]).

These intense debates finally lead to the introduction of a highly contentious form of partnership recognition in France. The ultimate compromises made by all parties lead to the creation of an institution situated somewhere in the no-man's land between status and contract. Although the PACS pretended to have no impact on the civil status of the parties involved, persons joined in a PACS were not permitted to enter a PACS with anyone else, and if they subsequently married (either each other or a third party), then the PACS was automatically terminated. As a result, many – including the present author – argued that the PACS ultimately should be regarded as a civil status affecting institution, regardless of whether this was the original intent of the legislature.[37]

After the Central European turbulence of 1998 and 1999, the beginning of the new millennium saw a return to the 'traditional' Scandinavian registered partnership schemes. Jurisdiction after jurisdiction began to introduce same-sex registered partnership, albeit each with their own unique national twist. The year 2000 saw Germany introduce a form of life partnership,[38] followed shortly by Finland with registered partnership in 2001,[39] Switzerland with registered partnership in 2005,[40] the three

---

[32]   French Senate, 25 June 1990 (Socialist), Act. No. 422.

[33]   French National Assembly, 25 November 1992 (Socialist), Act. No. 3066.

[34]   French Senate, 19 March 1997 (Socialist), Act No 274. Reintroduced in 1997: French Senate, 23 July 1997 (Socialist), Act No. 94.

[35]   French National Assembly, 23 July 1997 (Radical/Movement of Citizens), Act No 88.

[36]   See I Curry-Sumner, *All's Well that Ends Registered?* (Intersentia 2005) 79–80; F Ferrand, 'Frankreich', in JM Scherpe and N Yassari, *Die Rechtsstellung nichtehelicher Lebensgemeinschaften,* (Mohr Siebeck 2005) 211 ff. and F Ferrand, 'Die Stellung gleichgeschlechtlicher Partnerschaften in Frankreich', in J Basedow et al, *Die Rechtsstellung gleichgeschlechtlicher Lebensgemeinschaften* (Siebeck 2000) 113 ff.

[37]   See Curry-Sumner, *All's Well that Ends Registered?* (n 36) 318–35.

[38]   Gesetz zur Beendigung der Diskriminierung gleichgeschlechtlicher Gemeinschaften: Lebenspartnerschaften, BGBi I 2001, 266. See further Swennen, and Eggermont, (n 7) 25–6, §3.2.

[39]   Laki rekisteröidsystä parisuhteesta, nr. 95/2001. See further Lund-Andersen, (n 8) 4–9, §2.1.

[40]   Loi federale du 18 juni 2004 sur le partenariat enrégistré entre personnes du meme sexe.

jurisdictions of the United Kingdom[41] with civil partnership in 2005, Hungary with registered partnership in 2009,[42] Ireland with civil partnership in 2010,[43] Austria with life partnerships in 2010[44] and finally Liechtenstein with life partnerships in 2011.[45] The only exceptions to this general rule are Luxembourg and Andorra that introduced a civil partnership form in 2004 and 2005 respectively very similar to that previously created in France and Belgium.[46] In 2013, Malta also introduced a form of registered partnership open to same-sex and different-sex couples, although the rights and duties extended are very similar to marriage (thus a very similar solution to that ultimately adopted in the Netherlands).

At the same time as this general trend towards the introduction of same-sex registration schemes across Central and Western Europe, two other curious trends were taking place in Southern and Eastern Europe. In 1998 Catalonia had become the first autonomous region of Spain to also introduce a form of registration. This registration system bore similarities to that introduced in France and Belgium. The rights afforded to same-sex couples were not the same as those afforded different-sex married couples. Furthermore, the *union estable de pareja* scheme provided for three different establishment methods, namely a continuous period of cohabitation of two years, an undefined period of cohabitation and common children, or by a public declaration of their desire to be involved in such a union. This trend, therefore, also brought in new complexities to the concept of 'registered' partnership in the sense that in Catalonia, partners could also be grandfathered into the scheme simply on the basis of a period of unregistered cohabitation. Other autonomous

---

[41] England & Wales, Scotland and Northern Ireland. This scheme has since been extended to the Isle of Man (2011) and Jersey (2012). Currently this civil partnership legislation is not in force in Gibraltar or Guernsey.

[42] 2009. évi XXIX. Törvény a bejegyzett élettársi kapcsolatról, az ezzel összefüggő, valamint az élettársi viszony igazolásának megkönnyítéséhez szükséges egyes törvények módosításáról.

[43] Civil Partnership and Certain Rights and Obligations of Cohabitants Act 2010.

[44] Bundesgesetz von 18 december 2009 über die eingetragene Partnerschaft

[45] A referendum was held on the 17 and 19 June 2011, in which 68.8% of the voters voted for the enactment of the Life Partnership Act. The new Act entered into force on the 1 September 2011.

[46] Luxembourg: Loi du 9 julliet 2004 relative aux effets légaux de certains partenariats and Andorra: Llei qualificada de les unions estables de parella (see further K Boele-Woelki, I Curry-Sumner, M Jansen and W Schrama, *Huwelijk of geregistreerd partnerschap?* (Kluwer 2007) 105–7.

regions in Spain began to introduce similar schemes, although once again each with their own idiosyncrasies.[47]

At the same time, another trend was taking shape in Eastern Europe. The Czech Republic (2006) and Slovenia (2006) both introduced forms of registered partnership.[48] These schemes are both restricted to same-sex couples; however, unlike the Western European counterparts, these schemes are not intended to create an institution equivalent to marriage.[49] Instead both schemes enunciated the rights and duties that are extended to same-sex registered partners.

Currently forms of registered partnership are available in the following jurisdictions as the only possible formalized relationship open to same-sex couples: Andorra (2014), Austria (2010), Croatia (2014), Czech Republic (2006), Estonia (2016), Germany (2001), Hungary (2003), Ireland (2011), Liechtenstein (2011), Slovenia (2006) and Switzerland (2007).

2.4 Unregistered Relationship Forms

Alongside the above-mentioned formal registration forms, many juris-dictions also place same-sex couples on an equal footing with different-sex couples when addressing issues related to unregistered cohabitants.[50] However, the vast majority of these nations also provide for some form of registration system. This, therefore, means that same-sex couples wishing to access certain rights and benefits are provided with an option of doing so either via registration or via informal cohabitation. Until 2014, Croatia formed the only country in Europe, which allowed for the recognition of same-sex unregistered partnerships, without any formal

---

[47]   See further, Curry-Sumner, (n 36) 354. See also C Gonzalez Beilfuss, 'Spanien und Portugal', in Scherpe and Yassari, *Die Rechtsstellung nichte-helicher Lebensgemeinschaften* (Mohr Siebeck 2005) 249 ff. and S Schlenker, 'Die Stellung gleichgeschlechtlicher Lebensgemeinschaften in Spanien und in spanischen Teilrechtsordnungen', in Basedow et al, *Die Rechtsstellung gleichge-schlechtlicher Lebensgemeinschaften* (Siebeck 2000) 145 ff.

[48]   For more information on Slovenia see Boele-Woelki, Curry-Sumner, Jansen and Schrama, (n 46) 135–8.

[49]   See M Jagielska, 'Eastern European Countries: From Penalisation to Cohabitation or Further?' in Boele-Woelki and Fuchs (eds), *Legal Recognition of Same-sex Relationships in Europe* (Intersentia 2012) 42–4, §2.1 §§4.2 and 4.3.

[50]   With respect to Sweden, Norway, Iceland and Denmark, see Lund-Andersen (n 8) 14–16, §3 and with respect to France, Ireland and Scotland see Swennen and Eggermont (n 7) 37–8, §5.

registration scheme being available.[51] In 2014, Croatia passed legislation introducing a form of registered partnership, thus bringing an end to this unique status in Europe.

2.5 Summary

In summary it would appear that different trends are simultaneously palpable across the European continent. First, there is a distinct and obvious trend across the continent towards increased recognition of same-sex relationships. Currently, no fewer than 21 European jurisdictions have introduced some form of relationship registration scheme for same-sex couples. As time progresses legislatures have a propensity to create institutions akin to marriage (for example, Finland and Germany), or alternatively permit same-sex couples to marry (for example, Portugal and Sweden). Secondly, another trend is evident acknowledging that different-sex couples do not all desire to get married, yet many do wish to formalise their relationship. In some countries this has lead to the introduction of registration schemes for different-sex couples (for example, regions of Spain and the Netherlands). In other countries, different-sex couples have begun to complain that they are not permitted to register their partnership. In the United Kingdom and Austria different-sex couples have even gone so far as to submit their case to the European Court of Human Rights, with some jurisdictions going so far as to introduce schemes only open to different-sex couples, as in Greece.[52] In The Netherlands, where different-sex couples are also permitted to register their partnership, 2009 saw slightly fewer than 9,000 couples register their partnership.[53] The number of different-sex couples registering their partnership has increased steadily since the introduction of registered partnership in 1998.[54] A similar trend is also clearly evident with respect to the PACS in France. A third trend is noticeable namely towards the recognition or acceptance of unmarried, unregistered couples

---

[51] Zakon o istospolnim Zajednicama, Act of 14 July 2003.

[52] *Burden v United Kingdom*, App No 13378/05 (ECHR, 29 April 2008), (2008) 47 EHRR 38; *Ferguson and others v United Kingdom* (application lodged 2 February 2011).

[53] In 2009, only 576 registered partnerships were attributable to the 'lightning divorce procedure', which has been abolished since 1 March 2009. This means that the absolute number of partnership registrations in 2009 was 9,497 (of which 9,002 were opposite sex and 8,921 involved new registrations).

[54] In 1998: 1,500, in 1999: 1,322, in 2000: 1,670, in 2001: 3,044, in 2002: 4,305, in 2003: 4,305, in 2004: 5,148, in 2005: 5,744, in 2006: 6,315, in 2007: 6,804, in 2008: 7,450 and in 2009: 8,434.

who are (or should be granted) rights and benefits after a certain period of cohabitation. At present this movement would appear only to have gained limited legislative basis in some countries, for example, as was the case in Croatia until 2014. Other countries have, however, recognised these rights for a longer time, for example, Sweden.

3. COMMON THREADS AND MODELS

3.1 Introduction

At first glance, it would appear that there are few elements of commonality between the approaches adopted by the various legislatures across Europe.[55] However, this should not deter those wishing to compare these various institutions. Instead of looking at the broad picture and focusing on the differences, this section will provide a systematic analysis of the various approaches identifying common features and characteristics. These have enabled the creation of a number of models that can be used when comparing the various systems of formal registration.

3.2 Three Models of Registration

On the basis of extensive European research in 2005 and American research in 2008, it has been suggested by this author that three models of formal same-sex relationship recognition can be distinguished, the so-called 'monistic', 'dualistic' and 'pluralistic' models.[56] The question that can be posed is whether this theoretical framework can still be applied with the advent of 22 European jurisdictions having recognised same-sex relationship forms.

3.2.1 Monistic model

Under this approach, no separate registration scheme for same-sex couples is created. Instead the prohibition on same-sex marriage is removed, in turn creating a single, formalised institution open both to same-sex and opposite-sex couples, namely marriage. This approach has

---

[55] B Verschragen, 'The Right to Private and Family Life. The Right to Marry and to Found a Family, and the Prohibition of Discrimination', in Boele-Woelki and Fuchs (eds), *Legal Recognition of Same-sex Relationships in Europe* (Intersentia 2012) 255–83.

[56] Curry-Sumner (n 36) 266–78, 286–91, and 307–13, and Curry-Sumner and Curry-Sumner (n 6).

only been followed in a relatively small number of jurisdictions, namely in a number of provinces in Canada and states in the USA. Political resistance and sensitivity to making such a monumental change to existing legislation is part of the reason for the relatively low adoption of this model. As a result, this model was, until recently, restricted to common law jurisdictions where judges had taken the initiative to strike down gender-based marital restrictions, often on the basis of their unconstitutionality. In 2010 Portugal became the first country in Europe to adopt this approach. A decision of the Portuguese Constitutional Court held that it was not unconstitutional to deny same-sex couples the right to marry, but that the legislature had to act to ensure that the discrimination in treatment between same-sex and different-sex couples with respect to the rights stemming from marriage was removed. The Portuguese legislature ultimately opted to simply remove the prohibition on same-sex marriage.[57]

3.2.2 Dualistic model

Under this approach, a registry which is restricted to same-sex couples is created. Opposite-sex couples wishing to formalise their relationship are able to do so via traditional marriage. In this model, two institutions operate side-by-side; one for opposite-sex couples, that is, marriage, and one for same-sex couples, that is, 'registered partnership'. It should be noted that jurisdictions adhering to the dualistic model have also begun to make amendments to their legislation. In these jurisdictions, the distinction between marriage for different-sex couples, on the one hand, and registered partnership for same-sex couples, on the other, has increasingly come under pressure. Ultimately this pressure has led to the repeal of the registered partnership laws in some jurisdictions, for example in the Scandinavian jurisdictions.

Accordingly, the dualistic model should be divided into two time phases. In time phase 1, jurisdictions operate two systems side-by-side. As time elapses the necessity and justification for running two systems begins to ebb, and the legislature ultimately opts to repeal the registered partnership laws. At this stage, countries adhering to the dualistic model will be deemed to have entered time phase 2. Despite having a different origin, the second time phase of the dualistic model is also equivalent to the monistic model. One could, therefore, also argue that the dualistic model is perhaps also simply to be regarded as time period 1 of the monistic model.

---

[57] See Gonzalez-Beilfuss (n 9) 44, §2.1.

3.2.3 Pluralistic model

In the pluralistic model couples are offered two possibilities for formalising their relationship, irrespective of their gender, namely marriage or a
form of non-marital registered relationship. It must, however, be noted
that jurisdictions adhering to the pluralistic model tend to attain the end
phase of this model by virtue of a two-stage process, thereby necessitat-
ing the division of the pluralistic model into two time-periods. The first
time-period involves opening non-marital registration to both different
and same-sex couples, whilst leaving marriage legislation entirely intact
and unaltered. Once this has been achieved, the arguments for opening
civil marriage to same-sex couples are strengthened, since the discrimination originally faced by same-sex couples, in not being able to marry, is
simply replaced with a new form of discrimination; although different-
sex couples are offered a choice of relationship forms, same-sex couples
are not.[58] It is irrefutable that the option for different-sex couples to
register their relationship along identical lines to same-sex couples in The
Netherlands and Belgium, for example, played an important role in the
pressure placed on these Governments to amend the laws prohibiting
same-sex civil marriage. As Luxembourg moved to open up marriage to
same-sex couples, it too made the transition from stage 1 of the
pluralistic model to stage 2. The question is, according to this author, not
whether Andorra and Malta will make the transition, but more a question
of when.

At this moment in time, England & Wales, and Scotland provide
perhaps the most intriguing situation. Currently, the law in both of these
jurisdictions provide for marriage to both same-sex and different-sex
couples, yet the registration scheme is restricted to same-sex couples.
Accordingly, the law currently provides for family law institutions that
provide more options to same-sex couples! A situation that would have
been thought inconceivable 30 years ago. This situation will more than
likely not continue for much longer as a result of the recent decision in
Vallianatos & Others v Greece.

All these models can also be represented diagrammatically (see
Figures 4.1 to 4.3).

In analysing the legislation of various European jurisdictions, the
overview of jurisdictions in Table 4.1 can be produced.

---

[58]   See, for example, *Dutch Second Chamber,* 1995–1996, 23761, No 7, p 10.

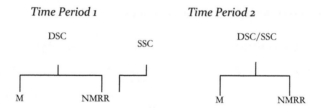

Figure 4.1   The pluralistic model of recognition of same-sex relationships

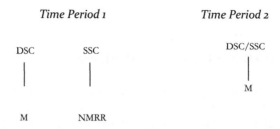

Figure 4.2   The dualistic model of recognition of same-sex relationships

Figure 4.3   The monistic model of recognition of same-sex relationships

Key: **DSC**: *Different-Sex Couples,* **SSC**: *Same-Sex Couples* **M**: *Marriage,*
NMRR: *Non-Marital Registered Relationship*

Table 4.1   Overview of registration schemes

PLURALISTIC		MONISTIC	
Time period 1	Time period 2	Time period 1 (Dualistic)	Time period 2
Andorra	Belgium	Czech Republic	Denmark
Malta	France	Germany	England & Wales (*)
	Luxembourg	Greenland	Finland
	Netherlands	Hungary	Iceland
	Spain	Liechtenstein	Ireland
		N. Ireland	Norway
		Slovenia	Portugal
		Switzerland	Scotland (*)
			Sweden

3.3   Rights and Duties Incumbent on Partners

With respect to the rights and duties incumbent on the same-sex registered partners or spouses enormous diversity exists. In some countries, the legal effects attributed are similar, if not almost identical, to those attached to the institution of marriage. In other jurisdictions only minimal protection is offered to the parties. Although the models described above are only suitable to the formal aspects of the relationship (that is, establishment and dissolution), a distinction can nonetheless be made between 'strong registration' and 'weak registration'. Strong registration involves the near assimilation of the legal effects attributed to registered partners and spouses. Although countries opting for this system often refrain, at least in the beginning, from amending the law relating to children (that is, adoption, parentage and parental responsibility), all the legal effects affecting the partners themselves are generally equalised. In contrast, weak registration entails the enactment of only minimal protective measures. These forms of registration often have no impact on the parties' personal law, for example, name law, nationality and civil status, or family and inheritance law, but are instead restricted to fiscal and property law issues, as well as the personal obligations that the parties have towards each other.

It would appear that the legal effects attributed to registered partners can be roughly divided into four categories:

- Property law and personal obligations;
- Fiscal law (tax, social security and pensions);

- Family and inheritance law; and
- Rights in relation to children.[59]

It would appear that those countries adopting a system of weak registration confine the effects of such a registration to the first two categories. Hence, the effect of registering a statutory cohabitation in Belgium or a PACS in France is restricted to fiscal and property law.[60] Strong registration, on the other hand, also reaches into rights and duties in the third and fourth categories. Hence in The Netherlands, the registration of a partnership also places registered partners in the same position as spouses with respect to inheritance law, name law and parental authority rights.

The rights and duties associated with the first category are generally of a low politically sensitive nature. It is assumed that parties involved in an intimate relationship wish to commit to each other, and by imposing duties such as a duty to cohabit or contribute to the costs of the household, the State is merely indicating its moral stance at little financial burden to the State. Although opinions as to the best or proper matrimonial property regime differ markedly and have resulted in protracted political debates in many countries, the question of whether to enact rules determining the property law effects of registering a non-marital relationship is by and large uncontroversial. Moreover, in the majority of legal systems, parties are in any case able to draw up a contract regulating such issues themselves.[61] The State simply provides for a default system to operate in the absence of such an expression of the parties' will.[62] In addition, it appears that in any debate concerning the protection that should be offered to cohabitants, discussion centres on this field of law.[63] It is, therefore, not

---

[59]   Curry-Sumner (n 36) 291–306. See further, E Rupp, *Die Lebenssituation von Kindern in gleichgeschlechtlichen Lebenspartnerschaften* (Bundesanzeiger Verlag 2009).

[60]   Swennen and Eggermont (n 7) 34–6, §4.3.

[61]   K Boele-Woelki et al., *Huwelijksvermogensrecht in rechtsvergelijkend perspectief* (Kluwer 2000) 248. The absence of such a system in the United Kingdom can be explained by fear on the part of the common law system that spouses could be bound by a contract which they made many years before. The principle of reasonableness, therefore, outweighs the principle of legal certainty in this system.

[62]   This, of course, does not detract from any disparity in the property regime applicable to spouses and registered partners.

[63]   See, for example, P Senaeve, 'Naar de invoering van het homohuwelijk in het Belgische recht?' (1992) *Echtscheidingsjournaal* 50–2; A Barlow, *Cohabitants and the Law* (3rd edn, Butterworths 2001); W Pintens, Van Der Meersch and Vanwinckelen, *Inleiding tot het familial vermogensrecht* (Universitaire Pers

surprising that this field of law is one of the first to be legislated upon for non-marital registered relationships.

Although rights and duties in the second category are generally of a less sensitive political nature than those in the third or fourth categories, the extension of fiscal benefits in the form of tax breaks, social security benefits and access to pension schemes, obviously comes at great financial cost to the State. The political will to remove fiscal discrimination is therefore often pitted against the available funds in the financial coffers.[64]

As one moves towards the third category of legal effects, one senses a shift in emphasis. If one accepts the extension of rights in this field it becomes difficult to make distinctions. Upon extending one right or duty, one must justify the almost unjustifiable in denying the extension of other rights in this category.[65] Rights and duties in this category also have a long-standing association with the law on marriage in many countries. On the European continent the celebration of a marriage has an important impact on those personal law rights associated with one's civil status, name and nationality. This is to some extent also true of common law countries, where according to old authorities the celebration of a marriage for many purposes fuses the legal personalities of husband and wife into one.[66] As a result, the extension of such rights to those outside of the marital bond is a much more sensitive matter than the rights in the first two categories.

The final category, untouched in many jurisdictions, is possibly the most sensitive of all. This sensitivity stems from a multiplicity of dynamic factors: biology, tradition, third party rights and moral values. The law on parentage was originally based on the presumption of

---

Leuven 2002) and W Schrama, *De niet-huwelijkse samenleving in het Nederlandse en Duitse recht* (Ars Notariatus Kluwer 2004).

[64] See, for example, the Annexes to the English proposal, Women and Equality Unit, *Civil Partnership: A Framework for the Legal Recognition of Same-sex Couples* (Department of Trade and Industry 2003) 75 (Tables 3 and 4, Annex A). In Table 3 it was estimated that introduction of the civil partnership schemes would cost the British Government £23-230 million per year by 2050 (for state pensions and bereavement benefits and public service pensions). In Table 4 it was estimated that the cost to private pension benefit schemes would be between £2.5–20 million.

[65] The only justification which has been offered (in Switzerland) is that the rules in the field of marriage are discriminatory. See further Curry-Sumner (n 36) 292–3.

[66] Blackstone, *Commentaries*, i. 442.

biology.[67] It was and still is simply presumed that the husband of a pregnant woman was the child's father: *pater is est quem nuptiae demonstrant.* The idea of extending such presumptions to same-sex couples involves an enormous excursion from reality. Even if the husband of the legal mother is not the father of the child, there is a biological possibility that he could be, whereas such a biological possibility is completely absent in same-sex couples.[68] The controversy surrounding children raised in same-sex families has even prevented gay rights groups from asserting the need for equality in this field.[69]

The necessary absence of parentage rights for same-sex couples does not explain a total lack of attention to this field. However, one must also note the State's interest in the raising of children. The State imposes its moral values on the opportunity for same-sex couples to adopt or raise children. In the majority of European countries to have introduced forms of non-marital registered relationship schemes, it has almost universally been accepted that children need to be raised by a mother and a father and that it is therefore undesirable for children to be raised by same-sex couples.[70] If one joins this with the often prevailing presumption that the marital home is the best place for the child to be raised, then it is not surprising that the rights in this category are the last to be extended to registered partners. It is, in addition, generally noted that a fundamental difference between same-sex and different-sex couples lies in the necessity for third party involvement in the case of same-sex relationships, either by means of sperm, egg or embryo donation or surrogacy. The traditional view that a child should remain in contact with, if not be raised by his or her biological parents, is therefore fundamentally besieged should one accept the proposition that same-sex couples are able to raise children. In avoiding the political quagmire associated with the venturing of an opinion in relation to these views, it is submitted that these reasons provide the explanation to the current absence of legislation with respect to children born or raised in non-marital registered relationships. Nonetheless, this initial reticence is gradually being eroded as

---

[67] See for example, MJ Vonk, *Children and their Parents: A Comparative Study of the Legal Position of Children with regard to their Intentional and Biological Parents in English and Dutch Law* (Intersentia 2007).

[68] Kortmann Commissie, *Commissie inzake openstelling van het burgerlijk huwelijk voor Personen van hetzelfde geslacht* (Dutch Ministry of Justice 1997) 5, §2.1.

[69] See, for example, Curry-Sumner (n 36) 189–94.

[70] See, for example, the Swiss legislature's discussion regarding adoption and artificial reproductive techniques: FF 2003, p. 1192 at 1223.

successive jurisdictions remove the prohibitions on same-sex adoption, stepchild adoption, joint parental authority and even the extension of the presumption of parentage.

Although this division into rough categories of rights is merely illustrative and does not profess to be used for any higher purpose, it is perhaps effective in helping to identify the crucial difference between those countries adhering to a system of strong registration and those adopting a system of weak registration. Of course, any global classification on this superficial basis will be subject to exception and it is admitted that this model is merely an aid in any attempt to discern general uniform trends in this field. In Switzerland, for example, despite having adopted a relatively strong registration form, the continued unequal treatment of men and women in the field of family law has led to unequal treatment of spouses and registered partners. This can lead to disagreement as to exact placement of a jurisdiction. For example Swennen and Eggermont, argue that Switzerland should be classified as a 'separate but unequal' jurisdiction, whereas in the classification proposed by this author it is regarded as a strong registration scheme. This difference in opinion is a result of respective weight given to the various rights and duties attributed. The classification is therefore not to be regarded as an exact science, but instead a guide to how countries relate to each other and how they may possibility develop in the future. On the basis of this classification as proposed in this chapter the division of jurisdictions shown in Table 4.2 can be made.

Table 4.2　Complete overview of registration schemes

	Pluralistic		Monistic	
	Time Period 1	Time Period 2	Time Period 1	Time Period 2
Strong	Malta	The Netherlands	Austria Finland Germany Greenland Hungary Ireland Liechtenstein N. Ireland Switzerland	Denmark England & Wales (*) Iceland Norway Portugal Scotland (*) Sweden
Weak	Andorra	Belgium France Luxembourg Spain	Czech Republic Slovenia	

3.4 Conclusion

The legal landscape with respect to same-sex couple registration is extremely volatile with the methods used by legislatures constantly evolving. Nonetheless, it is clear that distinct trends and groupings of legal systems are evident. Although it cannot be said that jurisdictions are all on the same path towards one common solution, it is possible to state that countries do appear to be on similar paths depending upon their original starting point. A distinction must be drawn between two groups of countries. On the one hand those countries that have opted to open their initial registration schemes to different-sex couples, such as France, Luxembourg and The Netherlands, (*Pluralistic Model*) and on the other, those jurisdictions that have restricted the scheme to same-sex couples (*Dualistic Model* leading to *Monistic Model*). Taking this distinction into account it would appear that countries are indeed moving along similar paths towards common goals, albeit with two different end results.

For those countries adhering to the pluralistic model, it would appear that the ultimate end result will be an institutional regulatory framework that provides for two formal relationship registration schemes open to both different-sex and same-sex couples. Already Belgium, France, Luxembourg, the Netherlands and Spain have made the transition from time period 1 to 2. For those countries adhering to the dualistic or the monistic systems, it would appear that the ultimate end result will be one single institutional framework (that is, marriage) open to all regardless of sexual orientation. It is already clear that countries are beginning to make the transition from dualistic to monistic (that is, Iceland and Sweden). At the same time it is also clear that jurisdictions to have originally extended only limited rights to same-sex couples (for example, Slovenia and the Czech Republic) are gradually extending and improving those benefits, and will at a certain point in the future perhaps have to be promoted to the category of 'strong registration'.

The question that obviously can – and should – be asked is whether one of these paths is more suitable, justifiable, less-discriminatory and so on. The answer to that question is: it depends! It depends on the legal, social, economic, political and demographic context in any given country. My personal preference is that provided by the pluralistic system in time period 2 whereby couples are offered the option of different formal relationship forms depending upon their own needs and desires at that moment in their lives. This system is non-discriminatory in all aspects and is therefore favourable over any system in time period 1. In comparison to the monistic system, the pluralistic model also provides the required deference to the pluralistic nature of family forms in today's society and, therefore, strikes a good balance between the sometimes-competing interests of legal certainty, non-discrimination and party autonomy. Perhaps, in the end we might be able to learn valuable lessons from the South African approach in which couples are provided with one legal institution, but are provided the option of two different nomenclatures. Party autonomy in a straitjacket!

4. CASE LAW OF THE EUROPEAN COURT OF HUMAN RIGHTS[71]

4.1 Respect for Private Life

Although the European Court of Human Rights has always tried to refrain from defining the exact ambit of the article 8 right to respect for private life, it is clear that 'elements such as gender identification, name and sexual orientation and sexual life are important elements of the personal sphere protected by Article 8'.[72] Nonetheless, the path to having reached this point has not been smooth. For more than 20 years the European Commission of Human Rights had consistently rejected all complaints by homosexuals as 'manifestly ill-founded'.[73] For the first time in *Dudgeon v UK*,[74] the European Court of Human Rights held that the criminalisation of homosexual acts by consenting adults did in fact affect the private life of the complainants; a decision that has since been endorsed in *X v United Kingdom*.[75] The Court has extended this decision by holding that consensual homosexual sexual activity, even if it falls outside the notion of 'private life' within the complainant's country, falls within the scope of 'private life' as defined by article 8. The court regarded the existence of

---

[71] On this see generally P Johnson, Homosexuality and the European Court of Human Rights (Routledge 2013); J Scherpe, 'From "Odious Crime" to Family Life – Same-sex Couples and the ECHR', in A-L Verbeke, J Scherpe, C Declerck, T Helms and P Senaeve (eds), Confronting the Frontiers of Family and Succession Law – Liber amicorum Walter Pintens (Intersentia 2012) 1225–40 and Scherpe (n 4).

[72] *Bensaid v United Kingdom*, App No 44599/98 (ECHR, 6 February 2001).

[73] C Forder, 'Civil Law Aspects of Emerging Forms of Partnership' (Fifth European Conference on Family Law 1999) 17.

[74] *Dudgeon v United Kingdom*, App No 7525/76 (ECHR, 22 October 1981), §§41 and 52.

[75] (1997) 24 EHRR 143. This was also affirmed in *Norris v Ireland*, App No 10581/83 (ECHR, 26 October 1988) and *Modnios v Cyprus* App No 15070/89 (ECHR, 25 March 1993).

legislation prohibiting sex with more than one person and the subsequent conviction for gross indecency to be an interference with the applicant's right to private life.[76]

The Court has also had to deal with a number of cases in which the age of consent for sexual activity between persons of the same-sex was set higher than for persons of a different sex. In *L and V v Austria* the Court unanimously held that this inequality constituted a violation of article 14 in conjunction with article 8 ECHR, and also unanimously ruled that there was no need to examine the complaints lodged under article 8 alone.[77] Similar decisions were also handed down in *BB v United Kingdom*[78] and *Sutherland v United Kingdom*.[79]

4.2 Respect for Family Life

In determining issues related to family life the court had ruled that a number of factors may be relevant, including: 'whether a couple live together, the length of their relationship and whether they have demonstrated their commitment to each other by having children together or by any other means'.[80] Although the Commission had held that homosexual unions did not concern 'family life' for the purposes of article 8,[81] in 1997 it was held that family life did exist between cohabiting unmarried heterosexuals.[82] In *Burden v United Kingdom*, the Court finally had the opportunity to consider whether same-sex couples could benefit from the protection of their family life as enshrined in article 8. In summary, the Court drew a bright line between formalised relationships on the one hand (for example, marriage and civil partnership), and non-formalised relationships on the other. It appeared at that time, that the Court was insinuating that formalised same-sex relationships should indeed be able to benefit from the protection offered by Article 8, by virtue of their family life. A decision later confirmed by *Courten v United Kingdom*.[83]

In 2010, the Court finally resolved the issue in the famous case of *Schalk and Kopf v Austria*. The case concerned an Austrian same-sex

---

[76] *ADT v United Kingdom* App No 35765/97 (ECHR, 31 July 2000) §26.
[77] *L and V v Austria* App No 39392/98 (ECHR, 9 January 2003).
[78] *BB v United Kingdom* App No 53760/00 (ECHR, 21 May 1996).
[79] *Sutherland v United Kingdom* App No 25186/94 (ECHR, 10 February 2004).
[80] *X, Y and Z v UK* (1997) 24 EHRR 143, §36
[81] *S v UK* (1986) 47 DR 274, No. 11716/85.
[82] *X, Y, and Z v. UK* 24 EHRR 143, §31.
[83] *Courten v United Kingdom* App No 4479/06 (ECHR, 4 November 2008).

couple's assertion that Austria had breached their convention obligation to respect their private and family life by denying their right to marry. The Court held:

> [T]he Court's case-law has only accepted that the emotional and sexual relationship of a same-sex couple constitutes 'private life' but has not found that it constitutes 'family life', even where a long-term relationship of cohabiting partners was at stake. In coming to that conclusion, the court observed that despite the growing tendency in a number of European States towards the legal and judicial recognition of stable de facto partnerships between homosexuals, given the existence of little common ground between the Contracting States, this was an area in which they still enjoyed a wide margin of appreciation.[84]

The Court went on to discuss the decisions of *Karner v Austria*, in which the Court had previously left open the question whether same-sex couples could fall within the scope of the notion of 'family life'. In *Schalk and Kopf*, the Court turned its attention to this unanswered question, stating:

> In view of this evolution the Court considers it artificial to maintain the view that, in contrast to a different-sex couple, a same-sex couple cannot enjoy 'family life' for the purposes of Article 8. Consequently the relationship of the applicants, a cohabiting same-sex couple living in a stable de facto partnership, falls within the notion of "family life", just as the relationship of a different-sex couple in the same situation would.[85]

The ECtHR has also reiterated this position in the recent case of *Vallianatos v Greece*.[86] It would, therefore, appear that the old-fashioned distinction between heterosexual couples and homosexual couples when addressing issues of 'family life' under the Convention has been banished to the history books.

4.3　Right to Marry

In 1986 in *Rees v UK*, where the right of a transsexual to marry was in issue, the Court made a broad statement regarding the right to marry derived from Article 12:

---

[84]　*Schalk and Kopf v Austria* App No 4479/06 (ECHR, 4 November 2008), §92.

[85]　*Schalk and Kopf v Austria* App No 4479/06 (ECHR, 4 November 2008), §94.

[86]　*Vallianatos v Greece* App No 29381/09 and 32684/09 (ECHR, 7 November 2013).

In the court's view the right to marry guaranteed by Article 12 refers to the traditional marriage between persons of the opposite biological sex. This appears also from the wording of the Article which makes it clear that Article 12 is mainly concerned to protect marriage as the basis of the family.[87]

However, the Court went on to say that the interpretation of article 12 may change in due course as the European Convention 'has always to be interpreted and applied in the light of current circumstances'.[88] However, even though the Court had expressed such progressive attitudes, the same case law was reiterated in 1990[89] and again in 1998.[90] However, in the recent judgments of *Goodwin v UK*[91] and *I v UK*,[92] the right of a transsexual to marry was upheld by the European Court of Human Rights. Under the then current law of the United Kingdom, transsexuals were prevented from being able to change their gender on their birth certificate. This prevented, therefore, post-operative transsexuals from celebrating a valid marriage (with a member of the opposite sex to their post-operative sex[93]), since marriage was (and still is) considered to be a heterosexual institution according to English law.[94] This reversal of previous case law best indicates the court's increasing awareness of the need to change and update old ideas concerning marriage, biological gender and gender reassignment.

The judgment in *Rees* and the subsequent judgment in *Cossey*[95] both indicate that the Court had regarded the two parts of article 12[96] as being closely related. However, while this was important when determining the meaning of 'marriage', it did not necessarily restrict the right to found a

---

[87]   (1986) 9 EHRR 56.

[88]   (1986) 9 EHRR 56, §49.

[89]   *Cossey v UK* (1991) 13 EHRR 622.

[90]   *X, Y and Z v UK* (1997) 24 EHRR 143.

[91]   *Goodwin v United Kingdom* App No 28957/95 (ECHR, 11 July 2002).

[92]   *I v United Kingdom,* App No 25680/94 (ECHR, 11 July 2002).

[93]   They are therefore allowed to enter into a marriage with a person of the same gender as their pre-operative sex, in which their sex change is not recognised and therefore this marriage would not be seen as a 'gay marriage' in the eyes of English law.

[94]   Compare with the definition under Dutch law in Article 1:30 of the Dutch Civil Code and also proposals recently laid before the Belgian Parliament *Parl. St. Kamer* 2001-2002, 14 March 2002, 1692/001.

[95]   (1991) 13 EHRR 622.

[96]   The right to marry on the one hand and the right to found a family on the other.

family to persons who are married.[97] Nonetheless, it has been argued by some commentators that article 12 does not actually denote two individual rights: the right to marry *and* the right to have children, but simply confers a single right, which in simple biological terms excludes homosexuals from the ambit of such a proviso.[98] The Charter of Fundamental Rights of the European Union employs the phrase 'the right to marry *and* the right to found a family'.[99] This provision, therefore, expressly states that these rights should be considered as two separate rights. This was recently endorsed by the European Court of Human Rights in *Goodwin v UK*,[100], where particular reference was made to the article 9 provision of the Charter[101].

McGlynn also highlights the removal of the words 'men and women' from the Convention provision in the charter.[102] She believes that this may well be of potential significance; however, it is submitted that the significance of this change in terminology must be interpreted with reference to *D and Sweden v Council*.[103] The Court of Justice held that it was 'not in question that, according to the definition generally accepted by the Member States, the term "marriage" means a union between two persons of the opposite sex'.[104] Consequently, if one takes this ECJ decision alongside the Charter's explanatory notes which clearly state that the 'article neither prohibits nor imposes the granting of the status of marriage to unions between people of the same sex', then the chance of article 9 being interpreted to include same-sex marriages is slim. This is especially so when one witnesses the conservative way in which the right to family life under article 8 has been interpreted.[105]

---

[97] DJ Harris et al, *Law of the European Convention on Human Rights* (Butterworths 1995) 440.

[98] In B Hoggett, *From the Test Tube to the Coffin* (Sweet & Maxwell 1996) 67.

[99] Article 9, emphasis added.

[100] *Goodwin v United Kingdom* App No 28957/95 (ECHR, 11 July 2002), §98.

[101] *Goodwin v United Kingdom* App No 28957/95 (ECHR, 11 July 2002), §§58 and 98.

[102] C McGlynn, 'Families and the European Union Charter of Fundamental Rights: Progressive Change or Entrenching the Status Quo?' (2001) *European Law Review* 582–98.

[103] Case C-122-125/99P *D and Sweden v. Council* (31 May 2001).

[104] Case C-122-125/99P *D and Sweden v. Council* (31 May 2001), §34.

[105] Reference has been made to this difference by the European Court of Human Rights in *Goodwin v UK* in §100 however further elaboration was not undertaken.

Only recently has the Court had to deal with the specific question of whether same-sex couples should have the right to marry according to the Convention. In *Schalk and Kopf,* as was stated earlier the Court was reticent to grant such rights with reference to articles 8, 12 and 14. Referring to the 'wide margin of appreciation' granted to States, the Court denied the applicants' complaint. Recently, the Court went one step further when dealing with the case of *Valliantos v Greece.*[106] Here, the applicants complained that the Greek legislation only provided for a form of registered partnership (or civil union as it was called in Greece) for different-sex couples. The Court, holding a violation of article 14 in conjunction with article 8 ECHR stated that the Greek State had failed to provide a justifiable reason for restricting the institution to different-sex couples. Perhaps most importantly in the context of this chapter the Court referred to the 'lack of consensus', but the 'increasing trend' amongst the Contracting States. This means that states will be under an obligation to provide same-sex couples with a legal framework in some form or another, enabling them to publicly gain access to the rights and duties associated with marriage. In referring to the comparative overview at the beginning of this chapter, it would appear that two main models could serve as a template for such frameworks.

This analysis has recently been further strengthened by the decision of the European Court of Human Rights in *Oliari and others v. Italy.*[107] In this case the ECtHR found that Italy had violated its Treaty obligations by failing to provide the applicants with a specific legal framework for the recognition and protection of their union. The ECtHR noted that the highest courts in Italy, i.e. the Italian Constitutional Court, had repeatedly pointed out the need for legislation to recognize and protect same-sex relationships. However, the Italian Government had failed to meet its obligations by failing to provide for a formalized relationship form for same-sex couples. Accordingly, Italy had violated Article 8 ECHR.

It is to be expected that the exact nature of this obligation will be tested time and time again in the coming years, as couples bring cases to the court requesting the court to explain why certain rights and duties are granted to different sex couples, whereas the right is not extended to same-sex couples. This incremental development, with cases debating each and every right, may well be the way in which the European Court

---

[106]   *Valliantos v Greece* App No 29381/09 and 32684/09 (ECHR, 7 November 2013).
[107]   App No 18766/11 and 36030/11 (ECHR, 21 July 2015).

of Human Rights is best able to deal with the steady and continuing trend towards full equality for same-sex couples.[108]

5. CONCLUSION

Who could ever have guessed it? In the lifetime of the European Convention on Human Rights, homosexuals have witnessed a change to their lives that can only really be termed monumental. At the end of the Second World War, and recovering from atrocities that they had suffered in Nazi concentration camps, European homosexual activity was still regarded as a criminal activity in many European jurisdictions. Sixty years on, and this chapter is able to signal the comparative legal overview of no fewer than 21 jurisdictions that now provide for formalised family relationships forms for same-sex couples. The world is truly a different place than 60 years ago. This obviously does not mean that the struggle for equal rights is over, or that there is no work to be done on continuing to ensure the respect for these rights, but one should not underestimate the progress that has been made in this field. In 60 years' time, who knows, maybe a legal scholar will be able to write a similar contribution in which inequality is simply an historical footnote.

RECOMMENDATIONS FOR FURTHER READING

J Basedow, K Hopt, H Kötz and P Dopffel (eds), *Die Rechtsstellung gleichgeschlecht-licher Lebensgemeinschaften* (Mohr Siebeck 2000).
K Boele-Woelki and A. Fuchs (eds), Legal Recognition of Same-sex Relationships in Europe (Intersentia 2012).
K Boele-Woelki, I Curry-Sumner, M Jansen and W Schrama, *Huwelijk of geregistreerd partnerschap?* (Kluwer, 2007).
S Cretney, *Same-Sex Relationships: From 'Odious Crime' to 'Gay Marriage'* (Clarendon Law Lectures, OUP 2006).
I Curry-Sumner, *All's Well That Ends Registered?* (Intersentia, 2005)
I Curry-Sumner and ST Curry-Sumner, 'Is the Union Civil? Same-sex Marriages, Civil Unions, Domestic Partnerships and Reciprocal Benefits in the USA' (2008) 4(2) *Utrecht Law Review* 236–78, accessed at *www.utrechtlawreview.org*
J Eekelaar, 'Perceptions of Equality: the Road to Same-Sex Marriage in England' (2014) 28 *International Journal of Law, Policy and the Family* 1.
J Scherpe, 'The Legal Recognition of Same-sex Couples in Europe and the Role of the European Court of Human Rights' (2013) 10 *Equal Rights Review* 83–96

---

[108] See, for example, the current case pending before the ECtHR: *Chapin and Charpentier v France* App No 40183/07 (ECHR, still pending).

(available 11 July 2015 at http://www.equalrightstrust.org/ertdocumentbank/ERR 10_sp1.pdf).

J Scherpe, From 'Odious Crime' to Family Life – Same-sex Couples and the ECHR, in: A-L Verbeke, JM Scherpe, C Declerck T Helms and P Senaeve (eds), *Confronting the Frontiers of Family and Succession Law – Liber amicorum Walter Pintens* (Intersentia 2012) 1225–40.

J Scherpe and N Yassari (eds), *Die Rechtsstellung nichtehelicher Lebensgemeinschaften/The Legal Status of Cohabitants* (Mohr Siebeck 2005).

K Waaldijk, 'Others may Follow: The Introduction of Marriage, Quasi-Marriage, and Semi-Marriage for Same-sex Couples in European Countries' (2004) 38 *New England Law Review* 569–90 and (2005) 5 *Judicial Studies Institute Journal* 104–27.

R Wintemute and M Andenæs (eds), Legal Recognition of Same-sex Partnerships (Hart Publishing 2001).

(2011) 19 *American University Journal of Gender, Social Policy and the Law* (special issue containing several national reports on the legal status of same-sex couples).

5. The financial consequences of divorce in a European perspective

Jens M. Scherpe

1. INTRODUCTION AND OVERVIEW

This chapter deals with the substantive law[1] of the financial consequences of divorce.[2] These consequences can (but do not have to) include
a division of property, certain periodical[3] or lump sum payments, a
sharing or division of pension rights (and similar) and the allocation of
the use of the marital home and other assets. No 'top-down' European
family law exists in relation to any of these,[4] as the European Union has
no competence to regulate such matters, and no cases on the financial
consequences of divorce have yet been decided by the European Court of
Human Rights. This chapter therefore is a purely comparative one.

The financial consequences of divorce are regulated in very different
ways amongst the European jurisdictions. Even the very basic understanding of the nature and structure of the financial consequences of
divorce appears to be fundamentally different. The most obvious contrast
here is between the common law jurisdictions of England and Wales,
Northern Ireland and Ireland[5] and the continental European jurisdictions
of the civilian tradition.[6] Only the latter know statutory matrimonial
property regimes which play a pivotal role in the financial consequences
of divorce. Without doubt, the division/allocation of (matrimonial and
other) property upon divorce is also central to the common law jurisdictions but it is embedded in a wholly different system and approach; it

---

[1] For Private International Law instruments see D Martiny (chapter 7 in
Volume I of this book set).

[2] Much and, in some cases, most or even all of what is described and
analysed in this chapter also applies to certain other legal regimes like the civil
partnership of the jurisdictions of the United Kingdom or the registered partnerships of the Netherlands and the Nordic Countries.

[3] Mostly so-called spousal maintenance, which is also often referred to as
alimony. In the following the term maintenance will be used.

[4] For an overview of international instruments touching this area see K
Boele-Woelki, F Ferrand, C González Beilfuss, and M Jänterä-Jareborg, N Lowe,
D Martiny and W Pintens, *Principles of European Family Law Regarding
Property Relations between Spouses* (Intersentia 2013) 18–24.

[5] On which see section 2.3 below.

[6] On which see sections 2.1 and 2.2 below.

is part of a holistic exercise which considers all the financial consequences of divorce at the same time.

By contrast, jurisdictions with a matrimonial property regime (irrespective of whether the regime applies by default or was chosen by the spouses) separate the various consequences outlined above into different remedies, usually beginning with a division of (matrimonial) property. The financial consequences of divorce in these jurisdictions is therefore commonly said to rest on several 'pillars',[7] whereas in the common law jurisdictions the financial consequences of divorce are delivered as a 'package'[8] (for a further discussion of this see 2.3 below).

Another obvious difference amongst the European jurisdictions relates to whether property consequences flow from the fact of marriage itself or only at the point of divorce. In most European jurisdictions, the act of marriage creates some form of community property (or at least the potential for one) whereas in other jurisdictions, notably the jurisdictions of the Germanic legal tradition and the Nordic Countries as well as the common law jurisdictions, marriage as such does not change the property relations of the couple. However, all jurisdictions in Europe have what are commonly referred to as 'default rules' for the financial consequences of divorce, that is, legal rules that apply in the absence of an agreement or contract,[9] and these rules are dealt with in this chapter first. Because the modalities of the division of property are the central distinguishing feature of these default rules, the jurisdictions are classified according to their default rules on this matter and property division on divorce is the main focus of this chapter.

---

[7] A Dutta, 'Marital Agreements and Private Autonomy in Germany', in JM Scherpe (ed.), *Marital Agreements and Private Autonomy in Comparative Perspective* (Hart Publishing 2012) 158–99, esp. 161 ff; see also JM Scherpe and A Dutta, 'Cross-border Enforcement of English Ancillary Relief Orders – Fog in the Channel, Europe Cut Off?' [2010] *Family Law* 385; JM Scherpe, 'A Comparative Overview of the Treatment of Non-matrimonial Assets, Indexation and Value Increases' [2013] *Child and Family Law Quarterly* 61–79; JM Scherpe, 'Towards a Matrimonial Property Regime for England and Wales?', in R Probert and C Barton (eds), *Fifty Years in Family Law – Essays for Stephen Cretney* (Intersentia Publishing 2012) 129–42.

[8] Cf. JM Scherpe, 'Marital Agreements and Private Autonomy in Comparative Perspective', in JM Scherpe (ed.), *Marital Agreements and Private Autonomy in Comparative Perspective* (Hart Publishing 2012) 443–518, esp. 476 ff, and references in the previous note.

[9] On which see section 3 below.

2. THE DEFAULT RULES ON FINANCIAL CONSEQUENCES OF DIVORCE

Focusing on the division of property in case of divorce, three distinctive approaches can be found in the European jurisdictions: those that create some form of community of property upon marriage (2.1 below), those where no such community is created but where there is a statutory regime governing the participation in the property of the other spouse in case of divorce (2.2 below) and those where all financial consequences of divorce, including the division of property, are subject to the discretion of the court (2.3 below). These three distinct approaches are now discussed in turn.

In addition, two approaches are considered that are more 'European' insofar as they are both meant to provide a potential basis for a common European approach to the financial consequences of divorce: the Franco-German Agreement on an elective 'community of accrued gains' matrimonial property regime (2.4 below) and the Commission on European Family Law's 'Principles on European Family Law Regarding Property Relations Between Spouses' (2.5 below).

2.1 Community of Property Jurisdictions

In the majority of European jurisdictions the act of marriage creates some form of community of property and marriage therefore has an immediate proprietary effect. The most extreme form of such a community is the Dutch universal community of property (2.1.1 below). However, by far the most common form is a community limited to the marital acquest (2.1.2 below).

2.1.1 Universal community of property
After Portugal abolished the universal community of property regime and replaced it with the community of acquest,[10] the Netherlands is now the only European jurisdiction to retain this regime. Several attempts to change and/or modernise the default regime have failed but it is not entirely unlikely that further attempts will follow.[11]

---

[10]   G de Oliveira, R Martins and P Vítor, 'Portugal' in K Boele-Woelki, B Braat and I Curry-Sumner (eds), *European Family Law in Action IV: Property Relations between Spouses* (Intersentia 2009) answer to Question 16.

[11]   Cf M Antokolskaia and K Boele-Woelki, 'Dutch Family Law in the 21st Century: Trend-Setting and Straggling behind at the Same Time', (2002) *Electronic Journal of Comparative Law* (available 12 July 2015 at http://

Under a universal community of property regime, all assets owned on the day of marriage in principle become community property. Everything acquired during the marriage, even through inheritance or gift, also becomes community property – unless the deceased or the donor has stipulated otherwise (see Figure 5.1).[12]

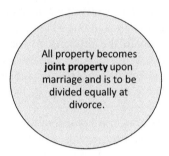

Figure 5.1   Universal community of property (The Netherlands)

In case of divorce the community property is divided equally. This, in theory, makes the Netherlands seem like a 'gold-diggers paradise', inviting people to 'marry into money' and then divorce relatively quickly. But while the courts can only deviate from equal sharing of the community property in exceptional cases, the socially accepted possibility of entering into binding matrimonial property agreements presumably prevents this 'paradise' from actually materialising.[13]

In the Netherlands pension rights are treated separately from other assets, but if such rights accrue during the marriage, they are shared equally as well. With regard to spousal maintenance the Dutch courts have a wide discretion, which is guided by a general principle of 'fairness' and two further principles, namely 'lack of means' and 'ability to pay'.[14] Unless there is a case of hardship, maintenance claims are limited to a maximum of five years in case of short, childless marriages, and to 12 years in other cases.[15]

---

www.ejcl.org/64/art64-5.txt or http://www.ejcl.org/64/art64-5.html) and K Boele-Woelki and B Braat 'Marital Agreements and Private Autonomy in The Netherlands', in JM Scherpe (ed.), *Marital Agreements and Private Autonomy in Comparative Perspective* (Hart Publishing 2012) 229–55, esp. 245 ff.

[12]   Boele-Woelki and Braat (n 11) 234.
[13]   Ibid, 230 ff, 248 ff.
[14]   Ibid, 241 ff.
[15]   Ibid, 243.

2.1.2   Community of acquests

The most common default matrimonial property regime in Europe is the community of acquest (sometimes also called 'community of acquisitions'). It is the default matrimonial property regime in most Romanic jurisdictions (for example, Belgium,[16] France,[17] Luxembourg[18] and Portugal,[19] in Spanish general law (*derecho común*), Aragon, Galicia, Navarre and the Basque Country[20]), as well as in most jurisdictions in Middle and Eastern Europe.[21] Needless to say, there are differences of detail in the separate jurisdictions, so in the following passages the focus is on common structures and principles.

The community of acquest essentially is a limited community of property and, as the name indicates, applies to the 'marital acquest' – that is, that which was generated during the marriage. Hence pre- (and post-) marital property is excluded from the community. There is also a general exclusion of money received through gift or inheritance during the marriage. These assets remain the separate or personal property of the spouses. Therefore, in a marriage to which the matrimonial property regime of a community of acquest applies, there are three groups of

---

[16]   See W Pintens, 'Marital Agreements and Private Autonomy in France and Belgium', in JM Scherpe (ed.), *Marital Agreements and Private Autonomy in Comparative Perspective* (Hart Publishing 2012) 68–88.

[17]   Ibid.

[18]   W Pintens, 'Matrimonial Property Law in Europe', in K Boele-Woelki, J Miles and J Scherpe (eds), *The Future of Family Property in Europe* (Intersentia 2011) 19–46, 22.

[19]   de Oliveira, Martins and Vítor (n 10).

[20]   In Spain family law is not unified and several regions have their own territorial laws (*derechos autonómicos* or *derechos forales*) in family law. On this see Albert Lamarca-Marqués, chapter 14 in Volume II of this book set, and J Ferrer-Riba, 'Marital Agreements and Private Autonomy in Spain', in JM Scherpe (ed.), *Marital Agreements and Private Autonomy in Comparative Perspective* (Hart Publishing 2012) 350–69; Pintens (n 18) 22 and W Pintens, 'Ehegüterstände in Europa', *Zeitschrift für Europäisches Privatrecht (ZEuP)* 2009, 268–81, 269.

[21]   See the national reports, especially the answers to Questions 16 and 18a in Boele-Woelki, Braat and Curry-Sumner (n 10); Pintens (n 18) 23 and Pintens (n 20) 269 ff. Notably Italy does not follow this approach but has a rather different regime which distinguishes between the personal property of the spouses, the communal property and the communal property *de residuo* (Art 177–79 *Codice civile*). Italy will not be discussed further in this chapter, but see the answers by S Patti et al for Italy in Boele-Woelki, Braat and Curry-Sumner (n 10).

property: the communal (or joint) property and the personal property of each spouse (see Figure 5.2).

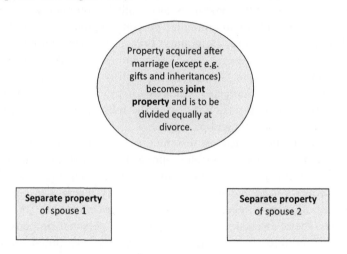

Figure 5.2   Community of acquest

Assets connected very closely to one spouse, such as clothes and other personal items, are also personal/separate property. In some jurisdictions damages received for pain and suffering are deemed to be part of the community property if they are received during the marriage. In other jurisdictions, however, this is not the case. A further main distinguishing factor is whether income generated by personal/separate property (such as interest, dividends and rents) during the marriage becomes community property (as is the case for example in Belgium, France, Spain and Portugal)[22] or not (as for example in Slovenia, Serbia and Croatia).[23] Indeed, it does seem debatable whether such income really is a 'fruit of the marriage' in all cases and thus should be considered a marital acquest. On the other hand, such income might well have a material impact on the marital standard of living and how the couple conduct their financial affairs.

---

[22]   For Belgium (Art 1405 Civil Code) and France (Art 1401 Civil Code) see Pintens (n. 16) 72 ff.; for Spain (Art 1347 Civil Code) see Ferrer-Riba (n. 20) 356 f.; for Portugal (Art 1728 Civil Code) see the answers to the questionnaire provides de Oliveira, Martins and Vítor (n 10); see generally Pintens (n 18) 23.

[23]   See the answers to the questions for those jurisdictions in Boele-Woelki, Braat and Curry-Sumner (n 10) and Pintens (n 18) 23 et seq.

The rules on whether debts incurred during the marriage count as personal or community 'property' differ greatly, but if these debts are incurred 'for the family' rather than in pursuit of a separate interest, they generally fall within/are subtracted from the community property. It is worth noting, however, that even where the debts are personal/separate, the creditors can of course go after the community property if the debtor defaults – which might be seen as the 'downside' of a matrimonial property regime based on a community of property. Indeed, this potential risk is often a reason why couples enter into a matrimonial property agreement (on which see 3 below).

When the marriage comes to an end through divorce, each spouse in principle retains his or her personal/separate property and the community property is divided equally. With very few and limited exceptions,[24] the courts are not afforded any discretion, even if the outcome is potentially unfair and/or creates hardship.

The court's role in dividing up the assets is limited to determining what the community assets are and then allocating them equally to the parties. That is often easier said than done because, in reality, the three groups of assets are often not as distinct as the underlying theory makes them sound. Frequently, payments will have been made from one group of assets to another, for example a spouse may pay the deposit for the purchase of the family home (which is in the couple's joint names and is, thus, community property) from his or her assets, or contributed to the upkeep or renovation of such property. In such situations, there is a need to calculate what the community property owes the separate property, and that then must be subtracted before an equal allocation of the community property takes place. The same of course applies if the community property was used for the benefit of the personal/separate property, and, indeed, when one spouse pays off the personal debts of the other. Again, there are slight differences between the jurisdictions, namely whether any gain (or indeed any loss) as part of the 'investment' into another property group is to be shared. For example, if a house is bought for €500,000, and the wife contributes half of the purchase price from money she inherited before the marriage, the question is whether she should receive just 'her money back' (that is, €250,000, potentially plus some inflation adjustment, would be considered her personal/separate property) in case of divorce, or whether she should benefit from a value increase of the

---

[24] Poland and Serbia allow for a limited discretion, but apparently, in practice, the courts do not very often depart from equal sharing; cf Pintens (n 18) 26.

property purchased (for example, if the property is worth €600,000 at divorce, €300,000 would be deemed her personal/separate property). This depends on whether the respective jurisdiction deems the contribution to be some sort of 'investment' leading to the acquisition of an (abstract) 'share' in the property (as would be the case for property purchases in France or Belgium)[25] or just a financial contribution.

It also worth noting that most community acquest jurisdictions allow the courts to allocate specific assets to a spouse, for example the matrimonial home might go to the spouse who will be the primary carer of the couple's children, or specific assets may be assigned to one spouse who particularly needs them for his or her profession. However, the recipient of such preferred allocation needs to compensate the other spouse so that he or she still nominally receives an equal share of the divided community property. Alternatively, the courts can frequently also order the use of the property by one spouse (which might or might not require payments to be made in return) rather than transferring the property.

As said at the beginning, the division of property is merely a 'pillar' and generally the starting point for the courts to determine the financial consequences of divorce. In addition to the division of property, all community of acquest jurisdictions allow for additional payments to be ordered, and it is these payments that are meant to compensate for any hardship or insufficiencies that the rather static division of property, according to the matrimonial property regime, might create. These payments can be periodical (then often referred to as 'maintenance' although their function can extend further) or in a lump sum, which is the case, for example, in France (*prestation compensatoire*)[26] and the federal law of Spain (*pension compensatoria*).[27] These payments can have a maintenance and/or compensation (for marriage-generated disadvantages) function. The courts' consideration will in many jurisdictions take into account the loss of pension rights due to the marriage.[28] The courts, in this regard, generally have a wide discretion, but will take into account the position of the spouses after the division of community property as just described.

---

[25] Pintens (n 16) 72 ff.

[26] Pintens (n 16) 76 f.

[27] Ferrer-Riba (n 20) 356 ff.

[28] Provided such pension rights were not already considered as part of the division of assets according to the matrimonial property regime.

2.2   Separation of Property/Participation Systems

Unlike those jurisdictions discussed in the previous section, for many European jurisdictions the default regime does not create any form of community of property, and the property of the spouses remains separate during the marriage (unless agreed otherwise at acquisition or by other contractual arrangement). However, this does not mean that the marriage has no subsequent proprietary consequences where one of the spouses dies (not dealt with in this chapter) or upon divorce. To the contrary, the spouse then participates in the property of the other according to specific statutory rules. Pintens therefore labels these jurisdictions as having 'participation systems' as their default matrimonial property regime.[29]

These jurisdictions can roughly be divided into those of the Nordic Countries, where a community of property is created in the event of divorce and the system therefore is a 'deferred community of property' (on which see 2.2.1 below), and those where no such community is created but the law stipulates that certain compensation payments need to be made (provided that specific statutory requirements are fulfilled). This is the case, for example, in the jurisdictions of the Germanic legal family (on which see 2.2.2 below).[30]

2.2.1   Deferred community of property

In the Nordic Countries, that is, Denmark, Finland, Iceland, Norway and Sweden, the default matrimonial property regime is that of a deferred (and universal) community of property.[31] During marriage the spouses

---

[29]   Pintens (n 20); W Pintens, 'Ehegüterrecht' in J Basedow, KJ Hopt and R Zimmermann (eds), *Handwörterbuch des Europäischen* Privatrechts (Mohr Siebeck, 2009) vol I, 350 ff; Pintens (n 18) 19 et seq; see also in the same volume K Boele-Woelki and M Jänterä-Jareborg, 'Initial Results of the Work of the CEFL in the Field of Property Relations Between Spouses', 47 et seq.

[30]   Space precludes a description and discussion of 'hybrid systems' such as Italy (on which see the answers by S Patti et al for Italy in Boele-Woelki, Braat and Curry-Sumner (n 10)) or of the separation of property systems of Catalonia, the Balearic Islands or Valencia (on which see Ferrer-Riba (above n 20); Martín-Casals and Ribot in Boele-Woelki, Braat and Curry-Sumner (n 10).

[31]   The matrimonial property regimes in the Nordic countries are quite similar and go back to the Nordic cooperation around 1910, there are some differences and, recently, significant efforts to modernise the law, particularly in Norway and Denmark. On the matrimonial property regimes in Nordic Countries generally see A Agell, *Nordisk äktenskapsrätt* (Nordiska Ministerrådet, 2003). See also M Jänterä-Jareborg, 'Marital Agreements and Private Autonomy in Sweden', in JM Scherpe (ed.), *Marital Agreements and Private Autonomy in*

live in a separation of property. However, upon divorce all the assets of the spouses (including pensions and so on) become community property – unless they were acquired by gift or inheritance, and the donor or the testator has expressly stated that the property should remain the separate property of one of the spouses.

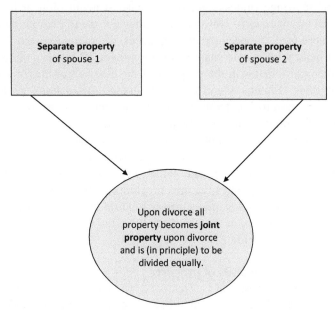

Figure 5.3   Deferred community of property (Nordic Countries)

Upon divorce the community property is in principle to be divided equally, but all of the Nordic jurisdictions give the courts discretion to deviate from equal sharing when not doing so would be inequitable.[32] However, the statutory provisions guiding the courts' discretion on when and how to deviate vary somewhat. In Denmark, such discretion is most restricted, allowing for a deviation from equal division only when the

Comparative Perspective (Hart Publishing 2012) 370–402; JM Scherpe, 'Privat-autonomie im Familienrecht der nordischen Länder', in S Hofer, D Schwab and D Henrich (eds), *From Status to Contract? – Die Bedeutung des Vertrages im europäischen Familienrecht* (Gieseking 2005) 209–54, esp. 212–19.

[32]   For details see see Agell (n 31) 373 ff and the answers to Question 127 for Denmark (I Lund-Andersen and I Magnussen), Finland (K Kurki-Suonio), Norway (T Sverdrup) and Sweden (M Jänterä-Jareborg, M Brattström and K Walleng), in Boele-Woelki, Braat and Curry-Sumner (n 10).

marriage was short (this is understood to be less than five years) *and* where there either was a considerable asset disparity between the parties at the beginning of the marriage or such a disparity arose during the marriage through an inheritance of gifts received by one of the spouses. This latter condition is not fulfilled if the disparity arose through other income generated during the marriage. In the East Nordic jurisdictions of Finland and Sweden, the deviation rules are broader and simply allow for a departure from equal sharing if sharing the assets equally would be inequitable. Icelandic law does the same when equal sharing would be 'unreasonable'. In all these jurisdictions, however, departure from equal sharing is seen as an exception, and is generally only applied if the assets are 'non-matrimonial' in the sense that they were acquired before the marriage or by gift or inheritance.

Norway reformed its law in 1991 and the statutory provisions expressly give a spouse the right to ask for non-matrimonial property (that is, pre-marital and inherited property and property received as a gift) to be exempted from equal sharing. However, a court may include these assets in the sharing if not doing so would be inequitable. So, in essence, the burden of proof in Norway (once it is shown that the assets indeed are non-matrimonial) lies on the spouse who wants the assets to be included, whereas in the other Nordic Countries it is the spouse who wants assets to be exempt who needs to argue that case. This may have the general effect that the deferred universal community of property in Norway essentially has been limited to what was acquired during the marriage, and the system therefore could be described as a deferred community of acquest.[33]

Maintenance payments for spouses play a very limited role in the Nordic countries. If they are awarded at all, it is usually for a very limited period of time. The law tries to avoid continuing financial ties between the spouses and promotes a 'clean break'. This reflects the attitudes on individuality, autonomy and gender equality in the Nordic Countries. Spouses are not considered as insurers for each other, and marriage not as a 'meal ticket for life' or a pension insurance. Cases of hardship therefore are dealt with by the (comparatively very generous) social welfare system and are not resolved by putting the burden on the ex-spouse (unless there are special circumstances).

---

[33]   Cf. Scherpe (n 8) 455.

2.2.2 Statutory compensation jurisdictions

In the jurisdictions of the Germanic legal family, marriage as such does not alter the property relations of the spouses. Property remains separate during the marriage. But, unlike in the matrimonial property regimes of the Nordic Countries, not even at divorce is a community of property created. Instead the matrimonial property regimes operate with statutory rules that allow the spouses to bring monetary claims upon divorce.

2.2.2.1 Community of accrued gains (Zugewinngemeinschaft) The name of the German default matrimonial property regime, the community of accrued gains (*Zugewinngemeinschaft*) is actually a complete misnomer. Contrary to what the name seems to indicate, at no time during (or after, of course) the marriage is a community of property created. The mechanism used by the statutory matrimonial property regime is one that allows the spouse to claim his or her share of the gains accrued during the marriage (the *Zugewinn*). In principle, this system is mathematically precise and determines with certainty who receives what (or rather who can claim what) in case of divorce, although there may well be problems regarding the valuation of certain assets.

In order to achieve this result, German law looks at the assets and debts of each of the spouses at two different points in time: the day of the wedding (initial assets) and the day a spouse has received the other's petition for divorce (final assets). However, gifts and inheritances received during the marriage are counted as initial assets, and debts are included in this calculation as well. This means that a reduction of debts during the marriage will count as a gain. As it is, therefore, in the interest of each spouse to have his or her assets regarded as initial assets, the burden of proof lies on that spouse to show that the assets indeed are 'initial'. In order to ensure that all assets are included, there are mutual duties of disclosure. The overall sum of the initial assets of a spouse[34] is then subtracted from the overall sum of his or her final assets to determine the accrued gain. The underlying idea of the German default matrimonial property regime is that each spouse should participate equally in the gains accrued during the marriage. So if one spouse has a higher gain than the other, this spouse then owes the other spouse an

---

[34] The actual sum is adjusted according to an index in order to reflect inflation etc.; on this see Scherpe (n 7; a Spanish translation published as 'Estudio comparativo del tratamiento de los bienes no matrimoniales, de su indexación y de sus aumentos de valor', in *Revista para el análisis del Derecho (InDret)* No. 2, 2014, is available at http://www.indret.com/pdf/1050___es..pdf (accessed 12 July 2015)).

equalisation payment. For example, if X's accrued gain is €70,000 and Y's gain is €50,000, then X must pay Y €10,000 so that the spouses both leave the marriage with the same accrued gain (see Figure 5.4).

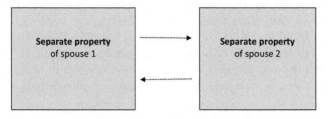

If at the time of divorce the accrued gain of one spouse is greater than the other spouse, the latter can bring a claim against the former as the accrued gain of the spouses is to be divided equally.

Figure 5.4   Community of accrued gains (Germany)

Apart from very extreme cases (for example, one spouse trying to kill the other)[35] the German courts cannot deviate from this equal sharing of the accrued gain. This can of course lead to hardship and also, in some cases, might be seen as manifestly unfair (for example, if the accrued gain is only due to a value increase of a pre-marital property or payments received as damages for pain and suffering). Yet, in recent reforms, the German legislature decided to maintain this aspect of the default regime and it must therefore be deemed to represent the German understanding of marital financial solidarity.

Germany has a rather sophisticated (or one might say complicated) system of dealing with pensions, which is completely detached from the division of assets under the matrimonial property regime, but the underlying principle is also one of (more or less) equal sharing.[36]

Hardships and/or needs are to be dealt with by (periodical) maintenance payments and, thus, such payments continue to play a central role in the German law on the financial consequences of divorce. The circumstances under which the court can exercise its (wide) discretion for such

---

[35]   § 1381 BGB. See e.g. the commentary by Brudermüller on this § in Palandt, *Bürgerliches Gesetzbuch* (73rd edn, CH Beck 2013).

[36]   See e.g. J Hauß and R Eulering, *Versorgungsausgleich und Verfahren in der Praxis* (Gieseking 2009); P Friederici, *Praxis des Versorgungsausgleiches* (Luchterhand 2010); F Ruland, *Versorgungsausgleich: Ausgleich, steuerliche Folgen und Verfahren* (CH Beck 2011).

payments are defined in statute and comprise, for example, maintenance needs because of ongoing childcare duties, old age, illness, unemployment, retraining and so on.[37] It is worth noting that the needs do not have to be generated by the marriage. Furthermore, at least in theory, the payments can also have a compensatory function.

2.2.2.2 Participation in acquests The matrimonial property regime of the participation in acquests (sometimes also referred to as participation in acquisitions; *Errungenschaftsbeteiligung*) is the default regime in Switzerland (and, in a slightly different form, in Greece[38]). It is in essence a combination of a 'community' of accrued gains and the community of acquest, but with an emphasis on the former model. Like in the 'community' of accrued gains, there never actually is a community of property. The property of the spouses remains separate at all times, but in the case of divorce each spouse is entitled to participate in the marital acquest of the other.

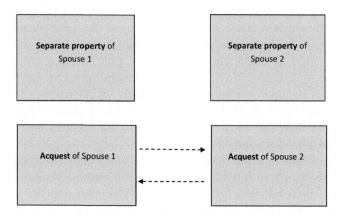

All of the property of the spouses remains separate at all times. But upon divorce each spouse participates in the acquest of the other.

Figure 5.5   Participation in acquests (Switzerland)

---

[37]   §§ 1570 ff. BGB
[38]   See Eleni Zervogianni, chapter 5 in Volume II of this book set, p 90.

This matrimonial property regime is generally regarded as somewhat complicated, as there are four groups of assets (the separate property ofeach spouse and the acquest [*Errungenschaft*] of each spouse), and contributions from each of these groups of assets to other groups of assets need to be calculated. This can involve a lot of difficult (and sometimes impossible) tracing and valuing of assets.[39] The system avoids the difficulties that the German 'community' of accrued gains encounters (for example, value increases of initial property which are counted as accrued gains). But it appears that while this is appealing on a theoretical level, there are considerable practical difficulties with this.[40]

In any event, once these calculations are done and the values of the acquests of each spouse have been determined, in Switzerland each spouse may claim one half of the acquest of the other. As these are monetary claims only, the respective claims are set off against each other and effectively only the spouse with the lower acquest can make a claim. Switzerland recently introduced pension splitting as a pillar separate from matrimonial property issues (although a further reform is pending), and now all pensions acquired during the marriage are to be shared equally between the spouses.[41] Spousal maintenance can be awarded and, despite a somewhat awkward statutory provision, the court essentially has full discretion.

Curiously, in Greece, spouses cannot claim half of the acquest but there is a (rebuttable) presumption that each spouse contributed one-third to the acquest of the other. This means that Greece is the only jurisdiction in Europe where there is a deviation from the general notion of equal sharing of the fruits of the marriage – as apparently the (admittedly rebuttable) presumption is that only one-third of the gain/acquest of the spouse is such a 'fruit'. It is also noteworthy that Greek law takes a rather harsh position regarding the family home and household goods as it makes no special provision for the primary carer of the children regarding these assets/items. Similarly, spousal maintenance (which can be awarded at the court's discretion) does not appear to be particularly generous.[42]

---

[39]   See I Schwenzer and T Keller (chapter 15 in Volume II of this book set), p 315ff.

[40]   Ibid, 316.

[41]   Art. 122(1) Civil Code. See Schwenzer and Keller (n 39) p 317.

[42]   Zervogianni (n 38) p 92.

2.2.3   The hybrid system of Austria – rule-based discretion

The default matrimonial property regime of Austria is also based on a separation of property during the marriage and perhaps therefore is often wrongly classed together with the other Germanic legal systems. But Austrian law is conceptually distinct as the division of assets does not follow strict statutory rules but, in principle, is discretionary.[43] This has led some[44] to compare the Austrian system with a deferred community of property, which indeed is quite apt given that in the Nordic default regimes the courts also retain a discretion to divide the matrimonial assets other than 50/50 between the spouses. However, the Austrian default matrimonial property regime actually has more in common with the default rules applied in common law jurisdictions, such as Singapore, New Zealand, some of the US-jurisdictions and the mixed jurisdiction of Scotland.[45]

The reason for this is that, unlike in the Nordic jurisdictions (perhaps with the exception of Norway, see above 2.2.1), in Austria and the jurisdictions just mentioned not all property is considered to be sharable community property in case of divorce, but just certain assets/property as defined in the statute. In Austria this is defined[46] as comprising property used during the marriage (*eheliches Gebrauchsvermögen*)[47] and marital savings (*eheliche Ersparnisse*).[48] The former particularly includes the household goods and the family home, but also anything that the spouses had at their disposal during the marriage (which has been held to include horses, holiday homes and even a castle).[49] 'Marital savings' are defined to include any form of savings or investment accumulated during the marriage.[50]

Specifically omitted from the 'sharing pool' are assets that were acquired before marriage (or indeed after separation), received as personal gifts or through inheritance, items that are for the personal or professional use of a spouse, and, curiously, assets that are owned by a

---

[43]   § 83(1) EheG.
[44]   E.g. Pintens (n. 18).
[45]   Cf Scherpe (n 8) 467 ff.
[46]   § 81(1) EheG.
[47]   § 81(2) EheG.
[48]   § 81(3) EheG.
[49]   See S Ferrari, 'Marital Agreements and Private Autonomy in Austria', in JM Scherpe (ed.), *Marital Agreements and Private Autonomy in Comparative Perspective* (Hart Publishing 2012) 51–67.
[50]   In practice this has been held to include not only savings and investments in the narrower sense, but also real estate, works of art and even a stamp collection, cf. Ferrari (n 49) 53.

business or shares of a company (provided that they are not merely an investment).[51] However, if the family home and/or the household goods were owned by one of the spouses before the marriage or acquired during the marriage through gift or inheritance (and therefore not normally included in the sharing pool), they can, in contrast with community of acquest jurisdictions, be included in the sharing pool if they are required by one spouse to maintain their standard of living, particularly where the spouses' child has a need for them.[52] So, if one were to make a comparison with other matrimonial property regimes, the Austrian system is better described as a 'deferred limited community of property', as the label 'deferred community of acquest' does not sufficiently capture the fact that assets, like the family home and household goods, can be included in the sharing, irrespective of when and how they were acquired.

In any event, the defining feature of the default Austrian matrimonial property regime is that the division of assets in the end remains discretionary, although in practice it seems to be the case that the assets are divided equally.[53] The statute offers certain criteria to guide the equitable exercise of the discretion. A court, therefore, ought to consider the contributions of the spouses to the acquisition of the assets, which expressly is defined to include housework, unpaid working in the other spouse's/the family business and child care,[54] and especially the welfare of the children. Interestingly, the statute even contains a provision stating that the division of assets should, if possible, be done in a way that the couple need not have any contact in the future,[55] so there is essentially a 'clean break principle' comparable to the Nordic Countries or England and Wales. Nevertheless, the aim appears to be that the spouses are to maintain their marital standard of living as far as is possible.[56]

---

[51]   § 82 (1) EheG.

[52]   § 82 (2) EheG.

[53]   Ferrari (n 49) 54; Pintens (n 16) 29.

[54]   § 83 (2) EheG. It is important to note that the Austrian Civil Code (ABGB) contains an additional provision according to which a spouse is entitled to appropriate compensation (*Abgeltung*) for the work he or she undertakes in the business of the other spouse (§ 98). The amount of compensation is at the discretion of the court, and the criteria listed that the court should consider is the length and nature of the work undertaken, the standard of living and particularly maintenance received.

[55]   § 84 EheG.

[56]   S Ferrari, G Hopf and G Kathrein, *Eherecht* (2nd edn, Manz 2005) § 83 EheG, Anm. 16.

The courts do not only have considerable discretion regarding the division of assets (that is, to allocate the shares) but also as to how the sharing should be undertaken. A court can actually order property transfers and so on.[57] In principle, the division should be effected by allocating specific assets to a spouse (that is, distribution in kind), and monetary claims (to compensate for the allocation of an asset to the other spouse) are regarded as an exception.[58]

As already mentioned, while there is no such rule in the statute, in practice the equal division of the assets concerned appears to be common. But, and this a crucial difference compared to the majority of the civil law jurisdictions in Europe, the court retains the discretion to decide otherwise. It appears that the Austrian Supreme Court tends to divide the assets differently if one of the spouses (in all decided cases it was the wife) not only took care of the household and the education of the children but also held a full-time job. Here the division was 2:1 in favour of that spouse, the obvious reason being that the spouse concerned really had two jobs (one inside and one outside the marital home) whereas the other only had one. Since the contributions therefore were very different, this had to be reflected in the award.[59]

Spousal maintenance in Austria is, in principle, paid for life[60] and it is determined without taking into consideration the division of assets. Whether a spouse is 'at fault' for the divorce still plays a considerable role for the amount to be awarded, and a spouse who is at fault cannot expect to be maintained – unless that spouse continues to be the primary carer or cared for a child or a relative during the marriage.[61] If maintenance is to be paid, the marital standard of living serves as a guideline.[62] However, in case law further guidelines have been developed, and generally a maximum of one-third of the income of the other spouse is deemed to be appropriate.[63] Where both spouses are deemed to

---

[57]   See §§ 85 ff.

[58]   See § 94 EheG.

[59]   Ferrari, Hopf and Kathrein (n 56) § 83 EheG Anm. 17 with further references.

[60]   § 77 EheG.

[61]   § 68a EheG. In the latter case the maintenance is usually limited to three years, § 68 (2) EheG. Maintenance claims under § 68 can also be barred completely if it would be inequitable considering the 'matrimonial offence'/ behaviour of the claimant spouse, § 68a (3) EheG.

[62]   § 66 EheG.

[63]   Ferrari (n 49) 54. See also M Schwimann and S Ferrari, in M Schwimann and B Verschraegen (eds), *Praxiskommentar zum Allgemeinen bürgerlichen Gesetzbuch I* (3rd edn, LexisNexis 2005) § 94 Rz 16 ff.

be at fault for the marriage coming to an end, then the economically weaker spouse can claim equitable maintenance provided that he or she cannot self-maintain, although the courts can impose a time-limit for such maintenance payments.[64] Where no spouse is at fault, maintenance claims can be made under certain circumstances for reasons of equity.[65]

2.3   Jurisdictions without a Matrimonial Property Regime

While in Austria (and indeed the Nordic Countries) the division of assets in case of divorce is at the court's discretion, there is no doubt that these jurisdictions nevertheless have a default matrimonial property regime. Despite certain similarities, this is not the case in the common law jurisdictions. It is true that in England and Wales, Northern Ireland and Ireland marriage as such does not change the proprietary relations of the spouses; it is also true that in case of divorce the courts have the power to redistribute this property.

However, to assume that these jurisdictions have a matrimonial property regime based on 'separation of property' is incorrect. Indeed, the case law is very explicit on this. In *Sorrell v Sorrell*,[66] Bennett J expressly rejected the suggestion, advanced by Professor Stephen Cretney,[67] that a community of property system had been 'imposed by judicial decision'. Baroness Hale, in *Miller v Miller; McFarlane v McFarlane* expressly held that '[w]e do not yet have a system of community of property, whether full or deferred'.[68]

Nevertheless it seems that particularly lawyers from the continental European jurisdictions find the idea that there could be jurisdictions without a matrimonial property regime inconceivable. Yet it is true. England and Wales, Northern Ireland and Ireland do not have a matrimonial property regime. Where a matrimonial property regime exists, it is looked at and the division of property dealt with separately and distinctly. This is emphatically not the case in England and Wales, Northern Ireland or Ireland. In these jurisdictions, the discretion of the court is exercised holistically, looking at the entirety of the facts and the circumstances of the case. No fixed rules or necessary distinctions between matrimonial property, maintenance, pensions and other financial remedies exist.

---

[64]   § 68 EheG.
[65]   § 69 (3) EheG.
[66]   *Sorrell v Sorrell* [2005] EWHC 1717 at [96].
[67]   S Cretney, 'Community of Property Imposed by Judicial Decision' (2003) 119 *LQR* 349, commenting on *Lambert v Lambert* [2002] EWCA Civ 1685.
[68]   [2006] UKHL 24 at [151].

Certainty and predictability are therefore not regarded as crucial elements of the law of financial consequences of divorce. On the contrary, the common law jurisdictions strive to be able to deliver a 'tailor-made package' for each individual case, and these packages may or may not contain transfer of property, pensions or periodical payments and so on. Which exact remedies the courts award varies from case to case, depending on the individual circumstances. This is essential to the understanding of the financial consequences of divorce in these jurisdictions and indeed to any meaningful comparison.

The approach taken by the common law jurisdictions of Europe has been described by Lord Denning (with regard to English law,[69] but his comments actually are equally apt for the other jurisdictions) as follows:

> The Family Court takes the rights and obligations of the parties all together and puts the pieces into a mixed bag. Such pieces are the right to occupy the matrimonial home or have a share in it, the obligation to maintain the wife and children, and so forth. The court then takes out the pieces and hands them to the two parties – some to one party and some to the other – so that each can provide for the future with the pieces allotted to him or to her. The court hands them out without paying any too nice a regard to their legal or equitable rights but simply according to what is the fairest provision for the future – for mother and father and the children.[70]

'Fairness' however, is a rather difficult and elusive concept as the one and only yardstick, as Lord Nicholls (again, with regard to English law) has pointed out:

> Everyone would accept that the outcome on these matters, whether by agreement or court order, should be fair. More realistically, the outcome ought to be as fair as is possible in all the circumstances. But everyone's life is different. Features which are important when assessing fairness differ in each case. And, sometimes, different minds can reach different conclusions on what fairness requires. Then fairness, like beauty, lies in the eye of the beholder.[71]

---

[69]   Any reference to 'English law' should be read as a reference to the law of England and Wales.

[70]   *Hanlon v Law Society* [1981] AC 124 (HL) 147.

[71]   *White v White* [2000] UKHL 5 at [1].

2.3.1   England and Wales[72]

In English law the understanding of fairness has undergone a radical change.[73] The Matrimonial Causes Act 1973 contains some limited guidance as to how overall fairness is to be achieved. According to s 25(1) first consideration is to be given to the welfare of any child of the family.[74] This criterion is taken very seriously and indeed in practice is given a very strong priority over other concerns. Nevertheless, all the circumstances of the case are to be taken into account, and s 25(2) then contains a list of non-exhaustive factors to which the court is 'to have regard':

(a)   the income, earning capacity, property and other financial resources which each of the parties to the marriage has or is likely to have in the foreseeable future, including in the case of earning capacity any increase in that capacity which it would in the opinion of the court be reasonable to expect a party to the marriage to take steps to acquire;

(b)   the financial needs, obligations and responsibilities which each of the parties to the marriage has or is likely to have in the foreseeable future;

(c)   the standard of living enjoyed by the family before the breakdown of the marriage;

(d)   the age of each party to the marriage and the duration of the marriage;

(e)   any physical or mental disability of either of the parties to the marriage;

(f)   the contributions which each of the parties has made or is likely in the foreseeable future to make to the welfare of the family, including any contribution by looking after the home or caring for the family;

(g)   the conduct of each of the parties, if that conduct is such that it would in the opinion of the court be inequitable to disregard it.

---

[72]   The Matrimonial Causes (Northern Ireland) Order 1978 is very similar to the Matrimonial Causes Act 1973 of England and Wales and will therefore not be discussed separately here.

[73]   For a brief overview see J Miles, 'Marital Agreements and Private Autonomy in England and Wales', in JM Scherpe (ed.), *Marital Agreements and Private Autonomy in Comparative Perspective* (Hart Publishing 2012) 89–121 and JM Scherpe, 'Land ohne Güterstand? Gegenwart und Zukunft des Scheidungsfolgenrechts in England und Wales', in I Schwenzer, I Götze, K Seelmann and J Taupitz (eds), *Familie – Recht – Ethik. Festschrift für Gerd Brudermüller* (CH Beck 2014) 643–52.

[74]   It is important to note that 'child of the family' includes children that have been treated by the couple as child of their family (Matrimonial Causes Act 1973, s 52(1)(b)), and thus can include children that are not the joint children of the couple.

There is no hierarchy or priority set out in the provision,[75] and in addition the court is under a duty to consider a 'clean break', that is, ending all ongoing financial relations between the spouses (s 25A).

This of course does very little to elucidate what 'fairness' might mean in an individual case, so it was for the judiciary to develop further guidance in the absence of legislative intervention.[76] Indeed, the approach to what is 'fair' changed radically at the beginning of this century through the decision in *White v White*.[77] In that case, the previous 'cap' or 'glass ceiling' of only awarding the financially weaker spouse his or her (but usually her) 'reasonable requirements' was abolished and replaced by a view of fairness which values the spouses' contributions equally:

> ... there is one principle of universal application which can be stated with confidence. In seeking to achieve a fair outcome, there is no place for discrimination between husband and wife and their respective roles ... There should be no bias in favour of the money-earner and against the home-maker and the child-carer.[78]

In the following years, the courts then developed this approach further in a string of cases,[79] culminating in the House of Lords decision in *Miller v Miller, McFarlane v McFarlane*.[80] Here, three 'strands' or 'rationales' of fairness were identified: needs, equal sharing and compensation (for relationship-generated disadvantages).[81] As Jo Miles rightly has pointed out, these 'strands' are difficult to reconcile, as each represents a different

---

[75] A Barlow, 'England' in Boele-Woelki, Braat and Curry-Sumner (n 10), answer to Question 161.

[76] On potential legislative changes see the Law Commission Report 'Matrimonial Property, Needs and Agreements' (Law Com No 343), available 12 July 2015 at http://lawcommission.justice.gov.uk/areas/marital-property-agreements.htm.

[77] [2000] UKHL 5.

[78] Ibid, at [24].

[79] On this see Miles (n 73) 93 ff.; Barlow (n 75); J Miles, '*Charman v Charman (No 4)* – Making Sense of Need, Compensation and Equal Sharing after *Miller/McFarlane*' (2008) 20 *Child and Family Law Quarterly* 378; Scherpe (n 7).

[80] [2006] UKHL 24.

[81] *Miller v Miller, McFarlane v McFarlane* [2006] UKHL 24 at [11]–[16] (Lord Nicholls) and [138]–[141] (Baroness Hale).

(and sometimes contradictory) view of the function of marriage. Moreover, the concepts overlap, so applying them consistently and clearly in practice appears difficult, if not impossible.[82]

That said, certain trends in their application are discernible from subsequent case law. Crucially, it appears that 'needs' is the dominant 'strand' in 'normal' cases, notwithstanding the difficulties in defining what 'needs' actually should entail.[83] As mentioned above, the welfare of the children of the family is the first consideration, and in practice this usually means that the needs of the children and thus those of the primary carer are met first. It is interesting to note that 'needs' in this context does not appear to be limited to 'relationship-generated needs (as for example in the Nordic countries).[84] So in England and Wales, 'fairness' first and foremost seems to mean covering the needs of the children and the spouses, particularly the primary carer. Hence, the other 'strands', and particularly 'equal sharing' really only come into play where the assets exceed the needs of parties.

In relation to 'equal sharing', both leading speeches in *Miller v Miller, McFarlane v McFarlane* distinguished between two groups of assets. Lord Nicholls termed them 'matrimonial and non-matrimonial assets' while Baroness Hale referred to them as 'family assets'[85] and 'other assets'. Subsequent case law seems to have adapted Lord Nicholls' terminology.[86] The leading speeches also appear to concur that the longer the marriage, the less important the distinction between the groups of property would be. While the exact definition of what constitutes each

---

[82] Miles (n 73) 93 ff; Miles (n 79). See also J Miles, 'Principle or Pragmatism in Ancillary Relief: The Virtues of Flirting with Academic Theories and Other Jurisdictions' [2005] *International Journal of Law, Policy and the Family* 242 et seq.

[83] On this see also the Law Commission report (n 76).

[84] *Miller v Miller and McFarlane v McFarlane* [2006] UKHL 24 at [11] per Lord Nicholls. Baroness Hale at [137]–[138] while focusing on relationship-generated needs also includes needs because of a disability if it arose during the marriage, and generally seems to accept that a temporal link rather than a causal link is sufficient.

[85] Building on a distinction developed by Lord Denning in *Wachtel v Wachtel* [1973] Fam 72 at 90, see *Miller v Miller and McFarlane v McFarlane* [2006] UKHL 24 at [149].

[86] See e.g. *K v L (Non-Matrimonial Property: Special Contribution)* [2011] EWCA Civ 550, [2011] 2 FLR 980; *AR v AR (Treatment of Inherited Wealth)* [2011] EWHC 2717 (Fam), [2012] 2 FLR 1; *N v F (Financial Orders: Pre-Acquired Wealth)* [2011] EWHC 586 (Fam), [2011] 2 FLR 533; *Jones v Jones* [2011] EWCA Civ 41, [2011] 1 FLR 1723.

group of assets appears to differ, there was a consensus between the leading speeches as to the policy issues which underlie the distinction. In the cases, there is a total of nine references to the 'fruits' of the marriage/matrimonial partnership/the couple's labours[87] and three to the 'joint/common endeavours'[88] of the spouses when describing the marital/ family assets. Hence the underlying policy is that only what was achieved jointly should, in principle, be subject to equal sharing, which excludes pre- (and post-) marital assets as well as gifts and inheritances received during or after the marriage.[89] However, both speeches agree that the family home should always be in the sharing pool, irrespective of how and when it was acquired.[90] So it appears that, while not having a matrimonial property regime as such, England and Wales now has embarked on a path that in practice distinguished between matrimonial and non-matrimonial property – but unlike in the continental European jurisdictions this approach is not fixed and formulaic but rather flexible and always subject to the needs of the spouses and the children. But where the needs are covered, non-matrimonial assets do not appear to be shared in practice anymore (if they ever were).[91] As Wilson LJ (as he

---

[87]   At paras [17], [19], [20], [21], [85], [141], [149] and [154] (twice).

[88]   At paras [22], [91] and [143].

[89]   On this see also Scherpe (n 7). For an example of the practical application see e.g. *S v AG (Financial Remedy: Lottery Prize)* [2011] EWHC 2637 (Fam) a recent lottery win was held to be non-matrimonial property rather than result of a joint endeavour – an interesting contrast to the decision by the German Federal Court of Justice (*Bundesgerichtshof*) (16.10.2013) XII ZB 277/12, NJW 2013, 3645 where the court held – somewhat formulaically – that a lottery gain even after separation but before the actual divorce constituted an accrued gain that needed to be shared in case of divorce.

[90]   Given property prices and the tradition of house ownership in England, the matrimonial home often is the most valuable asset of the spouses, and excluding it from the matrimonial pool (and from equal sharing) would often lead to needs not being covered. Cf. J Miles and JM Scherpe, 'The Future of Family Property in Europe', in Boele-Woelki, Miles and Scherpe (eds), *The Future of Family Property in Europe* (Intersentia 2011) 423–32.

[91]   See e.g. *B v B (Ancillary Relief)* [2008] EWCA Civ 543; *McCartney v Mills McCartney* [2008] EWHC 401 (Fam), [2008] 1 FLR 1508; *AR v AR (Treatment of Inherited Wealth)* [2011] EWHC 2717 (Fam), [2012] 2 FLR 1; *Robson v Robson* [2010] EWCA Civ 1171, [2011] 1 FLR 751; *K v L (Non-Matrimonial Property: Special Contribution)* [2011] EWCA Civ 550, [2011] 2 FLR 980; *N v F (Financial Orders: Pre-Acquired Wealth)* [2011] EWHC 586 (Fam), [2011] 2 FLR 533; *Jones v Jones* [2011] EWCA Civ 41, [2011] 1 FLR 1723; *S v AG (Financial Orders: Lottery Prize)* [2011] EWHC 2637 (Fam), [2012] 1 FLR 651. For a discussion of this the excellent summary

then was) pointed out in *K v L*, until now there does not seem to be a single 'reported decision in which the assets were entirely non-matrimonial and in which, by reference to the sharing principle, the applicant secured an award in excess of her or his needs'.[92]

The third 'strand' of fairness, compensation, receives little attention in practice and appears to be subsumed into either 'needs, generously assessed' or as achieved through equal sharing.[93]

As the author of this chapter has suggested elsewhere,[94] this in practice appears to lead to the following approach regarding the division of property in case of divorce:

- *Matrimonial property* is to be shared upon divorce unless consider-ations of fairness demand otherwise. Such considerations can include the (short) duration of the marriage and, very exceptionally, 'stellar' contributions, but primarily will be the aspects of needs and compensation.
- *Non-matrimonial property* is not to be shared unless considerations of fairness demand otherwise. Again, such considerations can include the duration of the marriage, but also the contributions made to the overall welfare of the family, particularly past and future child-care and related sacrifices, as well as other relationship-generated advantages and disadvantages and, of course, the needs of the spouses.

In any event, it is essential to keep in mind that the courts in England and Wales nevertheless not only retain full discretion regarding the division of assets in case of divorce, but regarding the entirety of the financial remedies. As mentioned at the outset of this section, the financial consequences of divorce are considered holistically and not separately. So, for example, it might well be that in a suitable case the primary carer of the children is awarded the family home (which represents 100 per cent of the family's assets) but then is not awarded any maintenance payments.

Interestingly this will in many cases lead to the primary carer of children being better off in low-money cases compared to his or her

---

and analysis by A Chandler, '"The Law is now reasonably clear": the Courts' Approach to Non-matrimonial Assets' [2012] Fam Law 163, and Scherpe (n 7).

[92]   [2001] 1 AC 596, [2000] 2 FLR 981 at [22].

[93]   See e.g. *Lauder v Lauder* [2007] EWHC 1227; *VB v JP* [2008] EWHC 112; *McFarlane v McFarlane (No 2)* [2009] EWHC 891. See Miles (n 73) 95.

[94]   Scherpe (nn 7 and 8).

continental European counterparts where the available matrimonial assets would merely be shared equally. Conversely, the financially weaker spouse may often be worse off in comparison in big-money cases where an equal sharing would give him or her a larger share of the assets, but considerations of fairness demand not sharing the assets equally. However, this is of course perfectly in line with the fact that the children are to be the 'first consideration' according to s 25(1) of the Matrimonial Causes Act 1973.

2.3.2 Ireland

As is well known, Ireland only introduced divorce in 1996. Therefore much of the law on the financial consequences of divorce has to be seen against the social, historical and constitutional background.[95] Similarly to England and Wales (and Northern Ireland), the determination of the financial consequences of divorce essentially is at the court's discretion, and s 20(2) of the Irish Family Law (Divorce) Act 1996 contains a list of factors that the court 'shall have regard to' when exercising its discretion:

(a) the income, earning capacity, property and other financial resources which each of the spouses concerned has or is likely to have in the foreseeable future,

(b) the financial needs, obligations and responsibilities which each of the spouses has or is likely to have in the foreseeable future (whether in the case of the remarriage of the spouse or otherwise),

(c) the standard of living enjoyed by the family concerned before the proceedings were instituted or before the spouses commenced to live apart from one another, as the case may be,

(d) the age of each of the spouses, the duration of their marriage and the length of time during which the spouses lived with one another,

(e) any physical or mental disability of either of the spouses,

(f) the contributions which each of the spouses has made or is likely in the foreseeable future to make to the welfare of the family, including any contribution made by each of them to the income, earning capacity, property and financial resources of the other spouse and any contribution made by either of them by looking after the home or caring for the family,

(g) the effect on the earning capacity of each of the spouses of the marital responsibilities assumed by each during the period when they lived with one another and, in particular, the degree to which the future earning

---

[95]   See Brian Sloan, chapter 5 in Volume II of this book set and L Crowley, 'Marital Agreements and Private Autonomy in Ireland', in JM Scherpe (ed.), *Marital Agreements and Private Autonomy in Comparative Perspective* (Hart Publishing 2012) 200–28.

capacity of a spouse is impaired by reason of that spouse having relinquished or foregone the opportunity of remunerative activity in order to look after the home or care for the family,

(h)   any income or benefits to which either of the spouses is entitled by or under statute,

(i)   the conduct of each of the spouses, if that conduct is such that in the opinion of the court it would in all the circumstances of the case be unjust to disregard it,

(j)   the accommodation needs of either of the spouses,

(k)   the value to each of the spouses of any benefit (for example, a benefit under a pension scheme) which by reason of the decree of divorce concerned, that spouse will forfeit the opportunity or possibility of acquiring,

(l)   the rights of any person other than the spouses but including a person to whom either spouse is remarried.

As in the other common law jurisdictions, there is no express hierarchy among these criteria, however it has been held that their consideration is mandatory.[96]

Unlike in England and Wales as well as Northern Ireland, the overarching principle is not one of 'fairness' but rather 'proper provision' for spouses and children.[97] This not only emphasises the protection of financially weaker family members (and thus 'needs') even more expressly than English law, but also makes express that the discretionary exercise is not focused on *division* (of property) but on *provision*, as was held in *T v T*.[98] In the same case, any notion that the financial consequences of divorce should be concerned with equality or equal sharing (and thus a more structured approach) was expressly rejected,[99] and it was affirmed that each case needed to be decided on the basis of its own particular circumstances.[100]

However, it has also been held that is not restricted to basic needs but should 'reflect the equal partnership of the spouses' and:

> ... should seek, so far as the circumstances of the case permit, to ensure that the spouse is not only in a position to meet her financial liabilities and obligations and continue with a standard of living commensurate with her

---

[96]   *MK v JPK* [2003] 1 IR 326.

[97]   Crowley (n 95) 204 ff.; Sloan (n 95); G Shannon, 'Ireland', in Boele-Woelki, Braat and Curry-Sumner (n 10), answer to Question 161.

[98]   3 IR 321, 383 (Denham J), and 398 (Murphy J).

[99]   Ibid, 398 (Murphy J), 417 (Fenelly J), and 407 (Murray J).

[100]   Ibid, 418 (Fenelly J), and 409 (Murphy J). See also Crowley (n 95) 208 ff.

standard of living during marriage but to enjoy what may reasonably be regarded as the fruits of the marriage so that she can live an independent life and have security in the control of her own affairs, with a personal dignity that such autonomy confers, without necessarily being dependent on receiving periodic payments for the rest of her life from her former husband.[101]

'Proper provision' in Ireland therefore includes participation in the 'fruits of the marriage' as well. In any event, as in the other European common law jurisdictions, there is no separate consideration of various remedies upon divorce, but the financial consequences are decided holistically and 'in a package'.

2.4 Franco-German Agreement on an Optional Matrimonial Property Regime of a Community of Accrued Gains

On 4 February 2010, France and Germany concluded an agreement on an optional matrimonial property regime (referred to hereafter as the 'FGA').[102]

---

[101]   Ibid, 408 (Murray J). See Crowley (n 95) 208 ff.

[102]   Abkommen zwischen der Bundesrepublik Deutschland und der Französischen Republik über den Güterstand der Wahl-Zugewinngemeinschaft (BGBl. 2012 II,   178;   (http://www.bmj.de/SharedDocs/Downloads/DE/pdfs/Abkommen_ zwischender_Bundesrepublik_Deutschland_und_der_Franzoesischen_Republik_ ueber_den_Wahl_Gueterstand.pdf).   Accord   entre   la   République   fédérale d'Allemagne et la République Française instituant un régime matrimonial optionnel de la participation aux acquêts (http://www.dnoti.de/DOC/2010/Abkommen_ deutsche_franzoesisch_gueterstand_fran_barrierefrei.pdf).   English   translation available at   http://www.bmj.de/SharedDocs/Downloads/DE/pdfs/Uebersetzung_ Abkommen_Wahlgueterstand.pdf. Explanatory notes can be found at http://www. bmjv.de/SharedDocs/Downloads/DE/pdfs/Erlaeuterungen_zum_deutsch_franzoe sischen_Abkommen_ueber_den_Guterstand_der_Wahl_Zugewinngemeinschaft. pdf (all last accessed 12 July 2015).
   On the agreement see M Giovanna Cubeddu Wiedemann, *The Optional Matrimonial Property Regime* (Intersentia 2014), with translations of the agreement and explanatory notes into English, Italian and Spanish); A Fötschl, 'The Common Optional Matrimonial Property Regime of Germany and France', (2009) *Yearbook of Private International Law* 395–404; A Fötschl, 'The Common Matrimonial Property Regime [COMP] of Germany and France: Epoch-Making in the Unification of Law' (2010) 18 *European Review of Private Law* 881–9; C González Beilfuss, 'El Acuerdo franco–alemán instituyendo un régimen económico matrimonial común', *Anuario Español de Derecho Internacional Privado (X)* 2010, 397–416; C González Beilfuss, 'The Franco-German Treaty Instituting a Common Matrimonial Regime of Participation in the Acquisitions: How Could Catalonia Opt In?', in A.-L. Verbeke et al (eds), *Confronting the Frontiers of Family and Succession Law. Liber Amicorum Walter Pintens* (Intersentia 2012) 623–32;

It entered into force on 1 May 2013,[103] and is the first bilateral agreement on substantive matrimonial property law in Europe. But it need not remain bilateral, as article 21 FGA expressly allows all member states of the European Union to accede to the agreement, and at least one, Luxembourg, has already expressed an interest in doing so.[104]

The FGA provides an optional regime, that is, the couple can choose this regime instead of the default regime that would otherwise apply to their marital relationship. That being so, it might more appropriately have been discussed below in the section on marital agreements (3 below); but it is addressed here owing to its comprehensive nature.[105] Spouses can choose this matrimonial property regime before or during their marriage,

---

P Simler, 'Le nouveau régime matrimonial optionnel franco-allemand de participation aux acquêts', Droit de la famille 2010-5, 9–19; E Becker, 'Ein europäischer Güterstand?', ERA Forum (2011) 12:103–18; Jäger, 'Der neue deutsch-französische Güterstand der Wahl-Zugewinngemeinschaft – Inhalt und seine ersten Folgen für die Gesetzgebung und Beratungspraxis', Deutsche Notar-Zeitschrift (DNotZ) 2010, 804; Klippstein, Der deutsch-französische Wahlgüterstand der Wahl-Zugewinngemeinschaft, Familie – Partnerschaft – Recht, FPR9 2010, 510–15; I Braeuer, 'Der neue deutsch-französische Wahlgüterstand', Forum Familienrecht (FF) 2010, 113–15; Meyer, 'Der deutsch-französische Wahlgüterstand', FamRZ 2010, 612–17; Schaal, 'Der neue Güterstand der Wahl-Zugewinngemeinschaft', Zeitschrift für die Notarpraxis (ZNotP) 2010, 162–72; Süß, 'Der deutsch-französische Güterstand der Wahl-Zugewinngemeinschaft als erbrechtliches Gestaltungsmittel', Zeitschrift für die Steuer- und Erbrechtspraxis (ZErb) 2010, 281; Krause, 'Die Wahl-Zugewinngemeinschaft als neuer Güterstand', Zeitschrift für Familien- und Erbrecht (ZFE) 2010, 247; Süß, 'Europäisierung des Familienrechts – Handlungsempfehlungen für den Notar zum status quo', ZNotP 2011, 282–91; Stürner, 'Der deutsch-französische Wahlgüterstand als Modell für die europäische Rechtsvereinheitlichung', Juristenzeitung (JZ) 2011, 545–55; Sengl, 'Die Auswirkungen des deutsch-französischen Güterstandes der Wahl-Zugewinngemeinschaft auf das deutsche Grundbuchverfahren', Der Rechtspfleger (Rpfleger) 2011, 125–28; D Martiny, 'Der neue deutsch-französische Wahlgüterstand – Ein Beispiel optionaler bilateraler Familienrechtsvereinheitlichung', ZEuP (Zeitschrift für Europäisches Privatrecht (ZEuP) 2011, 577–00; Braun, MittBay-Not 2012, 89. An English explanatory summary by the EU Directorate-General for Internal Policies (PE 425.658) can be found at http://www.europarl.europa.eu/RegData/etudes/note/join/2010/425658/IPOL-JURI_NT%282010%29425658_EN.pdf (accessed 12 July 2015).
[103]   In Germany the agreement has been incorporated into the Civil Code: § 1519 BGB.
[104]   Meyer (n 102) 617 and Klippstein (n 102) 511.
[105]   Furthermore, none of the other optional regimes available in the European jurisdictions are discussed in this chapter, but if they had been they would have been included in section 2 as well.

provided that the substantive law of a Contracting State to the agreement is applicable to their relationship (article 1 FGA) by virtue of the relevant rules of private international law.[106] The optional regime is therefore not limited to German or French nationals or to cross-border cases.

For the optional regime to apply the spouses must enter into a marital agreement/marriage contract choosing this regime for their matrimonial property relationship. No specific formal requirements are contained in the FGA for this, so it is the *lex loci contractus* which determines the required form; in both Germany and France this is a notarised agreement.[107]

The matrimonial property regime of the FGA is a 'community of accrued gains'.[108] The fact that such a matrimonial property regime was already known in both jurisdictions (as the default regime in Germany and an optional regime in France, the *participation aux acquêts*) made it easier to agree that it should be the basis for the new optional regime.[109] The regime is therefore one of a separation of property during the marriage but one which then allows the spouses to make monetary claims when the marriage ends (in principle for half of the accrued gain). The German default regime served as a basis for the new regime, subject to certain modifications reflecting the French law and legal traditions and, at least in the view of some observers, the modernisation of some certain provisions.[110] Since the German regime was already described above (2.2.2.1), this part will focus on how this FGA differs from German law.

---

[106] Cf. Klippstein (n 102) 512 and Jäger (n 102) 805 f for the possible applications combinations.

[107] On the role of notaries function of the notary see generally Center of Legal Competence, *Notaries in Europe – Growing Fields of Competence* (Intersentia, 2007) and particularly S Matyk, 'The European Union – A Driving Force for a European Notarial Profile' in the same volume, 15 ff. See Scherpe (n 8) 491 ff; and Ferrer-Riba (n 20) 360 ff; Dutta (n 7) 172 ff; Pintens (n 16) 38 f; N Dethloff, 'Contracting in Family Law: A European Perspective', in K Boele-Woelki, J Miles and JM Scherpe (eds), *The Future of Family Property in Europe* (Intersentia 2011) 65–94, 74 ff; G Brambring, 'Die Ehevertragsfreiheit und ihre Grenzen', in S Hofer, D Schwab and D Henrich (eds), *From Status to Contract? – Die Bedeutung des Vertrages im europäischen Familienrecht* (Gieseking, 2005) 17 et seq.

[108] The name was kept despite the fact that there is general agreement that it is somewhat inappropriate as there is no community of property at any time in this regime, cf. Becker (n 102) 109f.

[109] On these see the short descriptions by Becker (n 102) 106–9 and the EU Directorate-General for Internal Policies (n 102) 7–10.

[110] See e.g. Becker (n 102).

One of the central 'concessions' to the French legal tradition was the inclusion of specific protection for the family home and the family's household goods. According to article 5 FGA neither spouse can enter into binding agreements concerning such assets without consent (or later approval) from the other spouse.[111] This very much reflects the French *régime primaire*[112] whose rules cannot be altered by the spouses by marital agreement. Therefore adhering to this was essential for the FGA, which otherwise really only deals with matters which from a French perspective concern the *régime secondaire*. But the special protection of the family home was welcomed by the German delegation in any event and not controversial.[113]

Article 6 FGA allows each spouse to enter into contracts binding both of them regarding the management of the household and the needs of the children. The latter was particularly important for the French and reflects a modified version of the general French rules.[114]

Another crucial difference from the German community of accrued gains concerns the calculation and valuation of the assets. As described above (2.2.2.1), the gain is calculated by determining the initial assets (assets at the time of marriage) and the final assets (assets at the point when the divorce petition was made pending in a court of law). Assets acquired by inheritance and gift count as initial assets. But the difference between the German scheme and the FGA lies in the valuation of the assets.[115] In the German *Zugewinngemeinschaft* all assets are valued at the relevant points in time (day of marriage[116] and day of divorce petition) whereas in the French *participation aux acquêts,* the valuation is always undertaken on the day the matrimonial regime actually comes to an end. A 'compromise position' was adopted for the FGA: the German approach is followed, except for real property/immovables, in relation to which the French valuation rule prevailed (article 9 FGA). This means that an increase in the value of real property owned before the marriage

---

[111] The consequences of the ineffectiveness of such agreements are left to the respective applicable national law.

[112] Esp. Art. 215, 217 Code Civil.

[113] EU Directorate-General for Internal Policies (n. 102) 11 f.

[114] Esp. Art. 220 Code Civil; see Klippstein (102) 513 and Jäger (102) 808.

[115] Like the German *Zugewinngemeinschaft* the optional regime takes into account inflation and so on when determining the value of the initial and final assets by adjusting them by the average price-change rates for overall consumer prices in the Contracting States (articles 9(3), 11(3) FGA). On this see also JM Scherpe, 'A Comparative Overview of the Treatment of Non-matrimonial Assets, Indexation and Value Increases' [2013] *Child and Family Law Quarterly* 61–79.

[116] Or day of acquisition if acquired during the marriage.

or acquired during the marriage by gift or inheritance will not have to be shared. However, if the value increase is due to the actions of the spouses (such as building an extension, renovations and so on) this value increase nevertheless will be considered as a gain under the FGA.

This has been a contentious point about the German regime for some time. The approach of the optional regime may be said to meet spouses' actual expectations in contemporary society better, as 'pure' increases in value, which are external to the spouses' relationship, cannot really be considered as 'fruits of the marriage'.[117] Therefore it is somewhat surprising that according to article 8(3) FGA the fruits of such real estate, for example rent income and so on, are expressly *included* in the sharing (by not including them in the initial assets), as for these the same reasoning seems to apply.[118]

A minor but important difference is the treatment of damages received for pain and suffering. In the German regime, these are given no special treatment[119] so any such damages are treated as an accrued gain which needs to be shared. Given the deeply personal nature and purpose of such payments, this seems absurd. Therefore it is to be welcomed that the FGA adopts the French approach of including such payments in the initial assets (article 8(2) FGA) and thus exempts them from sharing.

A final and fundamental difference from the German regime is contained in article 14. The payments any spouse has to make as a result of the end of the matrimonial regime are capped at 50 per cent of the value of that spouse's assets (that is, after deduction of liabilities, and with safeguards against inappropriate behaviour such as squandering and so on, see article 10). Such a rule – which protects the payor by enabling him or her to retain at least half of his or her assets – was considered during the recent reforms in Germany but not implemented.[120] It was included in the FGA at the request of the French delegation.[121]

It needs to be added that matters such as pension sharing and maintenance are not covered by the FGA, and so the relevant national law applies.

---

[117]   Cf. Becker (n 102) 112.

[118]   A further difference is that according to the same provision gifts made to lineal relatives are not included in the calculation of the initial assets (but see article 10(3) on valuation in certain cases).

[119]   See e.g. Bundesgerichtshof NJW 1974, 137, and in the recent reforms it was decided not to address this issue/change the law, cf. EU Directorate-General for Internal Policies (n 102) 12.

[120]   Becker (n 102) 112; Klippstein (n 102) 514.

[121]   EU Directorate-General for Internal Policies (n 102) 12.

2.5   Principles of European Family Law Regarding Property Relations between Spouses

In 2013, the Commission on European Family Law (CEFL)[122] published its 'Principles of European Family Law Regarding Property Relations between Spouses'.[123] Like the earlier CEFL Principles, they are based on extensive comparative research and discussion amongst the national experts, particularly the members of the Organising Committee. Unlike previous Principles, and perhaps necessitated by the subject matter, the Principles do not merely offer one but actually two options[124] for matrimonial property regimes:[125] a participation in acquisitions (Principles 4:16–4:32) and a community of acquisitions (Principles 4:33–4:58). Both regimes are subject to the same rules on the General Rights and Duties of the Spouses (Principles 4:1–4:9)[126] and Marital Property Agreements (4:10–4:15). But, importantly, these rules have to be seen in

---

[122]   On the commission, its working method and the Principles in general see Katharina Boele-Woelki, chapter 6 in Volume I of this book set and www.ceflon line.net (Accessed 12 July 2015) where the national reports and the Principles (with translations into French, German, Spanish, Swedish and Dutch can be accessed).

[123]   K Boele-Woelki, F Ferrand C González Beilfuss, M Jänterä-Jareborg, N Lowe, D Martiny and W Pintens, *Principles of European Family Law Regarding Property Relations Between Spouses* (European Family Law No 31, Intersentia 2013). On these Principles see especially K Boele-Woelki and M Jänterä-Jareborg, 'Initial Results of the CEFL in the Field of Property Relations between Spouses', in K Boele-Woelki, J Miles and JM Scherpe (eds), *The Future of Family Property in Europe* (European Family Law No 29, Intersentia 2011) 47–62; K Boele-Woelki, 'General Rights and Duties in the CEFL Principles on Property Relations Between Spouses', in K Boele-Woelki, N Dethloff and W Gephart (eds), *Family Law and Culture – Developments, Challenges and Opportunities* (European Family Law No 35, Intersentia 2014) 3–12; N Lowe, 'Marital Property Agreements', in Boele-Woelki, Dethloff and Gephart (this note), 13–23; D. Martiny, 'The Participation in Acquisitions Regime', in Boele-Woelki, Dethloff and Gephart (this note), 25–35; F Ferrand, 'The CEFL Principles of European Family Law Regarding Property Relations Between Spouses – Community of Acquisitions', in Boele-Woelki, Dethloff and Gephart (this note), 37–61.

[124]   So neither regime is considered a 'default' one, cf. Boele-Woelki et al, *Principles* (n 123), Introduction, 26.

[125]   For the reasons for doing so see Boele-Woelki et al, *Principles* (n 123), Introduction, 24–7.

[126]   Comparable to the *régime primaire* in France and related jurisdictions and the German *allgemeine Ehewirkungen*. Cf. Boele-Woelki et al, *Principles* (n 123), Introduction, 16 and Boele-Woelki, 'General Rights and Duties' (n 123) 12.

conjunction with the other remedies available to a spouse in case of divorce, which are not dealt with by the Principles discussed here, including maintenance,[127] pension rights and so on. In that sense, the Principles only deal with one aspect of the financial consequences of divorce.

It is interesting to note at the outset that both matrimonial property regimes offered by the Principles expressly exclude from the sharing pool upon divorce property acquired (and debts incurred) before the marriage, as well as gifts or inheritances received during the marriage (Principles 4:19 and 4:36). This is an expression of a 'modern' view of marriage, where only 'marital contribution justifies marital solidarity', one of the cornerstones of the Principles.[128]

2.5.1 General rights and duties

The 'general part' of the Principles establishes the general equality of the spouses with regard to rights and duties (4:1–4:4). In line with the law in most European jurisdictions and the optional matrimonial property regime established by the Franco-German Agreement (above 2.4), the Principles also provide a strong protection for the family home. This protection is outside the matrimonial property regime as such; it is achieved not by subjecting it to the sharing exercise, but instead by limiting each spouses' ability to dispose of the family home (or to terminate or modify any lease of it) without the other spouse's consent (Principles 4:5–4:6). The general part also establishes spousal duties to inform each other about their assets and debts (Principle 4:8) and provides that spouses are free to enter agreements determining their marital property relations (Principles 4:9–4:15).

---

[127] On which there are separate Principles (2:1–2:10): K Boele-Woelki, F Ferrand, C González Beilfuss, M Jänterä-Jareborg, N Lowe, D Martiny and W Pintens, *Principles of European Family Law Regarding Divorce and Mainten-ance Between Former Spouses* (European Family Law Series No 7, Intersentia 2004), and K Boele-Woelki and D Martiny, 'Prinzipien zum Europäischen Familienrecht betreffend Ehescheidung und nachehelicher Unterhalt', ZEuP 2006, 6–20.

[128] See Boele-Woelki et al, *Principles* (n 123), Introduction, 27 and Boele-Woelki, 'Ziele und Wertvorstellungen der CEFL min ihren Prinzipien zum Europäischen Familienrecht', in A Verbeke, J Scherpe, C Declerck, T Helms and P. Senaeve (eds), *Confronting the Frontiers of Family and Succession Law – Liber Amicorum Walter Pintens* (Intersentia 2012) 167–85 and chapter 6 in Volume I of this book set by the same author; see also Martiny (n 123) 27 f.

2.5.2   The participation in acquisitions regime

The first regime offered by the Principles is that of a participation of acquisitions (Principles 4:16–4:32). The CEFL chose the term 'acquisitions' rather than 'acquest', but in substance the regime is based on the same principles as the Swiss default regime described above (2.2.2.2): a separation of property during the marriage and a participation in the acquisitions/acquest in case of divorce. So, during marriage there are four different groups of property: the acquisitions of each spouse and the 'reserved property' of each spouse.[129] While the participation of acquisitions regime is not one of the most common matrimonial property regimes in Europe, in many ways it reflects modern views on marriage adopted by those jurisdictions where separation of property is the default position.[130] The underlying policy is that by having separate property each spouse in principle is independent, has an incentive to be 'gainfully active' and has a duty to contribute equally to the welfare of the family. This is deemed by many (despite criticism) to promote self-sufficiency, autonomy and gender equality.[131] However, in order to ensure the 'necessary inter-spousal solidarity', the marital acquisitions/acquest in principle is to be shared equally in case of divorce (Principle 4:31).[132] The regime expressly recognises both spouses' contributions to the acquisitions, and provides for monetary compensation for such contributions in case of divorce (Principle 4:28).

Acquisitions are defined in Principle 4:18(1) to comprise all assets acquired during the marriage other than reserved property, and expressly include:

(a)   each spouse's income and gains whether derived from earnings or property;
(b)   assets acquired by means of either spouse's income or gains.

Hence it does not matter how the assets were acquired (unless the property/method of acquisition falls into one of the reserved property-categories), and – crucially – income derived from reserved property is

---

[129]   The latter is the functional equivalent of separate or personal (or 'non-matrimonial') property as described above, cf. Martiny (n 123) 28.
[130]   Cf. Martiny (n 123) 27.
[131]   Boele-Woelki et al, *Principles* (n 123) 147 f. and Boele-Woleki and Jänterä-Jareborg (n 122) 57.
[132]   The exact wording of Principle 4:31(1) is: 'If one spouse's net acquisitions exceed the value of that of the other, the latter participates in the surplus to the amount of one half.'

treated as an acquisition.[133] This is not the position taken by all jurisdictions with comparable regimes, but was deemed to be the 'better law' by the CEFL.[134] Importantly, pure value increases due to market fluctuations of 'reserved' (that is, separate/non-matrimonial) property are not included as an acquisition. But value increases that are the result of an 'investment' of the other spouse and so on[135] are included, which is clarified by Principle 4:19(e). Therefore the property to be shared is narrower than in the German default regime or the optional Franco-German regime.[136]

Reserved property is defined in Principle 4:19 as follows:

(a) assets acquired before the commencement of the regime;
(b) gifts, inheritances and bequests acquired during the regime;
(c) assets substituting reserved property;
(d) assets that are personal in nature;
(e) assets exclusively acquired for a spouse's profession;
(f) increases in value of the property included in (a) to (e)

In line with the Franco-German optional regime, but unlike the German default regime, assets that are personal in nature include damages received for pain and suffering.[137] The burden of proof that property falls into the 'reserved' category' rests on the spouse claiming such property, cf. Principle 4:18(2).

As already mentioned above, the marital acquisitions/acquest is in principle to be shared equally on divorce under Principle 4:31. However – and this is a novelty for most continental European jurisdictions – Principle 4:32 allows the competent authority to make an adjustment from equal shares in cases of 'exceptional hardship'. This implies that no deviation from equal sharing will be made in cases of merely 'ordinary hardship' – but one must of course keep in mind that there are other mechanisms in place (particularly maintenance payments) that may address such hardships. The Principles envisage that such an 'exceptional hardship' will arise if the marriage was 'extremely short' or in case of

---

[133] See Comment 2 to Principle 4:18 in Boele-Woelki et al, *Principles* (n 123) 154.

[134] Ibid.

[135] Comment 3 to Principle 4:18 in Boele-Woelki et al, *Principles* (n 123) 154 f.

[136] Comment 4 to Principle 4:18 in Boele-Woelki et al, *Principles* (n 123) 155.

[137] Comment 5 to Principle 4:19 in Boele-Woelki et al, *Principles* (n 123) 160.

'patrimonial damage based on extreme unfair behaviour of the other party'.[138] This is not particularly enlightening, but the commentary adds that the 'behaviour' exception to equal sharing is meant to be of very limited importance in practice.[139] Thus the exception is probably comparable to the German § 1381 BGB, where relying on behaviour of the other spouse rarely succeeds (successful examples include such extremes as attempts to kill the other spouse!).[140] Nevertheless, it is remarkable that the CEFL has allowed for an element of discretion regarding the property division, which, while present in the Nordic jurisdictions and Austria, is generally associated with common law jurisdictions and so jurisdictions without a matrimonial property regime as such.

2.5.3   The community of acquisitions regime

The other regime offered by the Principles is a community of acquisitions (Principles 4:33–4:58). The CEFL opted for the term 'community of acquisitions', but the term 'community of acquests' is commonly used to describe this type of matrimonial property regime, which is the prevalent regime in Europe and described above at 2.1.2. In essence, this regime is a limited community of property, namely a community limited to the marital acquest/acquisitions.[141] It creates community property for these assets from the day of the marriage and so is deemed to be appropriate particularly where there is economic inequality between the spouses, for example given their income, their financial situation and their access to employment, or when the spouses have organised their marriage such that one of them is employed full-time while the other is a homemaker or only working part-time.[142] The marital solidarity, it is argued, is immediate because the assets are shared from the very beginning of the marriage and not merely on divorce.[143] However, since the CEFL also wanted its Principles to also strike a balance between solidarity and each spouses' independence and self-sufficiency, the assets comprised by the community are somewhat more restricted than in most existing community of

---

[138]   Comment 2 to Principle 4:32 in Boele-Woelki et al, *Principles* (n 123) 216.

[139]   Ibid and Martiny (n 123) 35; Ferrand (n 123) 60.

[140]   See above n 35.

[141]   Ferrand (n 123) 38; Comment 2 to Principle 4:33 in Boele-Woelki et al, *Principles* (n 123) 220.

[142]   Ferrand (n 123) 39 f.

[143]   Ibid. See also Pintens (n 18) 42.

acquests/acquisitions regimes. The second regime offered by the Principles therefore is considered a 'modernised' version of these regimes.[144] This is particularly evident in the possibility given to the competent authority (usually the court) of deviating from equal sharing of the community property in cases of 'exceptional hardship' in Principle 4:57 (similar to Principle 4:32 discussed above). As already pointed out above, this element of discretion is alien to most[145] jurisdictions based on a community of acquest and so is a true innovation for this type of regime.

The community property is defined in Principles 4:34(2) and 4:35(1) to comprise everything acquired during the marriage which is not the 'personal property' of the spouses, and according to Principle 4:35(2) includes in particular:

(a) the spouses' income and gains whether derived from earnings, community property or personal property;
(b) assets acquired either jointly or individually by the spouses during the community of acquisitions by means of the spouses' income and gains;
(c) gifts and bequests to both spouses or to one spouse on the condition that they belong to community property.

As in the participation of acquisitions offered by the Principles, income deriving from 'personal property' is deemed to be part of the community property. This is not the norm among the existing regimes of a community of acquests/acquisitions, but was held by the CEFL to be the 'better law'.[146]

'Personal property' is then defined in Principle 4:36 as follows:

(a) assets acquired before entering into the community of acquisitions;
(b) gifts, inheritances and bequests acquired during the regime;
(c) assets acquired through substitution, investment or reinvestment in accordance with Principles 4:37 and 4:38;
(d) assets personal in nature, acquired during the regime;
(e) assets exclusively acquired for a spouse's profession.

Although it appears that the Comments on this Principle do not take a position on whether assets received as compensation for pain and

---

[144] Ferrand (n 123) 40 f.
[145] But not all: Poland and Serbia allow for a limited discretion, but apparently, in practice, the courts do not very often depart from equal sharing, see Pintens (n 18) 26.
[146] Cf. Ferrand (n 123) 44 and Boele-Woelki et al, *Principles* (n 123) 227.

suffering are personal and so leaves this to the national laws to define,[147] surely the 'better law' would have been to include them in the personal property, as is the case under Principle 4:19.[148] This would also have provided for greater consistency between the two optional regimes offered by the Principles.

Given that there is a community of property during the marriage, there must also be appropriate rules on debts[149] reflecting this position (Principles 4:40–4:43), which are necessarily more complicated than those for the other regime offered by CEFL (Principles 4:21 and 4:22). Under those Principles, the debts are allocated as either community debts (Principle 4:40, including in particular debts incurred for the maintenance of the children or to meet appropriate family needs, but also debts related to a spouse's professional activity) or personal debts (Principle 4:41). The recovery of community debts in Principle 4:42 is straightforward (from the community property and the personal property of the spouse who incurred the debt), but the recovery of personal debts in Principle 4:43 is more complex. Often perceived as a weakness of community of property regimes, there is the potential danger that the personal debts of one spouse might be borne by the other, at least in part, if they are recoverable from the community property. Therefore the CEFL opted for a 'better law' approach[150] by limiting recovery to certain community assets in Principle 4:43:

(1) Debts which are personal to one spouse can be recovered from
    (a) the debtor spouse's personal property;
    (b) the debtor spouse's income and gains;
    (c) the community assets to the extent of their merger with the debtor spouse's personal property.
(2) Personal debts related to tort or crime can also be recovered from half of the net value of the community property where the debtor spouse's personal property, income and gains are insufficient for recovery.

---

[147]   Comment 6 to Principle 4:36 in Boele-Woelki et al, *Principles* (n 123) 236.

[148]   See above and Comment 5 to Principle 4:19 in Boele-Woelki et al, Principles (n 123) 160.

[149]   See also the rules on administration of the property contained in Principles 4:44–4:48 which are not discussed here, but see Ferrand (n 123) 51–5.

[150]   Comment 1 to Principle 4:43 in Boele-Woelki et al, *Principles* (n 123) 271; Ferrand (n 123) 50.

Although no actual hierarchy is imposed, this Principle first favours recovery from the property of the debtor's spouse,[151] but also that spouse's income and gains which would otherwise become community property. Recovery from community property is only possible where the personal assets have been merged with those of the other spouse (for example, in a bank account), and only to the extent they have been merged. The only exception is in the case of personal debts related to a tort or crime: here it was decided that the victim should not bear the consequences of insufficient funds of the debtor's (that is, tortfeasor's/criminal's) personal property, income and gains.[152]

Apart from the element of discretion in Principle 4:57(2) mentioned above, the Principles offer no surprises regarding the division of assets on divorce: the basic principle is one of equal sharing of the community property (Principle 4:57(1)), with the possibility of allowing the competent authority to allocate specific assets – namely the family home and household goods and professional assets (Principle 4:56) – to one of the spouses in the interest of the family (without deviating from allocating equal shares).

2.6   Comparison – A Quest for Fairness?

2.6.1   Comparing the incomparable?

Sections 2.2–2.5 above have shown some key distinguishing features of the financial consequences of divorce which might be perceived as fundamental and unbridgeable differences:

- the fact that in some jurisdictions a form of community of property is created upon marriage whereas, in other jurisdictions, marriage as such does not change the property relations of the spouses;
- the fact that in some jurisdictions the financial consequences are fully discretionary, whereas in others there is no, or only limited, discretion with regard to the division of property; and
- the fact that the common law jurisdictions do not even have a matrimonial property regime as such but take a holistic view of all the financial consequences of divorce, whereas the civil law jurisdictions tend to separate those consequences into different, independent remedies.

---

[151]   Ferrand (n 123) p. 50; Comment 4 to Principle 4:43 in Boele-Woelki et al, *Principles* (n 123) 270.

[152]   Ferrand (n 123) 50.

These differences, at least at first glance, appear to be so fundamental that a meaningful comparison seems impossible. This certainly is true if one attempts to compare the details of the financial consequences of divorce. However, if one tries to see a broader picture and identify the underlying policies, the differences perhaps are not as great and insurmountable as they first appear.[153]

It is often argued by common law lawyers that their jurisdictions take a holistic and discretionary approach to the financial consequences of divorce because this is the best (or even the only) way to achieve a fair outcome for all situations.[154] While there might be some truth in this argument, it also implies that all regimes which actually operate with rigid or at least firmer rules therefore must come to 'unfair' outcomes. However, it is safe to assume that all jurisdictions actually aim to achieve fair outcomes, as it is difficult to imagine a jurisdiction which is content with a system that consistently generates unfairness or inequity. So if one assumes that all jurisdictions achieve (or at least aim to achieve) fair outcomes, then this is what all jurisdictions have in common. Taking this as a starting point, one then has two basic issues to compare: the methods for achieving a fair outcome and what is perceived as 'fair' in the respective jurisdictions.

2.6.2 Different paths to fairness

2.6.2.1 Different views on equality and fairness   There appears to be a divide in continental Europe (and indeed even amongst the members of the Commission on European Family Law) on whether a matrimonial property regime based on a community of property or on a separation of property is preferable to create 'fair' outcomes and also to create, or support, a partnership of equals. As already mentioned above, this is an ideological debate based on certain conceptions of marriage.[155] Community property systems create a pool of joint property from the very beginning and throughout the marriage; both spouses immediately acquire property rights. Thus it has been said that this ensures equality,

---

[153]   For a more detailed comparison see Scherpe (n 8) as well as J Miles and JM Scherpe, 'The Legal Consequences of Dissolution: Property and Financial Support between Spouses', in J Eekelaar and R George (eds), *Routledge Handbook of Family Law and Policy* (Routledge 2014) 138–52.

[154]   Although it is debatable whether this is actually achieved in these jurisdictions, given the unfortunate combination of legal uncertainty (as a necessary result of the basic discretion of the courts) and very high legal costs; cf. Miles and Scherpe (n 153) 142.

[155]   On this point see Scherpe (n 8) 474 f.

particularly for more 'traditional' marriages where only one of the spouses is generating an income or enjoys a significantly higher income.[156] On the other hand, a system based on a separation of property merely delays access to (usually) the very same assets until the divorce by stipulating participation rights. However, during the marriage no mandatory sharing takes place, thus promoting the independence of the spouses[157] and, in that sense, promoting equality – albeit, perhaps, a different kind of equality.

Thus which system is 'fairer' depends on one's views on marriage, and indeed on whether equality (and which kind of equality) is an element of 'fairness', but also on the lived reality of the marriage in question. As I have written elsewhere:[158]

> If equality primarily means that no distinction should be made between breadwinner and homemaker and that this should manifest itself during marriage through property ownership, then the community of property systems would be the better choice. If equality is seen as full autonomy of the spouses, and the partnership is seen as one of independents, the separation of property system seems appropriate where the objective of non-discrimination between breadwinner and homemaker is realised at divorce.

> It appears, therefore, that the policy message sent by the two systems is a very different one: the separation of property promotes a model of financially independent spouses with a safety net in case of divorce; the community of property system, it could be argued, promotes a model that better enables the spouses to choose to forgo financial independence to focus on the family, should they so wish.

However, as fundamental as these ideological differences seem to be (indeed, they have led the Commission on European Family Law to present two optional regimes in their Principles), the real practical differences might actually be minor. In an ongoing and well-functioning relationship, it presumably does not matter, at least most of the time, who owns what as the couple share their assets. Therefore the ideology-based views on which model better promotes independence and so on might actually not pass the reality test. For example, it would be difficult to argue that French women are, on the whole, less independent and 'less

---

[156] A Röthel, 'Die Zugewinngemeinschaft als europäisches Modell?' in V Lipp, E Schumann and B Veit (eds), *Die Zugewinngemeinschaft als europäisches Modell?* (Göttinger Juristische Reihe 2009) 66; Pintens (n 18) 42; Pintens (n 20) 279 ff.

[157] Pintens (n 18) 43; Pintens (n 20) 279 ff.

[158] Scherpe (n 8) 475.

equal' than their German counterparts. The higher labour market participation rates in France actually seem to suggest the opposite. In any event,
where the matrimonial property regime matters most is when the
relationship ends. Here, independent of which matrimonial property
regime governs the property relations of the spouses, if the parties are at
loggerheads it presumably requires the intervention of the court to secure
the property rights/compensation claims of the spouses in both systems.
So while admittedly claims *in rem* as the result of a community of
property might potentially be procedurally easier to pursue, the differences in practice might not be as fundamental as the (perceived) ideology
behind them suggests.

2.6.2.2 Discretion as a means to an end Each family is different. Each
divorce is different. Any system with fully fixed rules regarding the
financial consequences of divorce inevitably would create unfair outcomes. That is the reason why the common law jurisdictions have opted
for a fully discretionary system, at the expense of legal certainty, so that
every possible family situation can be resolved fairly. But that is also the
reason why all continental jurisdictions have incorporated elements of
discretion into their system for the financial consequences of divorce.
While only some jurisdictions (for example, the Nordic countries and
Austria) allow for a discretionary element with regard to sharing according to the matrimonial property regime, all jurisdictions allow for
discretion with regard to most other financial consequences of divorce,
most importantly maintenance payments and *prestation compensatoire/
pension compensatoria*. Hence the continental European jurisdictions
decided to prioritise certainty with regard to property ownership but at
the same time have ensured that potential hardships/unfair outcomes of
the property division could be compensated for (or at least mitigated by)
other discretionary remedies. Nevertheless, the underlying assumption of
the matrimonial property regimes is that, for the vast majority of spouses,
they create fair outcomes. It is also worth noting at this point that couples
for whom the 'default' matrimonial property regime might be inappropriate generally have the option of choosing a different property regime by
marital agreement (on which see 3 below). It is further worth noting that
the Principles drafted by the Commission on European Family Law
expressly include the possibility of adjusting the outcome of the division
of property in cases of 'exceptional hardship' (Principles 4:15 and 4:57).
While this cannot be regarded as the 'common core' of the European
jurisdictions, it was felt to be necessary to have a 'safety valve' for
exceptional cases.

2.6.2.3   Holistic view or separate remedies   The continental European jurisdictions all separate the financial consequences into different remedies, of which the division of the matrimonial property is often most central. However, sharing of pension rights, spousal maintenance, compensatory capital adjustments (such as the French *prestation compensatoire* or the Spanish *pension compensatoria*) or allocation of usage of the family home can be of equal importance. While treated and decided upon separately, together these different 'pillars' are meant to provide for a fair outcome.[159]

By contrast, the common law jurisdictions do not separate out these 'pillars' but take a 'holistic view' and deliver one 'tailor-made package' of financial consequences of divorce, which may (or may not) contain the different remedies available under the 'pillar' approach.[160] The courts are given an extensive 'tool box' of remedies by statute but they are left to exercise their own discretion as to which of the tools to use.[161]

The difference, therefore, is arguably only that the civil law jurisdictions mandate the courts to at least consider all of the remedies,[162] and in some areas (such as the division of property) orders have to be made, whereas in the European common law jurisdictions, the courts are at liberty not to do so and thus have greater flexibility. Nevertheless, the ultimate aim of both approaches remains a fair outcome, but any comparison of course needs to look at all the remedies together. It is also important to note that, as pointed out in the previous section, discretionary elements are found in all jurisdictions, although admittedly to varying degrees. And it is these discretionary elements that ensure that each system has the means to ensure fair outcomes.

2.6.3   Similar perceptions of fairness

'Fairness' of course is an elusive and ultimately subjective concept, and not only very likely to be different from jurisdiction to jurisdiction (and indeed from person to person) but also subject to change over time when the social realities of marriage change.[163] However, while societal changes within the European jurisdictions might not happen concurrently, there are certain general trends that can be observed, many of which are commented on in the different chapters of this book and that need not be

---

[159]   See references in n 7 above.

[160]   For a comparative discussion see Scherpe (n 8) 475 ff.

[161]   Miles and Scherpe (n 153) 141.

[162]   As of course, for example, maintenance payments or *prestation compensatoire/pension compensatoria* will only be ordered where appropriate.

[163]   Miles and Scherpe (n 153) 142.

iterated here, such as the general equality of spouses, the rise of the number of children born outside of marriage and the number of cohabiting couples and so on. Recognising the existence of these common trends, it is not unlikely that they will also find an expression in the law governing the financial consequences of divorce and particularly what is perceived to be 'fair' in the relevant jurisdiction.

In England and Wales, the House of Lords in *Miller v Miller; McFarlane v McFarlane*[164] expressly sought to bring greater clarity to the very abstract concept of 'fairness' and identified three 'strands' of fairness in the context of the financial consequences of divorce, namely sharing, needs and compensation.[165] These indeed appear to be the policies underpinning the financial consequences of divorce in all jurisdictions, albeit admittedly to varying degrees and with varying emphasis, and therefore they are now looked at in turn.

2.6.3.1 Sharing   Marriage – at least in law – in Europe is perceived to be a union of equals, where the couple share their lives and take responsibility for each other. Despite rising divorce rates, the underlying assumption remains that marriage is a union for life. However, all jurisdictions have rules on the financial (and other) consequences of divorce, as described above, to deal with the fact that the shared life might come to an end – and that the lives need to be divided and the assets shared.

'Sharing' is a hollow concept unless it is made clear what must be shared. In this regard, a number of common features can be observed,

---

[164]   *Miller v Miller; McFarlane v McFarlane* [2006] UKHL 24.

[165]   Arguably doing so after having noted New Zealand legislation and influenced by J Miles, 'Principle of Pragmatism in Ancillary Relief: The Virtues of Flirting with Academic Theories and Other Jurisdictions' (2005) 19 *International Journal of Law, Policy and the Family* 242–56, although neither New Zealand legislation nor Miles' article were expressly referred to in the judgment. But Miles' article was cited by Potter P (in a judgment given for the court which also comprised Thorpe LJ and Wilson LJ) in the influential case of *Charman v Charman* [2007] EWCA Civ 503 at [118] where Potter P in a (most unusual) postscript entitled 'Changing the Law' also draws attention to the fact that Counsel for Mr Charman, Singleton QC, had incorporated the article in his submission for Mrs McFarlane in the House of Lords. Potter P for the court also states here: 'The article is particularly interesting in that it demonstrates that the principles discussed in the article (needs, entitlement and compensation), were subsequently the principles identified by the House of Lords in deciding the conjoined appeals of *Miller* and *McFarlane*.' Potter P then also expressly refers to the discussion of New Zealand legislation in the article in [119].

namely that it appears to be the general view in Europe (with the notable exception of the Netherlands) that it is only the 'fruits of joint labour' that should be shared. Therefore, in almost all jurisdictions and in the CEFL Principles, assets owned before the marriage or inherited or received as a gift during the marriage, are either excluded automatically from the sharing (although in some jurisdictions the family home is given special consideration, for example in England and Wales)[166] or at least subject to potential discretionary adjustment to reflect the origin of the assets. In other words, all European jurisdictions seem to have some concept of 'matrimonial property' that is to be shared, even though what is considered as such property differs from jurisdiction to jurisdiction, and, in some jurisdictions, assets can 'become' matrimonial through usage over time.

As regards the actual sharing, apart from Greece (and some of the Spanish regional laws) the principle of equal sharing of the matrimonial assets is embedded in all European jurisdictions. Marriage is perceived as a partnership of equals, with both spouses assumed to be contributing equally to the welfare of the family, resulting in equal shares of the 'fruits of joint labour' should the relationship come to an end. So Greece, with its rebuttable presumption that a spouse has contributed one-third to the assets of the other spouse and is thus in principle only entitled to that share, stands virtually alone among the nations of Europe in not embracing the principle of equal sharing.

2.6.3.2 Need   Another policy that the European laws have in common is that the needs of the spouses play an important role. Unsurprisingly, the views on what constitutes 'needs' and how they should be covered differ,[167] but there is a consensus that needs ought to be covered. Not in all jurisdictions is this achieved through the law governing the financial consequences of divorce. In the Nordic Countries, for instance, and Sweden in particular, the understanding is that an ex-spouse is not responsible for the needs of his or her former spouse, but that providing for its citizens is the duty of the state. Hence maintenance, which in most jurisdictions plays a pivotal role in covering the needs of the spouses at

---

[166]   Miles and Scherpe (n 90).

[167]   See e.g. for England and Wales the report by the Law Commission (n 76). For a 'clash of cultures' regarding needs see A Dutta and JM Scherpe, 'Cross-Border Enforcement of English Ancillary Relief Orders: Fog in the Channel: Europe Cut Off?' [2010] *Family Law* 386–91, discussing a decision by the German Bundesgerichtshof *FamRZ* 2009, 1659 = *MDR* 2009, 1225 = *NJW-RR* 2010, 1. See generally Miles and Scherpe (n 153) 144–7.

least for a certain period of time (and thus 'compensating' for the hardships of the inflexible division of property) is rarely awarded in Sweden and the other Nordic Countries.[168] While this perhaps is at the extreme end of the spectrum, a general trend can be observed that the former spouse no longer is 'an insurer for all losses' and marriage no longer a 'meal-ticket for life',[169] as more and more European jurisdictions move towards time limiting spousal maintenance claims.[170] This reflects and promotes the view that marriage is, in principle, a union of two independent persons and that such independence is what the individuals concerned should strive for when the union comes to an end. Nevertheless, there is, of course, recognition of the spouses' inevitable – and indeed desirable – interdependencies during marriage, dealt with in the next section.

2.6.3.3 Compensation The final 'strand' of fairness is that of 'compensation', the underlying policy being that if one spouse makes sacrifices for the marriage/family, and thus incurs what might be called 'relationship-generated losses', this should be compensated for to a certain extent by the other spouse when the relationship comes to an end. Throughout Europe, such 'investments' in the family are considered to be beneficial for society, and without legal (and indeed financial) recognition there would be a disincentive to make such sacrifices for the family. However, not only determining what, if anything, should be compensated for, but also how this compensation should be quantified remains a difficult issue which is usually side-stepped by subsuming compensation considerations into sharing or needs. In most jurisdictions the division of property is already to a certain extent meant to incorporate elements of compensation in the property sharing exercise, particularly where a matrimonial property regime prescribes equal sharing (which of

---

[168] Cf. Scherpe (n 31) 233 ff; Jänterä-Jareborg (n 31) 377 ff.; S Schwarz and JM Scherpe, 'Nachehelicher Unterhalt im internationalen Privatrecht – Überlegungen zur Reformbedürftigkeit des Art. 8 des Haager Unterhaltsübereinkommens von 1973 anhand eines Beispiels aus dem deutsch-schwedischen Rechtsverkehr', *Zeitschrift für das gesamte Familienrecht (FamRZ)* 2004, 665–76.

[169] Miles and Scherpe (n 153) 146. See also the seminal article on this matter by I Ellman, 'The Theory of Alimony' (1989) 77 *California Law Review* 1–82, who also is the Chief Reporter for the American Law Institute's Principles of the Law of Family Dissolution (American Law Institute 2002).

[170] E.g. Germany and the Netherlands, on which see the national report on Germany by Martiny, chapter 4 in Volume II of this book set; Dutta (n 7) 164 ff, 179 ff; and Boele-Woelki and Braat (n 11) 243.

course is almost all European jurisdictions). In many jurisdictions there are additional compensatory mechanisms, such as the French *prestation compensatoire* or Spanish *pension compensatoria*, and maintenance or other periodical payments also contain an element of compensation.[171] Even in England and Wales, compensation is usually dealt with as part of 'needs, generously interpreted' or subsumed in the sharing.[172] So even if 'compensation' does not make an overt appearance in the express reasoning in many cases or statutes, it nevertheless is a strong rationale underpinning the financial consequences of divorce in Europe, including the matrimonial property regimes where they exist.

3. MARITAL AGREEMENTS

3.1 General Remarks

3.1.1 Terminology
After having looked at the 'default regimes', this chapter now turns to 'marital agreements', meaning an agreement or contract between the spouses by which they seek to regulate their property and other financial relationships,[173] often by selecting a different matrimonial property regime. Depending on the substance of the agreement, such agreements are often also referred to as 'matrimonial property agreements' (if just dealing with property) or 'maintenance agreements' (which nominally only deal with maintenance, although that may well also include some form of property allocation). Terminology-based distinctions can also be grounded on the point in time when the agreement was entered into, namely pre-nuptial or post-nuptial agreements. Finally, some jurisdictions give special consideration to agreements concluded at a point in time when the couple have already decided that they want to divorce and enter into an agreements regarding the financial consequences of divorce (referred to, perhaps somewhat confusingly, as 'separation agreements' in

---

[171] See generally Miles and Scherpe (n 153) 147–9.

[172] See e.g. *Charman v. Charman* [2007] EWCA Civ 503 at [76] and *VB v JP* [2008] EWHC 112 (Fam). But see also *Lauder v Lauder* [2007] EWHC 1227 (Fam) where consideration of compensation led to a higher claim.

[173] On such agreements see esp. Dethloff (n 107) and Scherpe (n 8). For an interesting collection of nine national reports on international marital agreements written by practitioners see D Salter, C Butruille-Cardew, N Francis and Stephen Grant, *International Pre-Nuptial and Post-Nuptial Agreements* (Jordan Publishing 2011).

England, or somewhat more precisely as *Scheidungsfolgenvereinbarungen* [agreements on the financial consequences of divorce] in Germany). This type of agreement is deemed to merit different treatment as the parties at that point are dealing with each other on the basis of known facts, whereas all other marital agreements are concluded some time (and sometimes even decades) before they are meant to apply (and, therefore, by necessity, involve an element of conjecture). So the factual assumptions of the parties when entering into the agreement might be wrong or the expected facts might have failed to materialise for most marital agreements, but for 'separation agreements' that is not the case as the facts are (or at least could be) known. Therefore these agreements generally are given greater weight/less scrutiny,[174] but what is said below on the legal evaluation nevertheless applies.

3.1.2   Fundamental differences in the function of marital agreements

One of the most important things to take into account when comparing marital agreements is that they apply against the background of the 'default rules'. So if the default rules stipulate some form of community of property, the effect of the agreement is immediate. The same of course is true if the default regime is one of a separation of property and the couple opts for a form of community of property (although this is very rare). This means that the function of the agreements is that they are meant not only to apply in cases of divorce but actually *during* the marriage as well. So such agreements are not, by any means, merely 'divorce agreements' but true 'marital agreements'. There may be many reasons for entering into such agreements, but one might well be to protect the other spouse from the 'negative effects' of a community of property, particularly the potential liability for the one spouse's debts. So the purpose (or at least one of the purposes) and function of the agreement in such cases is not to disadvantage or 'disenfranchise' the other spouse but rather to protect him or her. Another reason, and this applies equally to jurisdictions where a separation of property is the default position, might be that the personal and financial circumstances of the couple are such that the default regime is inappropriate for them, particularly in case of death of one of them (for example, because they have children from a previous relationship, or tax issues).

---

[174]   But oddly not in New Zealand, cf. M Briggs, 'Marital Agreements and Private Autonomy in New Zealand', in JM Scherpe (ed.), *Marital Agreements and Private Autonomy in Comparative Perspective* (Hart Publishing 2012) 256–88, esp. 277 ff and esp. *Harrison v Harrison* [2005] 2 NZLR 349 (CA).

That said, where there simply is no default regime, like in the common law jurisdictions of Europe, and all the financial consequences are at the discretion of the court, the very nature of the agreement is utterly different. As Lord Wilson has put it:

> a marital agreement which – as in a civil law country – replaces one defined outcome with another defined outcome is very different from one which – as in a common law country – replaces an undefined outcome, dependent on the future exercise of a court's discretion, with a defined outcome.[175]

The discretionary nature of the financial remedies in case of divorce also explains why marital agreements are not, and cannot be, binding on courts[176] in the common law jurisdictions. Since Parliament has decided to award the courts the discretion for these remedies, a private agreement between two parties cannot oust the jurisdiction of the courts. Therefore the 'status' and doctrinal nature of such agreements are different, although the outcomes in practice are somewhat similar when looking at the guiding principles.[177] In any event, even in common law jurisdictions, the agreements might have been concluded for estate and tax planning reasons, or having regard to the position of children from a previous relationship. Therefore, irrespective of the jurisdiction, it is essential not to pre-judge an agreement because of its content but actually to explore, as far as this is possible, the motivation for its conclusion.

The fundamental question underlying all these agreements, however, in each jurisdiction is how much freedom the parties should have to deviate from the 'default rules'. Needless to say, to a large extent, this will depend on the underlying default rules, but also on a society's view of marriage and what the inalienable, irreducible core of the marriage commitment is deemed to be.

---

[175] The Rt Hon Lord Wilson of Culworth, 'Foreword', in JM Scherpe (ed.), *Marital Agreements and Private Autonomy in Comparative Perspective* (Hart Publishing 2012) vii.

[176] In the absence of express statutory provisions to that effect, such as in Australia (on which see O Jessep, 'Marital Agreements and Private Autonomy in Australia', in JM Scherpe (ed.), *Marital Agreements and Private Autonomy in Comparative Perspective* (Hart Publishing 2012) 17–50) and New Zealand (on which see Briggs (n 174)). See also the Law Commission report (n 76).

[177] See below and Scherpe (n 8).

3.2   Legal Evaluation of Marital Agreements at the Time of Conclusion

3.2.1   Marital agreements are 'special'

A marital agreement dealing with the financial relations of the spouses is, first and foremost, to create a legal situation, legal rights and duties that are different from those that would otherwise apply, that is, the default situation. Given that in family law, and in particular the area of law concerned here, the law was created with the specific purpose to deal with the special situation of marriage and to create a legal framework that deviated from what the general law would otherwise stipulate, it might at first seem somewhat odd that a couple are allowed to 'opt out' of this protective system in the first place. Together with the perceived violation of marriage as a principally dissoluble union, this reasoning, for a long time in many jurisdictions, has led to such agreements being considered contrary to public policy.[178] While in a completely discretionary system this kind of argument might make sense (to a certain extent), it is out of place where a strict default matrimonial property regime applies. Simply put: the regime which applies by default cannot be suited for every marital relationship. Therefore the possibility and necessity for some

---

[178]   Cf. only the relatively recent legal development in England and Wales, esp. *Radmacher v Granatino* [2010] UKSC 42. On this case see e.g. J Miles, 'Marriage and Divorce in the Supreme Court and the Law Commission: for Love or Money?' [2011] 74 *Modern Law Review* 430 ff and JM Scherpe, 'Fairness, Freedom and Foreign Elements – Marital Agreements in England and Wales after Radmacher v. Granatino', [2011] *Child and Family Law Quarterly* 513–27 (translated into Spanish and published as 'Justicia, libertad y elementos extran-jeros. Los acuerdos matrimoniales en Inglaterra y Gales tras Radmacher vs Granatino', *Revista para el análisis del Derecho (InDret)* No. 2, 2012, available 12 July 2015 at http://www.indret.com/pdf/890_es.pdf) and 'Wirkung ohne Bindungswirkung – Eheverträge in England und Wales', *Zeitschrift für Euro-päisches Privatrecht (ZEuP)* 2012, 615–30 and 'Marital Agreements in England and Wales after Radmacher v Granatino – Implications for International Prac-tice', in W Pintens and C Declerck (eds), *Patrimonium 2012* (Intersentia 2012) 319–27; J Herring, PG Harris and R George, 'Ante-nuptial Agreements: Fairness, Equality and Presumptions' (2011) 127 *Law Quarterly Review* 335 ff. On the development of the law see see Miles (n 73) and 'Marital Agreements: "The More Radical Solution"', in R Probert and C Barton (eds), *Fifty Years in Family Law: Essays for Stephen Cretney* (Intersentia 2012) 93–102, N Lowe, 'Prenuptial Agreements – The Developing English Position', in A-L Verbeke, J Scherpe, C Declerck, T Helms and P Senaeve (eds), *Confronting the Frontiers of Family and Succession Law – Liber amicorum Walter Pintens* (Intersentia 2012) 867–86 and the Law Commission report (n 76).

couples to devise a matrimonial regime that better fits their needs was recognised relatively early on and relevant provisions have subsequently been included in various family law codifications.

Private agreements or contracts between the (future) spouses have been permissible in most jurisdictions for quite some time, and unsurprisingly, as a starting point, the general rules of contract law apply to these agreements. However, this in most jurisdictions is just a starting point. There is an awareness that (a) as just described, the couple contract out of a protective system (and generally to the detriment of one party who would otherwise be protected); and (b) the social situation is not necessarily one that is comparable to 'normal' contracts where the underlying assumption is that both parties have equal bargaining power and will negotiate with their own advantage in mind. In this regard, marital agreements are hardly unique. There are many situations where the laws of various jurisdictions have set up specific rules either because of a general structural inequality of the parties (for example in labour law, insurance law and consumer law) or because of the nature and importance of the transaction (for example the purchase of land or wills).

In their Principles of the Law of Family Dissolution, the American Law Institute said the following about the need for special rules for marital agreements:

> While there are good reasons to respect contracts relating to the consequences of family dissolution, the family context requires some departure from the rules that govern the commercial arena. First, the relationship between contracting parties who are married, or about to marry, is different than the usual commercial relationship in ways that matter to the law's treatment of their agreements. Persons planning to marry usually assume that they share with their intended spouse a mutual and deep concern for one another's welfare. Business people negotiating a commercial agreement do not usually have that expectation of one another ... These distinctive expectations that persons planning to marry usually have about one another can disarm their capacity for self-protective judgment, or their inclination to exercise it, as compared to parties negotiating commercial agreements. This difference justifies legal rules designed to strengthen the parties' ability and inclination to consider how a proposed agreement affects their own interest.[179]

---

[179]   American Law Institute, *Principles of the Law of Family Dissolution – Analysis and Recommendations* (American Law Institute Publishers 2002), comment c on § 7.02, 1063 et seq. See also I Mark Ellman, 'Marital Agreements and Private Autonomy in the United States', in JM Scherpe (ed.), *Marital Agreements and Private Autonomy in Comparative Perspective* (Hart Publishing 2012) 404–42.

The underlying assumption is that while there might be *nominal autonomy* by the standards of the general contract law, there might not be *actual autonomy* because of the special social situation the parties find themselves in. Somewhat paradoxically, most jurisdictions therefore have rules in place that restrict the autonomy of the parties procedurally in order to protect the actual autonomy of the parties. The most important of these rules are requirements concerning the form of the agreements and the requirement of legal advice (3.2.2 below), the disclosure of assets (3.2.3 below) and certain time requirements (3.2.4 below).

3.2.2   Formal requirements and legal advice

As for formal requirements, in civil law jurisdictions the most common requirement is that the agreement needs to be contained in a notarial deed. This has the purpose of bringing to the attention to the parties the importance of the agreement that they are about to enter and making the content of the agreement clear and easily proved. At the same time, the notary in the civil law jurisdictions is under a legal duty to provide neutral independent advice to both parties, and particularly the (future) spouse who is likely to be disadvantaged by the agreement compared to the default legal situation. This is generally regarded, rightly or wrongly, with some scepticism by lawyers from common law jurisdictions who instead require independent legal advice by different lawyers for the spouses. This is not the place to discuss the differences and advantages of the respective systems, and it suffices that there appears to be general agreement that some form of legal advice is desirable for marital agreements, unlike for most other agreements or contracts. This high-lights the fact that the law gives marital agreements special consideration.

There remains, however, a danger that the effectiveness of legal advice is overrated.[180] The parties generally suffer from what has been referred to as 'optimism bias'[181] regarding their marriage, namely that they assume that their marriage will be a success and, therefore, that the

---

[180]   See for example the Australian experience, on which see Jessep (n 176); see also B Fehlberg and B Smyth, 'Pre-Nuptial Agreements for Australia: Why Not?' (2000) 14 *Aust Jnl of Fam Law* 80–101; B Fehlberg and B Smyth, 'Binding Pre-Nuptial Agreements in Australia: The First Year' (2002) 16 *International Journal of Law, Policy and the Family* 127; O Jessep, 'Section 90G and Pt VIIIA of the Family Law Act 1975 (Cth)' (2010) 24 *Australian Journal of Family Law* 104; P Parkinson, 'Setting Aside Financial Agreements' (2001) 15 *Aust Jnl of Fam Law* 26–50.

[181]   See e.g. American Law Institute (n 179) comment b) on § 7.05, 1098; Dethloff (n 107) 87.

agreement they are about to conclude will be of little or no practical relevance.[182] While legal advice *might* help the parties (and specifically the party who is agreeing to a reduction to his or her rights on divorce) to better understand what they are doing, legal advice certainly is no guarantee that 'the message will sink in'. As I have said elsewhere,[183] even the best legal advice can never be more than *a* safeguard, but certainly never *the* safeguard.

3.2.3 Disclosure

As regards disclosure, common law lawyers often find it puzzling that there appear to be no duties to disclose assets when entering into marital agreements in many European jurisdictions. However, in this respect, one must keep in mind the default matrimonial property regimes. Most of these regimes expressly exclude pre-marital property from sharing, so there is nothing to be gained (and only costs generated) by requiring the parties to disclose such assets. That said, it generally is in the interest of the (future) spouse concerned to disclose such assets and if possible have them listed in the agreement as this can then later serve as proof that these assets indeed were pre-marital and that this was known at the time of the conclusion of the agreement. Otherwise, the burden of proof that these assets fall into the pre-marriage category attaches to the spouse benefitting from such proof, and providing that evidence might be significantly more difficult many years later when the marital agreements are eventually relied upon and/or challenged.

Several jurisdictions, notably those where the default regime is some form of community of property, require disclosure for post-nuptial agreements. This of course is due to the fact that when the spouses enter into such an agreement, there presumably has already been a phase in which some community property has been (or at least could have been) created. Post-nuptial agreements therefore essentially lead to a potential 'signing away' of existing rights and hence disclosure is a logical requirement in these situations. As for the jurisdictions without matrimonial property regimes, disclosure is a legal necessity, but (at least for England and Wales) only if the disclosure (or lack thereof) would be material to the agreement.[184] In principle all assets of the parties are

---

[182]   Although it might be of great relevance even in happy marriages for the reasons described above in section 2, as the agreement will not only apply in case of divorce but also during marriage in many jurisdictions.

[183]   Scherpe (n 8) 495.

[184]   *Radmacher v Granatino* [2010] UKSC 42 at [69]. See also Miles (n 73) and the references in n 178.

subject to the discretionary remedies of the courts. It therefore makes sense that a spouse should be informed about existing assets before entering into an agreement that (at least potentially) removes them from the pool of assets that is to be shared in case of divorce. In summary, it can be said that disclosure in all jurisdictions is required where it potentially might make a difference to the decision of at least one of the (future) spouses to enter the agreement.

3.2.4 Time requirement

Although much more common in common law jurisdictions, and almost absent in the civil law jurisdictions, Catalan law, for example, does also stipulate a rule that a pre-nuptial agreement must be entered into at least one month before the wedding.[185] While this is meant as another safeguard to ensure that a spouse is not suddenly confronted with and urged to sign an agreement shortly before the wedding, the effectiveness of such time requirements is very doubtful. The Law Commission of England and Wales when considering the issue quite rightly pointed out two main reasons against such time requirements:

> The first is a practical problem: with ceremonies commonly arranged – and deposits paid, for example, on reception venues – many months in advance, it would be hard to find an acceptable legal time limit that really addressed the issue of pressure. The second is a logical problem: any deadline for the making of prenuptial agreements simply diverts the pressure to another day. Rather than it being argued that one of the parties was compelled to sign on the day before the wedding, it could be argued with equal force that they felt compelled to sign the day before the deadline.[186]

3.3 Legal Evaluation of Marital Agreements at the Time they are Invoked

3.3.1 The substantive 'fairness challenge' to marital agreements

As pointed out at the beginning of the previous section (above 3.2), the purpose of a marital agreement is to create an outcome that differs from the outcome that otherwise would be achieved by the application of the default legal rules. While the previous section looked at certain procedural safeguards, this section deals with the substance of the agreement: when do the laws of the European jurisdictions allow the outcome of

---

[185] Ferrer-Riba (n 20) 363.

[186] Law Commission report (n 76) 109. See also the criticism of B Hooker, 'Prenuptial Contracts and Safeguards' [2001] *Family Law* 56, 57, who calls a deadline a 'mistake'.

such an (otherwise valid) agreement to stand? The answer to this
question is a reflection of the view on marriage in the respective
societies. The rules discussed in this section draw a line – a line that
cannot be crossed, a line which states clearly that there are some areas of
marital law that are not at the disposition of the parties and that will be
applied irrespective of their express agreements. In its most extreme
form– either all the default financial consequences are mandatory (as
apparently in Slovenia),[187] or none of them must apply (as apparently in
Scotland[188]). However, most jurisdictions do not hold these extreme
positions but rather place themselves somewhere in the middle – where
exactly again depends on what the view on marriage is, what is perceived
as the core of marriage out of which the parties cannot contract.

The comparison reveals certain common features in the European
jurisdictions. English law requires 'fairness' to prevail,[189] Irish law a
minimum of 'proper provision';[190] in Austria agreements can be set aside
if they are 'inequitable',[191] in Sweden if they are 'unreasonable',[192] in
Spain if they are 'seriously detrimental' to the other spouse.[193] The
Netherlands[194] and Germany[195] utilise the basic concept of an agreement
being against 'good faith' if it oversteps certain boundaries. All of these
terms can generally be summarised as expressing that, for each jurisdiction, an agreement between the spouses will be set aside if it is
'unfair' or 'unjust'. Still, all of this remains rather vague. Therefore it is
more rewarding to look at the actual circumstances in which the courts
have deemed it necessary to set aside marital agreements, and again
certain common themes emerge.

3.3.2   Fairness in marital agreements

It is unsurprising that, in considering the validity of marriage agreements,
a number of European jurisdictions look at whether there has been a
'change of circumstances'. By their very nature, marital agreements are

---

187   See the Barbara Novak, chapter 13 in Volume II of this book set, p. 272.
188   K McK Norrie 'Marital Agreements and Private Autonomy in Scotland',
in JM Scherpe (ed), *Marital Agreements and Private Autonomy in Comparative
Perspective* (Hart Publishing 2012) 289–310, esp. 301 ff.
189   Miles (n 73) and *Radmacher v Granatino* [2010] UKSC 42, esp. [75].
190   Crowley (n 95).
191   Ferrari (n 49) 64 f.
192   Jänterä-Jareborg (n 31), esp. 391 ff; Scherpe (n 31), esp. 228 ff.
193   Ferrer-Riba (n 20), esp. 363 f.
194   Boele-Woelki and Braat (n 11) 251 ff.
195   Dutta (n 7) 174 ff.

(also) regulating a (more or less) uncertain future event and may well have been concluded long before the marital breakup occurs. The factual basis on which this agreement was reached might therefore have changed completely, and assumptions about how the life of the couple develop might have been proved utterly wrong. While even in general contract law, this change can, in certain scenarios, lead to a contract being adapted or even declared void by the courts, there seems to be an even greater willingness to interfere if the agreement in question relates to marriage.

The paradigm case for a change of circumstance is the change of role in the marital relationship after the birth of a child, and many jurisdictions indeed make special reference in their legislation or case law to children and/or child care. If one of the spouses, still more often than not the woman in opposite-sex relationships, becomes the primary carer, this by necessity means that this spouse incurs certain detriments with regard to their income and ability to build up assets and a pension, and also to their career and employability in general. This is actually one of the main reasons why the default systems were set up in the way they were (as explained above, in modern times generally as a partnership of equals without regard to the role of the spouses in marriage), and hence one of the main areas where marital agreements might create outcomes which fundamentally oppose what policies in this area have historically sought to achieve.

Two jurisdictions provide a good example for this. The first is Germany with the fairly detailed 'core theory doctrine' (*Kernbereichslehre*) developed by the German Federal Court of Justice.[196] Essentially this doctrine puts all potential financial remedies on a scale and determines their 'closeness to the core of the protective scope of divorce law'. The closer to that core the remedy that the spouses agreed to contract out of or modify is, the less likely the courts are to allow that deviation to stand. According to the Federal Court of Justice, the division of matrimonial property is furthest removed from that core (and given that it is expressly regulated in the Civil Code this is not a surprise), but maintenance needs because of ongoing child care, or old age and infirmity are deemed to be closest to the core and thus, in practice, are almost impossible to contract away.

The second example is the approach developed by the UK Supreme Court for English law in the case of *Radmacher v Granatino*.[197] Building

---

[196] See Dutta (n 7) 174 ff.; JM Scherpe, 'A Comparative View of Pre-Nuptial Agreements' [2007] *International Family Law Journal* 18–23
[197] [2010] UKSC 42. See esp. [75] ff and also the references in n 178 above.

upon the three 'strands' of fairness that guide the courts' discretion when considering ancillary relief at the point of divorce (developed in the cases of *White v White*[198] and *Miller v Miller, McFarlane v McFarlane*[199]), namely 'needs', 'compensation', and 'equal sharing' the Court held:

> Of the three strands identified in *White v White* and *Miller v Miller*, it is the first two, needs and compensation, which can most readily render it unfair to hold the parties to an ante-nuptial agreement. The parties are unlikely to have intended that their ante-nuptial agreement should result, in the event of the marriage breaking up, in one partner being left in a predicament of real need, while the other enjoys a sufficiency or more, and such a result is likely to render it unfair to hold the parties to their agreement. Equally if the devotion of one partner to looking after the family and the home has left the other free to accumulate wealth, it is likely to be unfair to hold the parties to an agreement that entitles the latter to retain all that he or she has earned.

> Where, however, these considerations do not apply and each party is in a position to meet his or her needs, fairness may well not require a departure from their agreement as to the regulation of their financial affairs in the circumstances that have come to pass. Thus it is in relation to the third strand, sharing, that the court will be most likely to make an order in the terms of the nuptial agreement in place of the order that it would otherwise have made.[200]

So essentially, it is not generally possible to contract out of providing for existing needs and compensation. This is very much in line with not only the German approach just described, where spousal maintenance is meant to cover needs and compensation,[201] but also with the approach in most European jurisdictions. Where a matrimonial property regime is in place, parties may contract out of sharing assets, but not contract out of the other remedies which are meant to cover needs and compensation (although arguably often unfortunately are unsuited or insufficient to do so[202]). In many jurisdictions agreements about post-marital maintenance cannot be concluded in advance, and contracting out of the *prestation compensatoire* in France or *pension compensatoria* in Spain is not permissible either. Ensuring that the needs of the spouses are met in case of divorce and that certain disadvantages incurred are compensated appears to be the line that most of the European jurisdictions (perhaps

---

[198] *White v White* [2000] UKHL 54, [2001] AC 596.

[199] [2006] UKHL 24. On this see section 2.3 above.

[200] *Radmacher v Granatino* [2010] UKSC 42 at [81]–[82].

[201] But see the criticism by B Dauner-Lieb, 'Gütertrennung zwischen Privatautonomie und Inhaltskontrolle', 210 (2010) Archiv für die civilistische Praxis 580 ff., esp. 602 ff and Dethloff (n 107), esp. 90 ff.

[202] See references in the previous note and Scherpe (n 8) 517 f.

with Scotland being the most notable exception) draw. That therefore represents the common core of the law in Europe in this area. However, it is important to remember that while these principles might reflect the common core, the definitions and perceptions of what 'needs' are and what ought to be compensated vary greatly.[203]

3.4   Final Comparison – Protection *of* Autonomy and Protection *from* Autonomy

The commonalities and differences in approaches have been set out briefly above; space precludes a more detailed comparison.[204] What remains to be said is that the structural similarities actually extend beyond what has already been discussed above. It appears that in all European jurisdictions where marital agreements are permissible in principle, the technical approach to reviewing them is surprisingly similar and takes place in two stages.

In the first stage, the focal point is the time of the conclusion of the agreement, and in all jurisdictions certain specific formal and/or procedural requirements need to be met in order for the agreement to be able to have any legal relevance. All of these do not focus on the substance of the agreement as such; their main function is to ensure that the spouses are in a position to make an autonomous decision. This stage is about procedural rather than substantive fairness, about ensuring *actual* autonomy rather than realising the policy aims of family law in general and marriage in particular. Hence this stage could be called the 'protection *of* autonomy' stage.

The second stage only comes into play once the agreement has mastered the first hurdle and has satisfied the first stage – in other words, if the law is satisfied that the agreement actually was based on an autonomous decision of the spouses. The whole point of this stage is that the scrutiny now moves to the substance of the agreement, and therefore the court is essentially establishing whether, for policy reasons (as they are in the respective jurisdiction), it will set aside the agreement that the spouses had reached simply because of the outcome the agreement would create. It is, therefore, apt to call this stage the 'protection *from* autonomy' stage: whatever the agreement reached, for – ultimately paternalistic – general policy reasons, the courts will disregard the

---

[203]   Cf. Law Commission report (n 76).
[204]   For a more comprehensive comparison see Scherpe (n 8).

agreement in certain circumstances. This, in turn, reveals, for each jurisdiction, the inalienable core of marriage law.

4. SUMMARY – IS THERE A EUROPEAN REGIME FOR THE FINANCIAL CONSEQUENCES OF DIVORCE?

The answer to the question in the heading of this section quite clearly is a 'no' – there is no European regime for the financial consequences of divorce, although the CEFL Principles and the Franco-German Agreement on an optional matrimonial property regime might be seen as first tentative steps in that direction.[205] But what can be discerned from the comparison of the various matrimonial property regimes and functional equivalents is that there are certain common European elements.

As explained above, while the starting points and techniques used to achieve a fair financial outcome for the spouses differ fundamentally, and indeed the perceptions of what is fair are also fundamentally different, the European jurisdictions nevertheless do share *some* views on what makes an outcome fair. This shared view often is the result of similar views on marriage. Almost all European jurisdictions regard marriage as a partnership of equals, and this is reflected in some form of equal sharing of assets on divorce (the exceptions being Greece and some Spanish regional laws). There is therefore a broad European consensus that there is no room for any discrimination between the spouses based on the role they had during marriage, and that the main breadwinner (or the more financially successful spouse) should not be privileged simply because he or she managed to generate and retain more assets. Marriage is seen as a joint venture, and consequently at the end of a marriage the assets of this venture are to be shared equally (absent exceptional circumstances).

While there do, of course, remain significant differences in *exactly* which assets are to be shared, the underlying principles appear to be that only 'fruits of joint labour' are to be shared, that is, assets that have been generated by the spouses during the marriage (but not in all jurisdictions necessarily *by* the marriage; see for example the treatment of value increases of real estate in Germany). Therefore assets acquired by one of the spouses before the marriage (and obviously after the marriage) as

---

205 See also N Dethloff, Die Europäische Ehe, *StAZ* 2006, 253 and D Coester-Waltjen, 'Überlegungen zu einem europäischen Familienrecht', in C Müller-Magdeburg (ed.), *Unsere Aufgaben im 21. Jahrhundert – Festschrift für Lore Peschel-Gutzeit* (Nomos 2002) 35.

well as gifts and inheritances received during the marriage are generally excluded from the sharing exercise. Such assets are deemed to be extraneous to the marriage, and therefore not to be divided under the sharing principle should the marriage end.

A further, though less pronounced, consensus in most European jurisdictions seems to be that 'sacrifices' made for the family (the common but rather unfortunate terminology for 'undertaking family work') and resulting economic disadvantages ought to be addressed in some way. The underlying policy is that the choice to undertake family work should be incentivised and promoted to a certain extent, and that such work ought to be recognised as an important element in the financial consequences of divorce. However, there is equally a clearly discernible trend away from the 'meal ticket for life' marriage, which originated from the idea that the marital commitment was permanent and that this commitment persisted even if the marriage ended in divorce. Instead, the European jurisdictions have increasingly and explicitly turned away from this idea of marriage (and divorce) and have often limited the duration and quantum of post-marital obligations, particularly spousal maintenance. This is in line with the general acceptance of marriage as a partnership of equals and also promotes, to varying degrees, the view of the spouses as individuals rather than merely members of the marital unit – and, in principle, their autonomy. While there is an obvious tension between the policies described, this reflects the diversity of marriages in modern societies and the law's desire to accommodate all marriages.

The same can be seen in the way the jurisdictions allow – and do not allow – spouses to make their own arrangements regarding their financial relations. Most European jurisdictions allow the parties considerable freedom to enter into marital agreements and thus to opt out of the protective scheme that the default rules provide. There are, however, limits to this autonomy. The first limitation is that the European jurisdictions recognise that marital agreements concern a special social situation that merits special procedural and other safeguards in order to protect the spouses' actual autonomy. Social and other pressures, unrealistic expectations and other factors set this apart from 'normal' contractual negotiations and this is reflected in rules that aim for a protection *of* autonomy. But even where the marital agreement meets these requirements, a second layer of protection secures a protection *from* autonomy. This is the result of the view that there are certain elements of the default rules that for public policy reasons the spouses cannot contract out of. Whatever the spouses may have agreed, there are certain rights and duties that are mandatory and not at the disposition of the parties: these reflect the 'core' of marital obligations. In most European jurisdictions, this means the obligation to meet relationship-generated needs and compensation for relationship-generated disadvantages, particularly if those are the result of past or ongoing child care responsibilities.

So while there indeed is no common Europe regime for the financial consequences of divorce, there are certainly common themes and principles, and these – admittedly on a rather abstract level – constitute elements of a common European family law.

RECOMMENDATIONS FOR FURTHER READING

K Boele-Woelki, W Pintens, F Ferrand, C Gonzalez-Beilfuss, M Jänterä-Jareborg, N Lowe and D Martiny, *Principles of European Family Law Regarding Divorce and Maintenance Between Former Spouses* (Intersentia, 2004)

K Boele-Woelki, F Ferrand, C Gonzalez-Beilfuss, M Jänterä-Jareborg, N Lowe, D Martiny and W Pintens, *Principles of European Family Law Regarding Property Relations Between Spouses* (Intersentia, 2013)

K Boele-Woelki, B Braat and I Curry-Sumner (eds), European Family Law in Action. Volume IV – Property Relations Between Spouses (Intersentia 2009)

K Boele-Woelki, B Braat and I Curry-Sumner (eds), European Family Law in Action. Volume II – Maintenance Between Former Spouses (Intersentia 2003)

N Dethloff, 'Contracting in Family Law: A European Perspective', in K Boele-Woelki, J Miles and JM Scherpe (eds), *The Future of Family Property in Europe* (Antwerp, Intersentia, 2011) 65-94.

S Hofer, D Schwab and D Henrich (eds), *From Status to Contract? – Die Bedeutung des Vertrages im europäischen Familienrecht* (Bielefeld, Gieseking, 2005).

J Miles/J Scherpe, 'The legal consequences of dissolution: property and financial support between spouses', in: J Eekelaar/R George (eds.), *Routledge Handbook of Family Law and Policy* (Routledge 2014) pp. 138-152.

W Pintens, 'Ehegüterstände in Europa', *Zeitschrift für Europäisches Privatrecht (ZEuP)* 2009, 268-281.

W Pintens, 'Matrimonial Property Law in Europe', in K Boele-Woelki, J Miles and JM Scherpe (eds), *The Future of Family Property in Europe* (Antwerp, Intersentia, 2011) 19-46.

J Scherpe (ed.), *Marital Agreements and Private Autonomy in Comparative Perspective*, Hart Publishing 2012.

A Verbeke, S Cretney, F Grauers, P Malaurie, H Ofner, M Savolainen, F Skorini, G Van der Burght, 'European marital property law – Survey 1988–1994', (1995) 3 *European Review of Private Law* 445-482.

6. The child's welfare in a European perspective

Rob George*

1. INTRODUCTION

Family law in domestic legal systems across Europe gives special prominence to the welfare or best interests of children in disputes concerning their upbringing.[1] These domestic provisions receive support from the United Nations Convention on the Rights of the Child 1989, which provides that, in all actions concerning children, 'the best interests of the child shall be a primary consideration'.[2] The same language has, more recently, been used in the Charter of Fundamental Rights of the European Union.[3]

While domestic provisions often use slightly different language from these international documents, the idea that the child's welfare amounts to a special consideration in decisions regarding their upbringing is

---

* I have endeavoured to make the law as stated in this chapter up-to-date as at 17 January 2014.

[1] See, e.g., Children Act 1989, s 1(1) (England and Wales); Code Civil, article 373-2 (France); Bürgerliches Gesetzbuch, article 1671 (Germany); Civil Code, article 92 (Spain).

[2] United Nations Convention on the Rights of the Child 1989, article 3.

[3] Charter of Fundamental Rights of the European Union 2010, article 24(2).

widespread. However, despite the dominance of this welfare approach across Europe, there is a long-standing question about whether an approach to child law focused on the child's welfare is compatible with the requirements of the European Convention on Human Rights (ECHR) as interpreted by the European Court of Human Rights (ECtHR). The details will vary from jurisdiction to jurisdiction, but the widespread use of the welfare approach means that the core of the discussion is relevant across Europe. However, the question has been particularly well discussed by academics and judges in England, and so this chapter focuses on this debate as seen in the English context.

For some time, particularly in the aftermath of the implementation of the Human Rights Act 1998 in England (the Act gives the rights contained in the ECHR direct effect in English domestic law), there was a view amongst academic lawyers that the English welfare approach was inadequate from a human rights perspective.[4] However, this chapter suggests that a re-assessment of the meaning of the welfare principle in domestic law, coupled with an analysis of recent cases from the ECtHR, may call for further thought to be given to this conclusion.

2. THE RELEVANT LEGAL PROVISIONS

The focus of this chapter will be on two particular provisions of English law, coming from the Children Act 1989 and the Adoption and Children Act 2002. The former deals with both disputes between parents about children's upbringing and disputes between the state and the family about child protection matters, which English family lawyers refer to as 'private law' and 'public law' matters respectively. The Adoption and Children Act, on the other hand, applies only to adoption matters, which tend to come up as part of serious child protection matters. In all these cases, the welfare of the individual child is said to be the 'paramount consideration' in decisions concerning the child's upbringing.[5]

---

[4] While arguments to similar effect have been made in one or two cases (see, e.g., the arguments of Philip Cayford in *Payne v Payne* [2001] EWCA Civ 166, [2001] 1 FLR 1052), in general practising lawyers seem not to have favoured this line of attack.

[5] Different provisions about children's welfare apply in other contexts in English law, making welfare a consideration but not 'paramount' in the decision-making process. For example, when deciding whether to make a financial order after divorce, a court must 'have regard to all the circumstances of the case, first consideration being given to the welfare while a minor of any child of the family

Looking at these provisions in more detail, it is apparent that both Acts contain a statement about the child's welfare being the paramount consideration, although not in identical terms. The Children Act says:

> When a court determines any question with respect to –
>
> (a) the upbringing of a child ...
>
> the child's welfare shall be the court's paramount consideration.[6]

The Adoption and Children Act, by contrast, says:

> The paramount consideration of the court or adoption agency must be the child's welfare, throughout his life.[7]

Whether this difference is substantive or not is unclear. It has been held that a consideration of a child's welfare under the Children Act should focus not only on short-term questions, but should involve 'a medium-term and long-term view of the child's development'.[8] Indeed, it has been said that this assessment might, depending on the nature of the case, involve 'a judge dealing with a young child ... looking to the 22nd century'.[9] In such a case, it is hard to see that the Adoption and Children Act's instruction to consider welfare throughout the child's life would add much. The effect may be simply to make clear that adoption cases always involve life-long considerations; other decisions about children's upbringing may involve such questions, but equally may not depending on the nature of the case.[10]

In both Acts, these general statements of welfare paramountcy are then supplemented by lists of relevant considerations which decision-makers

---

who has not attained the age of eighteen': Matrimonial Causes Act 1973, s 25(1). For another example, when a trustee seeks an order relating to the exercise of the trustee's duties under s 14 of the Trusts of Land and Appointment of Trustees Act 1996, one of several matters 'to which the court is to have regard' under s 15(1) is 'the welfare of any minor who occupies or might reasonably be expected to occupy any land subject to the trust as his home'.

[6] Children Act 1989, s 1(1).

[7] Adoption and Children Act 2002, s 1(2).

[8] *Re O (Contact: Imposition of Conditions)* [1995] 2 FLR 124 (CA) at 129.

[9] *Re G (Education: Religious Upbringing)* [2012] EWCA Civ 1233, [2012] 3 FCR 524 at [26].

[10] In *Re G*, ibid, Munby LJ notes as an example that '[i]f the dispute is about whether the child should go on a school trip the judge will be concerned primarily with the present rather than the future'.

should take into account when assessing welfare.[11] The Children Act's list, in s 1(3), is known as the welfare checklist:

(a) the ascertainable wishes and feelings of the child concerned (considered in the light of his age and understanding);
(b) his physical, emotional and educational needs;
(c) the likely effect on him of any change in his circumstances;
(d) his age, sex, background and any characteristics of his which the court considers relevant;
(e) any harm which he has suffered or is at risk of suffering;
(f) how capable each of his parents, and any other person in relation to whom the court considers the question to be relevant, is of meeting his needs;
(g) the range of powers available to the court under this Act in the proceedings in question.

The list in s 1(4) of the Adoption and Children Act 2002 is in many ways similar to its Children Act counterpart:

The court or adoption agency must have regard to the following matters (among others) –

(a) the child's ascertainable wishes and feelings regarding the decision (considered in the light of the child's age and understanding),
(b) the child's particular needs,
(c) the likely effect on the child (throughout his life) of having ceased to be a member of the original family and become an adopted person,
(d) the child's age, sex, background and any of the child's characteristics which the court or agency considers relevant,
(e) any harm (within the meaning of the Children Act 1989) which the child has suffered or is at risk of suffering,
(f) the relationship which the child has with relatives, and with any other person the court or agency considers the relationship to be relevant including –
   (i) the likelihood of any such relationship continuing and the value to the child of its doing so,
   (ii) the ability and willingness of any of the child's relatives, or of any such person, to provide the child with a secure environment in which the child can develop, and otherwise to meet the child's needs,
   (iii) the wishes and feelings of the child's relatives, or of any such person, regarding the child.

---

[11] Similar lists of factors are found in other European jurisdictions: see, e.g., the French *Code Civil*, article 373-2-11.

At the European level, the key provision is in the European Convention on Human Rights and Fundamental Freedoms 1950 (ECHR), incorporated into English domestic law by the Human Rights Act 1998. Article 8 of the ECHR provides as follows:

1. Everyone has the right to respect for his private and family life, his home and his correspondence.
2. There shall be no interference by a public authority with the exercise of this right except such as is accordance with the law and is necessary in a democratic society in the interests of national security, public safety or the economic well-being of the country, for the prevention of disorder or crime, for the protection of health or morals, or for the protection of the rights and freedoms of others.

3. WELFARE AND HUMAN RIGHTS – THE ORIGINAL ANALYSIS

Much of this chapter focuses on asking whether recent developments in the jurisprudence of the ECtHR call for a reconsideration of some of the previous thinking about the inter-relationship between welfare and human rights which was seen in the English academic literature. In order to conduct such an analysis, it is necessary to have an idea of what that previous thinking was. A useful summary of the position is given by Claire Simmonds (Fenton-Glynn):

> commentators have argued [that] the approach to decision-making, the method of reasoning and potentially the result are fundamentally different under these laws. The English law requires the judge to start from the premise that the child's welfare will be the 'sole consideration' and thus will determine the outcome (*J v C* [1970] AC 688), and consider the rights of other parties only as far as they contribute to promoting the child's best interests. On the other hand, article 8 requires the judge first to evaluate the rights of the applicant (be that parent or child) to respect for family and private life, and then determine whether the infringement of this right has been in accordance with the law, pursued a legitimate aim, and was necessary in a democratic society.[12]

The English courts have long taken the view that there is no conflict between domestic law making the child's welfare 'paramount' (or

---

[12]   C Simmonds, 'Paramountcy and the ECHR: A Conflict Resolved?' [2012] *Cambridge Law Journal* 498, 498–99.

between the long-held interpretation of such provisions) and the requirements of the ECHR. For example, in *Re KD (Access: Principles)*,[13] it was
said that there was 'no inconsistency of principle' between a welfare
analysis and a rights analysis;[14] and such difference as was perceived was
'semantic only and lies only in differing ways of giving expression to [a]
single common concept'.[15] That was in the context of a child being
placed for adoption following wardship proceedings. More recently, in an
adoption case decided under the Adoption Act 1975, the House of Lords
reiterated this view:

> Under Art 8 the adoption order must meet a pressing social need and be a
> proportionate response to that need ... Inherent in both these Convention
> concepts is a balancing exercise, weighing the advantages and the disadvan-
> tages. But this balancing exercise, required by Art 8, does not differ in
> substance from the like-balancing exercise undertaken by a court when
> deciding whether, in the conventional phraseology of English law, adoption
> would be in the best interests of the child. The like considerations fall to be
> taken into account. Although the phraseology is different, the criteria to be
> applied in deciding whether an adoption order is justified under Art 8(2) lead
> to the same result as the conventional tests applied by English law. Thus,
> unless the court misdirected itself in some material respect when balancing
> the competing factors, its conclusion that an adoption order is in the best
> interests of the child, even though this would exclude the mother from the
> child's life, identifies the pressing social need for adoption (the need to
> safeguard and promote the child's welfare) and represents the court's consid-
> ered view on proportionality. That is the effect of the judge's decision in the
> present case. Article 8(2) does not call for more.[16]

In this passage, the House reflected the view taken just nine months
earlier in the Court of Appeal in a relocation case,[17] although the latter
attracted more academic attention and criticism despite – or perhaps
because of – its rather fuller engagement with the questions raised by the
ECHR.[18]

---

[13]   *Re KD (Access: Principles)* [1988] 2 FLR 139 (HL).
[14]   Ibid at 141 (Lord Templeman).
[15]   Ibid at 153 (Lord Oliver).
[16]   *Re B (Adoption: Natural Parent)* [2001] UKHL 70, [2002] 1 FLR 196 at
[31] (Lord Nicholls).
[17]   *Payne v Payne* [2001] EWCA Civ 166, [2001] 1 FLR 1052.
[18]   See, e.g., S Harris-Short, 'Family Law and the Human Rights Act 1998:
Judicial Restraint or Revolution?' [2005] *Child and Family Law Quarterly* 329; S
Choudhry and H Fenwick, 'Taking the Rights of Parents and Children Seriously:
Confronting the Welfare Principle Under the Human Rights Act' [2005] *Oxford*

In short, it is this view that was challenged by academics and, in understanding those criticisms, the work of four scholars might be thought particularly instructive. The most recent, and fullest, analysis comes from Shazia Choudhry and Jonathan Herring's 2010 book, *European Human Rights and Family Law*.[19] Two earlier works can also usefully be drawn on, in the form of articles by Sonia Harris-Short,[20] and by Choudhry and Helen Fenwick.[21] Between them, these works offer a complete and widely respected analysis of the state of the authorities and the legal arguments from first principles as they were at the times they were written.[22] It can therefore be accepted that they make the argument about the apparent conflict between welfare and human rights as well as it can be made, although only a brief summary of the argument is given here, and inevitably some of the nuance is thereby lost.

To a greater or lesser extent, these works draw on broader criticisms that are made in the common law literature of the welfare principle and the decision-making process undertaken in pursuit of welfare solutions.[23] These criticisms highlight a number of claimed deficiencies in the welfare approach, including its lack of predictability, the opaque nature

---

Journal of Legal Studies 453; J Herring and R Taylor, 'Relocating Relocation' [2006] *Child and Family Law Quarterly* 517.

[19] S Choudhry and J Herring, *European Human Rights and Family Law* (Hart Publishing 2010); see also J Herring, 'The Human Rights Act and the Welfare Principle in Family Law: Conflicting or Complementary?' [1999] *Child and Family Law Quarterly* 223; J Herring, 'Farewell Welfare?' [2005] *Journal of Social Welfare and Family Law* 159.

[20] Harris-Short (n 18); S Harris-Short, 'The Adoption and Children Act 2002, the Welfare Principle and the Human Rights Act 1998 – A Missed Opportunity' [2003] *Child and Family Law Quarterly* 119.

[21] Choudhry and Fenwick (n 18).

[22] See also J Eekelaar, *Family Law and Personal Life* (Oxford University Press 2007) 150: 'It seems certain that the interpretation given by the House of Lords to the duty to give paramount consideration to the best interests of the child when making a decision about the child's upbringing in *J v C* cannot be followed, because it allowed weight to be given to the parents' interests only to the extent that they had a bearing on those of the child. But now the standards of Article 8 will have to be applied to the interests of all parties.'

[23] The classic work was R Mnookin, 'Child-Custody Adjudication: Judicial Functions in the Face of Indeterminacy' (1975) 39 *Law and Contemporary Problems* 226, with more recent analysis by J Eekelaar, 'The Interests of the Child and the Child's Wishes: The Role of Dynamic Self-Determinism' [1994] *International Journal of Law and the Family* 42 and H Reece, 'The Paramountcy Principle: Consensus or Construct?' (1996) 49 *Current Legal Problems* 267, amongst others.

of the reasoning process, and the alleged[24] exclusion of an independent analysis of the interests of others concerned in the case because of the paramount consideration given to the child's best interests.[25] In other words, these criticisms are accepted as part of the background against which the welfare and human rights debate is conducted.

Because these criticisms of the welfare principle are accepted, the apparent differences in the analytical process called for under a human rights approach are easy to see. The human rights approach is said to call for a 'parallel analysis' of all the independently-held interests of all those affected by a decision. Each person's rights, or interests, are to be identified, assessed and weighed independently, and then the decision-maker is required to conduct an over-arching balance of all the relevant interests when making a decision.[26] Once these rights have been so analysed, the decision-maker is required to ask whether the interference is in accordance with law, is in pursuit of a legitimate aim, and is necessary in a democratic society.

It has long been clear that the interests of a child may be given some amount of priority in this process. As the ECtHR explained in *Johansen v Norway* in 1996, '[i]n carrying out this balancing exercise, the court will attach particular importance to the best interests of the child, which, depending on their nature and seriousness, may override those of the parent'.[27] However, the key point in this statement of principle for commentators was the phrase 'depending on their nature and seriousness'.[28] This point was said to demand a case-by-case assessment of the

---

[24]　For the reasons why I say 'alleged' in relation to this final criticism, see below, text from n 76.

[25]　So, for example, Choudhry and Fenwick say that under a welfare analysis, 'the welfare of the child is... the single deciding factor, that is, paramount over, and in fact displacing, all other considerations': Choudhry and Fenwick (n 18) 455.

[26]　See generally *Re S (A Child) (Identification: Restrictions on Publicity)* [2004] UKHL 47, [2005] 1 FLR 591.

[27]　*Johansen v Norway* (App No 17383/90) (1996) 23 EHRR 33 (ECtHR) at [78].

[28]　The omission of these words in *Payne v Payne* [2001] EWCA Civ 166, [2001] 1 FLR 1052 at [39] and by implication at [82] when referring to *Johansen* was a cause of particular criticism from commentators, since the selective quotation seemed so disingenuous: see S Harris-Short (n 18) 355; Herring and Taylor (n 18) 528. However, while the judges involved (Thorpe LJ and Butler-Sloss P) are, in the end, responsible for their judgments and for this serious omission, it is possible that the quotations adopted were taken, without further enquiry, from the submissions of counsel.

child's interests as compared with the interests of each other person involved in the case (primarily one or both parents, in most cases), rather than an assumption that the child's interests should always override anyone else's interests (which is what the welfare approach is said to involve).[29]

Consequently, while it was accepted that the child's interests could be given some degree of priority within a human rights analysis, it was not thought legitimate within that framework for the child's interests to be given 'paramountcy' in the sense in which that word is used in the English domestic context. ECtHR cases decided in the early part of the last decade that might have started to call some of these conclusions into question by taking a broader approach, such as *Yousef v The Netherlands* in 2002,[30] were explained as outliers and exceptions, rather than as the start of a change.[31] The question that this chapter explores is whether that conclusion should be revisited.

4. RECENT DECISIONS OF THE ECTHR

One reason why there may be reason to come back to the question of compliance between the English courts' approach to welfare and human rights stems from judgments from the ECtHR itself. Various decisions from the Grand Chamber and individual Chambers have re-stated a number of important principles and explored both the procedural and substantive contents of article 8 rights in relation to child law cases. From the English perspective, one case of particular interest is *YC v United Kingdom*,[32] decided in March 2012. However, before turning to that case, a broader discussion of the emerging principles is in order.

4.1 General Principles

First, it is clear that article 8 contains both procedural and substantive aspects. Although the procedural elements are not the focus of this chapter, it may be noted that the overall question asked by the ECtHR is

---

[29] See, e.g., Harris-Short (n 18) 355; Herring and Taylor (n 18) 528.

[30] *Yousef v Netherlands* (App No 33711/95) [2003] 1 FLR 210 (ECtHR).

[31] See, for example, Harris-Short (n 19); R Tolson, 'The Welfare Test and Human Rights: Where's the Beef in the Sacred Cow?' (2005) (available 31 July 2015 at http://www.familylawweek.co.uk/site.aspx?i=ed307).

[32] *YC v United Kingdom* (App No 4547/10) [2012] 2 FLR 332 (ECtHR) (hereafter, *YC v United Kingdom*).

'whether the decision-making process was fair and afforded due respect to the applicant's rights under Art 8'.[33] This requires the court to ask whether 'the decision-making process leading to the [decision] by the domestic court was fair and allowed those concerned to present their case fully'.[34] Court proceedings will often form only part of this assessment,[35] but in regard to court judgments they have to be read in the context of the case as a whole to assess whether the reasons given are relevant and sufficient for the decision being taken.[36] More broadly, it is necessary to ask:

> whether the domestic courts conducted an in-depth examination of the entire family situation and of a whole series of factors, in particular of a factual, emotional, psychological, material and medical nature, and made a balanced and reasonable assessment of the respective interests of each person, with a constant concern for determining what the best solution would be for the ... child ...[37]

As this quotation demonstrates, there is a strong link between the procedural requirements of article 8 and the substantive elements. In order to satisfy the procedural element, an 'in-depth examination of the entire family situation and of a whole series of factors' is demanded; and in order to know what those factors are, it will be necessary to have regard to the substantive requirements of article 8.

In terms of those substantive elements, it is fair to say that the European Court does not always speak with one voice. Indeed, insofar as this chapter suggests that recent cases may show a change in approach by the ECtHR, it is important to note that the Court has used many formulations over the years, and none appears to have become established for long. So for example, the ECtHR has described children's

---

[33] *YC v United Kingdom* at [133].

[34] *Neulinger and Shuruk v Switzerland* (App No 41615/07) [2011] 1 FLR 122 (hereafter, *Neulinger v Switzerland*) at [139]; see also *YC v United Kingdom* at [138].

[35] The assessment looks at the total interaction between the family and whatever parts of the state are involved in the decision-making. In *YC v United Kingdom* at [146], it is clear that the fact that the local authority had done work to try to 'rebuild the family through the provision of support for alcohol abuse and opportunities for parenting assistance' was one key consideration in finding no breach of article 8.

[36] See, e.g., *K and T v Finland* (App No 25702/94) [2001] 2 FLR 707 at [154]; *R and H v United Kingdom* (App No 35348/06) [2011] 2 FLR 1236 at [81].

[37] *Neulinger v Switzerland* at [139].

interests as being 'in every case of crucial importance',[38] and of 'particular importance', in addition to the *Johansen v Norway* 'nature and seriousness' approach.[39] Indeed, the *Johansen* formulation continues to be seen from time to time: a recent example is *Ahrens v Germany*, where the Court said: 'Consideration of what lies in the best interests of the child concerned is of paramount importance in every case of this kind; depending on their nature and seriousness, the child's best interests may override that of the parents'.[40]

Other cases, however, appear to adopt a broader approach and, in particular, do not use the phrase from earlier cases about the 'nature and seriousness' of the child's interests. For example, in the child abduction case of *Neulinger and Shuruk v Switzerland*, the Grand Chamber noted that 'there is currently a broad consensus – including in international law – in support of the idea that in all decisions concerning children, their best interests must be paramount'.[41] The Grand Chamber then proceeded to explain, in substantive terms, what the child's best interests might mean:

> The child's interest comprises two limbs. On the one hand, it dictates that the child's ties with its family must be maintained, except in cases where the family has proved particularly unfit. It follows that family ties may only be severed in very exceptional circumstances and that everything must be done to preserve personal relations and, if and when appropriate, to 'rebuild' the family ... On the other hand, it is clearly also in the child's interest to ensure its development in a sound environment, and a parent cannot be entitled under Art 8 to have such measures taken as would harm the child's health and development ...[42]

These points – both as to the general paramountcy of the child's welfare interests and as to the two limbs which need to be considered within that – have been paraphrased numerous times by individual Chambers hearing

---

[38]   *K and T v Finland* (App No 25702/94) [2001] 2 FLR 707 (Grand Chamber) at [154]; and similarly *Scott v United Kingdom* (App No 24745/97) [2000] 2 FCR 560 (ECtHR) at 572.

[39]   *Yousef v Netherlands* (App No 33711/95) [2003] 1 FLR 210 (EctHR) at [91].

[40]   *Ahrens v Germany* (App No 45071/09) [2012] 2 FLR 483 (ECtHR) at [63]. See also *C v Finland* (App No 18249/02) [2006] 2 FLR 597 at [54].

[41]   *Neulinger v Switzerland* at [135].

[42]   Ibid at [136]. This point can be seen to build on the earlier decision in *K and T v Finland* (App No 25702/94) [2001] 2 FLR 707 (Grand Chamber) at [155].

child law cases of various kinds.[43] Indeed, in *R and H v United Kingdom*, the Court said in terms that the principles from *Neulinger* have application beyond their immediate context: 'Although *Neulinger* ... concerned the relationship between Art 8 and the Hague Convention on Civil Aspects of International Child Abduction 1980, the court considers the principles set out above are equally applicable to domestic care and adoption proceedings'.[44]

4.2 YC v United Kingdom

As an application of these general principles, and in terms of advancing the discussion about the relationship between the English domestic law's concept of the welfare principle and the principles articulated by the European courts in relation to article 8, the case of *YC v United Kingdom* has particular interest. The case involved a child (aged 8 at the time of the domestic proceedings) whose parents were in a volatile, violent and alcohol-fuelled relationship, which was of sufficient seriousness for the local authority to be seeking a care order with a view to placing the child for adoption. Various support measures had been tried before court proceedings began, and on the verge of the trial the mother proposed that she should be assessed independently of the father, since she said that she was willing to separate from him if that would allow her to keep the child in her care. The local authority thought the mother to be incapable of effectively separating from the father within a realistic timescale given the child's needs because of the nature of her relationship with the father, but the Family Proceedings Court ordered further investigation and assessment.[45] The local authority and child's guardian appealed to the County Court, and the judge allowed the appeal and made a final care order[46] together with an order placing the child for adoption without the parents' consent.[47] The mother's application for permission to appeal to the Court of Appeal was refused.[48]

---

   [43]   See, e.g., *Šneersone and Kampanella v Italy* (App No 14737/09) [2011] 2 FLR 1322 at [85(v)]; *YC v United Kingdom* at [134].
   [44]   *R and H v United Kingdom* (App No 35348/06) [2011] 2 FLR 1236 at [74].
   [45]   Children Act 1989, s 38(6).
   [46]   Children Act 1989, s 31.
   [47]   Adoption and Children Act 2002, ss 22 and 52.
   [48]   Part of the Court of Appeal's reasoning is reproduced in *YC v United Kingdom* at [86]–[88].

As a test of the English approach to decisions about children's welfare, the process and reasoning in *YC v United Kingdom* provides a good example. The decision in the County Court – which, being the final substantive decision in the case, was the main focus of the ECtHR analysis – was brief and contained little by way of detailed analysis,[49] and therefore provides a good test case of the kind of process and reasoning which will survive review by the ECtHR.

For the majority in the ECtHR, the starting point was to ask what the judge ought to have done in order to comply with the requirements of article 8. Unsurprisingly, this analysis started by noting the standard three-stage approach to an assessment of whether the interference with the applicant's article 8 rights was justified, 'namely whether it was in accordance with the law, pursued a legitimate aim and was necessary in a democratic society'.[50]

While setting out the general principles seen in the previous section, the Court noted that in assessing a child's best interests, and in assessing the proportionality of measures proposed in the pursuit of those interests, many factors will have to be weighed; the Court had not previously thought it right to attempt to list those factors, since they will vary too much from case to case.[51] Nonetheless, in a very significant passage the Court went on:

> However, [the court] observes that the considerations listed in s 1 of the 2002 [Adoption and Children] Act ... broadly reflect the various elements inherent in assessing the necessity under Art 8 of a measure placing a child for adoption. In particular, it considers that in seeking to identify the best interests of a child and in assessing the necessity of any proposed measure in the context of placement proceedings, the domestic court must demonstrate that it has had regard to, inter alia, the age, maturity and ascertained wishes of the child, the likely effect on the child of ceasing to be a member of his original family and the relationship the child has with relatives.[52]

---

[49]　In the ECtHR, Judge de Gaetano's dissenting judgment described the County Court decision as 'most unorthodox' and as 'strange, to put it mildly': *YC v United Kingdom* at [2] and [4] of the minority judgment.

[50]　*YC v United Kingdom* at [130]; see generally Choudhry and Herring (n 19), ch 1.

[51]　*YC v United Kingdom* at [135]. It might be noted that the same view was taken by the Law Commission in its report that led to the Children Act 1989 – while general considerations could be listed in the welfare checklist, specific factors would have to be formulated on a case-by-case basis: Law Commission, 'Review of Child Law: Guardianship and Custody', Law Com No 172 (HMSO 1988).

[52]　*YC v United Kingdom* at [135].

Leaving aside for a moment the question of whether the 'checklists' of factors in either s 1(3) of the Children Act or s 1(4) of the Adoption and Children Act do in fact 'broadly reflect' an article 8 analysis,[53] it is worth noting that the majority judges supported their view on this point by reference to the English Court of Appeal decision in *EH v A London Borough Council*,[54] which also involved care and placement orders. The relevant part of that case is worth some attention. Giving the first judgment, Baron J said this:

> The judge was making a very draconian order. As such, he was required to balance each factor within the checklist in order to justify his conclusions and determine whether the final outcome was appropriate. Accordingly, because this analysis is entirely absent, his failure to mention the provisions of the 1989 Act and *deal with each part of s 1(3)* undermines his conclusions and his orders ...
>
> In a case where the care plan leads to adoption the full expression of the terms of Art 8 must be *explicit in judgment* because, ultimately, there can be no greater interference with family life. Accordingly, any judge must show how his decision is both necessary and proportionate. In this case what the judge said was 'removing the children from their mother without good reason ... would be a tragedy for them, quite apart from the mother'. With all due respect to him, this does not demonstrate that he had Art 8 well in mind.[55]

In other words, the relevant domestic authority on which the ECtHR made its assessment stated explicitly that a judge must go through and consider each factor on the checklist in turn.[56] This point appeared to be important for the majority's approach to *YC* because it meant that each factor within the welfare checklist – which 'broadly reflect the various elements inherent in assessing the necessity under Art 8 of a measure placing a child for adoption'[57] – would be expressly considered and weighed in the final analysis by the judge. However, it is at least

---

[53]　See below, text from n 68.

[54]　*EH v A London Borough Council* [2010] EWCA Civ 344, [2010] 2 FLR 661.

[55]　Ibid at [61] and [64] (emphasis added).

[56]　Wall LJ, agreeing with Baron J, similarly observed that 'these are not hoops imposed by Parliament and the appellate judiciary designed to make the life of the hard-pressed circuit judge even more difficult than it is already. They are not boxes to be ticked so that this court can be satisfied that the judge has gone through the motions': *EH v A London Borough Council* [2010] EWCA Civ 344, [2010] 2 FLR 661 at [96].

[57]　*YC v United Kingdom* at [135].

questionable whether the *EH* case is representative of the general approach of the English courts when it comes to welfare checklists.

Certainly, the House of Lords has said that 'in any difficult or finely balanced case … it is a great help to address each of the factors in the list';[58] but in the same paragraph, Lady Hale said that 'any experienced family judge is well aware of the contents of the statutory checklist and can be assumed to have had regard to it whether or not this is spelled out in a judgment'.[59] Much the same thought process is apparent from numerous Court of Appeal cases including,[60] just three months after *EH v A London Borough*, the evidently uncomfortable comments of a differently constituted Court of Appeal. In *M v Neath Port Talbot CBC*, Wilson LJ (giving the judgment of the Court) described Baron J's view as 'arresting'. Despite acknowledging the importance of not issuing conflicting views from the Court of Appeal where possible, his Lordship said this:

> it is, of course, unusual for a judge to be required to include any particular set of words in his judgment. The more usual approach is to assume, unless he has demonstrated to the contrary, that the judge knew how to perform his functions and what matters to take into account … Perhaps when the next appeal against a placement order arrives before us upon the basis of a complaint that there was no *express* reference to Art 8, we will have to consider whether, when considered in context, the instruction of this court in *EH*'s case is as absolutist as it at first appears.[61]

Two points arise from this discussion. First, it is far from clear that the domestic cases taken as a whole give much support to the ECtHR's view that English judges must demonstrate explicitly how they have considered, weighed and balanced all the factors on the checklist.[62] The general

---

[58]   *Re G (Residence: Same-Sex Parents)* [2006] UKHL 43, [2006] 2 FLR 629 at [40].

[59]   Ibid.

[60]   See e.g. *H v H (Residence Order: Leave to Remove from Jurisdiction)* [1995] 1 FLR 529 (CA) at 532: 'one should remember, that when one calls it a checklist, that it is not like the list of checks which an airline pilot has to make with his co-pilot, aloud one to the other before he takes off. The statute does not say that the judge has to read out the seven items in s 1(3) and pronounce his conclusion on each. Sometimes judges will do that, maybe more often than not; but it is not mandatory.'

[61]   *M v Neath Port Talbot CBC* [2010] EWCA Civ 821, [2010] 2 FLR 1827 at [22], citing *Piglowska v Piglowski* [1999] 2 FLR 763 (HL) at 784.

[62]   This view is also likely to dominate in future, since Lord Wilson has subsequently become a Justice of the Supreme Court, while Lady Hale (the other

view is rather that, as with any area of law where the judge is considering, weighing and balancing a well-known list of factors, his judgment should be 'read on the assumption that, unless he has demonstrated the contrary, the judge knew how he should perform his functions and which matters he should take into account'.[63]

Even leaving that point aside, though, some may wonder why the majority judgment in the ECtHR gave such focus to the *EH v A London Borough* approach, since it is clear that the County Court judge in *YC* had not, in fact, given the factors on the checklist any particular regard at all. As the majority judgment explains:

> The court acknowledges that ... the county court judge did not make express reference to the relevant considerations arising under Art 8 of the European Convention ... or to the various factors set out in s 1 of the 1989 Act and s 1 of the 2002 Act ... However, as outlined above, it is clear that he directed his mind, as required under Art 8 of the European Convention, to [the child's] best interests and that, in reviewing the applicant's application for a further assessment, considered whether in the circumstances rehabilitation of [the child] to his biological family was possible. He concluded that it was not. In reaching that decision he had regard to various relevant factors and made detailed reference to the reports and oral evidence of the social worker, the guardian (whose report was based on full consideration of the welfare checklist) and [a psychologist], all of whom identified the various issues at stake ... [64]

It is difficult to understand why the Court chose to emphasise the importance of assessing and weighing the individual factors identified by the checklist given that, when it came to analyse the decision under review, such an explicit process was clearly not judged to be necessary in order to make the process compliant with article 8. In his scathing dissent, Judge de Gaetano observed that this section of the majority judgment (like the Court of Appeal's 'cavalier' approach[65] when refusing

---

family law specialist on the Supreme Court) was already on record as taking a similar view about the checklist (see *Re G (Residence: Same-Sex Parents)* [2006] UKHL 43, [2006] 2 FLR 629 at [40]).

[63]   *Piglowska v Piglowski* [1999] 2 FLR 763 (HL) at 784. This point has been repeated frequently in recent Court of Appeal judgments, showing its ongoing application: see, e.g., *Re B (A Child)* [2012] EWCA Civ 1475 at [5]; *Re M (Children)* [2012] EWCA Civ 1710 at [47]; *Re TG (Care Proceedings: Case Management: Expert Evidence)* [2013] EWCA Civ 5, [2013] 1 FLR 1250 at [38]; *Re H (A Child)* [2013] EWCA Civ 72 at [69].

[64]   *YC v United Kingdom* at [147].

[65]   *YC v United Kingdom* at [1] of the minority judgment.

the mother permission to appeal) 'assumes that the judge had at some stage applied his mind properly in considering all the matters mentioned in s 1(4) of the 2002 Act',[66] despite the fact that the judge had not demonstrated such application in his judgment. For Judge de Gaetano, that 'gratuitous assumption' was inadequate to save the County Court judgment from violating article 8:

> There is no reference, specific or otherwise, to the checklist in s 1(4) of the 2002 Act. There is no reference to the rights enjoyed by both parents and children under the European Convention, to Art 8 or to any principle of proportionality. Whatever the guardian may have analysed and recommended in her report ... it was for the judge to apply independently his mind to the relevant and sufficient considerations and to show unequivocally in the judgment that he had done so.[67]

However, despite his criticism of the majority's assessment of the County Court judgment, there is little indication that Judge de Gaetano disagreed with the majority's construction of the question or, put another way, the view that the points in the welfare checklist would 'broadly reflect' the issues to be considered and weighed in an article 8 assessment.[68] This may be the most crucial part of *YC* in terms of the debate about the compatibility of the welfare principle as understood in English domestic law and the ECHR; and, as Simmonds says, 'this easy acceptance of the compatibility of English law with an article 8 analysis [by the Court in *YC*] may disappoint some authors'.[69] Indeed, defending the welfare principle against human rights arguments has been deeply unfashionable in academic circles but, as Simmonds says, *YC* and other recent cases suggest that 'paramountcy, in the English sense, may not be so alien to the ECtHR as it once was'.[70]

Simmonds cautions that one should be careful not to read too much into *YC* in two different regards. The first, with which no dispute could be taken, is regarding the crucial role of the procedural protections given under article 8, especially the meaningful participation in court and pre-court processes of all those involved. The second relates to the scope of the *YC* approach.

From a theoretical perspective, the question to be considered here is whether the ECtHR is right to say that the welfare checklist in the

---

[66] *YC v United Kingdom* at [5] of the minority judgment.
[67] *YC v United Kingdom* at [4] of the minority judgment.
[68] *YC v United Kingdom* at [135].
[69] Simmonds (n 12) 500.
[70] Ibid.

Adoption and Children Act (and, by implication therefore, the welfare approach more generally) does indeed 'broadly reflect' an article 8 analysis. The ECtHR's discussion of this point was brief. It noted simply that the checklist required judicial consideration, 'inter alia' of the child's age and wishes, the likely effect on the child of ceasing to be a member of the birth family, and the child's relationships with relatives.[71]

For some, this approach will be surprising because of its focus only on the child. There is no explicit mention in the checklist or in the Court's analysis at this point of the rights of the parents, separate from the child. It may be that the context of the case provides part of the answer to this question. The ECtHR was, of course, referring here to the issue of placing a child for adoption. It might be said that, by the time a case reaches this point, the rights of the parents have already been weighed and assessed, but have been required to give way to the child's interests because of the need to protect the child from harm. That reasoning is likely to be the basis for Simmonds' view is that *YC* is limited in scope to public law cases:

> although the ECtHR has been happy to sideline parental rights when dealing with abuse and neglect of children and the need for alternative care, it is less likely to do so in questions relating to, for example, contact, residence and relocation.[72]

It is in these central private law areas that, for Simmonds, the core of the difference between the English domestic cases and the ECtHR exists, and here 'the academic objections to the compatibility of the different approaches remain in this context as cogent as ever'.[73]

The question therefore is whether the ECtHR's analysis in *YC* will be applied, mutatis mutandis, to disputes between parents about the upbringing of the children (that is, private law disputes) as well. The complication in those cases is that there will be far less justification for focusing on the child's interests at the expense of the parents', and therefore the question of whether the English law's welfare approach, informed by its checklists, can be said, *in general*, to be a broad reflection of the article 8 requirements, or whether that is true only in the context of placing a child for adoption.

While there is no definitive evidence yet, one point that might support extending the same reasoning to private law cases comes from the fact

---

[71] *YC v United Kingdom* at [135].
[72] Simmonds (n 12) 501.
[73] Ibid.

that the source of many of the statements of principle in *YC* come from the child abduction (that is, private law) case of *Neulinger v Switzerland*. It remains at least possible, looking at the analysis in *YC* and other cases,[74] that the ECtHR may now see an English welfare analysis using the welfare checklist as asking questions and demanding analysis in much the same way as that demanded by the substantive limb of article 8.

In order to understand the argument for why this approach might yet be said to give due weight to the rights of parents and other family members in a welfare analysis, we must turn back to the domestic cases. It may be that part of the reason why there now appears to be less of a 'conflict' between domestic and ECtHR approaches is that we have a clearer understanding of what the domestic approach actually means.

5. WELFARE IN ENGLISH LAW

As noted earlier in this chapter,[75] many of the human rights criticisms that have been levelled against the English welfare approach take as their basis broader and well-established criticisms of the welfare principle. However, as I have suggested before,[76] it might be thought that some of the criticisms appear to be based on something of a parody of what that principle involves. For example, Choudhry and Fenwick's leading article on this debate starts by summarising the welfare approach in this way:

> its meaning is well understood amongst family lawyers: in decisions concerning children, the welfare of the child is to be the single deciding factor, that is, paramount over, and in fact displacing, all other considerations.[77]

However, while such a summary is not unusual, I would respectfully suggest that it lacks crucial nuance and, indeed, sets up something of a straw man in the welfare versus rights debate. Two particular questions

---

[74] See in particular *R and H v United Kingdom* (App No 35348/06) [2011] 2 FLR 1236 at [77], where the ECtHR explains that an assessment of the factors contained in the equivalent of the welfare checklist in Northern Ireland's adoption legislation (article 9 of the Adoption (Northern Ireland) Order 1987) would, so long as done properly, be compliant with article 8.

[75] Above, text at n 23.

[76] See R George, *Ideas and Debates in Family Law* (Hart Publishing 2012), ch 7.

[77] Choudhry and Fenwick (n 18) 456 citing, after the words 'single deciding factor', *J v C* [1970] AC 668 (HL).

might be raised. The first is whether the welfare of the child can be said to be a 'single … factor' and, perhaps following from that, whether it is right to say that welfare 'displac[es] all other considerations'.

When a judge, or anyone in fact, says that x is in the child's welfare, that statement represents the conclusion of an analysis of many factors – indeed, of all factors which bear on the decision about the child's upbringing, either directly or indirectly. This analysis expressly includes the rights of parents, and expressly requires a careful balancing of the competing considerations. In the leading interpretation of the welfare principle,[78] the House of Lords said this:

> in applying [the welfare principle], the rights and wishes of parents, whether unimpeachable or otherwise, must be assessed and weighed in their bearing on the welfare of the child in conjunction with all other factors relevant to that issue.[79]

It might be said that the instruction to consider these rights 'in their bearing on the welfare of the child' is where the welfare principle falls down. However, it must be remembered that the welfare principle applies only to disputes that are specifically about an aspect of the child's upbringing, not to disputes where the child is merely part of the case.[80] Any rights of a parent (or other party) that are in no way connected with the child's welfare[81] are also, ex hypothesi, in no way connected with the substantive aspects of the case when that case is only about the child's upbringing.[82] It therefore seems unsurprising that these factors should not be considered; conversely, any rights that are connected with the child will be relevant and will therefore be 'assessed and weighed'.

So, 'when all the relevant facts, relationships, claims and wishes of the parents, risks, choices and other circumstances *are taken into account*

---

[78]   Despite pre-dating the Children Act 1989, this case interprets a near-identical provision from earlier legislation and remains the leading understanding of the welfare approach.

[79]   *J v C* [1970] AC 668 (HL) at 715.

[80]   Above, n 5. See also J Eekelaar, 'The Role of the Best Interests Principle in Decisions Affecting Children and Decisions About Children' (2015) 23 *International Journal of Children's Rights* 3.

[81]   I suggest that the phrase 'connected with the child's welfare' is synonymous with having 'bearing on the welfare of the child'.

[82]   Rights to do with procedure, in particular those associated with the right to a fair trial under article 6 and the procedural aspects of article 8, might be different, though since these procedural rights exist because procedure is crucial to outcomes, their importance can be linked directly to the substance of the case.

and weighed,[83] the course of action to be followed is the one that most promotes the child's welfare. Does that mean that the courts assess welfare 'without regard for' the rights, interests or welfare of others?[84] Surely not. The fact that A's (qualified) rights do not prevail in the analysis does not mean that there was no 'regard' given to them. One might note that the child's (qualified) rights have not necessarily prevailed either. Consider, for example, a court order authorising a child to be taken into local authority care.[85] The article 8 rights of each parent are, of course, involved in such a decision; but so too are some of the child's article 8 rights. Welfare is a composite idea, whereas rights can be atomised.[86] I have a right to *x*, to *y* and to *z*, all of which are separate and freestanding, and which may indeed conflict with one another at times.[87] My welfare interest, on the other hand, is always made up of many considerations: those considerations may well be conflicting, but the welfare conclusion sits above such conflict, and reflects the end result of the analysis rather than a discussion about which factors should be included.

For these reasons, I would respectfully suggest that to say that welfare 'displaces' all other considerations risks conflating 'a welfare decision' with 'the factors which are used to make a welfare decision'. The conclusion of any gestalt, complex, multi-factorial analysis like a welfare analysis will overtake (or displace) the individual considerations which feed into it, but that does not mean that those considerations are unimportant, nor that they are not given their due weight and respect. It is the result of a balance – and if seen in this way, it may seem less surprising that the ECtHR would not see any inherent incompatibility between the English welfare approach and the substantive requirements of article 8.

In passing, it might be noted that this argument does not necessarily imply that the welfare checklist, by itself, reflects the requirements of an

---

[83]   *J v C* [1970] AC 668 (HL), 710 (emphasis added).

[84]   Herring, 'The Human Rights Act and the Welfare Principle in Family Law: Conflicting or Complementary?' (n 19) 225.

[85]   Children Act 1989, s 31.

[86]   That does not mean that either the idea of rights or a rights analysis in any given case is straightforward. Far from it. See generally Eekelaar (n 22) ch 6.

[87]   The child's rights in a care case, for example, may be in conflict with one another: as a basic example, the right to protection from inhuman and degrading treatment may be in conflict with the right to respect for family life; and different aspects of the right to respect for private and family life may be in conflict with each other: see *Neulinger v Switzerland* at [136].

article 8 analysis. The checklists are focused on issues from the child's perspective, but of course they are not exhaustive lists of considerations. They are expressly stated to be considerations for the court to take into account 'in particular', and so other factors can and should be included. It would go too far to say that the welfare checklist broadly reflects the requirements of article 8; but it may yet be arguable that the welfare principle, understood as suggested here, does reflect those requirements.

6. CONCLUSIONS

Given the central role of the welfare of the child as a legal concept across Europe, the question of whether this approach is compliant with the requirements of human rights instruments is of the highest importance. If there were an inherent incompatibility between this core legal approach and the right to respect for private and family life, there would be an urgent need to re-think domestic child laws across the Council of Europe member states.

However, the suggestion from this chapter is that such a reassessment is not in fact required. While there are still clearly issues to clarify – such as whether explicit discussion of individual factors within the decision-making process is required or whether, conversely, an overall assessment is adequate – the ECtHR's approach now seems to suggest that a best interests analysis that prioritises a child's welfare within a full assessment of the overall family situation will be compliant with article 8. The bigger challenge for states across Europe, to judge by those cases that succeed in the ECtHR, may be in ensuring that the procedural requirements of article 8 are complied with, and that the court is in a position in fact to undertake this wide-ranging assessment of the individual family's situation.

RECOMMENDATIONS FOR FURTHER READING

S Choudhry and H Fenwick, 'Taking the Rights of Parents and Children Seriously: Confronting the Welfare Principle under the Human Rights Act' [2005] *Oxford Journal of Legal Studies* 453.
S Choudhry and J Herring, *European Human Rights and Family Law* (Hart Publishing 2010).
J Eekelaar, *Family Law and Personal Life* (Oxford University Press 2007), ch 6.
J Eekelaar, 'The Interests of the Child and the Child's Wishes: The Role of Dynamic Self-Determinism' [1994] *International Journal of Law and the Family* 42.

J Eekelaar, 'The Role of the Best Interests Principle in Decisions Affecting Children and Decisions About Children' (2015) 23 *International Journal of Children's Rights* 3.

R George, *Ideas and Debates in Family Law* (Hart Publishing 2012), ch 7.

S Harris-Short, 'Family Law and the Human Rights Act 1998: Judicial Restraint or Revolution?' [2005] *Child and Family Law Quarterly* 329.

J Herring, 'The Human Rights Act and the Welfare Principle in Family Law: Conflicting or Complementary?' [1999] *Child and Family Law Quarterly* 223.

R Mnookin, 'Child-Custody Adjudication: Judicial Functions in the Face of Indeterminacy' (1975) 39 *Law and Contemporary Problems* 226.

H Reece, 'The Paramountcy Principle: Consensus or Construct?' (1996) 49 *Current Legal Problems* 267.

J Wallbank, S Choudhry and J Herring (eds), *Rights, Gender and Family Law* (Routledge 2010).

7. Parentage and surrogacy in a European perspective[1]

Katarina Trimmings and Paul Beaumont

---

[1] Parts 2 and 3 of this chapter draw on a previous publication of the authors: K Trimmings and P Beaumont, 'General Report on Surrogacy', in K Trimmings and P Beaumont (eds), *International Surrogacy Arrangements: Legal Regulation at the International Level* (Hart Publishing 2013) 439–549.

1. INTRODUCTION

Surrogacy completely disrupts traditional rules on legal parentage as it separates the three principal markers of legal motherhood: gestation, genetics and the intention to parent. Indeed, in surrogacy the woman giving birth may not be genetically related to the child and she has no intention of parenting the child she is carrying. Instead, it is planned that the child will be raised by a third party, who had instigated the child's conception. As a result, the normally imperceptible legal parentage rules traditionally based on an instinctive assumption that the gestational mother is the legal mother and her husband, if married, is automatically the legal father, are inevitably called into question.

A surrogate mother may be defined as a woman who carries a child, pursuant to an arrangement made before she became pregnant, with the sole intention of the resulting child being handed over to another person or persons and the surrogate mother relinquishing all rights to the child. There are two types of surrogacy: traditional surrogacy and gestational surrogacy.[2] In traditional surrogacy, the surrogate mother becomes pregnant with the sperm of the intended father (usually by insemination, and seldom through sexual intercourse) or is inseminated with donor sperm. As a result, the surrogate mother is genetically related to the child. In gestational surrogacy, an embryo is created by IVF, using the egg of the intended mother (or a donor egg) and the sperm of the intended father (or a donor sperm). Consequently, the surrogate mother has no genetic relationship with the child (though she does have an epigenetic relationship with the child). In the context of gestational surrogacy, the surrogate mother is sometimes referred to as a 'gestational carrier' or 'gestational host'.[3] Differences between traditional and gestational surrogacy must be taken into account when examining the legal and moral questions which arise in determining parentage. Most important is the question of whether traditional surrogacy should be treated differently from gestational surrogacy, given the existence of a genetic link between the surrogate mother and the child in the former case.[4]

---

[2]   See e.g. J Zuckerman, 'Extreme Makeover – Surrogacy Edition: Reassessing the Marriage Requirement in Gestational Surrogacy Contracts and the Right to Revoke Consent in Traditional Surrogacy Agreements' (2007–2008) 32 *Nova Law Review* 661, 662–5.

[3]   V Browne-Barbour, 'Bartering for Babies: Are Preconception Agreements in the Best Interest of Children?' (2004) 26 *Whittier Law Review* 429, 436.

[4]   See M Field, 'Reproductive Technologies and Surrogacy: Legal Issues' (1991–1992) 25 *Creighton Law Review* 1589, 1595. For an in-depth analysis see

Surrogacy agreements can also be classified into 'altruistic' and 'commercial' surrogacy arrangements. In altruistic surrogacy arrangements the surrogate mother is reimbursed by the intended parents up to the amount of her reasonable pregnancy-related expenses. In commercial surrogacy arrangements, the surrogate mother receives a payment beyond her reasonable pregnancy-related expenses.[5]

Domestic legal responses to surrogacy differ widely between jurisdictions. Generally speaking, some countries decide to regulate surrogacy, some to prohibit it and some to ignore it. Jurisdictions that choose to regulate surrogacy further differ on, for example, whether surrogate mothers should be allowed to receive payments beyond reasonable pregnancy-related expenses, whether surrogacy agreements should be legally enforceable and how the question of legal parentage should be approached in surrogacy cases.

The variety of domestic responses to surrogacy has led to widespread *forum shopping* where infertile heterosexual couples, homosexual couples or single people seeking to have a child through surrogacy travel from one country to another, purposely choosing 'surrogacy-friendly' jurisdictions as their destinations.[6] Cross-border surrogacy arrangements give rise to a variety of ethical and legal problems among which the most prevalent is the question of legal parenthood.

E Hisano, 'Gestational Surrogacy Maternity Disputes: Refocusing on the Child' (2011) 15 *Lewis & Clark Law Review* 517, 526–39.

[5] For a comment focused on the commercial aspect of surrogacy arrangements see C Luckey, 'Commercial Surrogacy: Is Regulation Necessary to Manage the Industry?' (2011) 26 *Wisconsin Journal of Law, Gender & Society* 213.

[6] By and large, the majority of these 'procreative tourists' are childless Western couples attracted by 'low-cost' surrogacy services and a 'ready availability of poor surrogates' in places like India and Eastern Europe. *Yamada v Union of India*, 2008 IND LAW SC 1554, 9 (29 September 2008) (known as 'The Baby Manji Case'). See also S Mohapatra, 'Stateless Babies & Adoption Scams: A Bioethical Analysis of International Commercial Surrogacy' (2012) *Berkeley Journal of International Law* 412, 422. It is to be noted that the cross-border surrogacy market, particularly in India, has been heavily criticised as surrogacy in this jurisdiction operates on an unregulated basis and thereby increases the risk of exploitation. See e.g. Trimmings and Beaumont (n 1) 530–1; U Smerdon, 'Crossing Bodies, Crossing Borders: International Surrogacy between the United States and India' (2008) 39 *Cumberland Law Review* 15; C London, 'Advancing Surrogate-Focused Model of Gestational Surrogacy Contracts' (2012) 18 *Cardozo Journal of Law & Gender* 391, 397; and A Malhotra, 'Commercial Surrogacy in India' [2009] *International Family Law Journal* 9.

Part 2 of this chapter examines theoretical approaches to legal parentage, with a particular focus on surrogacy. Part 3 explores the variety of national legal approaches to surrogacy, including domestic rules on legal parentage in surrogacy cases. Finally, Part 4 illustrates the problems associated with legal parentage in cross-border surrogacy cases and outlines how these issues are dealt with by judicial/administrative authorities in some European jurisdictions.

2. LEGAL PARENTAGE

The status of a legal parent is of great significance. Although a child can be in the care of a person without legal parental status (for example, a foster parent), legal parentage has supplementary advantages which ultimately manifest themselves in long-term stability for the child.[7] Legal parentage is an enduring status which does not end with the child's majority[8] and includes, inter alia, the attendant rights of inheritance from the legal parents.[9] From the perspective of the parents, legal parentage status confers on them a variety of exclusive rights that can be subsumed under the fundamental right to raise one's child.[10] Within the European Union, there exists a 'common core' of law concerning legal parentage, in particular the recognition of legal motherhood based on gestation and childbirth and of legal fatherhood for married men (the presumption of paternity) as described below.[11]

---

[7] D Purvis, 'Intended Parents and the Problem of Perspective' (2012) 24 *Yale Journal of Law & Feminism* 210, 213.

[8] N Lowe and G Douglas, *Bromley's Family Law* (10th edn, Oxford University Press 2007) 377.

[9] 'Explanatory Memorandum to the Human Fertilisation and Embryology (Parental Orders) Regulations 2010', SI 2010/985, para 2.1 (available 14 July 2015 at www.legislation.gov.uk/uksi/2010/985/pdfs/uksiem_20100985_en.pdf) ('Explanatory Memorandum'). See also N Lowe, 'The Establishment of Paternity under English Law' 82, available 14 July 2015 at http://ciec1.org/Etudes/ColloqueCIEC/CIEColloqueLoweAngl.pdf).

[10] M Byrn and J Vainik Ives, 'Which Came First, the Parent or the Child? (2010) 62 *Rutgers Law Review* 305.

[11] European Parliament, Directorate General for Internal Policies, 'Recognition of Parental Responsibility: Biological Parenthood vs. Legal Parenthood', i.e. Mutual Recognition of Surrogacy Agreements: What is the Current Situation in the MS? Need for EU Action?' prepared by V Todorova, 2010, p 16 (available 14 July 2015 at www.europarl.europa.eu/RegData/etudes/note/join/2010/432738/IPOL-JURI_NT(2010)432738_EN.pdf). See also N Lowe 'A Study Into the Rights and Legal Status of Children being Brought up in Various Forms of

2.1 General/Traditional Rules

Historically, one could become a parent only through sexual reproduction or adoption of a child.[12] With regards to the former, it was conclusively presumed that 'the act of giving birth necessarily resulted in motherhood'.[13] This presumption is embodied in the Latin maxim '*mater semper certa est, etiamsi vulgo conceperit*' or 'maternity is always certain, even of illegitimate children'.[14] As both gestation and birth can be witnessed, these two elements were considered as demonstrative of maternity and unequivocally applied to all births.[15] In 1977, in the UK House of Lords, in *The Ampthill Peerage* case, Lord Simon aptly remarked: 'Motherhood, although also a legal relationship, is based on a fact, being proved demonstrably by parturition. Fatherhood, by contrast, is a presumption.'[16]

Before the advent of DNA testing, paternity could not be conclusively established, unlike motherhood. Thus, in many legal systems the law

---

Marital and Nonmarital Partnerships and Cohabitation', Report for the attention of the Committee of Experts on Family Law, September 2009, CJ-FA (2008) 5), (available 14 July 2015 at www.coe.int/t/dghl/standardsetting/family/CJ-FA%20_2008_%205%20E%2025%2009%2009.pdf).

12   For an historical analysis of parentage rules from the continental and common law perspectives respectively see MT Meulders-Klein, 'Cohabitation and Children in Europe' (1981) 29 *American Journal of Comparative Law* 359 and R Mykitiuk, 'Beyond Conception: Legal Determinations of Filiation in the Context of Assisted Reproductive Technologies' (2001) 39 *Osgoode Hall Law Journal* 771, 779–790.

13   Mykitiuk (n 12) 778.

14   R Storrow, '"The Phantom Children of the Republic": International Surrogacy and the New Legitimacy' (2011–2012) 20 *American University Journal of Gender, Social Policy & the Law* 561, 593 (internal citation omitted). A recent High Court decision in Ireland stated that the presumption was 'irrebuttable' prior to the development of IVF based surrogacy arrangements; see Abbott J in *M.R & Anor v An tArd Chlaraitheoir & Ors* [2013] IEHC 91 at [100].

15   M Coleman, 'Gestation, Intent and the Seed: Defining Motherhood in the Era of Assisted Human Reproduction' (1995–1996) *Cardozo Law Review* 497, 501. This dates back to Roman law where a procedure existed 'for the examination of women who claimed to be pregnant and the witnessing of births to prevent fraudulent claims and substitution of babies', Justinian XXV, iv i 10, per JM Masson and others, *Principles of Family Law* (Sweet & Maxwell 2008) 527 fn 29. A similar process was in place in England. Ibid.

16   *The Ampthill Peerage* [1977] AC 547 at 577 (obiter).

presumed that the father of the child was the mother's husband.[17] The presumption originated in Roman law from the maxim '*pater est quem nuptia demonstrant*' or 'by marriage the father is demonstrated'.[18] If the child was born out of wedlock, no presumption of paternity applied.[19] The objective of the presumption of paternity was to further important policy goals: to protect children from the negative consequences of illegitimacy, to protect the conventional model of family and to stream-line family relationships.[20] In common law, the application of the marital presumption of paternity dates back to the 16th century.[21] Although at common law this presumption was rebuttable, it was close to impossible to overcome.[22] Today, some systems have created presumptions of parentage in cases where the gestational mother is in a registered partnership with someone or, in some cases, where the gestational mother is cohabiting with someone.[23]

---

[17]   F Kelly, 'Producing Paternity: The Role of Legal Fatherhood in Maintaining the Traditional Family' (2009) 21 *Canadian Journal of Women & Law* 315, 318. See also Hague Conference Prel Doc No. 11, Private International Law Issues Surrounding the Status of Children, including Issues arising from International Surrogacy Arrangements, 2011, para 19 (available 14 July 2015 at http://www.hcch.net/upload/wop/genaff2011pd11e.pdf).

[18]   Mykitiuk (n 12) 780.

[19]   N Bala and C Ashbourne, 'The Widening Concept of "Parent" in Canada: Step-Parents, Same-sex Partners & Parents by ART' (2011–2012) *American University Journal of Gender, Social Policy & the Law* 525, 530.

[20]   Purvis (n 7) 222 and J Dolgin, 'Choice, Tradition and the New Genetics: The Fragmentation of the Ideology of Family' (1999–2000) 32 *Connecticut Law Review* 523, 528.

[21]   B Rogers, 'The Presumption of Paternity in Child Support Cases: A Triumph of Law over Biology' (2002) 70 *University of Cincinnati Law Review* 1151, 1153 (internal citation omitted).

[22]   A Campbell, 'Conceiving Parents Through Law' (2007) 21 *International Journal of Law, Policy & the Family* 242, 250. Historically the prevalent view was that evidence beyond reasonable doubt was required to rebut the presumption. Lowe (n 9) 88. In the United States, for example, a married man could avoid the presumption only if he was impotent, sterile or could prove beyond reasonable doubt that he had no sexual access to his wife around the time of conception. *Godin v Godin*, 725 A.2d 904,910 (Vt. 1998), per Rogers (n 21) fn 15. Nevertheless, the English Family Law Reform Act 1969 departs from the principle of the necessity of proof beyond reasonable doubt, stating that it will suffice if the presumption is rebutted upon the balance of probabilities. Family Law Reform Act 1969 (England and Wales), s 26.

[23]   See Hague Conference Prel Doc No 11 (n 17) para 19. For example, some Commonwealth jurisdictions such as Tasmania, Ontario and New South Wales: Lowe (n 9) fn 6.

2.2   Surrogacy: Gestational/Birth Test, Genetics Test and Intent Test

Assisted reproductive technology, in particular surrogacy, presents a challenge to the traditional rules on legal parentage, in particular legal motherhood. Indeed, gestational surrogacy cases may involve as many as five 'procreators': a surrogate mother, two intended parents, a sperm donor and an egg donor.[24] This makes the application of the general parentage rules as described above rather problematic. Is the surrogate mother, who inevitably gives birth to the child, to be considered as the legal mother even if she has no genetic link with the child and no intention to parent? If she is married, is her husband to be regarded as the legal father? What is the role of an egg or sperm donor who has no intention of being the parent of the child when it comes to establishing legal parentage of a child born through a surrogacy arrangement?

In surrogacy cases, there is the potential for multiple claims of legal parentage based on biology (in other words, gestation and birth), genetics (in other words, by the person who contributes egg or sperm) and intention (in other words, by the person who initiated the child's conception and intends to raise the child).[25] In recognition of this reality, courts and legislatures in different jurisdictions have developed two novel approaches to legal parenthood in surrogacy arrangements: the 'genetics' test and the 'intent' test. Nevertheless, it must be pointed out that many countries continue to apply the general rules on legal parentage in surrogacy cases, as described above.[26] The section below examines the applicability of each of the approaches, including the traditional 'gestational/birth' test, to surrogacy cases.

2.2.1   The gestational/birth test

As explained above, according to the gestational/birth test, a woman who gives birth to a child is viewed as the legal mother of the child, even if

---

[24]   J Grossman and L Friedman, *Inside the Castle: Law and Family in the 20th Century America* (Princeton University Press 2011) 301.

[25]   Ministry of Attorney General Justice Services Branch, Civil and Family Law Policy Office (British Columbia), 'Family Relations Act Review: Discussion Paper' August 2007, available 14 July 2015 at http://www.courthouselibrary.ca/docs/default-source/asked-answered/ministry-of-attorney-general-justice-services-branch-civil-and-family-law-policy-office-2007-discussion-papers/chapter10-defining legalparenthood_apr9-2014.pdf?sfvrsn=2.

[26]   See section 2.1 above.

she is genetically unrelated to the child.[27] The award of legal motherhood to the birth mother is based principally on the assumption of an emotional and physical bond between the gestational mother and the baby developed during gestation.[28] Other arguments in favour of this approach include that it is generally in the best interests of the child to stay with his/her gestational mother[29] and that the gestational mother makes the largest contribution to the creation of the child.[30] In the context of the latter argument, it has been argued that the gestational/birth mother:

> ... risks sickness and inconvenience during pregnancy. She faces the certain prospect of painful labor. She even risks the small but qualitatively infinite possibility of death. Throughout all of this discomfort and uncertainty, it is her body, which remains the cradle for the growing fetus. By comparison, the physical involvement of the sperm donor is de minimis. While the egg donor physically risks more than the sperm donor, her level of physical involvement pales in comparison with the gestational host.[31]

The proponents of this approach also believe that a recognition of the gestational mother as the legal mother of the child will have the deterrent effect of discouraging surrogacy arrangements.[32] The allocation of legal

---

[27] It has been suggested that gestational motherhood is the 'purest form of parenthood' as the word 'parent' comes from the Latin *perere*, meaning 'to give birth'. M Pierce-Gealy, '"Are You My Mother?"': Ohio's Crazy-Making Baby-Making Produces a New Definition of "Mother"' (1994–1995) 28 *Akron Law Review* 535, 545.

[28] A Larkey, 'Redefining Motherhood: Determining Legal Maternity in Gestational Surrogacy Arrangements' (2003) 51 *Drake Law Review* 605, 625. See also K Horsey, 'Challenging Presumptions: Legal Parenthood and Surrogacy Arrangements' [2010] *Child and Family Law Quarterly* 449, 461–2.

[29] Horsey (n 28) 462, referring to Hill's comment that 'every US state has recognised a presumption that it is in the best interests of the child to remain with or be placed with its natural parent(s).' J Hill, 'What Does It Mean to Be a "Parent"? The Claims of Biology as the Basis for Parental Rights' (1991) 66 *New York University Law Review* 353, 400. Nevertheless, Horsey questions the term 'natural' as it is not clear whether the expression actually refers to the 'gestational' or the 'genetic' mother.

[30] Horsey (n 28) 463.

[31] Hill (n 29) 408.

[32] A Goodwin, 'Determination of Legal Parentage in Egg Donation, Embryo Transplantation, and Gestational Surrogacy Arrangements' (1992) 26 *Family Law Quarterly* 275, 291.

motherhood to the surrogate mother implicitly recognises that the surrogate's wishes must be prioritised should she change her mind and decide to keep the child.

The critics of the birth approach, on the other hand, assert that to accept gestation as the determinative factor of legal motherhood would employ a gender-specific constituent in the determination of legal parentage[33] and that it does not coincide with the pre-conception intent of the parties.[34] Opponents of the gestational test have likened the surrogate's task to that of a 'foster parent'[35] or a 'wet nurse'.[36]

Traditionally, the genetics test coincided with the birth test as genetics and gestation always met in one woman. Nowadays, in the era of assisted reproductive technologies, however, bearing a child is not always synonymous with being the child's genetic mother. It has therefore been suggested that, in establishing legal parenthood in surrogacy cases (or cases involving ART more generally), the genetics and gestational aspects of maternity should be split and valued separately.

2.2.2 The genetics test

According to the genetics test, the child's legal parents are determined on the basis of genetics. In this test, the genetics element should be accorded higher value than the gestational element. Ideologically, the genetics test stems from 'genetic essentialism' which is the belief that our genes are the core of who we are as human beings.[37] Therefore genetics should overcome any other factor when defining and establishing legal parenthood.[38]

A good illustration of the application of the genetics test can be found in the New York Supreme Court decision in the 'surrogacy-by-mistake'

---

[33]   M Garrison, 'Law Making For Baby Making: An Interpretive Approach to the Determination of Legal Parentage' (2000) 113 *Harvard Law Review* 835, 917. Horsey suggests that the gestational test 'prioritizes the mother whilst doing nothing for fathers': (n 28) 471.

[34]   Larkey (n 28) 625. See section 2.2.3 below.

[35]   *Johnston v Calvert*, 851 P.2d 776, 786 (Cal. 1993).

[36]   See A Hofheimer, 'Gestational Surrogacy: Unsettling State Parentage Law and Surrogacy Policy' (1992) 19 *New York University Review of Law & Social Change* 571, 591–2.

[37]   D Nelkin and S Lindee, *The DNA Mystique: The Gene as a Cultural Icon* (Michigan University Press 2004), per Hisano (n 4) 530.

[38]   L Bender, 'Genes, Parents and Assisted Reproductive Technologies: ARTs, Mistakes, Sex, Race and Law' (2003) 12 *Columbia Journal of Gender & Law* 1, 4.

case of *Perry-Rogers v Fasano*.[39] The Fasano and Rogers families were victims of negligence by a New York fertility clinic. Both couples were undergoing IVF treatment that resulted in viable pre-embryos. Due to a pre-embryo mix-up at the clinic, however, Mrs Fasano was implanted with six of the Rogers' pre-embryos along with one of hers and her husband's pre-embryos. All of the embryos Mrs Rogers was impregnated with were hers and her husband's. Unfortunately, these embryos did not implant in her uterus. Mrs Fasano, however, gave birth to twin boys. One of them was European-American like the Fasanos and the other was African-American like the Rogers. The Fasanos were happy to raise both children; however, in the meantime the Rogers learnt about the birth and sued for a declaration of parentage and custody. The Court took the stand that genetics was the core identity of the child and awarded custody to the Rogers.

A recent example of the genetics test being applied in Europe is the Irish High Court decision in the case of *M v An tArd Chláraitheoir*.[40] This case involved a domestic altruistic surrogacy arrangement where both intended parents were the genetic parents of twins born to a surrogate mother. The surrogate was the sister of the intended mother and was happy for her sister to be registered as the only mother of the child.[41] The intended parents initiated court proceedings seeking a declaration that the intended mother was the legal mother of the children. The court decided to grant the petition, abandoning the irrebuttable presumption deriving from the 'age-old maxim'[42] that the mother was always the woman who gave birth to the child. The High Court decision was, however, overturned by the Irish Supreme Court which ruled 6:1 against the intended parents and held that the birth certificate of the twins could not be changed to register the genetic mother as the legal mother.[43] The Court concluded that it was a matter for the Irish legislature to determine such rights by way of legislation.

---

[39] *Perry-Rogers v Fasano* 15 N.Y.S.2d 19 (App. Div. 2000). For a detailed analysis and a critique of the case see Bender (n 38).

[40] *M v An tArd Chláraitheoir* [2013] IEHC 91. For analysis of issues arising from this case see A Caffrey, 'Surrogacy – Genetics v Gestation: The Determination of "Mother" in Irish Law' [2013] *Medico-Legal Journal of Ireland* 34. See also n 107 below.

[41] *M v An tArd Chláraitheoir* [2013] IEHC 91 at [5] and [96].

[42] Caffrey (n 40) 34.

[43] *M.R. and D.R. (suing by their father and next friend O.R.) & ors v An t-Ard-Chláraitheoir & ors* [2014] IESC 60.

Proponents of the genetics test argue that it provides a clear and fair determination of parental rights[44] and encourages gender equality by placing the same value on the reproductive responsibilities of males and females.[45]

Critics argue that relying on the genetics test is 'sex-biased'[46] and creates a false impression that there is 'equity between the female and male role in the reproductive process'.[47] The underlying argument is that the genetics test considers only the means of contribution to reproduction that are common to both genders (in other words, contribution of their gametes), whilst ignoring gestation and birth as additional means of contributions to reproduction specific to women only.[48] In the context of the High Court decision in the Irish case of *M v An tArd Chláraitheoir*[49] it has been suggested that the genetics test was incompatible with the Irish Adoption Act 2010 as under this Act an unmarried (gestational) mother is allowed to place a child for adoption without the consent of the genetic father.[50] The question raised by the commentator was whether an unmarried father should have an equal right (to grant consent for adoption) if parentage is determined solely on the basis of genetics.[51] It was also argued that the genetics test challenged the nature of the birth certificate, by making it unclear whether a birth certificate should be regarded only as a historical record of birth capable of being amended or as irrefutable proof of legal parentage.[52]

More generally, the genetics test has also been scrutinised for degrading the status of the surrogate mother to a mere incubator, diminishing not only the biological value of gestation but also the significance of the bond that develops during gestation between the surrogate mother and the baby.[53] In the context of the former argument, it has been aptly remarked:

---

[44] Hofheimer (n 36) 601.
[45] See Hisano (n 4) 540.
[46] Bender (n 38) 44.
[47] Hisano (n 4) 531 (internal citation omitted).
[48] Bender (n 38) 44 and 47.
[49] *M v An tArd Chláraitheoir* [2013] IEHC 91. For analysis of issues arising from this case see Caffrey (n 40).
[50] Caffrey (n 40) 35.
[51] Ibid.
[52] Ibid.
[53] Bender (n 38) 51.

A pregnant woman intending to bring a child into the world is more than a mere container or breeding animal; she is a conscious agent of creation no less than the genetic mother, and her humanity is implicated on a deep level.[54]

It is arguable that the genetics test fails to give enough weight to the epigenetic effects of the gestational mother on the child which can certainly be significant in certain cases, for example, the consequences of significant drug use during pregnancy. Another concern associated with the genetics test is that it necessarily fails in surrogacy situations involving egg or sperm donors.[55] In such cases the test would lead to an absurd result where a donor would become the legal parent of any child that his or her gamete donation helped to create.[56]

It has also been suggested that the acceptance of the genetics test may result in property rights-based claims in relation to the resulting child.[57] Such claims would, however, be wholly unsuitable as one 'cannot have property rights in a child'.[58]

The genetics test can produce unjust outcomes in surrogacy cases where only one of the intending parents has a genetic link to the child.[59]

Finally, opponents of the genetics-based approach argue that genetics alone cannot be determinative as there might be other interests in establishing parenthood, as often demonstrated by non-surrogacy paternity cases.[60]

---

[54] *Johnson v Calvert* 851 P.2d. 776, 797-98 (Cal. 1993) per Justice Kennard (dissenting).

[55] See A Miller, 'Baseline, Bright-line, Best Interests: A Pragmatic Approach for California to Provide Certainty in Determining Parentage' (2002–2003) 34 *McGeorge Law Review* 637, 699. For such cases, Miller recommends the application of the intent-based approach with a judicially pre-approved surrogacy contract (see below).

[56] Horsey (n 28) 471.

[57] Ibid, 467.

[58] Ibid.

[59] Ibid, 459.

[60] S Rae, *The Ethics of Commercial Surrogate Motherhood: Brave New Families?* (Praeger 1994) 86. These interests include in particular the existence of a nurturing relationship between a child and father. Hisano (n 4) 541. To clarify the point, Hisano refers to a decision of the US Supreme Court in the case of *Lehr v Robertson* 463 U.S. 248, 250 (1983) where the Court refused the petition of a putative genetic father of a young child to veto the adoption of the child by the husband of the child's mother. The decision was based on the fact that the putative genetic father had almost no contact with the child and failed to support her. Ibid, 540. On the problem of establishment of legal paternity generally see for example K Baker, 'Bargaining or Biology? The History and

2.2.3   The intent test

According to the intent test, the intent of the parties as expressed in the surrogacy agreement controls the determination of the legal parenthood. The intent-based approach to the establishment of legal parenthood originated in 1993 in the United States from the California Supreme Court decision in the case of *Johnson v Calvert*.[61] The case involved a gestational surrogacy agreement between Mark and Crispina Calvert (the intended parents) and Anna Johnston (the surrogate mother). An embryo created from the Calverts' genetic material was implanted into Anna's uterus. In return for three payments totalling $10,000 and a life insurance policy, Anna agreed to relinquish all parental rights to the child. During the pregnancy, however, the relationship between the parties deteriorated. This prompted the intended parents to seek a court declaration that they were the parents of the child. In response, Anna filed a petition to be declared the mother. The two petitions were consolidated and the trial court ruled that the Calverts were the 'genetic, biological and natural father and mother', found the contract enforceable and denied Anna's claim to maternity. The Court held:

> Anna Johnston is the gestational carrier of the child, a host in a sense ... [She] and the child are genetic hereditary strangers. ... Anna's relationship to the child is analogous to that of a foster parent providing care, protection, and nurture during the period of time that the natural mother, Crispina Calvert, was unable to care for the child.

Anna appealed. The Supreme Court of California affirmed the first instance decision and resolved the issue by looking to the intent of the parties in signing the contract. The Court held that under the Federal Uniform Parentage Act 1973 (which, however, was not specifically

---

Future of Paternity Law and Parental Status' (2004–2005) 14 *Cornell Journal of Law & Public Policy* 1, in particular 9–16.

[61]   *Johnson v Calvert* 5 Cal 4th 84, 19 Cal Rptr 2d 494, 851 P2d 776 (cert denied 510 US 874, 114 S Ct 206, 126 L Ed 2d 163) (Cal 1993). For analysis of the case, see e.g. D Morgan, 'A Surrogacy Issue: Who is the Other Mother?' (1994) 8 *International Journal of Law and the Family* 386; A Vorzimer, 'The Egg Donor and Surrogacy Controversy: Legal Issues Surrounding Representation of Parties to an Egg Donor and Surrogacy Contract' (1999–2000) 21 *Whittier Law Review* 415, 415–17; L Behm, 'Legal, Moral and International Perspectives on Surrogate Motherhood: The Call for a Uniform Regulatory Scheme in the United States' (1999) 2 *DePaul Journal of Health Care Law* 557, 572–7; K Rothenberg, 'Gestational Surrogacy and the Health Care Provider: Put Part of the "IVF Genie" Back Into the Bottle' (1990) 18 *Law, Medicine & Health Care* 345, 345–6.

designed for surrogacy), both gestation and genetic ties can give rise to a presumption of motherhood. As both Anna and Crispina presented evidence of motherhood,[62] and the Court could find no clear preference in the Uniform Parentage Act as between the fact of physical gestation and birth and blood test evidence in determining motherhood, the Court decided to look at the intentions of the parties involved. The Court held that when gestation and genetics do not coincide in one woman, the woman who intended to bring about the birth of a child that she intended to raise as her own is the natural and legal mother of the child in California.[63] Although the intent test originally developed through common law, it is now regulated through a statute.[64] The statute contains a very broad definition of an 'intended parent' which covers 'an individual, married or unmarried, who manifests intent to be legally bound as the parent of a child resulting from assisted reproduction'.[65] An entry into a gestational surrogacy agreement that complies with the formal requirements laid down by the statute rebuts the legal presumption that the surrogate mother and, if applicable, her spouse or partner are the legal

---

[62] Anna through gestation and birth, and Crispina through her genetic link to the child.

[63] The application of the intent test in California was subsequently widened by the California Court of Appeal decision in the case of *Buzzanca v Buzzanca*, 61 Cal App 4th 1410, 72 Cal Rptr 2d 280 (Cal Ct App 1998). In this case, the intended parents, Luanne and John Buzzanca, decided to have an embryo genetically unrelated to either of them implanted in a surrogate mother, who would carry and give birth to the child for them. After the pregnancy, the intended parents split up, and the question arose as to who were the child's legal parents. The trial court concluded that the child had no legal parents. On appeal, this decision was reversed and the Court of Appeal held that even though neither of the intended parents was genetically related to the child, they were still her legal parents given their initiating role as the intended parents in her conception and birth. The intent test was later extended to include gay couples through the decision of the California Supreme Court in *Drewitt-Barlow v Bellamy* (per BSC, 'Surrogacy Laws in California', available 14 July 2015 at http://issgd.com/surrogacy-laws-in-california/) and lesbian couples through the following three decisions: *Elisa B. v Superior Court* 17 P.3d 660 (Cal. 2005); *Kristine H. v Lisa R.* 117 P.3d 690 (Cal. 2005); and *K.M. v. E.G.* 117 P.3d 673 (Cal. 2005).

[64] California Assembly Bill 1217, which came into force on 1 January 2013 as California Family Code, sections 7960–7962.

[65] California Family Code, section 7960 (c). All categories of potential intended parents (i.e. married, single, heterosexual as well as homosexual persons) are included in the definition. Importantly, there is no requirement of a genetic link between the intended parent and the child.

parents of the child.[66] In practice, the intent of the parties is often formalised through a 'pre-birth parentage order' which declares the intended parents as the legal parents before the child is born.[67] In practical terms, the order facilitates a pre-birth transfer of legal parentage.[68] In effect, the court order confirms the rebuttal of the presumption of the legal parentage of the surrogate mother and her spouse or partner. The order can only be contested on the basis of non-compliance with the formalities required by section 7962(2) of the California Family Code.[69]

The statutory regulation plausibly protects the interests of the surrogate mother, in particular through the requirements of separate legal representation[70] and evidence of how the intended parents will cover her medical expenses and the medical expenses of the newborn child.[71]

The application of the intent test in surrogacy cases has been widely endorsed by commentators.[72] Common arguments in support of the approach include:

---

[66] Ibid, section 7962 (f)(1).

[67] Ibid, section 7962 (f)(2): 'Upon petition of any party to a properly executed assisted reproduction agreement for gestational carriers, the court shall issue a judgment or order establishing a parent-child relationship ... .' It is to be noted that the order does not necessarily have to be issued before the child's birth but may be issued also after the birth of the child. Ibid. The use of pre-birth parental orders was common in California also prior to the entry into force of sections 7960–7962 of the California Family Code in January 2013. See S Snyder and M Byrn, 'The Use of Prebirth Parentage Orders on Surrogacy Proceedings' (2005–06) 39 *Family Law Quarterly* 633, 634.

[68] California Family Code, section 7962 f(2): 'Subject to proof of compliance with this section, the judgment or order shall establish the parent-child relationship of the intended parent or intended parents identified in the surrogacy agreement and shall establish that the surrogate, her spouse, or partner is not a parent of, and has no parental rights or duties with respect to, the child or children.'

[69] 'The judgment or order shall terminate any parental rights of the surrogate and her spouse or partner without further hearing or evidence, unless the court or a party to the assisted reproduction agreement for gestational carriers has a good faith, reasonable belief that the assisted reproduction agreement for gestational carriers or attorney declarations were not executed in accordance with this section.'

[70] California Family Code, section 7962 (b).

[71] Ibid, section 7962 (a)(4).

[72] See e.g. M Shultz, 'Reproductive Technology and Intent-Based Parenthood: An Opportunity for Gender Neutrality' (1990) *Wisconsin Law Review* 297; Hill (n 29); L Elrod, 'A Child's Perspective of Defining a Parent: The Case for Intended Parenthood' (2011) 25 *BYU Journal of Public Law* 245; Snyder and Byrn (n 67); Horsey (n 28); and J Herbie DiFonzo and R Stern, 'The Children of

(1)   Intended parents are the 'first cause' or the 'prime mover' of the procreative relationship.[73] Consequently, without the intended parents' initiative the child would never have been born.[74]

(2)   From the outset of the process the intended parents have intended to 'accept the responsibility of caring for [the child]'.[75]

(3)   The intent test provides all parties concerned with the benefit of legal certainty and predictability from the outset of the arrangement.[76] This is regarded as being in the interests of a child born through a surrogacy arrangement as 'children's interests are better served by enforcing parental ex ante intent than by making parental status hinge on an ex post assessment of parental suitability'.[77]

The intent test has, however, attracted criticism on the grounds that parental status should not be an object of private contracting.[78] The approach has also been disapproved for being inconsistent with a liability regime based on the right of the child to maintenance from a genetic parent[79] and for being unfit to adequately address the interests of children due to its inherent focus on adult intentions.[80]

The absence of the best interests of the child assessment in parentage determinations in gestational surrogacy cases in California appears to be the major weakness of the intent test as currently codified by ss 7960–7962 of the California Family Code. Section 3020 of the Family Code

---

Baby M' (2011) 39 *Capital University Law Review* 345 (pre-conception intent in conjunction with consistent behaviour).

[73]   Hill (n 29) 414 and Horsey (n 28) 455.

[74]   Horsey (n 28) 457. Nevertheless, it has also been submitted that without the surrogate mother the birth of the child would not happen. Horsey, however, suggests that this argument is not comparable to the argument for recognising the intended parents as the surrogate's position is 'more analogous to the position of a donor – she donates gestational time/use of her body – and should be treated similarly'. Ibid, 463.

[75]   J Levitt, 'Biology, Technology and Genealogy: A Proposed Uniform Surrogacy Legislation' (1992) 25 *Columbia Journal of Law and Social Problems* 451, 470. Also Horsey (n 28) 457.

[76]   Horsey (n 28) 458 and 470.

[77]   S Abramowicz, 'Contractualizing Custody' (2014) 83 *Fordham Law Review* 67, 120.

[78]   In this context, Hisano suggests that a surrogacy agreement is an 'extremely unique arrangement' which has 'emotional, physical, biological and psychological components, which can make it difficult to adhere to the pre-conception intent of the parties. Hisano (n 4) 538.

[79]   Baker (n 60) 11.

[80]   Garrison (n 33) 863–4.

requires courts to take account of the best interests of children when making an order concerning 'the physical or legal custody or visitation of children'. This obligation, however, does not extend to parentage determinations in surrogacy cases. Indeed, unlike in relation to custody agreements (premarital or postmarital) where courts are not bound by parents' custody agreements but must instead look to the welfare of the child, the determination of parentage in surrogacy cases in California is fully contractualised.[81] One of the reasons why premarital custody agreements (often incorporated into prenuptial agreements) have consistently been held to be unenforceable by courts is that such agreements are not 'knowing'.[82] The point can be formulated as follows: 'How ... can a parent possibly know what is best for a child who has not yet been born?'[83] In order for a custody agreement to be 'knowing', 'a custody agreement must be based on the needs of a particular, existing child, as well as on the relationship of each parent toward the child'.[84] Should similar rationale not be advanced in relation to determination of parentage through surrogacy agreements? The 'best interests of the child' argument in determining parentage has been raised by a number of scholars of which the most prominent one is Marsha Garrison.[85] In her view parentage contracts should not be recognised and parentage should instead be established as if the child had been conceived naturally through sexual intercourse, as opposed to assisted reproduction.[86] Other scholars have, however, maintained that although custody agreements should give way to a judicial assessment of the best interests of the child, parentage agreements should govern the establishment of legal parentage without the interference of the state which should not have the authority to decide who is fit to become a parent.[87]

---

[81] For a detailed analysis of the question of contractualising custody and parentage determinations see Abramowicz (n 77).

[82] Ibid, 77.

[83] Ibid.

[84] *In re Marriage of Littlefield* 940 P.2d 1362 (Wash. 1997) per Abramowicz (n 77) 78.

[85] Garrison (n 33).

[86] Ibid, 896.

[87] E.g. M Schultz, 'Reproductive Technology and Intent-Based Parenthood: An Opportunity for Gender Neutrality' (1990) 297 *Wisconsin Law Review* 323, 347–52.

2.2.4 Alternative approaches

Some commentators have, however, rejected all three approaches, arguing that none of them is sufficient as each of the three elements of legal parenthood (namely, genetics, birth and intent) only partially defines parenthood in surrogacy.[88] Several suggestions have been made for alternative solutions. These include the 'best interests of the child' test and the normative model of legal parenthood.

The application of the 'best interests of the child' test requires a determination as to who can best assume the parental responsibilities for a child born through a gestational surrogacy arrangement.[89] Alternatively, the 'best interests of the child' test should be applied in conjunction with an additional component: 'the intent-based tiebreaker'.[90] This means that if the court concludes that more than one woman (couple) is equally fit to take care of the child, the pre-conception intent should be conclusive.[91]

The normative model of legal parenthood implies that legal parenthood in surrogacy arrangements should be decided on the basis of a Lockean labour theory of property.[92] Following this model, parenthood should be awarded to the gestational mother or the intended parents, depending on who has 'invested the most labour in the developing foetus'[93] and therefore merits parenthood the most.

3. DOMESTIC APPROACHES TO SURROGACY AND LEGAL PARENTAGE

Countries differ considerably in their domestic legal approaches to surrogacy. Nevertheless, most jurisdictions consistently employ the general rules on legal parentage, including the gestational/birth test, when confronted with the establishment of legal parentage in surrogacy cases. These countries can be grouped into four broad categories: (1) countries where surrogacy in both its forms (namely, altruistic and commercial) is outlawed; (2) countries where surrogacy has been ignored by the legislature and remains unregulated; (3) countries where surrogacy is

---

[88] See for example Hisano (n 4) 528.

[89] *Johnson v Calvert*, 851 P.2d 776,799 (Cal. 1993) (Kennard, J., dissenting).

[90] Hisano (n 4) 543ff.

[91] Ibid.

[92] S Gillers, 'A Labour Theory of Legal Parenthood' (2000–2001) 110 *Yale Law Journal* 691.

[93] Ibid.

regulated whilst only an altruistic form of surrogacy is permitted; and (4) countries where commercial surrogacy is permitted.

3.1 Countries where Surrogacy (Altruistic and Commercial) is Outlawed

Countries where surrogacy in both its forms (altruistic and commercial) is outlawed can collectively be referred to as 'anti-surrogacy juris-dictions'.[94] In Europe, classic examples in this category are Germany and France.[95] Surrogacy arrangements (both altruistic and commercial) are void and unenforceable in these jurisdictions as they violate statutory prohibitions of surrogacy.[96] Commercial surrogacy arrangements are void also on the ground that they offend public policy.[97]

---

[94]   In Germany, for example, surrogacy is expressly prohibited by the Embryo Protection Act 1990 which bans 'medical methods used for abusive reproduction or those leading to 'split motherhood'. Certain prohibitive pro-visions related to surrogacy can be found also in the Adoption Placement Act 2001: S Gössl, 'National Report on Surrogacy: Germany', in Trimmings and Beaumont (n 1) 131–42, 131. In France, surrogacy is banned under the Bioethics Act 1994 (Loi n 94-653 du juillet 1994 relative au respect du corps humain): L Perreau-Saussine and N Sauvage, 'National Report on Surrogacy: France', in Trimmings and Beaumont (n 1) 119–30, 120.

[95]   For a detailed analysis of the French and German approach to surrogacy see Perreau-Saussine and Sauvage (n 94) and Gössl (n 94) respectively. For Germany see also R Wagner, 'International Surrogacy Agreements: Some Thoughts from a German Perspective' [2012] *International Family Law* 129. Examples of anti-surrogacy jurisdictions from outside Europe include China, Australia (Tasmania) and certain US States (e.g. Michigan, New York and the District of Columbia). For exhaustive analyses of the Chinese, Australian and American approach to surrogacy respectively see Z Huo, 'National Report on Surrogacy: The People's Republic of China', in Trimmings and Beaumont (n 1) 93–103; M Keyes, 'National Report on Surrogacy: Australia', in Trimmings and Beaumont (n 1) 25–48 and Snyder and Byrn (n 67) respectively. For recent calls for a departure from the restrictive approach to surrogacy in Michigan and New York see Ch VanWormer, 'Outdated and Ineffective: An Analysis of Michigan's Gestational Surrogacy Law and the Need for Validation of Surrogate Pregnancy Contracts' (2012) 61 *DePaul Law Review* 911 and A De Vito, 'Establishing and Rebutting Maternity: Why Women are at a Loss Despite the Advent of Genetic Testing' (2011) 74 *Albany Law Review* 1873 respectively.

[96]   For example, articles 16–17 of the French Civil Code expressly state that: 'Any agreements relating to procreation or gestation for a third party are void.' Perreau-Saussine and Sauvage (n 94) 120.

[97]   See e.g. Gössl (n 94) 134. In France even altruistic surrogacy arrange-ments are regarded as contrary to public policy. See Perreau-Saussine and

If, despite the ban, a surrogacy arrangement is entered into, the general rules on legal parenthood, including the gestational/birth test, as described above will apply. This means that the surrogate mother will be regarded as the legal mother and her husband (if married) will be viewed as the legal father of the child.[98] It might, nevertheless, be possible for the surrogate's husband to contest paternity and for the intended father to subsequently acknowledge his paternity[99] (or have his paternity established by a court).[100] The intended father also would be able to acknowledge his paternity or have his paternity judicially established if the surrogate mother was unmarried. The intended mother might then be able to adopt the child. This can, however, prove problematic as adoption legislation might be ineffective in cases where 'the adoptive parents took part in a procurement which is unlawful or contrary to public policy'.[101]

3.2 Countries where Surrogacy Remains Unregulated

Countries where surrogacy remains unregulated represent the largest proportion of European jurisdictions and include, for example, Belgium, Hungary, the Czech Republic, the Netherlands, Ireland and Spain.[102]

Sauvage (n 94) 120 where it is noted that such arrangements are 'contrary to two public policy principles, i.e. neither the human body nor the civil status of persons may be subject to private agreements'.

[98] For example, sections 1591 and 1592(1) of the German Civil Code. See also Gössl (n 94) 136.

[99] For example, section 1592(2) of the German Civil Code. See also Gössl (n 94) 136. An acknowledgment of paternity appears to be the only avenue to 'circumvent' the ban on surrogacy in France. See Perreau-Saussine and Sauvage (n 94) 128.

[100] For example, section 1592(3) of the German Civil Code. See also Gössl (n 94) 136.

[101] Gössl (n 94) 137. German courts have applied a strict standard based on the view that where the intended father is recognised as the legal parent, adoption by the intended mother is not indispensable. Adoption would be granted only if absolutely necessary for the child's well-being. Ibid. For a more liberal approach to recognition of a foreign judgment on paternity in a commercial surrogacy case see the German Federal Court of Justice decision of 10 December 2014 (Case XII ZB 463/13), analysed by Dina Reis in 'German Federal Court of Justice on Surrogacy and German Public Policy', 4 March 2015, available 11 August 2015 at http://conflictoflaws.net/2015/german-federal-court-of-justice-on-surrogacy-and-german-public-policy/.

[102] For exhaustive analyses of the legal approach to surrogacy in these jurisdictions see G Verschelden and J Verhellen, 'National Report on Surrogacy: Belgium', in Trimmings and Beaumont (n 1) 49–83; C Nagy, 'National Report

These countries neither expressly ban nor allow surrogacy; nevertheless, any surrogacy arrangement (whether commercial or altruistic) would be considered void and unenforceable.[103] Some countries falling within this category have recorded isolated occurrences of domestic altruistic surrogacy carried out by specialised medical facilities.[104] In the absence of regulation of altruistic surrogacy by legislation, internal guidelines of the clinics[105] or other relevant guidelines[106] normally apply to regulate the procedure. Legal parenthood in these altruistic surrogacy cases is established through the application of general parentage rules.[107] This means that the woman who gives birth to the child is regarded as the legal mother of the child.[108] If the surrogate mother is married, her husband is

---

on Surrogacy: Hungary', in Trimmings and Beaumont (n 1) 175–86; M Pauknerová, 'National Report on Surrogacy: Czech Republic', in Trimmings and Beaumont (n 1) 105–18; I Curry-Sumner and M Vonk, 'National Report on Surrogacy: Netherlands', in Trimmings and Beaumont (n 1) 273–94; M Harding, 'National Report on Surrogacy: Ireland', in Trimmings and Beaumont (n 1) 219–30; and P Orejudo, 'National Report on Surrogacy: Spain', in Trimmings and Beaumont (n 1) 347–56.

[103]   Either by an express provision (e.g. article 10 of the Spanish Act on ART – Ley 14/2006, sobre técnicas de reproducción humana asistida, BOE no 126, 27 May 2007) or under general principles of law (e.g. Ireland, the Czech Republic, Hungary, Belgium and the Netherlands).

[104]   For example, the Czech Republic. It is estimated that approximately 15 surrogate pregnancies are facilitated by IVF clinics in the Czech Republic annually; nevertheless, only one clinic openly admits to offering surrogacy services. The clinic requires that the intended mother provide her own genetic material. Pauknerová (n 102) 108.

[105]   For example, the Czech Republic and Belgium: see Pauknerová (n 102) 109 and Verschelden and Verhellen (n 102) 54 respectively.

[106]   For example, in Ireland, clinics operate under the guidelines of the Medical Council of Ireland. In the Netherlands, only one medical centre offers surrogacy and the procedure is carried out in accordance with relevant ministerial guidelines and the Guidelines on IVF-surrogacy issued by the Dutch Society for Obstetrics and Gynaecology. Harding (n 102) 219 and Curry-Sumner and Vonk (n 102) 280.

[107]   See *M v An tArd Chláraitheoir* discussed in section 2.2.2 above. See also Caffrey (n 40).

[108]   For example, the Czech Republic (s 50a of the Family Act), Spain (article 10 of the Act on ART – Ley 14/2006, sobre técnicas de reproducción humana asistida, BOE no 126, 27 May 2007, and article 116 of the Civil Code), Belgium (article 312 para 1 of the Civil Code) and the Netherlands (article 1:198 of the Civil Code). A new Hungarian Civil Code (which came into force on 15 March 2014) expressly provides that the woman who bore the child is to be treated as the legal mother. See Pauknerová (n 102) 111; Orejudo (n 102) 347; Verschelden

viewed as the legal father of the child.[109] Some countries have a specific provision for pregnancies achieved with the use of assisted reproductive technologies; in other words, the husband of the surrogate mother is regarded as the legal father if he consented to the fertility procedure. If the intended father is genetically related to the child, the intended parents might under certain conditions be able to obtain legal parenthood using provisions on determination of paternity (intended father) and adoption legislation (intended mother).[110] In particular, if the surrogate mother is married, her husband may be able to surrender or contest his paternity.[111] If the surrogate mother is not married or her husband has surrendered or contested his paternity, the paternity of the intended father may be established.[112] The intended mother may then be able to adopt the child through spousal adoption.[113] Nevertheless, alternative avenues to achieve the transfer of legal parenthood may be available in some jurisdictions.[114]

---

and Verhellen (n 102) 61; Curry-Sumner and Vonk (n 102) 276; and Nagy (n 102) 179.

[109] For example, the Czech Republic (s 51 of the Family Act), Spain (article 116 of the Civil Code), Belgium (article 315 of the Civil Code) and the Netherlands (article 1:199(a) of the Civil Code). Pauknerová (n 102) 112; Orejudo (n 102) 348; Verschelden and Verhellen (n 102) 64; Curry-Sumner and Vonk (n 102) 276.

[110] This appears to be possible, for example in the Czech Republic and Spain. See Pauknerová (n 102) 112 and Orejudo (n 102) 349.

[111] In the Czech Republic, for example, the husband of the surrogate mother may surrender his paternity by declaration. Pauknerová (n 102) 112.

[112] In the Czech Republic, for example, the intended father can become the legal father of the child through a consenting declaration of paternity made together with the surrogate mother. See Pauknerová (n 102) 112.

[113] For example, Spain and the Czech Republic (certain restrictions, however, apply; in particular, the surrogate mother must not be a relative of the intended mother and the intended parents are a married heterosexual couple). See Orejudo (n 102) 349 and Pauknerová (n 102) 112. It has been suggested that as a matter of practice domestic surrogacy arrangements are also implemented 'beneath the veil of adoption' in Hungary. Nagy (n 102).

[114] For example, a divestment of parental responsibility of the surrogate mother and her husband and a subsequent joint adoption of the child by the intended parents (the Netherlands) and a voluntary recognition of maternity by the intended mother/a judicial establishment of maternity initiated by the intended mother (both possible only if there is no mother listed on the birth certificate) (Belgium). Curry-Sumner and Vonk (n 102) 277 and Verschelden and Verhellen (n 102) 62–3 respectively.

3.3 Countries where Surrogacy is Regulated whilst only an Altruistic Form of Surrogacy is Permitted

3.3.1 United Kingdom[115]

In some European countries, for example in the United Kingdom and Greece, altruistic surrogacy is allowed and regulated by statute. The United Kingdom solves the problem of legal parenthood in surrogacy cases through the application of the general rules on legal parenthood.[116]

The underlying policy aim of the regulation of surrogacy in the United Kingdom is to prohibit commercial surrogacy arrangements and to limit surrogacy to a relatively small number of altruistic arrangements.[117] Altruistic surrogacy is available in the United Kingdom to specific qualified persons, with the eligibility criteria being set out in relevant statutory instruments.[118] The key piece of legislation that sets rules for the establishment of parenthood in cases of assisted reproduction, including surrogacy, is the Human Fertilisation and Embryology Act 2008

---

[115] For an in-depth analysis of the UK approach to surrogacy see M Wells-Greco, 'National Report on Surrogacy: United Kingdom', in Trimmings and Beaumont (n 1) 367–86. For empirical investigation into the incidence of surrogacy arrangements in the UK see M Crawshaw, E Blyth and O van den Akker, 'The Changing Profile of Surrogacy in the UK – Implications for National and International Policy and Practice' (2012) 34 Journal of Social Welfare and Family Law 267.

[116] For analysis of the Greek approach see section 3.3.2 below. Outside the EU, the 'UK approach' (i.e. altruistic surrogacy permitted by statute with legal parentage following the general rules on legal parentage) can be found for example in Australia (New South Wales, Queensland, South Australia, Victoria and Western Australia and the Australian Capital Territory), New Zealand and several US States. For exhaustive analysis of the regulation of surrogacy in Australia see Keyes (n 85). See also J Millbank, 'The New Surrogacy Parentage Laws in Australia: Cautious Regulation or "25 Brick Walls"?' (2011) 35 *Melbourne University Law Review* 165 and J Millbank, 'From Alice and Evelyn to Isabella: Exploring the Narratives and Norms of "New" Surrogacy in Australia' (2012) 21 *Griffith Law Review* 101 (the role of discourse in the recent wave of reforms to surrogacy laws in Australia). For an analysis of the US regulatory framework see Snyder and Byrn (n 67). See also D Hinson and M McBrien, 'Surrogacy across America' (2011) 34 *Family Advocate* 32; D Hinson, 'State-by-State Surrogacy Law Actual Practices' (2011) 34 *Family Advocate* 36 and Mohapatra (n 6) 424–30.

[117] Masson (n 15) 528.

[118] Surrogacy Arrangements Act 1985; Human Fertilisation and Embryology Act 1990 (HFEA 1990) and Human Fertilisation and Embryology Act 2008 (HFEA 2008).

(HFEA 2008). Although altruistic surrogacy is legal in the United Kingdom, the principal aspect of the surrogacy arrangement, namely the obligation of the surrogate mother to hand the child over to the intended parents, is unenforceable.[119]

Upon the birth of the child legal motherhood is established on the basis of the birth rule, with legal paternity depending upon the marital status of the surrogate mother. In particular, s 33(1) of the HFEA 2008 states:

> The woman who is carrying or has carried a child as a result of the placing in her of an embryo or of sperm and eggs, and no other woman, is to be treated as the mother of the child.

Section 35(1) of the same Act further states that if, at the time of the procedure, the woman 'was a party to marriage' and the embryo was not created with the sperm of 'the other party to the marriage', then 'the other party to the marriage' is to be treated as the father of the child unless it is shown that he did not consent to the procedure. In other words, the surrogate mother is regarded as the legal mother of the child (whether or not she is also the genetic mother) and her husband/partner (if applicable) is presumed to be the legal father of the child.

Nevertheless, an interesting feature of the United Kingdom system is that there is a specific statutory remedy available to the intended parents that allows for a transfer of legal parenthood from the surrogate mother (and her husband/partner as applicable) to the intended parents. In order to extinguish the legal status of the surrogate mother (and her husband/partner as applicable) and reassign legal parenthood to the intended parents, the intended parents must go through a post-birth legal process known as the 'parental order application'. The effect of a parental order is that it provides for a child to be treated as the legitimate child of the intended parents, with inter alia the attendant rights of inheritance from the intended parents and the right to be registered as a British citizen if one of the intended parents is a British citizen.[120] A parental order confers parental responsibility for the child exclusively on the intended parents and extinguishes the parental responsibility of anyone else.[121]

A parental order will be issued if:

---

[119] Surrogacy Arrangements Act (1985).

[120] Explanatory Memorandum (n 9) para 2.1. See also Home Office, UK Border Agency, 'Inter-country Surrogacy and the Immigration Rules', available 14 July 2015 at www.ukba.homeoffice.gov.uk/sitecontent/documents/residency/Intercountry-surrogacy-leaflet ('UK Border Agency Rules').

[121] Lowe and Douglas (n 8) 317.

(1)   the surrogacy arrangement is not commercial;[122]
(2)   at least one of the intended parents is domiciled in the juris-
       diction;[123]
(3)   the surrogate mother and her husband/partner (if applicable) have
       consented to the transfer of parentage;[124]
(4)   the application has been made less than six months after the birth of
       the child;[125]
(5)   there is a genetic link between at least one of the applicants and the
       child;[126]
(6)   the intended parents have attained the age of 18;[127]
(7)   the child is living with the intended parents at the time of the
       application;[128] and
(8)   the application has been made by a couple.[129]

Rather paradoxically, however, the HFEA 2008 gives courts a discretion
to grant a parental order even if more than reasonably incurred expenses
were paid to the surrogate mother as such payments can be retrospectively authorised by the court.[130]

---

[122]   HFEA 2008, s 54(8).
[123]   The requirement of domicile can be found in s 54(4)(b) of the HFEA
2008. The question of domicile surfaced in the case of *Re G (Surrogacy: Foreign
Domicile)* [2007] EWHC 2814 (in the context of the HFEA 1990), and in the
case of *Z and another v C and another* [2011] EWHC 3181 (Fam) (in the context
of the HFEA 2008).
[124]   HFEA 2008, s 54(6). The issue of consent by the surrogate mother arose
in the case of *D and L (Surrogacy)* [2012] EWHC 2631 (Fam). See also note
178.
[125]   HFEA 2008, s 54(3). The question of whether a parental order could be
granted even though the application was made after the expiration of the
statutory six-month period arose in the case of *In Re X (Surrogacy: Time Limits)*
[2014] EWHC 3135 (Fam). See also note 177.
[126]   HFEA 2008, s 54(1)(a) and (b).
[127]   HFEA 2008, s 54(1)(a) and (b).
[128]   HFEA 2008, s 54(4)(a).
[129]   The HFEA 2008 excludes single people from applications for a parental
order. Nevertheless, couples living in an enduring family relationship and not
within the prohibited degrees, regardless of whether they are married or not or in
a civil partnership, are eligible to apply: HFEA 2008, s 54(2).
[130]   HFEA 2008, s 54(8). The English courts have given the statute a very
liberal construction, see the case law discussed at 4.1 below (notes 164-181).

Where the intended parents do not meet the statutory requirements for application for a parental order,[131] alternative solutions must be resorted to. In particular, the intended parents might need to apply for adoption, special guardianship or a residence order.[132] A full transfer of legal parentage in a surrogacy situation can, nevertheless, be achieved only through a parental order under the HFEA 2008 as described above, or through adoption.[133] Although an adoption order produces the same effects as a parental order,[134] a successful application of adoption legislation to surrogacy cases in the United Kingdom (in particular cases involving commercial surrogacy) is rather uncertain.

3.3.2 Greece[135]

Not all jurisdictions that fall within the same category as the United Kingdom (in other words, surrogacy is regulated but only altruistic surrogacy is permitted) apply the general rules on legal parentage in surrogacy cases. A notable example of an alternative approach in Europe is Greece.

The core pieces of legislation through which surrogacy is regulated in Greece are Law No 3089/2002 on Medically Assisted Reproduction and

---

[131]　The most common reasons could be that neither of the intended parents is genetically related to the child, that the six-month time limit for the application for a parental order has passed, that neither of the intended parents is domiciled in the UK, or that the surrogate mother refused to give her consent to the transfer of legal parenthood.

[132]　Wells-Greco (n 115) 372.

[133]　Lowe and Douglas (n 8) 305, stating that generally legal parentage can be achieved in three ways: (1) it can be assigned automatically (not applicable to surrogacy); (2) it can be acquired through the making of a parental order under the HFEA 2008; or (3) it can be acquired through adoption. Nevertheless, there is a difference between a parental order and an adoption order in that the former 'triggers the re-issue of the child's birth certificate and effectively re-writes parentage from birth'. N Gamble, 'Made in the U.S.A. – Representing U.K. Parents Conceiving Through Surrogacy and ART in the United States' (2012) *Family Law Quarterly* 155.

[134]　In other words, that it reassigns legal parentage permanently.

[135]　For a detailed analysis of the Greek approach to surrogacy see K Rokas, 'National Report on Surrogacy: Greece', in Trimmings and Beaumont (n 1) 143–66. For further reading see D Papadopoulou-Klamaris, 'Medically-Assisted Reproduction in Greek Law' (2008) 61 Revue hellénique de droit international 521. For a comparison of the Greek and the British regulation of surrogacy see K Rokas, 'National Regulation and Cross Border Surrogacy in European Union Countries and Possible Solutions for Problematic Situations' (2014/2015) 16 Yearbook of Private International Law 217 (forthcoming).

Law No 3305/2005 on Application of Medically Assisted Reproduction.
In addition, the Greek Civil Code lays down the key principles that
govern access to medically assisted reproduction. Only altruistic gestational surrogacy is allowed in Greece.[136] In Greece, a surrogacy arrangement must be approved by a court prior to the fertility procedure to
confirm compliance with the requirements of the legislation.[137] If the
approval is granted, the parties are authorised to proceed with the
arrangement. The judicial approval of the surrogacy arrangement in
Greece will result in an automatic acquisition of legal parenthood by the
intended parents from the moment of the birth of the child, thereby
allowing for the application of the intent test to the establishment of legal
parentage in all surrogacy cases that fall within the scope of the relevant
statutory regulation.

3.4   Countries where Commercial Surrogacy is Permitted: Ukraine[138]

The intent-based approach to the establishment of legal parentage,
sometimes in combination with the genetics test, also applies explicitly or
implicitly in countries that allow commercial surrogacy. Such countries
can generally be termed as 'surrogacy-friendly' jurisdictions.

Only a small minority of countries around the world permit commercial surrogacy. The practice may either be expressly allowed in these
jurisdictions[139] or at least not explicitly banned and at the same time

---

136   Rokas (n 135) 144 stating that 'crucial is the altruistic character of the
process'.

137   Outside the EU, the 'pre-approval approach' can be found in Israel, South
Africa, Australia – Western Australia and Victoria, New Zealand and some US
States (e.g. Virginia and New Hampshire). See S Shakargy, 'National Report on
Surrogacy: Israel', in Trimmings and Beaumont (n 1) 231–46; M Slabert and C
Roodt, 'National Report on Surrogacy: South Africa', in Trimmings and Beau-
mont (n 1) 325–45; Keyes (n 85); C Achmad, 'National Report on Surrogacy:
New Zealand', in Trimmings and Beaumont (n 1) 295–310 and Snyder and Byrn
(n 67). In some of these jurisdictions, a special committee approval is required
instead of a court approval. See Trimmings and Beaumont (n 1) fn 106.

138   For a detailed analysis of the Ukrainian approach to surrogacy see G
Druzenko, 'National Report on Surrogacy: Ukraine', in Trimmings and Beaumont (n 1) 357–65.

139   For example, the US State of California where surrogacy, including
commercial, was expressly allowed on the basis of a judicial precedent, see
Johnson v Calvert 5 Cal.4th 84, 19 Cal.Rptr.2d 494, 851 P.2d 776 (cert. denied
510 U.S. 874, 114 S.Ct. 206, 126 L.Ed.2d 163) (Cal. 1993), and now on the basis
of legislation. For more information on the Californian approach to surrogacy see
above at section 2.2.3.

accepted by administrative/judicial authorities of the given country.[140] Other common features of these jurisdictions are that commercial surrogacy is performed there on a relatively large scale and that there are legal measures that allow the intended parents (or at least one of them) to obtain legal parentage. There are no surrogacy-friendly jurisdictions in Western or Central Europe, but, a small number of surrogacy-friendly countries can be found in Eastern Europe. The most prominent of these in terms of numbers of cross-border commercial surrogacy arrangements[141] is Ukraine, which will be the focus of the analysis below.[142]

Relevant statutory instruments that regulate surrogacy in Ukraine include the Family Code of Ukraine 2004 and the Instruction of the Order of the Ministry of Health of Ukraine No 771 of 23 December 2009[143] ('the Instruction'). There is no express provision on payments in surrogacy in Ukrainian legislation. The basis for the practice of commercial surrogacy therefore derives from the assumption that what is not prohibited is legal. This is used in combination with the principle of freedom of contract enshrined in the Ukrainian Civil Code.[144]

The Instruction imposes a number of requirements on the intended parents. In particular, only heterosexual couples are eligible to commission surrogacy in Ukraine.[145] There must also be a medical need for

---

[140] For example, India. For a detailed analysis of the Indian approach to surrogacy see U Smerdon, 'National Report on Surrogacy: India', in Trimmings and Beaumont (n 1) 187–18. See also Trimmings and Beaumont (n 1) 444–51; A Malhotra and R Malhotra, 'All Aboard for the Fertility Express' (2012) 38 *Commonwealth Law Bulletin* 31; A Malhotra, 'Earthquake rocks surrogacy', *The Daily Post*, 9 May 2015.

[141] For more information on the cross-border aspects of surrogacy see section 4 of this chapter below.

[142] Other Eastern European countries that can be termed 'surrogacy-friendly' include Russia, Belarus, Armenia, Moldova, Georgia and Kazakhstan (the last two to the extent they can be regarded as European countries given their geographic location at the dividing line between Europe and Asia): Trimmings and Beaumont (n 1) fn 22. For a detailed analysis of surrogacy in Russia see O Khazova, 'National Report on Surrogacy: Russia', in Trimmings and Beaumont (n 1) 311–24.

[143] The Instruction is a legally binding Act and was issued by the Ministry of Health pursuant to article 281 of the Ukrainian Civil Code ('Right to Life'): Druzenko (n 138) 357–58.

[144] Articles 6(1) and 627. Ibid, 358.

[145] Only heterosexual marriage is legal in Ukraine so surrogacy is not available to either same-sex couples or single persons. See article 21 of the Family Code which defines marriage as 'matrimony of a man and woman'. Druzenko (n 138) fn 15. A more liberal approach can, however, be observed in

surrogacy[146] and at least one of the intended parents must be genetically related to the child.[147] Traditional surrogacy is not envisaged by Ukrainian legislation.[148]

Article 123(2) of the Family Code states that the intended parents are to be regarded as the legal parents of a child born as a result of a surrogacy arrangement. This rule is reaffirmed by article 139(2) of the Family Code, which explicitly prevents a surrogate mother from claiming maternal affiliation to the child. Nevertheless, the Rules of Civil Registration require that a surrogate mother gives notarised consent for the intended parents to register as the legal parents of the child.[149] However, commentators believe that as the consent is only an administrative act, in the case of a refusal by the surrogate mother to consent to the registration, Ukrainian courts would look favourably on the intended parents.[150] Once consent has been granted by the surrogate mother, the intended parents will be listed on the child's birth certificate in any scenario that falls within the scope of Ukrainian legislation.[151]

4. CROSS-BORDER SURROGACY AND LEGAL PARENTAGE

The diversity in national approaches to surrogacy as described above has encouraged widespread *forum shopping* where intended parents from all

---

other surrogacy-friendly jurisdictions. For example, in California no eligibility requirements for the intended parents exist.

[146] Instruction, section 7, para 2. Druzenko (n 138) 361.

[147] It is a prerequisite for the registration of the intended parents as the legal parents of the child according to para 11 of section 1 of Chapter III of the Rules of Civil Registration in Ukraine approved by the Order of the Ministry of Justice of Ukraine of 18 October 2000 No 52/5. Druzenko (n 138) 360.

[148] The Family Code (article 123(2)) makes it clear that only cases where 'a human embryo conceived by the spouses (a man and a woman) by means of assisted reproductive technologies has been transferred to another woman's body' fall within the scope of surrogacy legislation. Druzenko (n 138) 360.

[149] Rules of Civil Registration, approved by the Order of the Ministry of Justice of Ukraine of 18 October 2000 No 52/5 as amended, Ch III, S 1, para 11. Druzenko (n 138) 361.

[150] Druzenko (n 138) 358.

[151] In other words: (1) Both intended parents are genetically related to the child; (2) Only the intended father is genetically linked to the child (ovum provided by a donor); (3) Only the intended mother is genetically linked to the child (sperm provided by a donor). As stated above, in all three situations, both intended parents will appear on the child's birth certificate as the legal parents.

over the world flock to 'surrogacy-friendly' jurisdictions with the intention of taking advantage of liberal local commercial surrogacy regimes. 'Surrogacy-friendly' jurisdictions are particularly attractive to foreign intended parents for the following three reasons:

(1) These countries do not impose nationality, domicile or habitual residence prerequisites for the intended parents.
(2) Legal parentage does not follow the general rules but instead is established on the basis of the intent test, often in combination with the genetics test. Consequently, intended parents (or at least one of them) are able to acquire legal parenthood in the country of birth.
(3) There is no shortage of willing surrogates given the commercial nature of surrogacy in these jurisdictions.

Although countries with a relatively neutral approach to surrogacy where altruistic surrogacy is permitted and regulated also allow intended parents in surrogacy cases to acquire legal parentage, either immediately upon the birth of the child (for example, Greece) or through a post-birth transfer of legal parentage (for example, the United Kingdom), these countries do not generally attract potential intended parents from abroad. The reason is that these jurisdictions commonly impose stringent requirements on the domicile/habitual residence/residence of the intended parents and/or the surrogate mother. The underlying rationale is to discourage 'procreative tourism'. An additional deterrent is the ban on commercial surrogacy in these countries as finding an altruistic surrogate is much more difficult than finding a commercial one.

Consequently, 'surrogacy-friendly' jurisdictions have become the 'hubs' of an international commercial surrogacy market, attracting intended parents from both anti-surrogacy countries and countries with a relatively neutral approach to surrogacy (see Figure 7.1).

There is a complete void in the regulation of surrogacy arrangements at the international level, as none of the existing international instruments contains specific provisions designed to regulate this emerging area of international family law.[152] In the absence of a global legislative

---

[152] Nevertheless, the problem of cross-border surrogacy arrangements is on the formal agenda of the Hague Conference on Private International Law as the Permanent Bureau of the Hague Conference is carrying out research into the topic, see chapter 5 in volume I of this book set. A report on the 'Desirability and Feasibility of Further Work on the Parentage/Surrogacy Project' Prel Doc No3B April 2014 and 'A Study of Legal Parentage and the Issues Arising from International Surrogacy Arrangements' Prel Doc 3C March 2014 were presented to

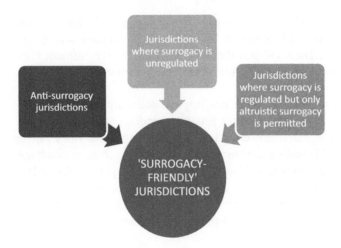

Figure 7.1 Dynamics of the cross-border commercial surrogacy market

response, highly complex legal problems arise from international surrogacy arrangements.[153] Among these problems, the most prevalent are the questions of legal parentage and the nationality of the child.[154] The focus of the following section is on legal parentage; the problem of the nationality of the child is beyond the scope of this chapter.

Problems associated with legal parentage in cross-border surrogacy cases arise essentially from the clash between differing approaches to

the Council on General Affairs and Policy of the Hague Conference in 2014. A further update (Prel Doc 3A) was presented to the Council in March 2015 and the Council then agreed to set up an Experts' Group to explore the feasibility of further work in the area of 'private international law issues surrounding the status of children, including issues arising from international surrogacy arrangements'. See the Hague Conference on Private International Law dedicated webpages on 'The Private International Law Issues Surrounding the Status of Children, Including Issues Arising from International Surrogacy Arrangements', available 14 July 2015 at www.hcch.net/index_en.php?act=text.display&tid=178.

[153] *X & Y (Foreign Surrogacy)* [2008] EWHC 3030 at 8. Hedley J warned that 'many pitfalls confront the couple who consider commissioning foreign surrogacy', and that 'potentially difficult conflict of law issues arise which may have wholly unintended and unforeseen consequences'. See also L Theis, N Gamble and L Ghevaert, '*Re X and Y (Foreign Surrogacy)*: "A Trek through a Thorn Forest"' (2009) 39 *Family Law Journal* 239.

[154] Ibid. See also D Howe, 'International Surrogacy – A Cautionary Tale' (2008) 38 *Family Law Journal* 61; and D Cullen, 'Surrogacy: "Commissioning" Parents Not Domiciled in UK – Matters To Be Borne in Mind by Those Contemplating Surrogacy Arrangements' (2008) 32 *Adoption & Fostering* 1.

legal parentage in the country of the birth of the child and the home country of the intended parents respectively. A very good example of such a conflict is the English case of *X & Y (Foreign Surrogacy)*.[155] In this case, a married British couple entered into a surrogacy agreement with a married Ukrainian surrogate. The surrogate mother was implanted with embryos created using donor eggs fertilised by the intended father's sperm. The surrogate mother gave birth to a set of twins. Under Ukrainian law, the British couple were considered the legal parents of the children and were registered as such on the birth certificates. Under English law, however, the legal parents of the twins were the surrogate mother and her husband.[156] The conflict between English and Ukrainian law resulted in parental status being lost for both couples. This left the children without legal parents and without rights to either British or Ukrainian citizenship. As a result, the children were, in the words of Mr Justice Hedley, 'marooned, stateless and parentless, whilst the couple could neither remain in the Ukraine nor bring the children to the UK'.

As the case illustrates, there are two dimensions to the problem of legal parentage in a cross-border surrogacy case: first, the acquisition of legal parentage in the country of birth and second, the transfer of the legal parentage to the intended parents in their home state. Indeed, the fact that the intended parents have been declared the legal parents in the country of birth does not automatically make them the legal parents in their home country. The intended parents will therefore seek to confirm the child's status as their child in their 'home' country. Generally, the problem of transfer of legal parenthood is treated differently in common law jurisdictions and in civil law countries. In most common law countries internal law (*lex fori*) will be applied to the establishment of legal parenthood where a child is born outside the jurisdiction (the '*lex fori*' method) because there is no foreign 'judgment' on legal parenthood that a court is being asked to recognise and because they do not apply foreign law to these types of issues of family law. In contrast, in most civil law countries the issue of the legal parenthood of a child born abroad will be approached through the application of relevant private

---

[155] *X & Y (Foreign Surrogacy)* [2008] EWHC 3030. Hedley J took this case into open court precisely in order to 'illustrate the sort of difficulties that currently can and do appear'.

[156] Under s 27 of the HFEA 1990, the woman who carries the child, regardless of genetics, is treated as the legal mother, even if the surrogacy takes place outside of the UK. In addition, despite the fact that the intended father was biologically related to the twins, because the surrogate mother was married, UK law presumed her husband to be the twins' father. See HFEA 1990, s 28.

international law rules on recognition of foreign judgments or the application of the relevant foreign law where there is no judgment to recognise (the 'conflict of laws' method).[157]

4.1 Common Law Countries

As mentioned above, in most common law jurisdictions, the law of the forum, in other words the *lex fori*, will be used to determine the legal parenthood of a child born as a result of a cross-border surrogacy arrangement. In some of these jurisdictions, the domestic law on parenthood expressly states that it has an extraterritorial effect, in other words it applies regardless of whether the child was born in the state concerned or abroad.[158] Available case law confirms that a foreign birth certificate does not suffice as proof of legal parenthood; instead, parenthood is to be decided in accordance with the *lex fori*.[159] In a number of common law jurisdictions, this approach has been reaffirmed through guidance issued by the state authorities for intended parents in cross-border surrogacy cases. For example, guidance issued by the UK Border Agency states that:

> ... anyone considering entering into an inter-country surrogacy arrangement must remember that if they reside in the United Kingdom, they are subject to United Kingdom law and the definitions which underlie it.[160]

Similarly, a guidance document published by the Irish Ministry for Justice, Equality and Defence provides that in considering the issue of legal parenthood in relation to children born as a result of a surrogacy

---

[157]   These two distinct methodological approaches were identified also in the preliminary report 'The Private International Law Issues Surrounding the Status of Children, Including Issues Arising from International Surrogacy Arrangements' prepared by the Permanent Bureau of the Hague Conference in March 2012. See http://www.hcch.net/index_en.php?act=text.display&tid=178 (accessed 14 July 2015) paras 35–41.

[158]   E.g. the UK (HFEA 2008, s 33(3)) and New Zealand (the Status of Children Act 1969, s 5(3)).

[159]   In the UK, for example, the issue was first tested before the High Court in *X & Y (Foreign Surrogacy)* [2008] EWHC 3030 (Fam). The Court made it clear that English law on parenthood applied to the determination of legal parenthood in a cross-border surrogacy case.

[160]   UK Border Agency Rules (n 110) para 10.

arrangement outside Ireland, '... the Irish authorities are required to apply Irish law'.[161]

Despite the fact that commercial surrogacy is illegal or against public policy in these countries, intended parents living in some common law jurisdictions have been able to achieve a full transfer of legal parentage in cross-border surrogacy cases.[162] In particular, in the United Kingdom, intended parents in cross-border commercial surrogacy cases have successfully relied on the existing United Kingdom legislation on surrogacy, which provides for the transfer of legal parenthood in altruistic surrogacy cases.[163] The analogous use of these provisions in cross-border commercial surrogacy cases has been made possible by the courts through the application of s 54(8) of the Human Fertilisation and Embryology Act 2008. This provision allows the courts a discretion to relax the statutory limit on the payment to the surrogate mother through a retrospective authorisation of payments exceeding reasonable pregnancy-related expenses in parental order applications.[164]

---

[161] Ministry for Justice, Equality and Defence, 'Citizenship, Parentage, Guardianship and Travel Document Issues in Relation to Children Born as a Result of Surrogacy Arrangements Entered into Outside the State' S 1, available 14 July 2015 at www.inis.gov.ie/en/JELR/20120221%20Guidance%20 Document.pdf/Files/20120221%20Guidance%20Document.pdf.

[162] A successful outcome is, however, often dependent on the existence of a genetic link between the child and at least one of the intended parents.

[163] The situation is, however, fundamentally different in another European common law jurisdiction – Ireland – where surrogacy remains unregulated. It has been suggested that the only potential avenue available to Irish intended parents in cross-border surrogacy cases to regularise the relationship between themselves and a surrogate child is through domestic adoption. See C Lindsay-Poulsen, 'Surrogacy: The Quest for Legal Recognition – Part 3' (2012) 30 *Irish Law Times* 38. For a comprehensive analysis of surrogacy in Ireland see Harding (n 102). See also C Lindsay-Poulsen, 'Surrogacy: The Quest for Legal Recognition – Part 1' (2012) 30 *Irish Law Times* 12 and C Lindsay-Poulsen, 'Surrogacy: The Quest for Legal Recognition – Part 2' (2012) 30 *Irish Law Times* 26. See also the *M v An tArd Chláraitheoir* case discussed above at n 40 et seq. In some non-European common law jurisdictions, for example New Zealand and to some extent Australia, some intended parents in cross-border surrogacy cases have been able to achieve a full transfer of legal parenthood through domestic adoption. Trimmings and Beaumont (n 1) 525.

[164] Section 54 of the HFEA 2008 replaced s 30 of the HFEA 1990 and permitted civil partners and couples in an enduring family relationship to apply for a parental order, in addition to married couples. Applications for a parental order under s 30 of the HFEA 1990 in the cross-border context included *Re X &*

The landmark decision was the case of *Re L (a minor)*[165] where legal parenthood was awarded to a British couple who had entered into a surrogacy arrangement in Illinois, USA. The court held that, despite the fact that payments to the surrogate mother had exceeded reasonable expenses, the child's welfare dictated that the parental order be made. The court concluded that one of the effects of the HFEA was that the child's welfare should not only be taken into consideration but should be the court's paramount consideration in parental order proceedings involving international surrogacy arrangements.[166] The court held:

> The effect of that must be to weight the balance between public policy considerations and welfare ... decisively in favour of welfare. It must follow that it will only be in the clearest case of the abuse of public policy that the court will be able to withhold an order if otherwise welfare considerations support its making.[167]

The court, nevertheless, acknowledged the tension between the public policy against commercial surrogacy and the paramountcy of the welfare principle, and expressed the view that applications for authorisation under s 54(8) of the 2008 Act should continue to be scrutinised carefully on a case-by-case basis.[168]

Y (Foreign Surrogacy) [2008] EWHC 3030 (Fam); *Re S (Parental Order)* [2009] EWHC 2977 (Fam); and *Re G (Surrogacy: Foreign Domicile)* [2007] EWHC 2814.

[165]   *Re L (A Minor)* [2010] EWHC 3146 (Fam).

[166]   Para 9. Justice Hedley explained that the Human Fertilisation and Embryology (Parental Orders) Regulations 2010 apply certain provisions of current adoption legislation (i.e. the Adoption and Children Act 2002) to applications for parental orders under s 54 of the HFEA 2008. In particular, the application of s 1 of the Adoption and Children Act 2002 to parental order applications means that the child's welfare is the court's paramount consideration when deciding whether or not to make a parental order. Ibid. See also *Re X Children* [2011] EWHC 3147 (Fam) para 30. The Human Fertilisation and Embryology (Parental Orders) Regulations 2010 give effect to s 54 of the HFEA 2008 and replace the Parental Orders (Human Fertilisation and Embryology) Regulations 1994 and the Parental Orders (Human Fertilisation and Embryology) (Scotland) Regulations 1994. For more information see Explanatory Memorandum (n 9).

[167]   *Re L (A Minor)* [2010] EWHC 3146 (Fam) at [10].

[168]   Ibid, at [12].

The line of reasoning established in *Re L (a minor)* was followed in later cases: *Re X (Children)*[169] involved two separate commercial surrogacy arrangements between a British couple and two Indian surrogate mothers. One child was born as a result of each of these arrangements, and parental orders were awarded to the British couple. In the case of *A and A v P, P and B*[170] a British couple entered into a surrogacy arrangement in India. Sadly, the intended father, who was also the genetic father, died unexpectedly during the parental order proceedings. Although it was not clear whether the intended mother was genetically related to the child,[171] the court concluded that the paramountcy of the welfare principle required that a parental order be made.[172] The case of *IJ (A Child)*[173] concerned a surrogacy arrangement entered into between a British couple and a married Ukrainian surrogate. The child was conceived as a result of the fertilisation of an egg from an anonymous egg donor by sperm from the intended father. The intended parents experienced difficulties in obtaining immigration clearance for the child to enter the United Kingdom;[174] however, once in the country, they were able to apply successfully for a parental order. Finally, *J v G (Parental*

---

[169] *Re X (Children)* [2011] EWHC 3147 (Fam). For a comment on this case see F Cranmer, 'International Surrogacy: Parental Orders – Commercial Surrogacy vs Interests of Child' (2012) 168 *Law & Justice* 150.

[170] *A and A v P, P and B* [2011] EWHC 1738 (Fam); [2012] Fam 188.

[171] The uncertainty was due to the fact that five embryos were transferred to the surrogate mother's womb, two of which were formed from the intended mother's eggs and three from donor eggs. All eggs were fertilised with the intended father's sperm.

[172] A consideration was given also to the UNCRC, in particular article 8 of that Convention which requires contracting states to protect the child's right to identity. The court held that the concept of identity included the legal recognition of a relationship between a child and his/her parents (see paras 27–28). If the application for a parental order was rejected, it would seriously impact the child's right to have his identity protected. In particular, the consequences of not making an order in this case would be as follows: '(i) There is no legal relationship between the child and his biological father; (ii) The child is denied the social and emotional benefits of recognition of that relationship; (iii) The child may be financially disadvantaged if he is not recognized legally as the child of his father (in terms of inheritance); (iv) The child does not have a legal reality which matches the day to day reality; (v) The child is further disadvantaged by the death of his biological father.' *A and A v P, P and B* [2011] EWHC 1738 (Fam) para 26 (Theis J).

[173] *Re IJ (A Child)* [2011] EWHC 921 (Fam).

[174] Ibid, at [3].

Orders)[175] concerned an application for parental orders in relation to twins born from a surrogacy arrangement commissioned in California by two men who were United Kingdom nationals and civil partners. Mrs Justice Theis granted a parental order to both men on the basis of the welfare of the children. She encouraged intending parents in cross-border surrogacy cases to apply for a parental order in the United Kingdom within six months of the birth of the child as required by United Kingdom law.[176] Nevertheless, the six months requirement has recently been waived in *Re X (A Child) (Surrogacy: Time Limit).*[177]

Lately, a move towards an even more lenient approach towards cross-border commercial surrogacy was made by the High Court in the case of *D and L (Surrogacy).*[178] The court not only agreed to retrospectively authorise payments exceeding reasonable pregnancy-related expenses as in the previous cases but also to dispense with the need to obtain the surrogate mother's consent to the transfer of parentage. The case concerned a surrogacy arrangement between a male couple and an Indian surrogate. Following the birth of twins, the surrogate mother could not be located to give her consent as required by s 54 of the Human Fertilisation and Embryology Act.[179] Under this provision, the consent of the surrogate is required at least six weeks after the birth of the children. Despite the lack of a valid consent, the court decided to grant a parental order to the applicants as the welfare of the children required it. Nevertheless, Baker J pointed out that the authority to waive consent should not be exercised lightly:

> [a]lthough a consent given before the expiry of six weeks after birth is not valid for the purposes of s54, the court is entitled to take into account evidence that the woman did give consent at earlier times to giving up the baby. The weight attached to such earlier consent is, however, likely to be limited. The courts must be careful not to use such evidence to undermine the legal requirement that a consent is only valid if given after six weeks.

---

[175] *J v G (Parental Orders)* [2013] EWHC 1432 (Fam).

[176] *J v G (Parental Orders)* [2013] EWHC 1432 (Fam) at [30].

[177] *Re X (A Child) (Surrogacy: Time Limit)* [2014] EWHC 3135 (Fam). For a detailed comment on this case see K Trimmings, 'Six Month Deadline for Applications for Parental Orders Relaxed by the High Court' (2015) *Journal of Social Welfare and Family Law* (forthcoming); and M Welstead, 'Surrogacy: One More Nail in the Coffin' (2014) *Family Law Journal* 1637.

[178] *D and L (Surrogacy)* [2012] EWHC 2631 (Fam). For a comment on this case see A Conroy, 'Surrogate Children Born in India' (2012) 36 *Adoption & Fostering* 119.

[179] See section 3.3.1 above.

The principles formulated in the above cases now seem to be firmly established and have recently been succinctly summarised by Theis J in *Re WT (A Child)*.[180]

To summarise, reported case law shows that despite the underlying public policy against commercial surrogacy in the United Kingdom, the courts have generally been sympathetic to the situation of the intended parents. The rationale behind this approach has been explained by Hedley J as follows:

> The difficulty is that it is almost impossible to imagine a set of circumstances in which by the time the case comes to court, the welfare of any child (particularly a foreign child) would not be gravely compromised (at the very least) by a refusal to make an order ... If public policy is truly to be upheld, it would need to be enforced at a much earlier stage than the final hearing of a section 30 application.[181]

4.2 Civil Law Countries

As mentioned above, in civil law countries, the issue of legal parenthood in cross-border surrogacy cases is usually approached from the private international law perspective, often through the method of recognition. Depending on the availability of legal remedies in the country of birth (often conditioned upon the genetic make-up of the child), the intended parents will normally seek recognition of a judgment issued in the country of birth that accorded them legal parenthood there or they will argue that the applicable law to govern the parentage of the child is the law where the child was born and use, for example, a birth certificate from that country and a disavowal of paternity or maternity by the surrogate mother and her husband as evidence that under the foreign law the intended parents are the legal parents.[182] The recognition of the foreign judgment or the application of the foreign law will, however,

---

[180]   *Re WT (A Child)* [2014] EWHC 1303 (Fam) at [35].

[181]   *X & Y (Foreign Surrogacy)* [2008] EWHC 3030 Fam at [24]. Section 30 refers to HFEA 1990.

[182]   In cases where legal parenthood was acquired in the country of birth through adoption, recognition of a foreign adoption order will be sought instead. It, however, appears that this scenario occurs in a small minority of cross-border surrogacy cases so the analysis will focus on the alternative, more common situations as listed above. See also Curry-Sumner and Vonk (n 102) 283, noting that the vast majority of Dutch intended parents in cross-border surrogacy cases seek recognition of their legal parentage established in the country of birth on the basis of 'the alleged creation of legal familial ties, i.e. parentage'.

often be refused on the grounds of public policy, placing the intended parents in a precarious situation.[183] Examples include cases from a variety of jurisdictions.

4.2.1 Spain[184]

In one Spanish case, a Spanish gay couple entered into a gestational surrogacy arrangement with a surrogate mother in California. Twins were born as a result of the arrangement and the intended fathers sought the registration of the births at the Spanish consulate in Los Angeles. The request was denied on the grounds that the applicable law was Spanish law and that the surrogate mother was the legal mother under Spanish law. Interestingly, the consulate took the 'applicable law' approach. The couple successfully appealed to the administrative body in Spain in charge of the Civil Register (DGRN) which ordered the births of the twins to be registered in Spain.[185] The Public Prosecutor launched a successful appeal in the Court of First Instance in Valencia, which was confirmed by the Court of Appeal in Valencia. There was no California judgment to recognise and under the Spanish applicable law the gay couple were not the legal parents.[186]

4.2.2 The Netherlands[187]

In the Netherlands, courts have consistently refused to register foreign birth certificates where there was no mother stated in the document. In one case, a Dutch surrogate mother decided to take advantage of the possibility of an anonymous birth in France in order to avoid being listed

---

[183] For a detailed analysis of public policy in the context of cross-border surrogacy arrangements see D Gruenbaum, 'Foreign Surrogate Motherhood: *mater semper certa erat*' (2012) 60 *American Journal of Comparative Law* 475, 494–500.

[184] For more information on the cross-border aspects of surrogacy in Spain see Orejudo (n 102) 349–55. See also E Farnós Amorós, 'Surrogacy Arrangements in a Global World: The Case of Spain' [2013] International Family Law 68.

[185] Decision of the Ministry of Justice, Madrid, 18 February 2009, No 2575/2008.

[186] Decision of the Tribunal de Primera Instancia No 15 of Valencia, 15 September 2010, No 193/2010. The decision was upheld on appeal: Audiencia Provincial de Valencia (Seccion 10a), 23 November 2011, No 826/2011. See also the analysis of Orejudo (n 102) 349–55. For administrative developments see 4.2.7 below.

[187] For more information on the cross-border aspects of surrogacy in the Netherlands see Curry-Sumner and Vonk (n 102) 283–93.

on the child's birth certificate as the mother of the child she was carrying for a gay Dutch couple. Upon the birth of the child, the intended fathers returned to the Netherlands with a French birth certificate where only one parent, that is, the biological father, was listed. The Dutch authorities refused to register the birth certificate on the grounds of public policy. The District Court of The Hague concurred with the registrar's view, opining that to register a birth certificate where no details about the mother were available would violate the child's right to know his or her parents guaranteed by article 7 of the United Nations Convention on the Rights of the Child (UNCRC).[188]

A different line of reasoning was used by the same court in another case which concerned a 'typical' cross-border commercial surrogacy arrangement commissioned by a Dutch gay couple in California. In this case a pre-birth order was issued by the Superior Court of California which ordered that, upon the birth of the child, the intended fathers be placed on the child's birth certificate as the legal parents. Once back in the Netherlands, the men sought recognition of the birth certificate. Their application was, however, refused by the court with the following reasoning:

> The judicial decision from the Superior Court of California of 15th August 2008 cannot be recognised since it is contrary to Dutch public policy, bearing in mind the aforementioned fundamental rule of family law (*mater certa semper est*) and the fact that the judicial decision was ordered without the legal mother first being determined.[189]

4.2.3 France[190]

Normally, the first step for French intended parents involved in cross-border surrogacy arrangements is to apply to the French consulate for the registration of a foreign birth certificate or a foreign judgment that accorded them parentage in the French civil status records.[191] If the application is successful, the intended parents will obtain 'a French public document of the highest standard of proof that firmly establishes parentage according to French law'.[192] A decision of the consulate to register the birth can, however, be questioned by the Ministère public,

---

[188] Ibid, 291.

[189] Ibid, 293. For developments see 4.2.7 below.

[190] For more information on the cross-border aspects of surrogacy in France see Perreau-Saussine and Sauvage (n 94) 122–30.

[191] French intended parents can also apply for recognition of a foreign birth certificate before the Conseil d'Etat. See section 4.2.5 below.

[192] Perreau-Saussine and Sauvage (n 94) 126.

which can request that the registration be annulled on the grounds of public policy. The ultimate decision is then to be taken by the Cour de cassation. Such a situation arose in two recent cases, each of which involved a surrogacy arrangement commissioned in the United States (California and Minnesota respectively) by a French married couple. In both cases, there was a genetic link between the intended father and the child, and legal parenthood was established in the United States by a judgment.[193] The Cour de cassation accepted the request of the Ministère public and held that a registration of the judgments would violate public policy as 'according to current law, it is contrary to the principle by which the status of persons may not be subject to private agreements ... to give effect, in relation to parentage, to an agreement on surrogacy'.[194] The cases were, however, then brought before the European Court of Human Rights (ECtHR) (see section 4.2.9 below).

4.2.4   Toward a more liberal trend
Consistent with the general trend towards an increased focus on the 'best interests' of the child, more liberal developments have emerged recently in some civil law jurisdictions. Judicial and administrative authorities in these countries have 'invented' various ad-hoc partial solutions, eventually leading to (at least) partial recognition of the legal parenthood established in the country of birth.

4.2.5   Use of a foreign birth certificate as evidence of the genetic father being the legal father under the applicable law
In a recent French case which concerned a child born to a gay couple through surrogacy in India, the court held that as a DNA test proved a genetic link between the child and one of the intended fathers and he was registered as the father on the Indian foreign birth certificate the court could presume that the child was French and entitled to a French travel document to leave India to go to France.[195] The fact that surrogacy arrangements are contrary to French public policy does not affect the obligation of the authorities to give primary consideration to the best interests of the child in all actions concerning children in accordance with article 3(1) of the UNCRC.[196]

---

[193]   Cour de Cassation, Chambre Civile 1, 6 April 2011, 09-66.486, Publié au bulletin, and Cour de cassation, civile, Chambre civile 1, 6 avril 2011, 10-19.053, Publié au bulletin. Per Perreau-Saussine and Sauvage (n 94) 125.
[194]   Ibid. See also D Gruenbaum (n 183) 496.
[195]   Perreau-Saussine and Sauvage (n 94) 123.
[196]   Ibid.

A similar approach was taken in a series of court decisions in Belgium: *Samuel*,[197] *AM&ND*[198] and *C*.[199] The case of *Samuel*[200] involved a traditional surrogacy arrangement in Ukraine, with the intended father being genetically related to the child. A Ukrainian birth certificate listed the surrogate mother and the intended father as the legal parents of the child. The intended father then sought acceptance of his parentage in Belgium relying on the evidence of the Ukrainian birth certificate. The court granted the request, pointing out that the decision was not meant to give effect to the surrogacy arrangement (which was contrary to public policy), but only concerned the establishment of the intended father's paternity. The acceptance of the birth certificate as an authentic instrument was seen as desirable in the light of the child's interests and, as required by Belgian private international law, in accordance with the applicable law (Belgian law as the law of the nationality of the person whose parenthood is at stake).[201]

Both *AM&ND*[202] and *C*[203] concerned surrogacy arrangements commissioned in India by Belgian single men as the intended parents. In both cases an egg donor was used and the respective intended fathers provided sperm. In each case, an Indian birth certificate listed the intended father as the legal parent but there was no mention of a mother on the birth certificate. Despite this, however, in both cases, the Indian birth certificate was accepted in Belgium as an authentic instrument and in accordance with Belgian law as the applicable law the fathers were accepted as the children's fathers on the grounds of the best interests of each of the children. In the case of *C*,[204] human rights arguments were also used to justify the decision. In particular, it was held that a refusal to accept the evidence of the birth certificate would infringe the child's and the

---

[197]   *Samuel*, Court of First Instance Brussels, 15 February 2011. Per Verschelden and Verhellen (n 102) 52.

[198]   *AM & ND*, Court of First Instance Nivelles, 6 April 2011. Per Verschelden and Verhellen (n 102) 52.

[199]   *C*, Court of First Instance Brussels, 6 April 2010. Per Verschelden and Verhellen (n 102) 52.

[200]   *Samuel*, Court of First Instance, Brussels 15 February 2011. Per Verschelden and Verhellen (n 102) 60.

[201]   See Verschelden and Verhellen (n 102) 69–70.

[202]   *AM & ND*, Court of First Instance Nivelles, 6 April 2011. Verschelden and Verhellen (n 102) 69–70.

[203]   *C*, Court of First Instance Brussels, 6 April 2010. Verschelden and Verhellen (n 102) 69–70.

[204]   *C*, Court of First Instance Brussels, 6 April 2010. Verschelden and Verhellen (n 102) 69–70.

intended father's right to family life guaranteed by article 8 of the European Convention on Human Rights (ECHR).

In *H & E*[205] a surrogacy arrangement was entered into between a Belgian married couple and a Ukrainian surrogate mother. Embryos were created using the intended parents' gametes and the surrogate mother gave birth to a set of twins. Birth certificates were issued in Ukraine, listing the intended parents as the legal parents of the children. The couple then sought acceptance in Belgium of the birth certificates as authentic instruments and for the court to find them to be the legal parents in accordance with Belgian law as the applicable law. The court held that it could not accept the intended mother as the legal mother of the child as this would undermine the Belgian domestic rule on legal motherhood (the rule that the woman who gives birth to a child is to be regarded as the legal mother). The court, however, opined that there was nothing wrong with accepting the legal parenthood of the intended father.

Belgian courts have applied the acceptance of a birth certificate as an authentic instrument in accordance with the applicable law approach to cases involving gay couples as intended parents, with the outcome that only the man who was genetically related to the child was found to be the legal father under Belgian law. An example is the case of *M&M*,[206] which involved a surrogacy arrangement commissioned by a Belgian gay couple in California. Donor eggs were used to create embryos. The arrangements resulted in the birth of a set of twins. Before the birth of the children, the Californian Supreme Court declared both men to be the genetic and legal parents and ordered that their names be placed on the birth certificates after the birth of the children. The children were brought to Belgium on US passports. Once in Belgium the couple sought registration of the birth certificates in the civil register. The registration was, however, opposed by the public prosecutor so the men decided to initiate legal proceedings to both be accepted as the children's legal parents in Belgium. Although the first instance court refused to do so on the grounds of public policy, this decision was overturned on appeal. The appellate court acknowledged that surrogacy contracts were void under public policy principles, however, it held that the illicit nature of such contracts could not infringe on the superior interests of the child. Consequently, the court accepted the legal parenthood of the genetic father but not of the non-genetically related member of the gay couple.

---

[205] *H & E*, Court of First Instance Antwerp, 19 December 2008. Per Verschelden and Verhellen (n 102) 70.

[206] *M & M*, Court of Appeal Liège, 6 September 2010. Per Verschelden and Verhellen (n 102) 70.

4.2.6 Recognition of a judgment on parenthood issued in the country of birth

In December 2011, the Austrian Constitutional Court was called upon to decide a case involving a cross-border surrogacy arrangement between an American surrogate mother (resident in the US state of Georgia) and Austrian/Italian intended parents.[207] The couple were Austrian residents, although only the intended mother was an Austrian citizen. As surrogacy is prohibited in Austria, the couple decided to explore the option of cross-border surrogacy. Consequently, two surrogacy arrangements were commissioned by the couple in the United States (in 2006 and in 2009 respectively), with the same surrogate mother and in both cases the couple using their own genetic material. Two children were born as a result of these arrangements. The children became United States citizens by birth and both later obtained Austrian citizenship as well. However, when the intended mother claimed child benefits, the Austrian Ministry of Interior requested that the Austrian nationality be withdrawn on the basis that surrogacy was illegal in Austria, that under Austrian law the surrogate mother remained the children's legal mother and that the US court's decision establishing legal parenthood of the intended mother could therefore not be recognised in Austria. These arguments were, however, rejected by the Austrian Constitutional Court among others on the following grounds:

(1) the US judgment determining legal parenthood of the intended mother was taken without reference to Austrian law and was therefore valid under norms of private international law;

(2) the Austrian law prohibiting surrogacy was not a part of Austrian public policy and therefore recognition of the US judgment was not contrary to public policy;

(3) the surrogate mother could not be forced by Austrian law into the position of the legal mother against her will;

---

[207] Decision of the Constitutional Court (Verfassungsgerichtshof) No B 13/11-10, 14 December 2011, full text in German is available at http://eudo-citizenship.eu/caselawDB/docs/AT%20VfGH%20B1311_10.pdf, and a summary of the decision in English can be found at http://eudo-citizenship.eu/databases/citizenship-case-law/?search=1&name=&year=&country=Austria&national=1 (both accessed 14 July 2014). For a comment on this case see E Bernat, 'Staatsangehörigkeit eines von einer Österreicherin und einem Italiener abstammenden Kindes, das von einer amerikanischen Leihmutter im amerikanischen Gliedstaat Georgia geboren worden ist' (2012) 3 *Recht Der Medizin* 104.

(4)   when determining the issue of nationality, the Ministry of Interior had acted arbitrarily by ignoring scholarly views and case law on public policy and by failing to consider the welfare of the children.

4.2.7   Administrative initiatives

In Spain, a more lenient approach has recently been taken at the administrative level. In October 2010, the Dirección General de los Registros y del Notariado (DGRN), which is an administrative body in charge of the Civil Register, issued a resolution to instruct civil registrars on how to proceed in cases involving cross-border surrogacy.[208] Normally, civil registrars in Spain register legal parenthood established by a foreign judgment only if the judgment has first been formally recognised by a Spanish court. The resolution, however, instructs the registrars that in cross-border surrogacy cases, the prior recognition of the foreign judgment by the court is not necessary. Instead, if certain conditions are met, the civil registry is competent to pronounce the authenticity of the foreign judgment and to register the birth in Spain without recognition of the foreign judgment by a court. The resolution requires, for example, that:

(1)   the foreign judgment was issued in uncontested proceedings;
(2)   procedural rights of the parties, in particular the surrogate mother, were guaranteed in the foreign proceedings;
(3)   there was no infringement of the best interests of the child and the surrogate mother; and
(4)   the surrogate mother gave her consent freely and voluntarily, without error, violence or fraud.[209]

Importantly, the resolution does not require that the foreign judgment is not contrary to Spanish public policy.[210]

---

[208]   Instrucción de 5 de octubre de 2010, de la Dirección General de los Registros y del Notariado, sobre regimen registral de la filiación de los nacidos mediante gestación por sustitución. Per Orejudo (n 102) 350.

[209]   Ibid, 353.

[210]   Ibid, 352. However, in a ruling made in February 2014, the Spanish Supreme Court held that the civil registry had to examine not only the authenticity of the birth certificate but also whether the certificate was contrary to Spanish public policy. The Court acknowledged that the best interests of the children had to be taken into account in this scrutiny; however, a balance had to be achieved between the children's interests and the interests of the Spanish State to prevent commodification of children and women. See Permanent Bureau of the Hague Conference, 'A Study of Legal Parentage and the Issues Arising from

Administrative initiatives in the Netherlands indicate that in due course the country might also move towards a more permissive approach to cross-border surrogacy. In particular, in a letter from the Secretary of State for Safety and Justice addressed to the Chairman of the House of Representatives dated 16 December 2011,[211] the Secretary summarised the problems that arise from cross-border surrogacy arrangements in the Netherlands and proposed among others the following measures:

(1)   cross-border surrogacy arrangements where at least one of the intended parents shares a genetic link with the child should be accepted in the Netherlands; and
(2)   no judgment should be passed on the expenses paid to the surrogate mother in cross-border scenarios.

Undoubtedly, the proposed approach goes against the current Dutch policy on surrogacy[212] and it is unclear whether the proposed regulation would extend also to domestic surrogacy cases.

4.2.8   Acknowledgement of paternity

In some countries a more liberal approach has been taken in relation to acknowledgment of paternity by intended fathers in cross-border surrogacy cases. It has been reported that in Germany, for example, 'the public

---

International Surrogacy Arrangements' Prel Doc No 3 C, 76, March 2014, available 14 July 2015 at http://www.hcch.net/upload/wop/gap2014pd03c_en.pdf. Nevertheless, in response to the ECtHR decisions in *Mennesson* and *Labassee* (see section 4.2.9. below), the DGRN has issued a Circular stating that the 2010 DGRN Instruction must now be applied again by registries regardless of the contradictory Supreme Court decision.

[211]   F Teeven (Ministry of Justice), 'Onderwerp Draagmoederschap', 16 December 2011 (available 14 July 2015 at www.google.co.uk/url?sa=t&rct=j&q= &esrc=s&frm=1&source=web&cd=1&ved=0CE0QFjAA&url=http%3A%2F%2F www.rijksoverheid.nl%2Fbestanden%2Fdocumenten-en-publicaties%2Fkamer stukken%2F2011%2F12%2F16%2Fbrief-tweede-kamer-draagmoederschap%2F draagmoederschap.pdf&ei=8agGUMCvAoTPhAeR8ZHYBw&usg=AFQjCNE3 nkzqBGfBJYlliGSBP10Y8aihiw&sig2=j494p4s9wS8hlDU06i7U_A).

[212]   Currently, surrogacy is not regulated in the Netherlands; nevertheless, commercial surrogacy is criminalised under Dutch law. For a detailed overview of the Dutch domestic approach to surrogacy see Curry-Sumner and Vonk (n 102) 274–83.

policy exception seems to be handled less strictly [in cases of acknowledgment of paternity] than in questions of motherhood as a whole'.[213] In at least one reported German cross-border surrogacy case, German authorities applied foreign (Russian) law to decide whether the intended father had undertaken a valid acknowledgment of paternity in Russia. This resulted in the acknowledgment undertaken by the intended father in Russia being held valid in Germany.[214]

In two cases in Switzerland, intended fathers successfully acknowledged the child before a Swiss court following a refusal by a Swiss consulate to recognise the foreign birth certificate.[215] In one of these cases, the acknowledgment of paternity was possible even though the intended father was not the genetic father of the child.[216]

Finally, according to French law, it is open to French intended fathers in cross-border surrogacy cases to acknowledge paternity to establish their legal parenthood.[217] This avenue was advocated by the Conseil d'Etat during the review of the French Bioethics Act 1994 in July 2011. In particular, the Conseil d'Etat suggested that 'the prohibition of the establishment of maternity between the intending mother and the child should be maintained'; however, 'acknowledgment of paternity should become the main alternative to the prohibition of surrogacy'.[218]

4.2.9 The European Court of Human Rights

In June 2014, the ECtHR took a decision in two French cross-border commercial surrogacy cases – *Mennesson v France*[219] and *Labassee v France*[220] (see section 4.2.3 above for details of these cases). In these

---

[213] Gössl (n 94) 141. For a comprehensive analysis of the German approach to paternity see S Kamei, 'Partitioning Paternity: The German Approach to a Disjuncture Between Genetic and Legal Paternity With Implications for American Courts' (2009–2010) 11 *San Diego International Law Journal* 509.

[214] AG Nürnberg, UR III 0264/09, 14 December 2009. Per Gössl (n 94) 140.

[215] 2012 Hague Report (n 157) para 37.

[216] Ibid.

[217] See Perreau-Saussine and Sauvage (n 94) 129.

[218] 'La Révision Des Lois de Bioéthique', étude du Conseil d'État parue à la Documentation française, in particular pp 47–54, per Perreau-Saussine and Sauvage (n 94) 128.

[219] ECHR, 26 June 2014, App. no. 65192/11.

[220] ECHR, 26 June 2014, App no. 65941/11. For a comprehensive comment on these cases see G Puppinck, 'ECHR: Towards the Liberalisation of Surrogacy' (2014) 118 *Revue Lamy de Droit Civil* 78, English translation available 14 July 2015 from http://papers.ssrn.com/sol3/papers.cfm?abstract_id=2500075. See also P Beaumont and K Trimmings, 'Recent jurisprudence of the European Court of

cases the Court faced the problem of the refusal by France to grant legal recognition to parent-child relationships that had been lawfully established in the US between children born as a result of commercial surrogacy arrangements where the intended father was also the genetic father of the child. The applicants relied on article 8 of the ECHR which guarantees the right to respect for private and family life. The Court first explored the applicability of article 8 to the given situation – that is, did 'family life' and 'private life' exist in the cases in question? The Court found that article 8 was applicable as 'there was no doubt that the Mennessons had cared for the twins as parents since the children's birth and that the four of them lived together in a way that was indistinguishable from "family life" in the accepted sense of the term'.[221] In relation to 'private life' the Court found that the right of identity was 'an integral part of the concept of private life and there was a direct link between the private life of children born following a surrogacy treatment and the legal determination of their parentage'.[222] The Court noted that France's refusal to recognise the legal parent-child relationship stemmed 'from a wish to discourage French nationals from having recourse outside France to a reproductive technique that was prohibited in that country with the aim, as the authorities saw it, of protecting the children and the surrogate mother'.[223] The interference pursued two legitimate aims listed in article 8: the 'protection of health' and the 'protection of the rights and freedoms of others'. Consequently, the interference had been 'in accordance with the law' within the meaning of article 8.

The Court noted the fact that approaches to surrogacy within Europe differ widely and that surrogacy raised 'delicate ethical questions'.[224] The Court indicated that the prohibition of surrogacy was acceptable in principle; however, this liberty was 'mitigated' by the practical need to 'take into account the fact that an essential aspect of the identity of individuals is at stake when it comes to kinship'.[225] Consequently, the

---

Human Rights in the area of cross-border surrogacy: is there still a need for global regulation of surrogacy?' University of Aberdeen, Centre for Private International Law Working Paper No 2015/2 available on 11 August at http://www.abdn.ac.uk/law/documents/Recent_jurisprudence_of_the_European_Court_of_Human_Rights_in_the_area_of_cross-border_surrogacy.pdf

[221] European Court of Human Rights, 'Press Release' (185) 2014, 26 June 2014, 3.

[222] Ibid.

[223] Ibid.

[224] ECHR, 26 June 2014, App no. 65192/11 para 79, per Puppinck (n 220).

[225] Ibid, para 80.

margin of appreciation was narrow when it came to parentage, which involved a key aspect of an individual's identity.[226]

The Court examined the issues separately from the perspective of the applicant parents and from the perspective of the children. No violation of article 8 was found in relation to the applicant parents' right to respect for their family life. This was because France enabled the family to settle in the country with the children and to live with them together in circumstances which were similar to other families. There was no risk of the applicant parents and the children being separated by the authorities. The Court, however, found a violation of article 8 concerning the children's right to respect for their private life due to the refusal by France to recognise the children's legal relationship with their genetic fathers. The Court held that given the significance of genetic parentage as an element of a person's identity, it was contrary to the best interests of the children to deprive them of the legal relationship with their genetic fathers.[227] It is not clear if the Court would extend the same rights to the

---

[226]   European Court of Human Rights (n 220).

[227]   The decision of the ECHR in the *Menesson* and *Labassee* cases can be contrasted with a recent decision of the Italian Court of Cassation from 11 November 2014, No 24001 (thanks to Professor Costanza Honorati for translation of key aspects of this judgment) where the Court refused to recognise the existence of a parent-child relationship between a couple that had commissioned surrogacy in Ukraine and a child born as a result of this surrogacy arrangement. Italy, like France, forbids surrogacy. Italian authorities took a decision to remove the child from the intended parents and to place him for adoption. Moreover, criminal proceedings were initiated against the intended parents in Italy. In the light of the ECHR decisions in *Menesson* and *Labassee* this approach might appear harsh; however, it is thought that it is justifiable. This is in particular on the grounds that the present case differs from the French cases in two important respects: first, there was no genetic connection between the child and either of the intended parents (i.e. the child was conceived using donor eggs and donor sperm); and second, such an arrangement was illegal also in Ukraine as only surrogacy where at least one of the intended parents is genetically linked to the child is permitted in that jurisdiction. For a discussion of the decision of the Chamber of the ECtHR in a similar case of *Paradiso and Campbell v Italy*, ECHR 27 January 2015, App no. 25358/12, and for suggestions as to how the Grand Chamber should decide that case, see P Beaumont and K Trimmings (n220).

Similarly, the liberal approach taken by the ECHR in the *Menesson* and *Labassee* cases can be contrasted with two decisions of the Court of Justice of the European Union (CJEU) on the interpretation of the Equal Treatment Directives (Directive 2000/78/EC of 27 November 2000, establishing a general framework for equal treatment in employment and occupation and Directive

child of an intending mother who is the genetic mother of the child given the existence of a different birth mother.

5. CONCLUSION

For a number of reasons, the above examples of solutions 'invented' by judicial and administrative authorities of different countries to fill the existing legal vacuum on surrogacy are, unfortunately, far from adequate. First, in many jurisdictions, procedures used to achieve these solutions were originally not designed for surrogacy situations and are therefore not suitable for application to surrogacy cases. As a result, the procedures are often very complex and lengthy, adding additional stress and costs on the intended parents who might be forced to stay in the country of birth for an extended period of time. Second, in addition to their ad-hoc nature, these remedies normally offer only partial solutions in relation to legal parenthood whereby it is only the position of the intended father that is regularised. The recent development of a human rights remedy by the ECtHR so far only confers rights on genetic fathers. The position of intended mothers (genetic or otherwise) and non-genetic fathers remains uncertain, with often no, or only limited, options of acquiring legal parenthood.[228] This is particularly true in relation to some civil law countries. Finally, it has rightly been pointed out that many cross-border surrogacy cases are further complicated by a 'catch 22' dimension, meaning that the intended parents must return from the country of birth in order to establish legal parentage in their home country but often find it difficult to bring a child into their home country before first establishing legal parentage.[229]

2006/54/EC of the European Parliament and of the Council of 5 July 2006) – Case C-363/12 *A Government Department and the Board of Management of a Community School* ECLI:EU:C:2014:159 and Case C-167/12 *C.D. v S.T.* ECLI:EU:C:2014:169. Both cases raised the issue of the entitlement to paid maternity leave of a woman who had commissioned surrogacy. The CJEU held that EU law did not provide for commissioning mothers to be entitled to paid leave equivalent to maternity leave as there was no sex (2006 Directive) or disability (2000 Directive) discrimination and that adoption leave for a commissioning mother is outside the scope of the 2006 Directive.

[228] One of the options might be adoption, however, in some countries the adoption process might be far from straightforward where the child was born as a result of a commercial cross-border surrogacy arrangement.

[229] Millbank, 'The New Surrogacy Parentage Laws in Australia' (n 116) 198.

In jurisdictions where the ad-hoc, partial remedies have been crafted, there is a trend to focus primarily on the best interests of the child, with the result of the welfare principle trumping the public policy concerns that surround cross-border (in particular commercial) surrogacy. Despite the obvious tension between the two policy goals, the inclination to favour the best interests of the child is based on the objective to lessen the detrimental impact of the legal limbo for children born as a result of a cross-border surrogacy arrangement. Given the absence of a regulatory framework, this line of reasoning is considered reasonable. Indeed, courts in cross-border surrogacy cases are quite often faced with a *fait accompli* where the welfare of a very young child is at stake, and it would therefore be unrealistic to expect them to strictly implement the policy considerations against commercial surrogacy at this late stage. However, recent decisions of the highest courts in France, Italy and Spain show that the public policy concerns can still play a decisive role and in certain cases may lead to the child being removed from the intending parents if neither of them have a genetic link with the child.

Nevertheless, the current status quo raises the question of whether it is acceptable to retrospectively give effect to a cross-border commercial surrogacy agreement whilst prohibiting such arrangements domestically for serious ethical reasons.[230] Against this background, the current situation is wholly unsatisfactory and clearly points to the need for a global regulatory mechanism of cross-border surrogacy not least in order to ensure that the legal status of children born through cross-border surrogacy is 'remedied by a more direct, transparent and inclusive legislative response.'[231] It would also have the significant benefit of preventing a situation where the intended mother has no parentage rights when the intended father does, even where both are the genetic parents.

---

[230] On the problem of 'circumvention tourism' more generally see I Cohen, 'S.H. and Others v. Austria and Circumvention Tourism' (2012) 25 *Reproductive BioMedicine Online* 660.

[231] Millbank, 'The New Surrogacy Parentage Laws in Australia' (n 116) 203. Recent resources that address the problem of surrogacy arrangements in a transnational context include Trimmings and Beaumont (n 1); 2014 Hague Report (n 152); K Boele-Woelki, '(Cross-Border) Surrogate Motherhood: We Need to Take Action Now!', in Permanent Bureau of the Hague Conference on Private International Law, *A Commitment to Private International Law: Essays in Honour of Hans Van Loon* (Intersentia Publishing 2013); E Farnós Amorós, (n 184); D Gruenbaum, (n 183); Storrow (n 14) and E Stehr, 'International Surrogacy Contracts Regulation: National Governments' and International Bodies' Misguided Quests to Prevent Exploitation' (2012) 35 *Hastings International Law & Comparative Law Quarterly* 253.

RECOMMENDATIONS FOR FURTHER READING

P Beaumont and K Trimmings, 'Recent jurisprudence of the European Court of Human Rights in the area of cross-border surrogacy: is there still a need for global regulation of surrogacy?' University of Aberdeen, Centre for Private International Law Working Paper No 2015/2 available on 11 August at http://www.abdn.ac.uk/law/documents/Recent_jurisprudence_of_the_European_Court_of_Human_Rights_in_the_area_of_cross-border_surrogacy.pdf and the final version in G Biagioni et al (eds), *Migrant Children in the XXI Century. Selected Issues of Public and Private International Law* (Editoriale Scientifica 2016).

D Berthiau and L Brunet, 'L'ordre public au préjudice de l'enfant' (2001) *Dalloz* 1522–9.

M Coester, 'Ersatzmutterschaft in Europa' in H-P Mansel, T Pfeiffer, H Kronke, C Koehler and R Hausman (eds) *Festschrift für Erik Jayme* (Sellier 2004).

European Parliament, 'A Comparative Study on the Regime of Surrogacy in EU Member States', 2013, available 13 July 2015 at http://eurogender.eige.europa.eu/sites/default/files/EST93673.pdf.

European Parliament, Directorate General for Internal Policies, 'Recognition of Parental Responsibility: Biological Parenthood vs. Legal Parenthood', i.e. Mutual Recognition of Surrogacy Agreements: What is the Current Situation in the MS? Need for EU Action?' prepared by V Todorova, 2010, p 16, available 13 July 2015 at www.europarl.europa.eu/RegData/etudes/note/join/2010/432738/IPOL-JURI_NT(2010)432738_EN.pdf.

P Hammje, 'Maternité pour autrui, possession d'état et état civil' (2011) *Revue Critique De Droit International Privé* 722.

K Horsey, 'Challenging Presumptions: Legal Parenthood and Surrogacy Arrangements' (2010) 22 *Child and Family Law Quarterly* 449–74.

N Lowe, 'A Study Into the Rights and Legal Status of Children Being Brought up in Various Forms of Marital and Nonmarital Partnerships and Cohabitation', Report for the attention of the Committee of Experts on Family Law, September 2009, CJ-FA (2008) 5), available 13 July 2015 at www.coe.int/t/dghl/standardsetting/family/CJ-FA%20_2008_%205%20E%2025%2009%2009.pdf.

B Lurger, 'Das österreichische IPR bei Leihmutterschaft im Ausland-das Kindeswohl zwischen Anerkennung, europäischen Grundrechten und inländischem Leihmutterschaftsverbot' (2013) *IPrax* 282–9.

Permanent Bureau of the Hague Conference, 'Desirability and Feasibility of Further Work on the Parentage/Surrogacy Project' Prel Doc No3B April 2014 and 'A Study of Legal Parentage and the Issues Arising from International Surrogacy Arrangements' Prel Doc 3C March 2014 available 13 July 2015 at http://www.hcch.net/index_en.php..

K Trimmings and P Beaumont (eds), *International Surrogacy Arrangements: Legal Regulation at the International Level* (Hart Publishing 2013).

8. Parental responsibility in a European perspective

Josep Ferrer-Riba

1. INTRODUCTION

Parental responsibility is commonly understood as a set of powers, rights and duties with regard to children that the law allocates to parents or to third persons. These powers, rights and duties are aimed at protecting and promoting the rights and welfare of children and substantially encompass the provision of personal care, education, administration of the child's property, and exercise of legal representation. The consensus around the notion of parental responsibility extends to the idea that parental powers must be exercised for the benefit of children, taking into primary consideration the child's best interests and respecting and furthering the child's progressive maturity and autonomy.

These widely shared understandings have been favoured and reinforced in Europe by international instruments from the Council of Europe,[1] the

---

[1] The most important of these instruments is undoubtedly the European Convention on Human Rights (1950) (ECHR). In the particular field of parental responsibilities mention should be made of Recommendation (84)4 of 8 February

Hague Conference on Private International Law,[2] the European Union,[3] and by the case law of the European Court of Human Rights (ECtHR). They have also been advanced by academic work in the field of family and comparative law undertaken by the Commission on European Family Law (CEFL), which has led to the publication of Principles of European Family Law Regarding Parental Responsibilities (CEFL Principles).[4] These Principles – like those previously drafted and now being reworked at the instigation of the Council of Europe – have been designed to serve as a guide for legislatures at the national and international level and to provide a model for the harmonisation of family law in Europe.[5] This package of law and soft law materials is contributing to the consolidation

---

1984 on parental responsibilities, adopted by the Committee of Ministers (CM), and the White Paper on Principles concerning the Establishment and Legal Consequences of Parentage 2002 (hereafter White Paper) drafted by the Committee of Experts on Family Law (CJ-FA) [CJ-FA (2006) 4e]. On the basis of the White Paper and some more recent materials, in 2010 and 2011 the CJ-FA drew up a Draft recommendation on the rights and legal status of children and parental responsibilities (hereafter Draft CM/Rec 2011), which is currently being examined by the Committee of Ministers of the Council of Europe with a view to its adoption. For a full list of all Council of Europe conventions and recommendations with regard to matters concerning children see Part II of the Report 'Council of Europe Achievements in the Field of Family Law (Family Law and the Protection of Children)' [CJ-FA (2008)2] and chapter 3 in Volume I of this book set by Nigel Lowe.

2 See particularly the Hague Convention on Jurisdiction, Applicable Law, Recognition, Enforcement and Cooperation in Respect of Parental Responsibility and Measures for the Protection of Children (1996) (HCPC) and chapter 5 in Volume I of this book set by Hannah Baker and Maja Groff.

3 See Council Regulation (EC) No 2201/2003 of 27 November 2003 concerning jurisdiction and the recognition and enforcement of judgments in matrimonial matters and matters of parental responsibility, repealing Regulation (EC) No 1347/2000 ([2003] OJ L338/1), commonly known as 'Brussels II *bis* Regulation'. On this see chapter 1 in Volume I of this book set by Geert de Baere and Kathleen Gutman.

4 K Boele-Woelki, F Ferrand, C González Beilfuss, M Jänterä-Jareborg, N Lowe, D Martiny, W Pintens, *Principles of European Family Law Regarding Parental Responsibilities* (Intersentia 2007).

5 On CEFL organisation and activities see chapter 6 in Volume I of this book set by Katharina Boele-Woelki. Concerning the CEFL's working method and its application to the field of parental responsibilities, see K Boele-Woelki and D Martiny, 'The Commission on European Family Law (CEFL) and its Principles of European Family Law Regarding Parental Responsibilities' [2007] ERA Forum 8: 125–43; K Boele-Woelki, 'The CEFL Principles Regarding

of common European patterns of legal development in this field and will be taken as a valuable reference point in this chapter.

As a topic for legal research, parental responsibility poses multiple challenges given the diversification of family models in modern European societies and these societies' commitment to recognising children's rights and promoting children's welfare. These circumstances influence decisions regarding the attribution of parental responsibility, its breaking down into different collections of rights and duties, its opening up to third persons, the way in which it is exercised and also its termination. The diversity of approaches to these matters found in European national laws, from the perspectives of both legal technique and family policy, confirms the need to engage in further research on these topics.[6]

2. MEANING AND SCOPE OF PARENTAL RESPONSIBILITY

Parental responsibility (or parental responsibilities, in the plural, as proposed by the Council of Europe and endorsed by the CEFL)[7] is an expression that has been shaped by international law. It is rarely used by national legal systems, with the important exceptions of England and Wales and, more recently, Denmark and Portugal.[8] Its meaning and scope

---

Parental Responsibilities: Predominance of the Common Core', in K Boele-Woelki and T Sverdrup (eds), *European Challenges in Contemporary Family Law* (Intersentia 2008) 63–84.

[6]   J Ferrer-Riba, 'Parental Responsibility', in J Basedow et al (eds), *The Max Planck Encyclopedia of European Private Law,* vol II (Oxford University Press 2012) 1247–50.

[7]   On the terminology question see J Scherpe, 'Establishing and Ending Parental Responsibility: A Comparative View', in R Probert, S Gilmore and J Herring (eds), *Responsible Parents and Parental Responsibility* (Hart Publishing 2009) 45.

[8]   For England and Wales see Children Act 1989, ss 2, 3 and J Scherpe, 'Elterliche Sorge von nicht miteinander verheirateten Eltern in England und Wales', in D Coester-Waltjen, V Lipp, E Schumann and B Veit (eds), *Alles zum Wohle des Kindes? Aktuelle Probleme des Kindschaftsrechts* (Göttinger Juristische Schriften, Universitätsverlag Göttingen 2012) 71–84. For Denmark see Act No 499 of 6 June 2007 and J Scherpe, 'Das neue dänische Gesetz über elterliche Verantwortung', *Zeitschrift für das gesamte Familienrecht (FamRZ)* 2007, 1495–6, and extensive information in JCG Jeppesen de Boer, *Joint Parental Authority (A comparative legal study on the continuation of joint parental authority after divorce and the breakup of a relationship in Dutch and Danish law and the CEFL principles)* (Intersentia 2008), 65–8. In Portugal see Act No

have evolved significantly over time. Two phases can be identified from the time it was first used in various Council of Europe recommendations (1979, 1984)[9] to its consolidation in the CEFL Principles.

In the first phase, which ended around the turn of the century, the term 'parental responsibility' was essentially used to rename in a more child-focused manner the set of powers and duties attributed by the law to parents in relation to their minor children. As in the United Nations Convention on the Rights of the Child (1989) (UNCRC),[10] the concept's emphasis on responsibility aimed to highlight that these powers, traditionally known as parental authority, are attributed only insofar as they are necessary for fulfilling the duties of protection and assistance to children, and therefore must always be exercised in children's best interests. Today this concept is taken for granted.

The notion of parental responsibility in both the Council of Europe recommendations cited above and the UNCRC encompasses not only the position of the parents but also that of other family members or close persons taking their place should the parents be absent or unable to exercise their rights and duties. This is also clearly stated by the Hague Convention on Jurisdiction, Applicable Law, Recognition, Enforcement and Cooperation in Respect of Parental Responsibility and Measures for the Protection of Children (1996) (HCPC), which defines the term 'parental responsibility' as including 'parental authority, or any analogous relationship of authority determining the rights, powers and responsibilities of parents, guardians or other legal representatives in relation to the person or the property of the child' (article 1(2)). In all these texts the expression 'parental responsibility' must be conceived of mainly as a terminological update, a more suitable way of referring to the set of powers, rights and duties that belong to parents, as well as to persons placed *in loco parentis*.

---

61 of 31 October 2008 modifying the regulation of divorce. Other countries that have introduced the term, using either the singular or the plural form but with no relevant shift in content from its traditional meaning of parental authority, are Norway (Children Act 1981), Scotland (Children Act 1995, s 1), and Catalonia (Civil Code, articles 233-8, 235-2.2, 236-1). For a comparative overview on terminology see also Boele-Woelki et al (n 4) 26–7.

[9] (PA) Recommendation 874(1979) on a European Charter on the Rights of the Child (Principle II, c: 'The concept of "parental authority" must be superseded by "parental responsibility"'), and (CM) Recommendation (84)4 of 8 February 1984 on parental responsibilities.

[10] Article 18(1): '... both parents have common responsibilities for the upbringing and development of the child'.

The second phase began with the publication of the White Paper on Principles concerning the Establishment and Legal Consequences of Parentage (2002) drafted by a Committee of Experts on Family Law, also on the Council of Europe's initiative, continued with the passage of the Brussels II*bis* Regulation 2003, and was conclusively consolidated in 2007 with the publication of the CEFL Principles.

In these texts the concept of parental responsibilities broadened and came to refer to the position of any person to whom rights and duties aimed at promoting and safeguarding the welfare of a child are attributed, regardless of whether the position has greater or lesser content. In this sense, parental responsibilities include the right to determine the child's residence (which is the most important component of the rights of custody), the right to maintain personal relationships with the child where appropriate (which describes the essence of a right of access or contact) and all other functions of any person or institution aimed at taking care of the child's person or property.[11] In accordance with this wider meaning, parental responsibilities may be vested in persons other than the child's parents (for example, grandparents, step-parents, foster parents and even public institutions).[12]

The creation of an all-encompassing concept that includes any person's position targeted at promoting and safeguarding the child's welfare is particularly useful for the purposes of private international law. It greatly simplifies the way in which the qualification problems that typically arise in conflict of laws cases are dealt with, and guarantees the equal treatment of children in cross-border relationships whose circumstances require the recognition or enforcement of judgments affecting their personal and family lives.

From the perspective of substantive family law, its usefulness is not so evident. On the one hand, the recognition that all forms of legally relevant relationship with a child, even though they may not be based on biological or adoptive parenthood, may constitute parental responsibility enhances the intrinsic value of the different forms of affective and social parenting, and does not discriminate between them on grounds of their greater or lesser intensity. When it is applied to parents, it helps to highlight the fact that their parental duties remain after they have ceased to live with their children, even if they do not have custody and their contact with them changes or reduces in frequency or intensity. On the

---

[11]   Article 1.2 of the Brussels II *bis* Regulation; principle 3:1 of the CEFL; principle 20 of the Draft CM/Rec 2011.

[12]   Article 1(1)(b), (c), (d) of the Brussels II *bis* Regulation; CEFL principles 3:2 and 3:9; principles 22 and 24 of the Draft CM/Rec 2011.

other hand, however, the concept's very breadth undermines its normative value. The Principles' drafters emphatically state that 'concepts like guardianship and custody, that are still used in national systems, have been left behind'.[13] However, their substitution by the concept of parental responsibility does not obviate the need to lay down criteria for deciding upon the residence of the child in separating families, articulating custodial and decision-making responsibilities, regulating access rights or coordinating parents' powers with those held by other persons vested with more limited protective functions. It is no wonder that in these areas the White Paper and the CEFL Principles are less illuminating than the guidance and wealth of ideas provided by the Principles of the Law of Family Dissolution drafted at the initiative of the American Law Institute.[14]

The normative use of the European concept of parental responsibility requires a certain degree of functional deconstruction. This responsibility may extend to powers and duties concerning decision-making, relationships based on living together with the child, relationships based on personal contact, interim protection functions and even supervisory functions over the exercise of other functions. They are all aimed at promoting and safeguarding the rights and welfare of the child, but to very different extents. To mention one example, although the CEFL Principles dealing with the content of parental responsibilities as regards the child's person or property[15] aim to be general in application, they cannot be applied to persons who take on interim protection functions or who have mere contact rights: they apply only to the parent or parents (or other persons in their place) who hold wide decision-making powers.

In the following pages I will focus on parental responsibility in the strict sense, namely on the position occupied by the parents or, in their absence, other persons assuming a parental role, at the core of which are duties to act in the sphere of the children's personal lives and property and autonomous decision-making with effects vis-à-vis both the child and third parties.

---

[13] Boele-Woelki et al (n 4) 14.

[14] American Law Institute, *Principles of the Law of Family Dissolution: Analysis and Recommendations* (Matthew Bender & Co 2002) Chapter 2, 92–408.

[15] See CEFL principles 3:19, 3:22, 3:23 and 3:24.

3. ATTRIBUTION OF PARENTAL RESPONSIBILITY

3.1　Holding vs. Exercising Parental Responsibility

Before looking at how and to whom parental responsibility is attributed, it is useful to tackle the distinction between 'holding' it and 'exercising' it. This is an unclear area in the theory of parental responsibility, which hovers over its normative structuring as carried out by some legal systems. The CEFL Principles, for instance, refer separately to the attribution and the exercise of parental responsibilities and comment that they 'are namely not synonymous expressions', but also admit that the instruments from which they draw inspiration are not at all clear about the distinction and do not define what is meant by them.[16]

One source for the distinction can be traced back to private international law.[17] The HCPC, for example, sets different criteria for determining the law governing the attribution of parental responsibility and the law governing its exercise. In both instances the applicable law is the law of the state of the child's habitual residence (at the time of attributing or exercising parental responsibility). However, in the second instance (unlike in the first one) the applicable law may change should the place of residence change.[18] Treating the attribution and exercise of parental responsibility separately thus reflects the fact that attribution of parental responsibility is a one-off event, while its exercise has a recurring nature.

The rationale of the distinction just outlined, although accurate, does not explain why some legal systems distinguish between the holding and the exercise of parental responsibility. The distinction, which is common in systems that attribute parental responsibility to the parents as soon as legal parentage is established[19] (although not exclusive to these

---

[16]　Boele-Woelki et al (n 4) 77.

[17]　See, for example, the explanatory memorandum to the Draft CM/Rec 2011 [CDCJ (2011) 15, para 79].

[18]　See articles 16 and 17 of the Convention, which deal with the law governing the attribution or termination of parental responsibility and the law governing its exercise, respectively.

[19]　It applies for instance in France, Italy and Spain. See, respectively, Bénabent, *Droit de la famille* (2nd edn, Montchrestien 2012) 451; T Auletta, *Diritto di familia* (Giappichelli 2011) 370; L Díez-Picazo, A Gullón, *Sistema de derecho civil,* vol IV (11th edn, Tecnos 2012), 256–9.

systems),[20] recognises the suitability in the abstract of the holder of parental responsibility for assuming parental functions, without pre-judging the appropriateness of the exercise of parental functions being decided according to the specific circumstances of the family setting. The holder, therefore, may lack the powers of exercise if the child's best interests justify the other parent or a third party having exclusive exercise. This may happen, for instance, as a consequence of one parent's personal circumstances, both parents living apart, or the need to adopt measures to protect the child. The legal position of the 'passive holder' of parental responsibility, then, has only limited content: given that it typically is attributed to one of the parents, he or she has the duty of maintenance, contact rights, the power to oppose the adoption of the child by a third party, supervisory powers and an expectation of assuming or reassuming the full exercise of parental responsibility should the appropriate circumstances arise (for example, the death of the other parent or the lifting of foster care measures).

Conversely, legal systems that allow the holding of responsibilities with no actual exercise usually also contemplate the reverse case: the exercising of responsibilities without holding them. This situation may arise in cases in which the responsibilities are delegated to third persons, either at the request of the holders of parental responsibility or by imposition of a competent authority in order to protect the child.

3.2 The Attribution to Parents

Nowadays it is generally agreed that the primary responsibility for caring for and bringing up children falls equally on both parents. Article 18 of the UNCRC enshrines this principle and commits states to using their best efforts to ensure its recognition.

The consensus around this idea, however, does not translate into the unconditional automatic attribution of parental responsibility to both parents as soon as paternity and maternity have been legally established.

---

[20] It is also known in countries that do not automatically attribute parental responsibility to both parents, such as Germany and the Netherlands, but to a different extent. In Germany the distinction provides for the possibility of transferring the exercise to third persons or suspending the exercise on the grounds of incapacity: see J Gernhuber and D Coester-Waltjen, *Familienrecht* (6th edn, CH Beck 2010) § 57 I, 674-9, § 64 III, 819–22. In respect of the Netherlands see Jeppesen de Boer (n 8) 149–51.

Recent comparative law reports drafted on the initiative of the CEFL[21] enable us to distinguish between two broad types of legal systems in this context:

(a)　Legal systems that attribute parental responsibility to both parents on a general basis once parentage has been established.[22]

　　　This approach, which implies a principled stand on the suitability of parents for assuming the parenting role, is compatible with the regulation of rather exceptional cases where parents may be excluded from parental responsibility from the outset because of the circumstances in which the parentage has been established. In the legal systems belonging to this first type, the holding of parental responsibility does not necessarily imply its effective exercise either, as mentioned previously.

(b)　Legal systems that distinguish between the parents of children born in and out of wedlock.[23]

　　　These legal systems are reluctant to attribute automatic parental responsibility to fathers who are not married to the mothers of their children, on the grounds that in the absence of marriage the fathers' willingness to assume their responsibilities and cooperate with the mothers in bringing up the children may vary greatly according to circumstances, and in some cases may be non-existent. For this reason the law makes the acquisition of parental responsibilities on the part of a father who has children outside wedlock conditional on the existence of an indicator confirming his suitability. The European Court of Human Rights has concluded that this more rigorous treatment of unmarried fathers with the aim of identifying those who could be considered 'meritorious' (and who thus might be accorded parental rights) is a differentiation that respects the

---

[21]　K Boele-Woelki, B. Braat and I Curry-Sumner (eds), *European Family Law in Action*, vol III (Intersentia 2005), 265 ff.

[22]　Automatic attribution exists in Belgium, Czech Republic, Croatia, Denmark, France, Hungary, Italy, Lithuania, Poland, Russia and Spain. In this respect see Scherpe (n 7) 46, with reference to the national reports published in Boele-Woelki et al (n 21). It should be borne in mind that in some countries establishing maternity outside marriage requires the mother's acknowledgment or a judicial decision (France and Italy) and that automatic attribution may be conditional on the parents' living together (Italy, Hungary).

[23]　See Scherpe (n 7) 46. According to the author – filtering and updating the data provided by the CEFL reports published in Boele-Woelki et al (n 21) – the distinction is used in Austria, England and Wales, Finland, Germany, Ireland, the Netherlands, Norway, Sweden and Switzerland.

proportionality principle and therefore does not constitute a form of discrimination prohibited by the ECHR.[24]

In these legal systems the father's access to parental responsibility may derive primarily from the mother's endorsement: the law normally attributes parental responsibility to the father if he marries the mother or if the parents reach an agreement to share these responsibilities,[25] either explicit or inferred from certain conduct (such as the father's name being recorded on the child's birth certificate).

If the mother is opposed to sharing parental responsibility national laws usually make available to the father the alternative option of acquiring parental responsibility by means of a court order.[26] Some legal systems, such as those in Germany and Austria, traditionally rejected this alternative, on the basis that the attribution of joint responsibilities against the will of one parent and without the least spirit of cooperation between the parents had more disadvantages than advantages and could run counter to the child's welfare. This approach, which had generated a great deal of criticism,[27] was finally rejected by the ECtHR in *Zaunegger* (2009)[28] and *Sporer* (2011).[29] The Court did not share the assumption 'that joint custody against the will of the mother is prima facie not to be in the child's interests', and held the treatment of a father who was not married to the mother to be discriminatory compared with that of a separated or divorced father. In cases of separation or divorce, even in highly confrontational scenarios, both parents retain their parental rights unless the court, on the request of either

---

[24]   *McMichael v United Kingdom* (App No 16424/1990) [1995] (24 February 1995); *B v United Kingdom* [2000] 1 FLR 1, [2000] 1 FCR 289 (14 September 1999).

[25]   See, for example, Children Act 1989, s 4(1)(a)–(b) (England and Wales); *Bürgerliches Gesetzbuch* (BGB) § 1626a (1) 1 (Germany); *Allgemeines Bürgerliches Gesetzbuch* (ABGB) § 177 (2) (Austria); *Burgerlijk Wetboek* (BW) article 1:252 (Netherlands).

[26]   See for example Children Act 1989, s 4(1)(c) (England and Wales); BW article 1:253c (Netherlands).

[27]   See M Coester, 'Nichteheliche Elternschaft und Sorgerecht' (2007) 14 *FamRZ* 1137–45; J Scherpe, 'Nichteheliche Kinder, elterliche Sorge und die Europäische Menschenrechtskonvention' (2009) 73 RabelsZ 950-960; *idem* (n 7) 57–8, with additional references.

[28]   *Zaunegger v Germany* (App No 22028/04) [2009] (3 December 2009) = FamRZ 2010, 108 with notes by D Henrich and J Scherpe.

[29]   *Sporer v Austria* (App No 35637/03) [2011] (3 February 2011).

party, awards sole custody in accordance with the child's best interests. According to the court, there is no good reason to justify making unmarried fathers worse off than their married counterparts. Although there is no consensus as to whether the fathers of children born out of wedlock should have the right to request joint custody without the mother's approval, decisions on the attribution of custody should be based on the child's best interests and, in the event of conflict between the parents, an opportunity for judicial scrutiny should be provided. Following these judgments both Austria and Germany changed the law in order to allow fathers who are not married to the children's mothers to obtain parental responsibility, whether wholly or in part, by means of a judicial decision.[30]

The White Paper on parentage favours the attribution of parental responsibilities to both parents but, acknowledging that in some legal systems only one parent holds parental responsibilities by operation of the law, proposes that the other parent should have an opportunity to acquire them unless it is against the child's best interests.[31] The CEFL Principles, for their part, hold that 'parents, whose legal parentage has been established, should have parental responsibilities for the child', with no other constraints.[32] This principle is consistent with the power of the competent authority to discharge the holder of parental responsibilities where his or her behaviour or neglect causes a serious risk to the person or the property of the child and with the possibility of establishing a sole exercise regime by agreement between the parents or a decision by the competent authority.[33]

The rule of automatic attribution of parental responsibility, with the safeguards just mentioned, appears to be clearly superior to the rules of selective attribution. If the child's interests require limits to be imposed on one parent's position, it is preferable to restrict or cancel his or her powers of exercise rather than exclude him or her from all responsibility

---

[30] See ABGB, § 180 (1) Nr 2 and (2) (Austria), as amended by the *Kindschafts- und Namensrechts-Änderungsgesetz* 2013 (BGBl. 11 January 2013), and BGB § 1626a (1) Nr 3 and (2) (Germany) as amended by the *Gesetz zur Reform der elterlichen Sorgen nicht miteinander verheirateter Eltern* of 16 April 2013 (BGBl. 19 April 2013).

[31] Principle 19. The Draft CM/Rec 2011 goes further in this direction by adding that 'lack of consent or opposition by the parent having parental responsibilities should not as such be an obstacle for such acquisition'.

[32] Principle 3:8. See Boele-Woelki et al (n 4) 59–65.

[33] Principles 3:32 and 3:15, respectively.

from the outset. This helps to avoid a feeling of disempowerment in the parent whose position is restricted and may help to reinforce a positive attitude towards the fulfilment of basic parenting duties (such as maintenance and contact).[34] Legal systems that do not automatically attribute parental responsibility may in any event reach similar outcomes through the courts, which feel drawn to award parental responsibility using very generous criteria, as the practice of English law shows.[35] This practice distorts the meaning of the attribution of responsibility and in some cases degrades it to the point where it is merely a sort of official approval.[36] Accordingly it seems preferable to make all parents 'passive holders' of parental responsibility across the board, with very strict exceptions, and adjust eligibility requirements for becoming an 'active holder' of parental responsibility either by means of an agreement between the parents or an act of authority such as a court order.

3.3 Third Persons

The participation of third persons in the exercise of parental roles is leading to new developments in the law of parental responsibilities. Comparative law findings show that an increasing number of European legal systems take non-traditional forms of social parenting into consideration when regulating parental responsibility.[37] The European principles acknowledge that parental responsibilities may in whole or in part be attributed to and exercised by persons other than the parents, in addition to or instead of them.[38]

This acknowledgement, expressed in very broad terms, covers at least three groups of cases. First, it includes persons exercising contact rights, in line with the idea that the maintaining of personal relationships with the child falls within the scope of parental responsibility.[39] Second, it includes persons called upon to assume parental roles 'instead of the parents', in other words to replace them. Substituting other persons to

---

[34]   M Coester, 'Sorgerecht nicht miteinander verheirateter Eltern' (2012) 17 *FamRZ* 1344.

[35]   See e.g. J Herring, *Family Law* (5th edn, Pearson 2011), 357–61; Scherpe (n 7 and n 28).

[36]   H Reece, 'The Degradation of Parental Responsibility', in Probert et al (eds) (n 7), 85–102.

[37]   Boele-Woelki et al (n 21) 389–476.

[38]   Principle 20.3 of White Paper 2002 and CEFL principles 3:9 and 3:17.

[39]   Boele-Woelki et al (n 4), 67, 68. On these relationships see CEFL principles 3:25 to 3:29.

take the place of parents as a result of death, incapacity or any other grounds leading to the termination of their parental responsibility, is a necessary consequence of continuity in the protection of the child, which historically has always been provided for and has been regulated in widely varying terms. Finally, in certain circumstances there may be intervention from third parties 'in addition to the parents'. This is a more recent phenomenon, which can be accounted for by the increasing complexity of family relationships in present-day societies and the importance attached by states to ensuring a safe environment for the care and upbringing of children. The third group includes two cases which are socially clearly defined: alternative care arrangements with the intervention of foster carers, and the participation of the parent's spouse or partner in the exercise of parental responsibility.

3.3.1   Foster carers
Placing the child in alternative care has implications for the position of the legal parents (whose responsibility is necessarily affected), the position of the carers, and, as the case may be, the position of the public authorities at whose initiative or under whose supervision the protective measures are usually taken. The institutional design of these situations in Europe is very diverse.[40] Generally, foster carers are attributed some responsibilities, which may range from deciding on matters relating to everyday life to exercising wide parental rights and duties. The diversity of their functions does not relate to the level of trust that the law places in them, but to family circumstances. If the reasons leading to the foster placement are envisaged to be permanent, the parents are frequently discharged from their responsibilities and the foster placement then leads to the constitution of a guardianship or adoption. If, on the other hand, the need for protection is temporary or at least conceived as reversible, the responsibilities assumed by foster carers may coexist with responsibilities that continue to be held by the parents.

The distinction between holding and exercising parental responsibility is useful for articulating the relationship between parents and foster carers. Parents may continue to hold responsibility at the same time as the foster carers exercise (in full or in part) the rights and duties that it entails. The fact that parents retain their responsibility means the possibility remains that they will exercise it again in the future, and that

---

[40]   See Boele-Woelki et al (n 21) 389–476. See also J Ferrer-Riba, 'Child Protection', in J Basedow et al (eds), *The Max Planck Encyclopedia of European Private Law,* vol I (Oxford University Press 2012) 179–82, with additional references.

their consent is required before the child can be given up for adoption. However, it seems unfortunate to apply the distinction between holding and exercising parental responsibility to carers, as the CEFL Principles insist on doing.[41] Foster parents are appointed to exercise parental rights and duties by virtue of parental delegation or an order issued by the competent authority. It makes little sense to say that they can be mere holders of parental responsibilities, when they are always appointed to undertake protective duties immediately.

3.3.2 Parent's spouse or partner

The proliferation of blended families in European societies has highlighted the position of parents' spouses or partners (hereafter, for simplicity, step-parents). Step-parents become involved *de facto* in children's daily care and support. Legal systems are becoming progressively more cognisant of this informal role, not only by acknowledging that a relationship with a spouse or partner's children constitutes family life and deserves the legal protection conferred on families, but also by allowing step-parents to participate in parenting responsibilities. The willingness of legislatures and courts to recognise such participation is still by no means universal – it has not yet reached a significant number of countries – and is materialising in very different ways. A glance at national legal systems reveals substantial divergences with regard to the requirements that must be fulfilled for step-parents to be able to assume responsibilities, to the sources of their legal powers and duties (it may be the law, a court or administrative order, or a private agreement), and to the content of the powers and duties that can be awarded to step-parents.[42]

The CEFL Principles propose that 'the parent's partner living with the child may take part in decisions with respect to daily matters unless the other parent having parental responsibilities objects'.[43] The rule is based on the German *kleines Sorgerecht* model,[44] which was recently followed in Catalonia,[45] and on the model applied in other countries which limit

---

[41]   Compare principles 3:9 and 3:17, and see the comments to principle 3:9, in Boele-Woelki et al (n 4) 66–7.

[42]   For comparative law information see Boele-Woelki et al (n 21), Questions 27–30, 389–428.

[43]   Principle 3:18.

[44]   BGB, §1687 b, which extends also to a right of representation in emergency situations.

[45]   Catalan Civil Code, article 236-14, including both participation in making decisions about daily life and the taking of urgent measures if there is imminent risk to the child.

step-parents' legal involvement to participation in the children's upbringing and the duty to stand in for the other spouse or partner if circumstances so require.[46] These models of participation translate a standard
social role into legal terms. Other countries have opted for more
ambitious approaches, to the point of providing that step-parents can
assume full parental responsibilities. This is the case in Danish law,
which for this to occur requires the partner to be married to the legal
father, the latter to be the sole holder of parental authority and the
agreement between the spouses to have official approval.[47] This model,
which formally integrates step-parents into the family, clearly functions
as an alternative to adoption and brings to the forefront a topic of
considerable interest for family law research, namely, the interchange-
ability between parental responsibilities and adoption. In a similar
direction, English law allows step-parents to assume parental responsibilities in full or to a limited extent, whether there are one or two holders of
parental responsibilities. In this model the law envisages that step-parents
will assume parental responsibilities through the consent of the legal
parents, but it can also take place by a court order. In any event, the
assumption of parental responsibilities by the step-parents has no extinc-
tive effect on the pre-existing responsibilities held by legal parents.[48]

These examples confirm the lack of a common core in this area, both
in terms of the requirements for attributing parental responsibility to a
spouse or partner and the content of that responsibility. It is a field in a
state of transition, where proposals for regulation based on private
autonomy coexist with approaches based on judicial intervention or
based in the production of effects by direct operation of the law (*ope
legis*). The *ope legis* award of parental responsibilities to a step-parent
appears to be highly unusual.[49] Comparative law data indicate that where
it occurs it is usually limited to the power to take daily or urgent
decisions. The Council of Europe's most recent endeavours favour the
operation of private autonomy and suggest allowing binding agreements
to be made between one parent and her spouse or registered partner in

---

[46]   As provided by Czech law (s 33 of the Family Code) and Swiss law
(article 299 of the *Zivilgesetzbuch* – ZGB).

[47]   Act on Parental Responsibility, article 13(2). See also Jeppesen de Boer
(n 8) 200–1.

[48]   Children Act 1989, s 2(6); on this see Herring (n 35) 345–6.

[49]   In the Netherlands this is possible in respect of a child born to one of the
spouses during a marriage (typically, of a lesbian couple) not having family ties
with another parent: see the Dutch report by K Boele-Woelki, W Schrama and M
Vonk, in Boele-Woelki et al (n 21), Q 27, 403.

order for the spouse or partner to assume parental responsibility, provided that the other parent, should he also hold responsibility, consents in writing.[50] The normative models that predominantly rest on the private autonomy of the parties involved are theoretically plausible but are not always suitable for the informal dynamics of family life. If they are to become operational they need to be combined with the possibility of having recourse to the competent authority, be it to circumvent the veto of a non-resident parent or to reject agreements that are contrary to the best interests of the child.

4. ENDING PARENTAL RESPONSIBILITY

Parental responsibility may end for reasons involving the child on the one side or the parents or any other holder of responsibility on the other side. Both classes of grounds for termination follow similar patterns in all European legal systems.[51] From the child's perspective, parental responsibility ceases when the child reaches majority, marries or enters into a registered partnership (with exceptions in a few jurisdictions), or dies.[52] From the perspective of the holders of parental responsibility, responsibility is clearly brought to an end by their death, by the adoption of the child (when parental responsibility is transferred from the birth parents to the adoptive parents), and by an order from a competent authority (for example, an order reversing a prior resolution entrusting parental responsibility to a specific person). Finally, although it is not usually treated as a ground for termination of parental responsibility, it is important to note that in most legal systems parental responsibility can be discharged or removed. Removal of parental responsibility takes place by an act of authority on the basis that the child's person or property is at serious risk or has in fact been harmed.

With regard to the termination of parental responsibility, three topics can be envisaged for research. The first relates to the child's personal autonomy: the law must establish at which time or period in the child's

---

[50]   Principle 24 of the Draft CM/Rec 2011.

[51]   Boele-Woelki et al (n 21), Q 3, 55–63.

[52]   See CEFL principle 3:30, which also includes the child being adopted. Bearing in mind that the Principle enumerates the grounds for termination from the child's perspective, the inclusion of adoption seems unwarranted. Adoption implies substitution by the adoptive parent or parents in the holding of parental responsibilities and, in cases of adoption by a parent's partner, only a partial substitution (on account of the other parent's being supplanted).

life he or she can assume powers of self-determination and parental responsibilities must reasonably come to an end. The second relates to the parents or other holders of parental responsibilities: the law must establish the grounds for and procedures through which the holders of parental responsibility can be discharged from it. The third relates to the continuity of the protection when the persons exercising parental responsibility cease to hold it and must be replaced. In legal systems that distinguish between holding and exercising parental responsibility the right of exercise is passed on to another holder of parental responsibility, if there is one, and the question therefore arises as to whether this effect should be automatic or not. If there is no other holder of parental responsibility, the question, then, is who should assume the responsibility and how this should take place: whether with subjection to the same status of rights and duties or to a different legal framework.

4.1 Coming of Age and Emancipation

Parental responsibilities generally end when minors come of age and assume full responsibility over their person and property. As the Draft Recommendations issued by the Council of Europe acknowledge, 'states may provide that parental responsibilities continue beyond the age of majority or end before that age under conditions determined by national law'.[53] The formula takes into account both the possibility of shifting the ending of parental responsibilities forward, due to marriage or via emancipation, and also of extending it should the child suffer from a disability that limits or impedes his or her capacity for self-management.

There is no agreement in Europe over whether the law has to allow parental responsibility to be terminated before a child reaches the age of 18, based on the degree of the child's maturity shown or on his or her personal and family circumstances. Some legal systems provide an institutional response to this question, namely emancipation.[54] Emancipation both extinguishes parental responsibility and brings about the child's acquisition of full or limited contractual capacity. It may be granted by the parents, under the assumption that they are in a better position than legislatures to assess the child's aptitude for self-determination. It may

---

[53] Principle 25 of the Draft CM/Rec 2011.
[54] See information about the systems allowing emancipation in Boele-Woelki et al (n 21), Q 3, 55–63, and particularly in the reports by F Ferrand (France), S Patti, E Bellisario and L Rossi Carleo (Italy), V Mikelenas (Lithuania), K Boele-Woelki, W Schrama and M Vonk (Netherlands), G de Oliveira (Portugal), M Antokolskaia (Russia), and C González Beilfuss (Spain).

also be granted by the courts in the presence of indicators of independence and personal maturity, such as the fact of the child having left home, cohabiting with a partner, or living by his own means.

European law's lack of uniformity on this question is not particularly problematic. On one hand, lowering the age of majority to 18 throughout the continent has narrowed the space in which national differences used to be able to manifest themselves. Many legal systems that do not provide for emancipation do, however, allow the fact of a minor's marriage or entry into a registered partnership to end parental responsibility. Finally, all European legal systems are today opening up autonomous decision-making spaces to minors, both in the area of rights affecting the personal sphere (education, vocational training, privacy, religion, freedom of association, medical treatment) and in the area of contractual capacity, taking into consideration maturity, age, the type of contract to be entered into and social practices.[55] Although there is tremendous legislative diversity in this area,[56] there is a clear common underlying trend to favour the autonomy of minors without excluding the continuity of parental responsibilities, weakened though these may be.

4.2 Discharge and Restoration

If a holder of parental responsibility exercises it in a way that is detrimental to the child's person or property he or she may be partially or completely discharged of it. The possibility of removing parental responsibility is generalised throughout European legal systems[57] and is also incorporated in texts of uniform law.[58] As an alternative to removing

---

[55] See P Hellwege, 'Capacity', in Basedow et al (eds) (n 40) 138–40.

[56] To appreciate the diversity, see L Francoz-Terminal, *La capacité de l'enfant dans les droits français, anglais et écossais* (Stämpfli 2008) 145–93 comparing French, English and Scottish law. French law allows emancipation at the age of 16 by judicial decree at the request of one parent (article 413-2 of the *Code civil*); in Scottish law the child becomes legally capable at the age of 16 (s 1 of the Age of Legal Capacity (Scotland) Act 1991); English law does not lay down age thresholds but is based on the principle that a minor's natural capacity should always prevail. Scottish and English legal systems retain mechanisms to protect minors in the exercise of their contractual capacity, while French law excludes them for emancipated minors. Besides these varied formulas of access to 'pre-majority', all three systems have different mechanisms to facilitate the exercise of personal rights by minors themselves before they reach majority.

[57] Boele-Woelki et al (n 21), Q 51, 669–92.

[58] CEFL principle 3:32; principle 24 of the White Paper; principle 27 of the Draft CM/Rec 2011.

parental responsibility when circumstances arise that justify relieving parents of their responsibilities, some legal systems restrict themselves to issuing protection measures or other types of orders that limit or suspend the exercise of parental rights and transfer them to other persons without formally removing parental responsibility.[59] This less common option should be subject to further research and taken into consideration in future developments of the law of parental responsibility.

The removal of parental responsibility presupposes ill-treatment, abuse, neglect, or any other form of behaviour on the part of the holder which causes harm to the minor or risks serious harm to his or her person or property. The grounds for the divestment of parental responsibility do not necessarily require fault or blame on the part of the parents. Although views in Europe differ on this question, there is a current trend towards conceiving the deprivation of parental responsibility as a protective measure and objectivising the requirements for its application.[60] Of course the circumstances leading to the deprivation of parental responsibility are frequently punishable. In some legal systems the deprivation of parental responsibility actually constitutes an ancillary penalty to sentences for committing certain crimes. Even in these cases, however, deprivation of parental responsibility mainly fulfils – or should fulfil – a preventive and protective function. In this regard the ECtHR has rejected the possibility of its removal being ordered for reasons relating purely to punishment and which have no bearing on children's welfare.[61]

The protective rationale of the discharge of parental responsibility means that in practice the measure is only advocated when the child may derive some benefit from it. The constellations of cases brought before the ECtHR show that a discharge is almost always considered within the context of the implementation of other child protection measures that involve the prospect of a permanent severance of family ties, such as placing a child in foster care with a view to adoption, or the adoption of the child outright. Depending on the legal system and the circumstances of the case, the discharge of parental responsibility may anticipate the

---

[59]   In this respect see the reports by I Lund-Andersen (Denmark), N Lowe (England and Wales) (regarding persons on whom parental responsibility has been automatically conferred at the time of the child's birth) and A Koutsouradis (Greece) (describing that a person may be deprived of the exercise but not the holding of parental care, except as the ancillary consequence of a criminal judgment) in Boele-Woelki et al (n 21), Q 51, 673, 678–9.

[60]   Boele-Woelki et al (n 4) 214–15.

[61]   *Sabou and Pircalab v Romania* (App No 46572/99) [2004] (28 September 2004).

decision to place a child for adoption, may be the object of a claim exercised in child protection proceedings or may be the consequence of implementing a foster care order. The ECtHR has had the opportunity to formulate and consolidate very elaborate case law concerning the substantive standards and procedural safeguards which the competent authorities must observe in these cases, and has thus contributed to the harmonisation of this area to a great extent at European level.[62]

The case law established by the ECtHR sets forth both procedural and substantive requirements. Among the former, the Court recognises not only the traditional guarantees encompassed by the right to a fair trial but also the right 'to a sufficient involvement in the proceedings', which has become one of the pillars upon which European child protection systems are based.[63] From the point of view of the substantive requirements the decision to deprive parents of their rights and responsibilities is always considered to be an exceptional measure motivated by an overriding requirement pertaining to the child's best interests. Consequently, the degree of discretion enjoyed by national authorities is limited and subject to strict scrutiny.[64] These restrictions to administrative discretion are thrown into especially sharp relief when the circumstances motivating the need for intervention are not attributable to the holders of parental responsibility, such as when they suffer from an intellectual disability.[65] In these cases all possible measures of educational or financial support must be exhausted before making a decision to deprive parents of parental responsibility and separate them from their children, which intrudes so greatly in the personal sphere.

Parental responsibility that has been removed from parents may also be restored. The legal systems regulating discharge of parental responsibility always allow for this possibility, should there be a change in circumstances that justifies the restoration and so long as it is in the minor's best

---

[62] On these standards and safeguards see J Ferrer-Riba, 'Principles and Prospects for a European System of Child Protection' [2010] InDret 2: 15–21; S Choudry and J Herring, *European Human Rights and Family Law* (Hart Publishing 2010) 299–308 (in relation to the decision to take a child into care).

[63] On both sets of rights and the differences between them see Ferrer-Riba (n 62) 16–17; Choudry and Herring (n 62) 309–16. The fact that a parent is not represented in the proceedings divesting him or her of parental rights violates article 8 of the ECHR: *A.K. and L. v Croatia* (App No 37956/11) [2013] (8 January 2013).

[64] *Johansen v Norway* (App No 17383/90) [1996] (7 August 1996); *P., C. and S. v the United Kingdom* (App No 56547/00) [2002] (16 July 2002); *Aune v Norway* (App 52502/07) [2010] (28 October 2010).

[65] *Kutzner v Germany* (App No 46544/99) [2002] (26 February 2002).

interests.[66] According to the ECtHR, the lack of access to a court to challenge the deprivation of parental rights in the event of a change of circumstances fails to strike a fair balance between the interests of the child, those of the person divested of his or her rights and those of society at large, thus infringing article 8 of the ECHR.[67] As has been pointed out previously, the cases that reach the European Court consistently demonstrate that deprivation of parental responsibilities regularly only takes place when a child's separation from his or her own family environment is perceived to be irreversible and a return cannot reasonably be envisaged: 'the deprivation of parental rights … is inconsistent with the aim of reuniting them [parent and child]'.[68] As long as the possibility of a child being reunited with his or her parents exists, the measures adopted usually involve suspension of the exercise of parental responsibility (or its partial discharge), but not its total deprivation. For this reason, although the rationale for restoring parental responsibility is clear and convincing, in fact it rarely comes about.

Common practice regarding the discharge of parental responsibility leaves its utility open to serious questioning, which is a good reason to look more closely at legal systems that have no recourse to it. If a child is harmed or at risk of being harmed by his or her carer's behaviour, the exercise of parental responsibility can be transferred in full or in part to another carer (the other parent, under a sole parental responsibility order, or a foster carer) without formal discharge of the holding of the responsibility. The primary aim of deprivation when – as is usually the case – the parent affected by the measure has already lost custody of the child and the exercise of decision-making powers, is to put an end to his or her residual rights and legal expectations as a 'passive holder' of parental responsibility, namely, the right to regain the exercise of responsibility if the other parent dies and the right to oppose the child's adoption by a third person. There are, however, other means of deactivating these rights. First, the prospect of assuming or regaining the exercise of parental responsibility may be subject to pre-emptive judicial control. Secondly, the right to oppose adoption may be dispensed with during the adoption process itself on the same grounds that allow for the discharge

---

[66] Boele-Woelki et al (n 21), Q 54, 707–13. See also CEFL principle 3:34; principle 28 of the Draft CM/Rec 2011.
[67] *M.D. and others v Malta* (App No 64791/10) [2012] (17 July 2012).
[68] *Johansen v Norway* (n 64); *M.D. and others v Malta* (n 67).

of parental responsibility, thus avoiding the need for a previous discharge of parental responsibility.[69]

4.3 Subsequent Allocation of Parental Responsibility in Cases of Early Termination

The law must provide systems of substitution in the exercise of parental responsibility in the event of a parent or third person dying, being impeded from exercising parental responsibility or ceasing to exercise it for any other reason. This eventuality is dealt with in different ways depending on the circumstances involved at the time the early termination takes place. For these purposes it is useful to distinguish between three groups of cases:[70] (a) termination of parental responsibility in respect of one parent who exercised it jointly with the other parent or another holder of responsibility; (b) termination of parental responsibility in respect of one parent who exercised it solely, while the other parent is still available; (c) termination of parental responsibility in respect of one or both parents, there being no additional holders of responsibility.

In case (a) the responsibilities continue to be exercised solely by the remaining holder of responsibility (typically the surviving parent) by operation of the law. The legal treatment of this type of case leaves little room for doubt in all European jurisdictions.[71] Given that the surviving partner was already entrusted with the parental functions there is no reason to question his or her suitability to carry on exercising them alone. The only objection to this approach could be the upheaval caused to a child by the significant change to his or her life if he or she did not previously live with the surviving parent. Some legal systems (Denmark and Norway) address this difficulty by allowing a third person to apply for parental responsibility.[72] This option permits a departure from the

---

[69] See the comparative law information confirming this point in *A.K. and L. v Croatia* (n 63).

[70] Cf. CEFL principle 3:31; principle 23 of the White Paper; principle 26 of the Draft CM/Rec 2011. Although the CEFL Principles and the White Paper refer only to the parents and deal only with the hypothetical death of one or both of them, the proposed rules may be applied *mutatis mutandis* to other holders of parental responsibility and to other cases of termination of responsibility for reasons other than death.

[71] Boele-Woelki et al (n 21), Q 33, 455–66.

[72] Boele-Woelki et al (n 4), 205, referring to the national reports by I Lund-Andersen and C Jeppesen-De Boer (Denmark) and T Sverdrup and P Lødrup (Norway).

default rule but puts the onus on the third person to demonstrate that there are sound reasons for allowing it, based on the child's best interests.

Situations in group (b) do not permit an entirely satisfactory unified response. According to the CEFL Principles, if a parent with sole parental responsibilities dies, the responsibilities should be attributed to the surviving parent or a third person upon a decision by the competent authority.[73] The comments to the relevant principle indicate that adopting this solution deviates from the European common core, which opts to automatically attribute the exercise of parental responsibilities to the surviving parent.[74] In reality, national jurisdictions only attribute parental responsibility automatically to the surviving parent if he or she already held (but did not exercise) the responsibility. Should circumstances arise that render this allocation undesirable, this may justify another person (for example, a step-parent) to demand that the public authority change the allocation. What the CEFL Principles propose, however, is much more suitable for cases in which the surviving parent did not hold parental responsibility. In such cases it is undoubtedly preferable to avoid automatic reactions and instead defer the decision to the competent authority to assess whether a third person is more suitable to assume the responsibilities. Nonetheless, this is not 'a better solution' that departs from the common core: it is the general rule when the deceased parent held sole parental responsibilities.[75] To summarise, when the parent that exercised sole parental responsibility dies, it seems reasonable to propose that the responsibility be passed on by operation of law either to the surviving parent or, by a decision taken by the competent authority, either to the surviving parent or to a third person, depending on whether the surviving parent was the holder of parental responsibility or not.[76]

In the last group of cases (c), the termination of parental responsibility leads to the appointment of another person or persons to substitute for the parents in the exercise of their protective functions. These functions are encompassed within the concept of 'parental responsibilities' in the European principles and international instruments, but are regulated by national legislation in a different institutional framework: that of the guardianship of minors. Giving persons who are placed *in loco parentis* a different legal status from that held by parents has its historical roots in

---

[73] Principle 3:31 (2).

[74] Boele-Woelki et al (n 4) 210–11; idem, 'The CEFL Principles' (n 5) 78.

[75] See for instance the national reports by M Roth (Austria), N Lowe (England and Wales), N Dethloff and D Martiny (Germany), K Boele-Woelki (the Netherlands) and H Hausheer (Switzerland), in Boele-Woelki et al (n 21).

[76] See in this respect principle 23(2) of the White Paper.

Roman law. It can be explained by the diversity of situations in which a guardianship may arise, but also by an outdated understanding of a guardian's functions being centred on wealth management. The law of guardianship has remained of only marginal relevance in comparative law.[77] The efforts towards European harmonisation in the area of parental responsibilities go above and beyond the scope of guardianship: the principles dealing with the content of these responsibilities apply to any person holding them, irrespective of whether they are the parents or third persons.[78] This approach, which standardises the basic legal content of rights and duties over the child's person and property regardless of the holder, seems to be right insofar as it gives parents or, failing this, the competent authority, an opportunity to order more intense monitoring of the exercise of parental responsibilities by third persons should circumstances relating to a minor's personal life or property require it.

There is a growing consensus in favour of allowing parents to appoint a substitute holder of parental responsibilities in anticipation of their deaths.[79] Parents are in a much better position than the law or a public authority to judge what is best for their children. Given the risk that their proposals may not be the most suitable, some legal systems treat them simply as desires or recommendations that the authority must take into account.[80] However, bearing in mind that the risk is small, it seems more consistent with the pre-eminent position of parents in most legal systems to characterise their intervention as an exercise of a right, and place the burden of proving that their proposal is not in the minor's best interests on whomever objects to the appointment or instructions, including the minor herself if she is mature enough.

5. CONCLUDING REMARKS

The overview of the main trends in European national legal systems shows parental responsibility to be a complex institution characterised by

---

[77] See A Röthel, 'Guardianship of Minors', in Basedow et al (n 40), 812.

[78] See CEFL principles 3:19 to 3:24, which apply to holders of (full) parental responsibilities without distinguishing between parents and third parties.

[79] Principle 23(3)-(4) of the White Paper; principle 26 (2) of the Draft CM/Rec 2011. The CEFL Principles do not take a stance on this issue and leave it to national law to resolve.

[80] This is the case in Bulgaria, the Czech Republic, France, Lithuania, Norway, Poland, Russia, and Switzerland, as exposed by the national reports in Boele-Woelki et al (n 21), Q 34, 467–76.

a remarkable normative diversity, which makes it particularly challenging for comparative law research purposes. In spite of the valuable steps taken towards its harmonisation in the international arena by international institutions, courts and academic bodies, its legal design in European civil and family codes is still highly heterogeneous.

From a European perspective, parental responsibility in its current form appears to be a child-centred institution. The progressive embrace of the term 'responsibility', instead of 'authority' or '*potestas*', reflects the paradigm shift that has imposed itself in Europe after a long process of social and legal evolution. According to this view the core of parental responsibility is made up of duties of caring for and bringing up children, and by the powers to make and implement decisions that must be exercised both in the child's interests and for the fulfilment of these duties. Parental powers are limited not only by the commitment to the child's welfare but also to the child's autonomy; this leads to the demise of parental responsibility during the last stage of children's minority through the effects of various legal techniques that make it possible for children to make their own decisions. More theoretical and empirical research should be conducted on the relative effectiveness of these techniques in promoting minors' interests in personal and property-related matters.

While the responsibility towards minors is child-centred, there is also consensus on affirming its 'parental' nature, in other words its allocation to a child's parents on a principled basis. This allocation is based on the deep natural or emotional bonds that the parent/child relationship normally entails and the presumption of unconditional parental commitment deriving from these bonds. It is important to note that in the current European landscape the allocation of this responsibility is becoming increasingly separated from parents' family status. Its allocation has already been disassociated from gender criteria and we are now witnessing a clear trend towards its also becoming disassociated from the parents' marital status or their living together. Adjustments or exceptions to the rule attributing parental responsibility to both parents on an equal footing are only justified by the child's best interests and, particularly as the child grows up, by the way in which the parent/child relationship actually develops, but not primarily by the parents' family status.

The primacy of parents in assuming responsibility for their children is also embodied in the upholding of their private autonomy to agree on ways of exercising parental responsibility, to agree to its being conferred or shared with third persons, or to make binding appointments or give instructions in anticipation of their future absence. The recognition of parental autonomy to regulate the shape and the performance of parental powers and duties has not yet been fully consolidated in European legal systems and is usually subject to different degrees of judicial oversight. It is nevertheless fertile ground for research and one in which future developments are to be expected.

The unconditional attribution of parental responsibility to parents, tied to the need to weigh up the circumstances in which a child lives and the quality of his or family attachments, explains the growing trend towards the breaking up of parental responsibilities into bundles of duties and powers of varying content and intensity. A significant number of jurisdictions have traditionally distinguished between a suitability to assume this responsibility in the abstract and a 'better suitability' to exercise it in view of the specific family circumstances, by means of the distinction between holding responsibility and exercising it. Systems that do not recognise this distinction are forced to adapt the content and attribution of parental responsibility to take account of personal and family positions, which sometimes differ significantly. On the other hand, it should not be forgotten that parents' authority must be combined with the state's protective role and the power of judicial or administrative authorities to order protection measures, allow the participation of third persons in the exercise of parental functions or, as a matter of last resort, discharge parents from their responsibilities. This interference in the holding or exercise of parental responsibility also contributes to its functional unbundling: at times it requires distinctions to be drawn between powers related to daily matters and those related to matters of long-term impact; between executive powers and supervisory powers, or between residence-based powers and powers that can be exercised aside from child custody. This breaking up of parental responsibility – which to many justifies the preference for the plural term 'responsibilities' – adds to its image as complex institution and also opens up multiple spaces for comparative analysis.

RECOMMENDATIONS FOR FURTHER READING

A Bainham, S Day Sclater and M Richards (eds), *What is a Parent?* (Hart Publishing 1999).

K Boele-Woelki, B Braat and I Curry-Sumner (eds), *European Family Law in Action, vol III, Parental Responsibilities* (Intersentia 2005).

K Boele-Woelki, F Ferrand, C González Beilfuss, M Jäntera-Jareborg, N Lowe, D Martiny, W Pintens, *Principles of European Family Law Regarding Parental Responsibilities* (Intersentia 2007).

K Boele-Woelki, 'The CEFL Principles Regarding Parental Responsibilities: Predominance of the Common Core', in K Boele-Woelki and T Sverdrup (eds), *European Challenges in Contemporary Family Law* (Intersentia 2008) 63.

J Eekelaar, 'Rethinking Parental Responsibility' (2001) 31 *Family Law* 426.

C Jeppesen de Boer, *Joint Parental Authority (A Comparative Legal Study on the Continuation of Joint Parental Authority after Divorce and the Breakup of a Relationship in Dutch and Danish Law and the CEFL Principles)* (Intersentia 2008).

E Örücü and J Mair (eds), *Juxtaposing Legal Systems and the Principles of European Family Law on Parental Responsibilities* (Intersentia 2010).

R Probert, S Gilmore and J Herring (eds), *Responsible Parents and Parental Responsibility* (Hart Publishing 2009).

J Scherpe, 'Nichteheliche Kinder, elterliche Sorge und die Europäische Menschenrechtskonvention' (2009) 73 RabelsZ 935.

I Schwenzer (ed), *Tensions Between Legal, Biological and Social Conceptions of Parentage* (Intersentia 2007).

MJ Vonk, *Children and their Parents (A Comparative Study of the Legal Position of Children with Regard to their Intentional and Biological Parents in English and Dutch Law)* (Intersentia 2007).

9.   Adoption in a European perspective

Claire Fenton-Glynn[*]

1.   INTRODUCTION

Europe is a continent with diverse traditions concerning adoption. The prevalence of adoption varies greatly throughout: while in each of England, France and Italy there are around 3,000 to 4,000 adoptions per year, in each of Austria, Albania, Cyprus, Czech Republic, Georgia and Iceland there are less than 100.[1] Further, while some countries have a strong tradition of domestic adoption, others focus predominantly on inter-country placements, either as sending (for example, Russia and Ukraine) or receiving (for example, Netherlands, Sweden and Norway) states.

This diversity may go some way to explaining why the European Convention on the Adoption of Children of 1967, and its revised 2008

---

[*]   Accurate to 1 October 2013.
[1]   See Hague Conference on Private International Law, 'Adoption Statistics' (available 13 July 2015 at http://www.hcch.net/index_en.php?act=conventions.publications&dtid=32&cid=69).

version, have been so ill received, obtaining only 16 and seven ratifications or accessions respectively.[2] On the other hand, adoption has been an area in which the European Court of Human Rights (ECtHR) has generated a considerable body of jurisprudence, and in relation to the procedural aspects of adoption has established important safeguards to protect the rights of children, birth parents and prospective adopters involved in the practice. However, with regard to the substantive law, there remains considerable variation among European states, and the Court has been cautious in its approach, leaving a wide margin of appreciation to domestic authorities.

This chapter will consider the jurisprudence of the Court in three principal areas of adoption practice. First, it will discuss how consent to adoption is regulated, and the procedures put in place to protect both the birth parents,[3] and the adopted child. It will analyse the assistance given to parents who voluntarily give their consent to the adoption of their child, as well as the mechanisms by which adoption can be undertaken without parental consent. Further, it will consider how and when the child is heard in adoption proceedings, and the weight that is given to his or her wishes and opinions in various jurisdictions across Europe. Second, it will examine the conditions under which a person may become an adoptive parent, looking at key issues of marital status and sexual orientation, and the ways in which the Court has limited the discretion of states in this area. Finally, it will look at issues that arise post-adoption, focusing on the child's access to information regarding his or her birth parents, including the controversial issue of anonymous birth.

2. CONSENT TO ADOPTION: PROTECTING THE RIGHTS OF THE PARENTS AND CHILD

2.1 Adoption without Consent: Ensuring Proportionality

The placement of children for adoption without the consent of their parents has been an area in which the European Court of Human Rights has been particularly influential, establishing strong safeguards to ensure

---

[2]   The 1967 Convention has been renounced by Norway and Sweden, and partially renounced by the United Kingdom.

[3]   In this chapter, I will use the term 'birth parents' to refer to the child's legal parents at birth. This does not necessarily respond to the child's biological parents, as there may be reasons why the child's biological origins are not reflected in law.

not only that the right of parents to respect for family life is not interfered with unjustly, but also that the child's right to stay with his or her parents wherever possible is not intruded upon.

The key element in such cases is the issue of proportionality, which dominates the evaluation of child protection measures under article 8 of the ECHR. In essence, it obliges the state to ensure that any action taken to protect the child is no more than is necessary in that particular situation, meaning that adoption cannot be ordered without the consent of the parents unless there is no less intrusive alternative that would similarly satisfy the child's needs.

Under the ECHR, adoption without parental consent is the most extreme form of interference with family life. As the Court stated in the case of *Görgülü v Germany*, 'it is in a child's interest for its family ties to be maintained, as severing such ties means cutting a child off from its roots, which can only be justified in very exceptional circumstances.'[4] The state will therefore in principle require serious justification before allowing an adoption order to be finalised, and the strictest standard of review will be used under the ECHR.[5] While affording the state a wide margin of appreciation when taking a child into care in the first place, in theory, the Court proclaims to examine much more stringently the need to grant an adoption order, and whether it can be considered proportionate to the individual child's situation.

However, in practice, the 'exceptional circumstances' test has not proved difficult to overcome. When examining whether an adoption order is proportionate, and the reasons behind it are relevant and sufficient, Choudhry and Herring suggest that the test will be satisfied where the state's measures are deemed to be in the best interests of the child.[6] This is coupled with a wide margin of appreciation given to domestic authorities that are in direct contact with the parents and child involved, and who are best placed to make a decision concerning the child's welfare.[7]

It is thus not in the area of substantive guarantees that the ECHR is most effective, but in the procedural safeguards that it places on authorities to ensure that parents are adequately involved in the decision-making process. This is a well-established principle of ECtHR jurisprudence, and is one from which unmarried fathers in particular have

---

[4] [2004] ECHR 89 at [48] (citations omitted).

[5] See *Johansen v Norway* [1997] 23 EHRR 33.

[6] S Choudhry and J Herring, *European Human Rights and Family Law* (Hart Publishing 2010) 331–2.

[7] See, for example, *Söderbäck v Sweden* [1998] 29 EHRR 95.

benefitted. Since the seminal case of *Keegan v Ireland,* a father who has established 'family life' under article 8 has the right to be consulted about any placement for adoption, and to be involved in any proceedings that occur.[8] Further, both parents have a procedural right to legal assistance to ensure a fair trial under article 6, where the case raises difficult points of law and emotive issues,[9] and the right under article 8 to have access to the material relied on by the authorities when making the adoption decision.[10]

These principles are, however, relatively well established and this is an area that has been admirably covered by other authors.[11] In the area of adoption with consent, however, there have been number of recent decisions that have been particularly influential in providing greater protection to birth parents, and through them, children.

2.2   Adoption with Consent: Procedural Requirements and State Assistance

Similarly to adoption without consent, where a child is voluntarily placed for adoption by his or her parents, procedural safeguards are particularly important, in this case to ensure that the parents' consent to adoption is free, informed and truly voluntary.[12] The European Court of Human Rights has focused on two key areas of procedural rights for parents giving their consent to adoption: first, the timing of consent after the mother has given birth; and second, the assistance and counselling given by states to assist the birth parents in coming to a decision.

---

[8]   [1994] 18 EHRR 342 (although it should be noted that this case involved the placement of a child for adoption with the consent of the mother). There is insufficient space in this chapter to consider the circumstances in which family life can be found under article 8, although it should be noted that some fathers are now recognised to have private life under this article through the intention of having a relationship with their children that is thwarted by the mother. It is unclear whether such private life will extend to requiring participation in adoption proceedings. See *Anayo v Germany* [2010] ECHR 393; *Schneider v Germany* [2012] 54 EHRR 12.

[9]   See *P, C and S v the United Kingdom* [2002] 35 EHRR 31.

[10]   *TP and KM v the United Kingdom* [2002] 34 EHRR 2.

[11]   See Choudhry and Herring, (n 6); U Kilkelly, *The Child and the European Convention on Human Rights* (Ashgate 1999).

[12]   In this instance, I refer only to 'voluntariness' in legal terms. Whether a decision is truly voluntary given the situation in which a mother (or indeed father) finds themselves in is an important issue, but space precludes its discussion in this chapter.

The timing of consent given by a mother for the placement of her child for adoption is crucial to ensuring that her rights, and those of the child, are not violated. Women need to be protected from making life-changing decisions in the immediate aftermath of birth, and the practice of allowing birth mothers to give their consent at this time exploits their weakness when they are most vulnerable. A mother needs time to recover from the effects of the birth and the hormones involved with pregnancy, and time should be given for her to reflect on her decision in a less stressful and emotionally charged situation.

This will be of benefit to both the mother and the child, as it means that they will not be separated prematurely and as such, the mother and child have the greatest chance of maintaining the integrity of the family, where at all possible. The revised European Convention on Adoption of Children (ECA) (2008) has addressed these concerns, and requires that a mother's consent cannot be given until six weeks after birth.[13] The explicit reasoning behind the inclusion of this requirement was to 'avoid premature adoptions to which mothers give their consent as a result of pressure exerted before the birth of the child or before their physical health and psychological balance have been restored after the child's birth'.[14]

However, it is also important for the sake of the child that an adoption is not delayed for too long. Especially where a child is placed in institutional care in the intervening period, it is well established that the longer he or she remains, the greater the risk of harm, attachment disorder and developmental delay.[15] Thus the right of the child to not be separated from his or her birth family prematurely must be balanced against the right to be placed in a secure and stable environment as soon as possible.

While some European jurisdictions have attempted to strike this balance by placing required waiting periods ranging from 30 days

---

[13] Article 5(5).

[14] Explanatory report to the European Convention of the Adoption of Children (Revised) 2008, [37].

[15] C Hamilton-Giachritsis and K Browne, 'Identifying Good Practices in the Deinstitutionalisation of Children under 5 Years from European Institutions' (Daphne Programme, 2005) (available 13 July 2015 at http://ec.europa.eu/ justice_home/daphnetoolkit/html/projects/dpt_2003_046_c_en.html); K Browne, 'The Risk of Harm to Young Children in Institutional Care' (Save the Children 2009) (available 13 July 2015 at http://resourcecentre.savethechildren.se/content/ library/documents/risk-harm-young-people-institutional-care); K Browne, C Hamilton-Giachritsis, R Johnson, M Ostergren, 'Overuse of Institutional Care for Children in Europe' (2006) 332 *British Medical Journal* 485.

(Spain[16] and Bulgaria[17]) to six weeks (Cyprus,[18] Czech Republic,[19] England,[20] Hungary,[21] Latvia,[22] Malta,[23] Portugal,[24] Serbia,[25] Switzerland[26] and Turkey[27]), eight weeks (Estonia[28] and Germany[29]), 60 days (Romania),[30] two months (Belgium,[31] Norway[32] and Ukraine[33]) and three months (Denmark,[34] Greece,[35] Iceland,[36] Lithuania[37] and Montenegro[38]), others have taken a more permissive approach, allowing consent to be given immediately after birth (Slovenia),[39] or even before the birth (Slovakia).[40]

Only in Finland and Sweden is there any reference to the emotional and physical state of the mother, with consent only permitted after she

---

[16]   Civil Code, article 177.
[17]   Family Code 2003, article 89(2).
[18]   Adoption Act 1995, s 6(3)(a).
[19]   Act No 94/1963 Sb on Family, s 68a.
[20]   Adoption and Children Act 2002, s 52(3).
[21]   Family Act 1952, s 48(3).
[22]   Civil Law, article 169.
[23]   Civil Code, article 118(2).
[24]   Civil Code, article 1982(3).
[25]   Family Act, article 98(3).
[26]   Civil Code, article 265(b)(1).
[27]   Civil Code, article 310.
[28]   Family Law Act 2009, s 152(2). The parent's consent can be given before this, but it will not enter into force until eight weeks after birth.
[29]   Civil Code, s 1747. However, the father may consent to the adoption of the child before birth if the parents are not married to each other.
[30]   Law 273/2004, article 16(1).
[31]   Civil Code, article 348-5.
[32]   Act of 28 February 1986 No 8 relating to adoption, s 7.
[33]   Family Code, article 217(3).
[34]   Adoption (Consolidation) Act, article 8(2).
[35]   Civil Code, article 1551.
[36]   Adoption Act no 130/1999, article 8.
[37]   Civil Code, article 3.209(3).
[38]   Family Law, article 124.
[39]   There is no law regarding the time after birth that the mother can consent to adoption, therefore it is possible for her to give consent from the moment the child is born (Y Brulard and L Dumont, *Comparative Study Relating to Procedures for Adoption among the Member States of the European Union, Practical Difficulties Encountered in this field by European Citizens within the Context of the European Pillar of Justice and Civil Matters and Means of Solving these Problems and of Protecting Children's Rights* (European Union 2007) 449).
[40]   Ibid, 444.

has sufficiently recovered from the child's delivery (and in Finland, in any case no earlier than eight weeks after birth).[41]

In 2009, the European Court of Human Rights found a positive obligation on states to ensure that mothers have sufficient time to reflect so that they can make an informed and considered decision. In the case of *Todorova v Italy*, involving children declared adoptable 30 days after birth, the Court found that:

> in disputes of this nature, where the consequences are of extreme importance as they affect the family relationship, the State had a positive obligation to ensure that the consent given by the applicant to the abandonment of her children was informed, and had been surrounded by adequate safeguards.[42]

In doing so, the Court approved the six-week rule in the ECA (2008),[43] and recognised that although the interests of children required that their future be decided as soon as possible, the right of the mother to have time to reflect on her decision requires a more delicate balance to be struck.

However, while giving the mother time to consider her decision after birth is important, this by itself is not enough. Many mothers who are considering giving up children at birth are young, single and economically vulnerable,[44] and it is important that they are provided with sufficient assistance during the adoption process to ensure that they understand the decision that is being made, and have been given an opportunity to consider its implications.

---

[41] Finland: Adoption Act 22/2012, s 15; Sweden: Children and Parents Code, s 5a.

[42] [2009] ECHR 69 at [82] (my translation).

[43] Despite the fact that Italy is not yet party to this Convention, although it is party to the original 1967 European Convention on the Adoption of Children which has the same requirement (article 5(4)).

[44] FJ Pilotti, 'Intercountry Adoption – Trends, Issues and Policy Implications for the 1990s', in *Childhood* (Instituto Interamericano del Nino 1993) 165–77. A 2005 report found that in Romania, 29% of mothers who abandoned their children were under the age of 20; another 28% were between 20 and 24. 63% were single mothers, and 94.2% were unemployed (UNICEF, *The Situation of Child Abandonment in Romania* (2005) 31–2). Likewise, 67% of children in Bulgarian institutions in 2008 came from single parent families (University of Nottingham, *Child Abandonment and its Prevention in Europe* (Daphne Programme 2012) 8). In a survey of 89 maternity units across nine European countries, 75% cited poverty and financial hardship as among the causes of child abandonment (University of Nottingham, *Child Abandonment and its Prevention in Europe* (Daphne Programme 2012) 11).

The content of this procedural requirement in relation to assistance to birth mothers was explored in the case of *Kearns v France*.[45] This case involved an Irish woman who fell pregnant in an extra-marital relationship. In February, she travelled to France with her mother and a French lawyer, and requested an anonymous birth under French law. On the day after the child's birth, in the presence of a nurse acting as an interpreter, she signed the record placing the child in state care. In May, the child was placed for adoption with a new family. However, in July, the mother returned to the hospital seeking the return of her child. When this was refused, as the two-month time period within which she could revoke her consent had passed, she made an application to the ECtHR, alleging a violation of her right to respect for family life under article 8. She argued that the French authorities had a positive obligation to make all necessary arrangements to ensure that she understood the precise implications of her actions, including a clear and accurate translation of the technical legal provisions concerning her.[46]

The Court rejected her argument on the grounds that as an Irish national she had specifically chosen to give birth in France to take advantage of the anonymous birth laws in that jurisdiction. Furthermore, it held that the presence of a doctor and nurse with knowledge of English was sufficient, and article 8 cannot be construed as requiring the authorities to ensure the presence of qualified interpreters.

Although the application failed on the facts, this case opens the door to the possibility of requiring states to ensure that birth parents sufficiently understand the consequences of placing a child for adoption. The fact that the applicant had chosen to travel to France for the birth was extremely detrimental to her case, but it is arguable that a mother who was already living in the country concerned and did not understand the procedure due to language or the complicated nature of the law in this area may be in a strong position to claim a violation of article 8. This case made clear that sufficient information and advice in a language that the parent can understand is a vital component of this provision.

In compliance with this requirement, some European states have included specific obligations for counselling for both mothers and fathers in their legislation and practice. Finland is a particularly good example of this, with the Adoption Act requiring that before consent is given, a consultation be arranged with the parents to explain the purpose, conditions and legal consequences of adoption. Parents must also be informed

---

45   *Kearns v France* [2008] 50 EHRR 33.
46   Ibid, [52].

of the financial assistance and social services available to them if they wish to keep their child.[47] Belgian law makes similar provision, requiring the mother and father to be informed of the consequences of adoption by both social services and the tribunal before whom they give their consent. Such information must relate to their rights, as well as the assistance and advantages offered to families and possible ways to resolve social, financial, psychological or other problems that may be posed by their situation.[48]

In other states, counselling is not required, but the court (or authority) taking the parents' consent must explain the consequences of adoption and its legal effects.[49] This is the case in England, where a Children and Family Court Advisory and Support Service (Cafcass) officer must witness the consent of a parent or guardian to adoption.[50] In the organisation's guidance document, the officer is required to ensure that the consent given is unconditional, and given with a full understanding of the nature and effect of the order. Furthermore, the officer is advised to be vigilant about factors that might invalidate consent, such as incapacity due to mental ill health or learning disability.[51] By placing this obligation on government officials, the English Parliament has placed an additional check to ensure that the rights of children and their parents are protected.[52]

The European Court of Human Rights is thus playing an important role in determining the timing and manner of voluntary consent to adoption, through interpreting procedural safeguards for birth parents into article 8. This protects not only the rights of the birth parents whose consent is

---

[47] Adoption Act 22/2012, ss 14, 21, 24.

[48] Civil Code, article 348.4.

[49] For example: Portugal: Civil Code, article 1982(1); Malta: Civil Code, article 119(1); Lithuania: Civil Code, article 3.212(4); s 3; Estonia: Family Law Act 2009, s 152(6); Cyprus: Adoption Act 1995, s 7.

[50] Family Procedure Rules 2010, rule 16.32.

[51] CAFCASS, *Guidance for Witnessing Consent to the Making of an Adoption Order (in Partner and other Non-Agency Adoptions* (2007) [6.4] (available 13 July 2015 at http://www.cafcass.gov.uk/media/6524/CONSENT%20TO%20THE%20MAKING%20OF%20AN%20ADOPTION%20ORDER%20300312.pdf).

[52] Of course, government regulation of consent does not necessarily ensure protection of rights, and has been one of the major problems in intercountry adoption in countries such as Cambodia, Guatemala and India. See, for example, DM Smolin, 'Child Laundering: How the Intercountry Adoption System Legitimizes and Incentivized the Practices of Buying, Trafficking, Kidnaping, and Stealing Children' (2006) 52 *Wayne Law Review* 113.

needed, but also the rights of the child to stay with his or her birth parents where they are willing and capable of caring for him or her. This is still an emerging area of jurisprudence, however, as the cases brought before the Court in this area have been few and far between. Nevertheless, the Court shows important signs of progress in protecting birth parents in vulnerable positions.

2.3 The Child's Voice in Adoption Proceedings

When considering whether to grant an adoption order, it is not only the wishes of the birth parents that should be considered, but also the views and opinions of the child him- or herself. Article 12 of the United Nations Convention on the Rights of the Child (UNCRC) makes clear that children who are capable of forming their own views have the right to express them, and have them given due weight in accordance with their age and maturity.

The child's voice in adoption proceedings can be considered in two different ways: the first concerns the age at which a child must give his or her consent to adoption; the second concerns the way in which children below this age of consent are listened to, and their opinions weighed.

The most common way in which authorities decide whether to obtain the child's consent is through the use of a set age limit, after which the child is deemed capable of making an autonomous decision on the matter. This is seen in 30 European states, although the age that this is set differs widely, from ten (Armenia,[53] Azerbaijan,[54] Bosnia and Herzegovina,[55] Estonia,[56] Georgia,[57] Lithuania,[58] Moldova,[59] Romania,[60] Russia[61] and Slovenia[62]) to 11 (Malta),[63] 12 (Albania,[64] Andorra,[65] Belgium,[66]

---

[53] Family Code 2004, article 24.
[54] Family Code 1999, article 124.5.
[55] Family Law 1990, articles 142–171.
[56] Family Law Act 2009, s 151.
[57] Civil Code, article 1255.
[58] Civil Code, article 3.125.
[59] Family Code, article 127.
[60] Law No 273/2004.
[61] Family Code 1995, article 132(1).
[62] Marriage and Family Relations Act 1976, article 137(2).
[63] Civil Code, article 115(3)(d).
[64] Law No 9695 of 19 March 2007, article 15(2).
[65] Qualified Law on Adoption of 21 March 1996; Regulations for Adoption of 10 June 1998.
[66] Civil Code, article 348-1.

Croatia,[67] Greece,[68] Latvia,[69] Former Yugoslav Republic Of Macedonia,[70] Norway,[71] Portugal[72] and Spain[73]),[74] 13 (Poland[75] and France[76]), 14 (Bulgaria,[77] Germany,[78] and Italy[79]) and 15 (Luxembourg[80] and Monaco[81]).

On the other hand, in Cyprus,[82] the Czech Republic,[83] Slovakia,[84] Switzerland,[85] Turkey,[86] and Ukraine,[87] there is no fixed age of consent. In each of these countries, the child's consent is required for adoption if he or she has the capacity, or is of sufficient maturity, to understand and

---

[67] Family Act 2003, article 134.

[68] Civil Code, article 1555.

[69] Civil Law, article 169.

[70] Family Law 2004, article 123.

[71] Act of 28 February 1986 No 8 relating to adoption.

[72] Civil Code, article 1981.

[73] Civil Code, article 177(1).

[74] Finland, Netherlands, Denmark, Iceland and Sweden also set their age of consent at 12, but allow qualifications to this. When reviewing its adoption law in the 1990s, England also considered setting 12 as the minimum age at which a child's consent would be needed, but did not include this in the final Act, as it was considered that any age limit would place an unnecessary burden on the child. (Review of Adoption Law, Report to Ministers of an Interdepartmental Working Group (Department of Health and Welsh Office 1992), [9.5]).

[75] Family Code, article 118(1). The Guardianship court may exceptionally declare that consent is unnecessary if the child is not capable of giving consent (i.e. suffers from mental disabilities).

[76] Civil Code, article 345.

[77] Family Code 2003, article 89(4).

[78] Civil Code, section 1746.

[79] Law 184 of 4 May 1983, article 7.

[80] Civil Code, article 356.

[81] Civil Code, article 249.

[82] If his or her age and maturity permits (Adoption Act 1995, article 4c).

[83] If he or she is able to understand and consider the effects and consequences of the adoption, except in cases where it would frustrate the purpose of adoption (Act No 94/1963 Sb on Family, s 67).

[84] When, having regard to age and maturity, he or she is able to assess the impact of the adoption (Act No 36/2005 Act on Family; Act No 305/2005 Social and Legal Protection of Children and Social Nurture; Act No 99/1963 Code of Civil Procedure). See also Slovakia, *Country Profile for Intercountry Adoption: State of Origin* (available 13 July 2015 at http://www.hcch.net/index_en.php?act=publications.details&pid=5095&dtid=42).

[85] If the child has the capacity to consent (Civil Code, article 265).

[86] If the child has capacity to act on his or her own behalf (Civil Code, articles 305–320).

[87] Family Code, article 218(1).

consider the decision being made. In a similar fashion, several European countries have no rules regarding the child's consent, and instead must simply listen to the views of the child (Liechtenstein[88] and Austria).[89] These requirements fit most closely with the position of the UNCRC, allowing for the evolving capacities of the child, and acknowledging that each child develops differently, and will be ready to make such a decision at different times.

The jurisprudence of the ECtHR concerning the right of the child to participation has been noticeably lacking, and where the Court has considered the issue, it has relied on outdated notions of parental and state authority. This was first seen in the case of *Nielsen v Denmark*,[90] decided shortly after the English case of *Gillick* that had allowed the child the right to autonomously make decisions where he or she was of sufficient capability and maturity.[91] However, contrary to the English approach, the ECtHR found in *Nielsen* that a child's hospitalisation against his will was a reasonable exercise of parental authority, even though he was capable of expressing his views clearly and maturely.

The only ECtHR case that has explicitly considered the child's consent to adoption has been that of *Pini v Romania*, which concerned two nine-and-a-half-year-old girls who were placed in intercountry adoption, without seeking their views. Under the law at the time that the adoption order was made, consent of children was only needed once they reached ten years of age, but by the time the adoptive parents tried to enforce the decision (which was being contested by the orphanage in which the children were living) the girls were between ten and 12. As such, the Court ruled that they 'had reached an age at which it could reasonably be considered that their personality was sufficiently formed and they had attained the necessary maturity to express their opinion as to the surroundings in which they wished to be brought up',[92] and could not be forced against their will to form an alternative family.

What is interesting about this case is that the majority of the Court did not question the fact that the children were not asked for their opinions of the adoption at the age of nine and a half, although this was something that the judges in dissent relied on. As judges Thomasson and Jungwiert pointed out, the difficulties in this case largely arose from the lack of

---

[88]   Civil Code, article 181a.

[89]   Civil Code, article 181a.

[90]   *Nielsen v Denmark* [1988] 11 EHRR 175.

[91]   *Gillick v West Norfolk and Wisbech Area Health Authority* [1986] 1 AC 112 (HL).

[92]   *Pini and Others v Romania* [2005] 40 EHRR 13 at [157].

participation of the children in the first place, and lengthy judicial proceedings could have been avoided if the children's views had been ascertained.

Children's participation is not simply about giving consent to an adoption, however. Many children who are not capable of making a decision concerning their future care still have views and opinions that should be taken into account, and given due weight, even if they do not determine the outcome. Unfortunately, this is not possible across all European jurisdictions, with only a handful giving an unimpeded right to all children to participate if they so wish.[93] Some do not permit children under the age of consent to participate at all,[94] while others place age restrictions on this right.[95]

The participation of a young child in custody proceedings was considered by the ECtHR in the case of *Sahin v Germany*.[96] The applicant in this case was an unmarried father, who was challenging the German law that fathers of children born out of wedlock could only have access to their children with the consent of the mother, or if the court ruled that it was in the child's best interests. When deciding on whether contact would be in the child's interests, the court did not hear the applicant's five-year-old son directly, but relied on the evidence of a psychological expert who had met with the child, and recommended that questioning him would involve a risk to his psychological health and should thus be avoided. The father challenged this, claiming that the failure of the court to hear the child directly constituted a procedural violation of article 8.

Relying on the margin of appreciation given to domestic authorities, the Court found that it was within the discretion of courts to assess the evidence before them, and decide what form of participation would best protect the interests of the child. It held that:

---

[93] For example, Denmark (Adoption (Consolidation) Act, s 6(1)), Estonia (Family Law Act 2009, s 151), Hungary (Family Act 1952), Iceland (Adoption Act no 130/1999, article 6), Latvia (Procedures of Adoption, articles 5.3 and 10; however, the child must be able to 'formulate an opinion' before this is heard (Civil Law, article 169)).

[94] For example, in Armenia, Azerbaijan, Georgia, Malta, Moldova, Serbia, Slovakia and Turkey, there is no legislative requirement concerning adoption that the child be heard, except once he or she reached the age of consent.

[95] Albania (over 10 – Law No 9695 of 19 March 2007, article 15), Andorra (over 10 – Qualified Law on Adoption of 21 March 1996; Regulations for Adoption of 10 June 1998), Austria (over 5 – Civil Code, article 181a), Liechtenstein (over 5 – Civil Code, article 181a).

[96] *Sahin v Germany* [2003] ECHR 340.

> It would be going too far to say that domestic courts are always required to hear a child in court on the issue of access to a parent not having custody, but this issue depends on the specific circumstances of each case, having due regard to the age and maturity of the child concerned.[97]

While this decision focused on the procedural rights of the father to a fair hearing, rather than the right of the child to participate in a decision concerning his or her welfare, it establishes an important precedent for domestic courts to ensure that the child is heard in some manner, either directly or indirectly.

This is an area in which the jurisprudence has been particularly slow to develop, which is not surprising given that it goes to the heart of the rights of the child and child autonomy, an issue that the Court has been loath to engage with. However, through the enforcement of parental rights, children's rights are beginning to be introduced through the back door, and it is hopefully an area that will continue to develop in the future.

3.   ADOPTIVE PARENTHOOD: PRIVILEGE OR RIGHT?

It is in the area of the selection of adoptive parents that the jurisprudence of the European Court of Human Rights has been most influential, particularly in the area of single homosexual adopters. However, the Court has made clear that the ECHR, like every other international human rights instrument, does not provide prospective parents with a 'right to adopt'. In its 1975 decision of *X v Belgium and the Netherlands*, the Commission held that:

> a State cannot separate two persons united by an adoption contract, or forbid them to meet, without engaging its responsibility under Article 8 of the Convention. But one should not deduce from this a positive obligation on the State to grant a particular status – that of adoption – to the applicant and the person in his care.[98]

Adoption is not a fundamental right analogous to an individual freedom, which would oblige the state to provide it to all citizens, but rather a privilege voluntarily extended. However, where the state extends a privilege falling within the scope of one of the Convention rights, it must

---

[97]   Ibid, at [73].
[98]   App no 6482/74 (European Commission of Human Rights, 10 July 1975).

do so in a non-discriminatory manner.[99] As such, if adoption is permitted by the state, the restrictions on the eligibility and suitability of prospective adopters must comply with article 14 of the ECHR. To withstand scrutiny under this article, any difference in treatment must have an objective and reasonable justification (that is, pursue a legitimate aim), and there must be a reasonable relationship of proportionality between this aim and the means employed to pursue it.[100] This is a less strict level of scrutiny than that imposed by the principle of proportionality under article 8: the means employed do not have to cause the least interference possible, merely be a reasonable response to the objective pursued.

3.1 Adoption by Single Parents

Every European state allows adoption by single persons;[101] however, in several states such restrictive conditions are placed on single adopters that this right is illusory in practice. For example, in Cyprus,[102] Croatia,[103] Serbia[104] and Slovakia,[105] single persons are permitted to adopt only in exceptional circumstances or for special reasons, while in Lithuania single persons are only permitted to adopt where the child has extremely serious health problems and no married couple wish to adopt,

---

[99] In *Fretté v France*, the Court held that the desire to adopt fell within the scope of article 8, and thus could be examined for compliance with article 14. However, the partly concurring opinion of Judge Costa joined by Judges Jungwiert and Traja disagreed with this analysis. They argued that because there is no right to adopt or form a family under international law or the ECHR, there was no interference by the state in the applicant's private or family life, and there could be no link between article 14 and article 8 ([2002] 38 EHRR 21). This was reiterated by Judge Zupančič in the case of *EB v France*, which will be discussed below. While these judges made a valid point that the reasoning behind the majority's decision that the matter fell within the scope of article 8 was lacking, their own argument relied too greatly on whether there had been a *violation* of article 8, rather than whether the desire to found a family could fall within its scope ([2008] 47 EHRR 21).

[100] See, for example, *Fretté v France*, ibid, at [34].

[101] At least when it comes to domestic adoption: Ukraine only permits foreign citizens who are married to adopt (Family Code, article 212(1), (9)), although single Ukrainian citizens may adopt.

[102] Brulard and Dumont, (n 39) 77.

[103] Family Act 2003, s 74(2).

[104] Family Act, article 105.

[105] Brulard and Dumont (n 39) 433.

or where the child is over eight years of age and unable to be placed with another family.[106]

Further, in Ireland, adoption for a single person will only be permitted where the Adoption Authority considers it desirable, taking into account the welfare of the child,[107] while in Montenegro and Luxembourg, single persons are only permitted to enter into a simple adoption, rather than a full one.[108] In Armenia, only single females can adopt, while in Malta, a single person cannot adopt a female child.[109] In Georgia, Lithuania and Russia, if the child is adopted by a single person, he or she will retain links with the birth parent of the opposite sex to the adopter, so that he or she will continue to have one male and one female 'parent'.[110]

The claims of single persons to be permitted to adopt were first addressed by the European Commission on Human Rights in 1975 in the case of *X v Belgium and the Netherlands*.[111] In this case, involving the application of an unmarried man to adopt, the Commission based its decision on article 12, which confers a right to 'men and women of a marriageable age' to 'marry and to found a family, according to the national laws governing the exercise of this right'. It found that the existence of a couple was fundamental to the exercise of this right, and thus this article could not be relied on.

As discussed above, the Court went on to find that article 8 did not place a 'positive obligation on the State to grant a particular status – that of adoption – to the applicant and the person in his care'. While it is true that the ECHR does not require adoption to be recognised within the jurisdiction, and therefore establishes no 'right to adopt' recent jurisprudence suggests that where adoption *is* permitted, domestic authorities must grant sufficient legal safeguards to parent-child relationships that are already established.

This was seen in the seminal case of *Wagner and JMWL v Luxembourg*, which involved a single mother who was a Luxembourger citizen, who travelled to Peru to adopt a child. The adoption order was granted by the Peruvian provincial family court, but the mother's attempt to have

---

[106] Civil Code, article 3.210(2).

[107] Adoption Act 2010, s 33.

[108] Family Law, article 134 (Montenegro); Civil Code, article 367 (Luxembourg).

[109] See *Wagner and JMWL v Luxembourg* App no 76240/01 (ECHR, 28 June 2007) at [68].

[110] Ibid, at [69].

[111] App no 6482/74 (European Commission of Human Rights, 10 July 1975).

this recognised as a full adoption in Luxembourg failed, as only simple adoptions were available to single persons.

The applicant argued that the distinction between married and single adopters was discriminatory and thus in contravention of article 14 taken in conjunction with article 8. The government, on the other hand, contended that the distinction had the legitimate aim of protecting the child, as two parents were better able to care for an adopted child, especially one who had come from abroad and had been uprooted from everything he or she knew.[112]

Interestingly, the Court based its findings under article 14 not on the claims of the *mother* not to be discriminated against, but on the situation of the *child*, and in particular the child's right not to be treated differently from other children who had been the subject of a judgment of full adoption in Peru resulting in a complete break from the family of origin. It held that although these biological ties had been legally broken, because of the decision of the Luxembourg authorities no alternative legal link had been forged with the adoptive mother, leaving the child in a legal vacuum. The Court found that there was no reason to justify such discrimination in this case, especially since other Peruvian children adopted by single mothers had previously obtained full adoptions in Luxembourg.[113]

In this rather contrived way, the Court avoided the difficult issue of discrimination on the grounds of marital status in adoption.[114] Although there appears to be near consensus in Europe that single people *should* be permitted to adopt, the question remains unanswered whether there is a right for a single person to adopt *on an equal basis* with a married couple.

---

[112] *Wagner and JMWL* (n 109) at [146]–[147].

[113] This decision was partly aided by the fact that prior to the applicant's adoption application, all Peruvian adoptions, including those by single parents, were automatically approved. It was only at the time of her application that new rules were applied to strictly scrutinise judgments. The Court found that she had thus entered into the adoption in good faith, and was not trying to avoid Luxembourger laws, and had a legitimate expectation that the adoption would be approved.

[114] This is hardly surprising, as the Court tends to avoid findings on the most difficult issues if it can base its decisions on more clear-cut grounds (for example, *X v Belgium and the Netherlands* (n 111)).

3.2   Same-Sex Adoption: An Evolving Field

The issue of same-sex adoption is somewhat more controversial than that of adoption by single persons, with opinions still divided across Europe as to the extent to which this should be accommodated. A 2006 European Union study showed that although 69 per cent of respondents in the Netherlands and 51 per cent in Sweden supported the authorisation of adoption for same-sex couples throughout Europe, these were the only countries in which a majority was of that opinion.[115] A very clear divide can be seen in the survey of the 27 EU states (as there were at the time), with Western European jurisdictions showing higher support than those in Eastern Europe. Denmark and Austria both had 44 per cent in favour, with Belgium and Spain close behind at 43 per cent, and Germany at 42 per cent. On the other hand, in Estonia only 14 per cent of respondents were in favour, with 13 per cent in Hungary, 12 per cent in Bulgaria, Lithuania and Slovakia, 11 per cent in Greece, 10 per cent in Cyprus, 8 per cent in Latvia and Romania and 7 per cent in Malta and Poland.[116]

Despite this lack of popular support, there has been a small, but growing, number of countries that have now permitted joint adoption by homosexual couples: for example, Belgium,[117] Denmark,[118] England,[119]

---

[115]   It should be emphasised that the respondents were asked whether 'adoption of children should be authorised for homosexual couples throughout Europe', rather than simply whether they would support same-sex couples being authorised to adopt within their jurisdiction. As such, it is unclear whether respondents disagreed with the proposition because they were against adoption by same-sex couples, or because they did not feel this was an issue upon which there should be an EU wide mandate. European Commission, *Eurobarometer 66: Public Opinion in the European Union* (2006) (available 13 July 2015 at http://ec.europa.eu/public_opinion/archives/eb/eb66/eb66_en.pdf) 45.

[116]   Ibid.

[117]   Civil Code, article 343.

[118]   Denmark, *Country Profile for Intercountry Adoption: Receiving State* (available 13 July 2015 at http://www.hcch.net/index_en.php?act=publications.details&pid=5128&dtid=42).

[119]   Adoption and Children Act 2002, articles 49–50.

France,[120] Iceland,[121] Netherlands,[122] Norway,[123] Spain[124] and Sweden.[125] However, no matter how restrictive the laws on joint adoption for same-sex couples in the majority of jurisdictions, as was seen above, all countries permit adoption by single persons, and for many years, this has been used by prospective homosexual parents as a simpler route to forming a family.

The European Court of Human Rights has examined the right of single homosexuals to adopt on two occasions, coming to vastly different results in each.

In the first case, *Fretté v France* in 2002, the Court upheld the decision of the French authorities to refuse permission to adopt based on questions raised concerning 'his particular circumstances as a homosexual man'.[126] It found that the scientific community, and particularly experts on childhood, psychiatrists and psychologists, was divided on the consequences for a child of being adopted by one or more homosexual parent, and that the French authorities were legitimately allowed to limit the right to adopt in the interests of children.[127]

This view was strongly challenged by the joint partly dissenting opinion of Judge Sir Nicholas Bratza and Judges Fuhrmann and Tulkens, who found no evidence to suggest that homosexual parents would be harmful to children, and suggested that where single persons were permitted to adopt, any rejection of an application based solely on the grounds of sexual orientation was in breach of article 14 of the ECHR.

It was this dissenting view that was endorsed six years later in the case of *EB v France*, which effectively overruled *Fretté*. In a short section, with very little explanation, the Court found that the arguments of the French government regarding the consequences of a child being brought up by a homosexual parent were not convincing or weighty enough to

---

120 Following the passing of Law 2013-404 allowing same-sex couples to marry.
121 Law of June 27 2006.
122 Civil Code, article 1:227.
123 Norway, *Country Profile for Intercountry Adoption: Receiving State* (available 15 July 2015 at http://www.hcch.net/index_en.php?act=publications.details&pid=5090&dtid=42).
124 See Civil Code, article 44, which allows same-sex couples to marry.
125 Children and Parents Code, s 3.
126 [2002] 38 EHRR 21 at [10].
127 Ibid, at [42].

justify refusing to accept a homosexual's application.[128] It held that 'in rejecting the applicant's application for authorization to adopt, the domestic authorities made a distinction based on considerations regarding her sexual orientation, a distinction which is not acceptable under the Convention'.[129] Given the detailed analysis undertaken in *Fretté* concerning the practice of other member states and the opinions of the scientific community regarding homosexual adoption, the reasoning behind this decision, and the lack of detailed consideration of these issues, seems particularly weak.

However, it does show the marked shift in attitudes towards homosexual parenting in Europe. While *Fretté* allowed the government to focus on the legitimate aim of 'protecting' children from homosexual parents, such arguments were not given any weight by the Court six years later. Only one of the dissenting judges relied on the 'negative' role that the 'erotic relationship with its inevitable manifestations and the couple's conduct towards each other' would have on the personality of the child,[130] while the rest of the dissenting judges considered that a refusal of adoption on the grounds of sexual orientation alone would have violated article 14, had not other legitimate reasons been put forward for refusing the application.[131]

As a result of this case, any state that permits adoption by a single parent cannot prevent a homosexual applicant from adopting on the grounds of his or her sexual orientation, although restrictions on homosexual couples remain unchallenged. Given the slow development of this area of law, it may be some time before these restrictions are lifted; however, the Court appears to have laid to rest the myth that homosexual

---

[128]   [2008] 47 EHRR 21. This case has been extensively criticised for its reasoning, and for its position on the so-called 'contamination' of the decision-making process. The majority decided that where two grounds were relied on to reject the applicant, it was sufficient for one to be invalid to find the decision in violation of article 8 (see, for example, A Bainham, 'Homosexual Adoption' (2008) 67(3) *Cambridge Law Journal* 479).

[129]   *EB v France*, ibid, at [96] (footnotes omitted).

[130]   Dissenting opinion of Judge Loucaides.

[131]   Judge Zupančič argued that adoption was a privilege, and not a right, and therefore distinctions could be made on grounds that were not affected by arbitrariness, prejudice or frivolity. He held that a decision is arbitrary when it is not based on reasonable grounds and reasonable decision-making, but instead rests on prejudice, such as prejudice against homosexuals. However, he did not subscribe to the 'contamination' theory of the majority, and found that it was sufficient that one ground was valid for the refusal to adopt to be legitimate.

parents are in some way harmful to their children, or less able to provide a loving and nurturing home.[132]

4. INFORMATION ON ORIGINS: ANONYMOUS BIRTH AND THE RIGHT TO IDENTITY?

The final area of adoption practice in which the Court has been particularly influential has been that of a child's access to information about his or her origins, although in this area it has been the *denial* of the child's right that has been notable, rather than the protection provided by the Court.

The right of the child to have access to information about his or her birth parents has gained increasing academic attention in recent years. Studies have shown that without this information, the child may have difficult forming his or her own identity, and the ensuing state of uncertainty fundamentally undermines the child's security and mental health.[133] It is also an important element in a child's psychological balance,[134] as evidence suggests a manifest need in all people 'to know about their background, their genealogy, and their personal history if they are to grow up feeling complete and whole'.[135] The less information concerning his or her origins that the child has, the greater the problems experienced.[136]

Unfortunately, there are only a handful of countries in Europe that fully recognise the importance to a child of knowing his or her origins

---

[132] See M Rupp, *Die Lebensituation von Kindern in gleichgeschlechtlichen Lebenspartnerschaften* (Bundesanzeiger Verlag 2009).

[133] HJ Sants, 'Genealogical Bewilderment in Children with Substitute Parents' (1964) 37(2) *British Journal of Medical Psychology* 133, 133.

[134] S Besson, 'Enforcing the Child's Right to Know Her Origins: Contrasting Approaches under the Convention on the Rights of the Child and the European Convention on Human Rights' (2007) 21 *International Journal of Law, Policy and the Family* 137, 140.

[135] J Triseliotis, 'Obtaining Birth Certificates', in P Bean (ed.), *Adoption: Essays in Social Policy, Law, and Sociology* (Tavistock 1984) 38.

[136] J Triseliotis, *In Search of Origins: The Experiences of Adopted People* (Routledge & Kegan Paul 1973) 54–5. It is acknowledged that this need may be a socially constructed phenomenon that may not be present in children brought up in societies where the nuclear biological family is not the established norm. The nuclear biological family is, however, the model that adoption attempts to emulate, and for the purposes of this chapter, there will be no further consideration of the social impetus behind this need.

and thus require adoptive parents to tell their child that he or she is adopted, including Croatia,[137] Iceland,[138] Italy,[139] Montenegro[140] and Norway.[141] Croatia and Montenegro require that this be done before the child reaches the age of seven, while the other states rely on the discretion of parents to choose when this is advisable, or when the child is mature enough.[142] This approach is consistent with research by Triseliotis that suggests that the longer the secret of their adoption was kept from the child, the more serious the consequences when this was subsequently revealed.[143]

On the other end of the scale in Ukraine, however, a child has the right *not* to have his or her adoption disclosed, even to him- or herself.[144] Similarly, in the Former Yugoslav Republic of Macedonia, legislation permits adopted children to be registered with the names of the adoptive parents in place of the birth parents, and does not require the preservation of information concerning the child's origins.[145] In Russia, even if a child is informed of his or her adoptive status, there is no legal mechanism for obtaining access to information about his or her origins.[146]

In all other European countries, however, there is a general acceptance that the child should in principle be able to access information about his or her origins, although the extent to which this is restricted by age or parental authority varies greatly from state to state.

---

[137]   Family Act 2003, article 124.
[138]   Adoption Act, article 26.
[139]   Law No 149/2001.
[140]   Family Law, article 122.
[141]   Act of 28 February 1986 No 8 relating to adoption, s 12. This is also the case in domestic Dutch adoptions, which are not conducted in secret and it is standard practice for the child to be informed about its natural parents. Committee on the Rights of the Child, *Concluding Observations: Netherlands* (24 July 1997) CRC/C/51/Add.1, [76]; MJ Vonk, 'Tensions between Legal, Biological and Social Conceptions of Parenthood in Dutch Family Law' (May 2007) 11(1) *Electronic Journal of Comparative Law* 18, (available 13 July 2015 at http://www.ejcl.org/111/abs111-21.html).
[142]   Although the Icelandic legislation advises that, as a rule, this should be done before the child reaches six years of age.
[143]   Triseliotis (n 136) 36. This is in line with the current English jurisprudence on establishing paternity (see, for example, *Re R (A Minor) (Contact)* [1993] 2 FLR 762).
[144]   Family Code, article 226(2).
[145]   Committee on the Rights of the Child, *Concluding Observations: FYR of Macedonia* (11 June 2010) CRC/C/MKD/CO/2 [34].
[146]   See Family Law 1995.

The most common restriction is that of age. The majority of countries allow an unrestricted right to access information once the child reaches 18 (Andorra,[147] Czech Republic,[148] Greece,[149] Hungary,[150] Iceland,[151] Lithuania,[152] Norway,[153] Poland,[154] Slovakia,[155] Spain,[156] Switzerland[157] and England),[158] although this is lowered to 15 in Serbia,[159] 14 in Austria[160] and Ukraine[161] and 12 in the Netherlands.[162] However, Italy requires the adopted person to be 25 before he or she can apply to access

---

[147] Not regulated by law.

[148] Czech Republic, *Country Profile for Intercountry Adoption: State of Origin* (available 13 July 2015 at http://www.hcch.net/index_en.php?act=publications.details&pid=5116&dtid=42).

[149] Civil Code, article 1559.

[150] *Extracts of the Legislation on Adoption: Hungary* (available 13 July 2015 at http://www.childoneurope.org/issues/adoption/adoption_legislation/hungary.pdf).

[151] Adoption Act no 130/1999, article 27.

[152] Civil Code, article 3.221. Information can be accessed earlier if this is required for reasons of health, or other important reasons.

[153] Act of 28 February 1986 No 8 relating to adoption, s 12.

[154] Poland, *Country Profile for Intercountry Adoption: State of Origin* (available 13 July 2015 at <http://www.hcch.net/index_en.php?act=publications.details&pid=5093&dtid=42).

[155] Slovakia, *Country Profile for Intercountry Adoption: State of Origin* (available 13 July 2015 at http://www.hcch.net/index_en.php?act=publications.details&pid=5095&dtid=42).

[156] Civil Code, article 180(5).

[157] Civil Code, article 268c (although information can be accessed earlier if a legitimate interest is shown).

[158] Adoption and Children Act 2002, s 60.

[159] The child must also be 'able to reason' (Family Act, article 59).

[160] Austria, *Country Profile for Intercountry Adoption: Receiving State* (available 13 July 2015 at http://www.hcch.net/index_en.php?act=publications.details&pid=5083&dtid=42).

[161] Family Code, article 226(3). Although as discussed above, under Ukrainian law the child has a right *not* to know about his or her adoption, so may not know to access the files.

[162] Access is permitted if the child is younger and is considered able to reasonably assess his or her own interests (Act on the Adoption of Foreign Children, article 17d). It is interesting to note that this legislation covers only children adopted into the Netherlands through inter-country adoption. In the Netherlands, in contrast to many other European countries, adoption is not conducted in secret and it is standard practice for the child to be informed about his or her natural parents. (See Initial Report to the Committee on the Rights of the Child, Netherlands (24 July 1997) CRC/C/51/Add.1, [76]; Vonk, (n 141) 18).

official files, and even then permission must be granted by the Juvenile Court after listening to the interested parties.[163]

On the other hand, many states still leave the ability to control information concerning the child's origins solely in the hands of adoptive parents. In Armenia[164] and Azerbaijan,[165] the child cannot access any information regarding his or her origins with the permission of the adoptive parents, and as stated above, in Russia, Ukraine and the Former Yugoslav Republic of Macedonia, it is entirely up to the adoptive parents whether the child will be informed if he or she is adopted at all. The power is also placed in the adoptive parents' hands in Estonia,[166] Hungary,[167] Latvia,[168] Portugal[169] and Spain,[170] where legislation requires that if the child is younger than 18, access to information about the child's origins is granted only with the adoptive parents' consent.[171] While in the latter case, adoptive parents may act as a safeguard to ensure that the child does not find out information before he or she is sufficiently mature to understand and cope with it, the same power can

---

[163]   Law No 149/2001. However, where the mother has refused to be named, this cannot be overturned (see discussion below).

[164]   Family Code 2004, article 169. The Committee on the Rights of the Child have criticised this approach (*Concluding Observations: Armenia* (26 February 2004) CRC/C/15/Add.225, [38]).

[165]   Family Code 1999, article 130.

[166]   Family Law Act 2009, s 164(7). Even then, the birth parents must also have consented to their information being revealed.

[167]   The child must be over 14, and this may be refused in his or her interests. ChildONEurope, *Extracts of the Legislation on Adoption: Hungary* (available 13 July 2015 at http://www.childoneurope.org/issues/adoption/adoption_legislation/hungary.pdf).

[168]   Civil Law, article 162.

[169]   Civil Code, article 1985. The consent of the birth parents is also needed in this case.

[170]   Civil Code, article 180(5).

[171]   In Denmark, Finland and Germany the adoptive parents' rights must also be considered. In Finland the authorities may deny access to information if it would be contrary to the private interests of another party; in Germany, access may be denied if there is overriding opposition from one of the other parties to the adoption (Civil Code, article 9b) and Danish authorities will decide whether to allow access to records on an individual assessment, balancing securing individual privacy with securing access for any party with a legitimate interest (Denmark, *Country Profile for Intercountry Adoption: Receiving State* (available 13 July 2015 at http://www.hcch.net/index_en.php?act=publications.details&pid=5128&dtid=42)).

also be used to protect the parents' position, to the detriment of mature and capable children.[172]

4.1 Anonymous Birth

In addition to the weight that is given to the interests of the adoptive parents in this area, the birth parents also play a significant, and sometimes overriding, role in some states. In this context, the debate concerning access to information for adopted children is inextricably linked with the debate regarding anonymous birth, as this precludes information being recorded concerning the child's parents and interferes with the very essence of this right of a child to know his or her origins, making it a virtual impossibility that this will ever be achieved. This issue goes beyond whether adoption records should be sealed or not, to whether or not there will be a record to access in the first place.

Anonymous birth is the practice by which mothers can give birth in a hospital without stating their identity, and the child is then placed for adoption. While France is the most prominent exponent of this practice,[173] it is also legal in Luxembourg and Austria.[174] Other European countries also incorporate secrecy not simply as a facet of the adoption process, when files are sealed, but at the time of birth. In Italy there is no requirement that the mother be entered onto the birth certificate of the

---

[172] The best interests principle has also been invoked to place restrictions on the access of children to information. In Albania, access to records may be restricted or rejected on 'special occasions', where there are reasons to believe that it will bring about grave consequences (Law no 9695 of 19 March 2007, article 37). In addition, in Croatia, all children have the right to examine their adoption files and birth register, if the social welfare authorities establish that this would be in the child's interests (Family Act 2003, article 142). It is not clear in these countries on what grounds the authorities may decide that the knowledge would be contrary to the child's best interests. If he or she wishes to know the information, any denial would have to be founded on particularly serious projected consequences for these to outweigh the damage to the child at having the request refused.

[173] Provided for in the Civil Code, article 341.

[174] In Austria, the practice is somewhat different however, as while the mother is not required to provide proof of her identity or register with the health services, she must leave her details to be accessible to the child at the age of 14. This provides a compromise between the two sets of interests, and will be discussed below.

child,[175] and in the Czech Republic and Greece, although the mother's identity is recorded, the birth records can be kept secret.[176]

As a result, an increasing number of children are being denied the right to ever receive any information on their origins, as it is simply not known, even by the authorities. Even in situations where the information has been collected upon the child's birth, however, and retained by the authorities, in some countries the birth parents can veto the release of this information if the child searches for it at a later date. In Portugal,[177] Estonia,[178] France,[179] Georgia,[180] Italy[181] and Slovenia,[182] the identity of a birth parent cannot be revealed to the child if he or she opposes it, leaving the child in the same situation as he or she would be if no records had been collected at all. These countries do not engage in a balancing process, and simply leave all the power in the hands of the birth parents to decide what rights a child can have access to.[183]

---

[175]   Article 250 of the Civil Code does not make it mandatory for parents to recognise an illegitimate child, and if they choose not to do so, they will not be named on the birth certificate. If the child searches for information on his or her parents at a later date, this will not be disclosed if the parent wished for anonymity.

[176]   University of Nottingham, Child Abandonment and its Prevention in Europe (Daphne Programme, 2012) 21.

[177]   Civil Code, article 1985.

[178]   Family Law Act 2009, s 164(7).

[179]   Law No 93 of 22 January 2002, article 147-6.

[180]   Georgia, *Country Profile for Intercountry Adoption: State of Origin* (available 13 July 2015 at http://www.hcch.net/index_en.php?act=publications. details&pid=5118&dtid=42).

[181]   Law No 149/2001.

[182]   Slovenia, *Country Profile for Intercountry Adoption: Receiving State* (available 13 July 2015 at http://www.hcch.net/index_en.php?act=publications. details&pid=5096&dtid=42).

[183]   An argument has been put forward that this is justified on the grounds that it protects the rights of women to refuse motherhood and escape socially defined roles. Especially in countries where access to birth control is limited, and abortion is only permitted under strict circumstances, a secret adoption gives a woman the chance to take back control of her own reproductive autonomy (see N Lefaucheur, 'The French "Tradition" of Anonymous Birth: The Lines of Argument' (2004) 18 *International Journal of Law, Policy and the Family* 319, 331). However, while the ability of women to control their reproductive autonomy is an essential right, once the child is born, it can no longer be considered absolute. The rights and well-being of the child must be a primary consideration, as has been agreed by 193 states that are parties to the UNCRC, and as such, arguments of maternal autonomy cannot unilaterally extinguish the right to receive information on his or her biological origins.

The balance between parental rights, public policy considerations and the right of the child to information concerning his or her identity has been central to the jurisprudence of the European Court of Human Rights, and was at the heart of the decision of the Court in the (in)famous case of *Odièvre v France*. This case concerned an application brought by a French woman, born in 1965, whose mother had requested that her birth be kept secret, and who was thus placed for adoption anonymously. In 1990, the applicant was able to obtain non-identifying information about her natural family, but her applications for further identifying information about her parents and her natural siblings were refused. She made an application to the ECtHR, complaining that her inability to obtain this information prevented her from finding out her personal history, in violation of article 8 of the Convention.

The majority in *Odièvre* took a very restrictive approach to the child's right to information on his or her biological origins, deeming that it was sufficient that non-identifying information be provided to the child, which would enable her to trace some of her roots.[184] In particular, the concurring opinion of Judge Rozakis argued that balance had been achieved between the child's rights and the mother's, because the authorities counselled the mother of the difficulties the child may face without knowledge of his or her origins, encouraged her to leave non-identifying information, and allowed her to waive confidentiality at a later stage.

Several of the majority and concurring judgments also went on to suggest that the balance should not be seen just as between parental and child rights, but between the competing rights of the child him- or herself.[185] In this respect, Judge Greve argued that: 'The primary interest of the child is to be born and born under circumstances where its health is not unnecessarily put at risk by birth in circumstances in which its mother tries to secure secrecy even when that means that she will be deprived of professional assistance when in labour.'[186]

This presents an appealing, but ultimately false, dichotomy. As Austria has shown, it is possible to both protect the identity of the mother, and provide information for the child at a later date, by allowing the mother to remain anonymous at the hospital, but requiring her to leave identifying information with the child welfare authorities for the child to access

---

[184]   *Odièvre v France* [2003] 38 EHRR 43 at [48].

[185]   This has been how the debate has been framed in Belgium, where a debate on anonymous birth began as a result of the large number of women crossing the border into France to give birth anonymously (see ibid, at [19]).

[186]   Ibid.

when he or she reaches 14 years of age.[187] A similar law has recently been passed in Germany, which allows women to give a false name to give birth in hospital and for the birth certificate, but requires that their correct personal data be sealed and stored in a central agency for access by the child once he or she turns 16.[188]

Anonymous birth allows the mother to decide whether the child will be able to access his or her rights, not only in relation to information on origins, but also concerning the right to stay with his or her wider family group where possible. It thus circumvents the child protection system, and, particularly worryingly, deprives the child and his or her father of the chance to establish a relationship. As the dissent in *Odièvre* pointed out, it precludes any balancing of interests, and allows the mother's decision to constitute an absolute defence to any request for information, irrespective of the reasons for, or legitimacy of, that decision. In an emotive judgment, they stated that: 'The mother thus has a discretionary right to bring a suffering child into the world and to condemn it to lifelong ignorance.'[189]

In 2012, the Court revisited the question of anonymous birth in the context of the Italian system, which does not allow the release of either non-identifying information or the mother's identity, even *with* the consent of the birth mother. In *Godelli v Italy*,[190] the Court differentiated the case from *Odièvre*, stating that by allowing the mother to later consent to the release of information, the French system allowed an element of balance that the Italian system did not.

While this decision is a step in the right direction, the Court nevertheless continues to judicially approve a system that denies the child the right to know and be cared for by his or her birth parents, and the right to preserve his or her identity. As a result, the European Convention on Human Rights, which in principle should be an optimal instrument for dealing with an issue involving the balancing of competing rights, has

---

[187] This was (cautiously) approved by the Committee on the Rights of the Child, *Concluding Observations: Austria* (5 October 2012) CRC/C/AUT/CO/3-4, [30].

[188] Gesetz zum Ausbau der Hilfen für Schwangere und zur Regelung der vertraulichen Geburt (SchwHiAusbauG) v. 28.08.2013, BGBl. I S. 3458.

[189] Joint dissenting opinion of Judges Wildhaber, Sir Nicholas Bratza, Bonello, Loucaides, Cabral Barreto, Tulkens and Pellonpää, *Odièvre* (n 184) at [7].

[190] [2012] ECHR 2035. See C Simmonds, 'An Unbalanced Scale: Anonymous Birth and the European Court of Human Rights' (2013) 72(2) *Cambridge Law Journal* 263.

failed to evolve in line with current understandings of the importance of knowledge concerning biological origins to an adopted child, and allowed states to sidestep obligations to both mothers and children to deal with the underlying social and economic issues that drive the wish to remain anonymous, both before and after birth.

5. CONCLUSION

This chapter has not attempted to set out every detail of the European Court of Human Right's jurisprudence regarding adoption, but to highlight some of the principal areas of development in recent years, both positive and negative.

The development of law in this area has been limited by two key factors. First, the very nature of the Court itself as a supranational body means that it is unwilling to fully examine some of the substantive issues surrounding adoption, in particular adoption without parental consent. Second, the adult-centred focus of the jurisprudence limits the scope of issues discussed and leaves children very much sidelined. In some ways, this is unsurprising, as it is adults who predominantly take cases before the Court, and thus the issues are analysed from the perspective of their rights. Although the Court is slowly starting to promote the welfare of the child, this only comes into play as a limitation on parental rights under article 8, rather than as a decision-making principle in its own right. More worryingly, the Court has taken a substantially paternalistic approach to children's rights when they have been brought before the Court, particularly in terms of children's autonomy and decision-making capacity.

This does not mean that the ECHR does not provide many important safeguards in relation to adoption. The procedural safeguards established by the Court concerning the timing of consent and assistance provided to birth mothers have been vital steps forward, not to mention the rights secured for unmarried fathers. However, until it evolves to more fully recognise and respect the rights of children, the Convention will remain an imperfect instrument for dealing with issues of such importance in a child's life.

RECOMMENDATIONS FOR FURTHER READING

American Bar Association Child Custody and Adoption Pro Bono Project, 'Hearing Children's Voices and Interests in Adoption and Guardianship Proceedings' (2007) 41(2) *Family Law Quarterly* 365.

S Besson, 'Enforcing the Child's Right to Know Her Origins: Contrasting Approaches Under the Convention on the Rights of the Child and the European Convention on Human Rights' (2007) 21 *International Journal of Law, Policy and the Family* 137.

Y Brulard and L Dumont, *Comparative Study Relating to Procedures for Adoption among the Member States of the European Union, Practical Difficulties Encountered in this field by European Citizens within the Context of the European Pillar of Justice and Civil Matters and Means of Solving these Problems and of Protecting Children's Rights* (European Union 2007).

S Choudhry and J Herring, *European Human Rights and Family Law* (Hart Publishing 2010).

C Fenton-Glynn, Children's Rights in Intercountry Adoption – A European Perspective (Intersentia 2014).

Jane Fortin, 'Rights Brought Home for Children' (1999) 62 *Modern Law Review* 350.

U Kilkelly, *The Child and the European Convention on Human Rights* (Ashgate 1999).

University of Nottingham, *Child Abandonment and its Prevention in Europe* (2012).

EJ Samuels, 'Time to Decide? The Laws Governing Mothers' Consents to the Adoption of their Newborn Infants' (2004–2005) 72 *Tennessee Law Review* 509.

E Steiner, 'Odièvre v France – Desperately seeking mother – anonymous births in the European Court of Human Rights' (2003) 15 *Child and Family Law* Quarterly 425.

A Warman and C Roberts, 'Adoption and Looked after Children – an International Comparison', *Working Paper 2003/1*, Department of Social Policy and Social Work, University of Oxford.

10. Family law and older people in a European perspective

Jonathan Herring

1. INTRODUCTION

The European Union is getting older, not only as an institution but as a people. This raises issues of fundamental importance. While the ageing of Europe is sometimes presented as a crisis, in fact, it is great news that we can enjoy life longer. Longer life expectancy produces challenges, but also exciting opportunities.[1] These have been recognised by the European Union, which has presented a series of declarations and policy initiatives to deal with the ageing population and to encourage active and healthy

---

[1] European Commission, *2012 to be European Year for Active Ageing* (EC 2010).

ageing.[2] Indeed, 'healthy ageing' has been listed as one of priority themes for Europe 2020.[3]

There are certainly some grand-sounding statements to be found within the European documentation about the rights of older people. At the heart of the European response is article 23 of the Revised European Social Charter:

> With a view to ensuring the effective exercise of the right of elderly persons to social protection, the Parties undertake to adopt or encourage, either directly or in cooperation with public or private organisations, appropriate measures designed in particular:
>
> – to enable elderly persons to remain full members of society for as long as possible, by means of:
>   a adequate resources enabling them to lead a decent life and play an active part in public, social and cultural life;
>   b provision of information about services and facilities available for elderly persons and their opportunities to make use of them;
> – to enable elderly persons to choose their life-style freely and to lead independent lives in their familiar surroundings for as long as they wish and are able, by means of:
>   a provision of housing suited to their needs and their state of health or of adequate support for adapting their housing;
>   b the health care and the services necessitated by their state;
> – to guarantee elderly persons living in institutions appropriate support, while respecting their privacy, and participation in decisions concerning living conditions in the institution.

This is reinforced by article 10 of the Lisbon Treaty, which outlaws unjustified discrimination on the basis of age.

The 2012 Vienna Ministerial Declaration welcomed the increasing rates of life expectancy and the growing proportion of older people. One of the commitments was as follows:

> We are committed to meet individual and societal challenges triggered by population ageing through adequate and sustainable measures of financial security in old age, life-long continuum of health and social care, including long-term care, and provisions of inclusive systems and support for active ageing, life-long learning, and participation in various spheres of society without discrimination, particularly with regards to older women.

---

[2] European Commission, *Active and Healthy Ageing: Concrete Action Plans for a Better Life for Older Europeans* (EC 2012).

[3] European Commission, *Europe 2020* (EC, 2010) 546.

A good example of the range of policies that might be required to address these issues is the EURAGE[4] Charter on the Rights of the Elderly.[5] This proposes formal recognition of rights for older people concerning a wide range of issues including autonomy and self-determination; respect; equal treatment; social participation; active citizenship; financial security; personal development, social contact and meaningfulness; access to information; housing and living environment; and care and service provision.

This chapter will focus on the European response to family law issues relating to older people. If the goals in the Declaration and Social Charter are to be achieved state interaction with the family is crucial.[6] As Walker and Maltby argue:

> an effective strategy on active ageing would be based on a *partnership* between the citizen and society. In this partnership, the role of the state is to enable, facilitate and motivate citizens and, where necessary, to provide high quality social protection for as long as possible. This will require interrelated individual and societal strategies. As far as individuals are concerned, they have a duty to take advantage of lifelong learning and continuous training opportunities and to promote their own health and well-being throughout the life course. As far as society is concerned, the policy challenge is to recognise the thread that links together all of the relevant policy areas: employment, health, social protection, social inclusion, transport, education and so on. A comprehensive active ageing strategy demands that all of them are 'joined-up' and become mutually supportive.[7]

Of course, legal responses can only be a small part of the solution to the broader issues concerning ageing. Ageist attitudes are rife across Europe, with 46 per cent of older people in one survey reporting have experienced age prejudice.[8] The role that the law and the EU can play in producing a successful older population is limited, but is nevertheless significant, in

---

[4]   The European Research Group on Attitudes to Age, an international project investigating attitudes to age across Europe.

[5]   European Council, *Council Conclusions on Active Ageing* (EC, 2010).

[6]   H Meenan and G Broadbent, 'Law, Ageing and Policy in the United Kingdom' (2007) 2 *Journal of International Ageing, Law and Policy* 67.

[7]   A Walker and T Maltby, 'Active Ageing: A Strategic Policy Solution to Demographic Ageing in the European Union' (2012) 177 *International Journal of Social Welfare* 21.

[8]   D Abrams, P Russell, C-M Vanclair and H Swift, *Ageism in Europe: Findings from the European Social Survey* (Age UK 2011).

providing the circumstances in which healthy ageing can take place.[9]
This chapter will start by summarising some of the demographic issues,
before then examining the response of family law to some of the main
issues.

2. DEMOGRAPHICS

It is clear that the population of the European Union is growing, and that
its age structure is changing.[10] We are seeing low fertility levels and
higher life expectancy. All the signs are that the share of older person in
the total population will increase. On 1 January 2010 the estimated
population of 27 member nations of the European Union (EU-27) was
501.1 million, an increase of 1.4 million from the previous year. The
increase is in partly due to net immigration, but also due to longer life
expectancy. On 1 January 2010 0–19 year olds made up 21.3 per cent of
the population of EU-27; the age range 20–64 made up 61.3 per cent and
over 65s were 17.4 per cent. The percentages of those over 65 are set to
increase in the years ahead. Eurostat projects that the share of population
aged 65 or over will increase from 17.4 per cent in 2010 to 30.0 per cent
in 2060. The proportion of those over 80 is set to treble by 2060.[11]

Particular attention should be paid to dependency ratios: the ratio of
those deemed dependent on account of their youth or old age versus
'working age' (15–64) people. Across the EU the dependency ratio is
28.4 per cent, meaning EU-27 had around four working people for each
dependent person. But the ratio varies between countries: it is 18.5 per
cent in Ireland and 34.1 per cent in Germany. Between 1990 and 2010
the 'working age' population (those aged 20–64) decreased by 1.8
percentage points across the EU-27, while the older population (65 and
above) increased by 3.7 per cent. There was also a 5.4 per cent decrease
in the number of younger people (those below 16). It has been estimated
that the total 'working age' population will fall by 20.8 million from the
year 2005 to 2030. The number of older people aged over 80 is set to
increase by 12.6 million in the same period.[12] It is estimated that by 2060

---

[9]   M Hartlapp, 'Deconstructing EU Old Age Policy: Assessing the Potential
of Soft OMCs and Hard EU Law' (2012) 16 *European Integration online
Papers* 3.

[10]   Eurostat, *The Greying of the Babyboomers: A Century-Long View of
Ageing in European Populations. Statistics in Focus* (Eurostat 2011).

[11]   Ibid.

[12]   Ibid.

there will be only two people of working age in the EU for every person aged over 65, compared to a ratio of around four to one today.[13]

Another demographic shift, which will be clear from other chapters in this book, is the changing nature of family life. There are fewer marriages and increased rates of divorce, unmarried cohabitation, births outside marriage and living alone. These changes in the nature of family life all impact significantly on older people. For example, divorce can cause a notable reduction in the likelihood that an older person will have a partner to care for them in old age. In Italy, the proportion of women aged 65 or older who are living alone doubled from 22 per cent in 1970 to 40 per cent in 2000. In England the increase was from 34 per cent to 48 per cent over the same time period.[14]

3. OLDER PEOPLE, FAMILIES AND CARE ISSUES

The key issues that arise with an ageing population are significant.[15] With old age often comes an increased need for care, both in terms of medical care; social care (such as the preparation of food, assistance with the tasks of daily living); and emotional care. This is a central issue for family lawyers because across Europe it is family members who provide the majority of care of older and disabled adults. Notably, much of that care is provided by family members who are older themselves, and is predominantly performed by women. This care work has historically been unrecognised and has played a substantial role in the marginalisation of older people and of women.[16] The familial provision of care is coming under strain from various directions. Increasing rates of paid employment by women; later age at childbirth; and increased rates of family breakdown have all put pressure on the assumptions that families (and women in particular) will provide care for older relatives.

In 2005 it was estimated that across Europe 19 million people provided at least 20 hours of care work a week to elderly, disabled or chronically

---

[13] Ibid.

[14] J-L Fernández, J Forder, B Trukeschitz, M Rokosova and D McDaid, *How can European States Design Efficient, Equitable and Sustainable Funding Systems for Long-Term Care for Older People?* (WHO 2009).

[15] See J Herring, *Older People in Law and Society* (Oxford University Press 2010) and J Herring, *Caring and the Law* (Hart Publishing 2013) from which some of the following material is taken.

[16] See Herring, *Caring and the Law* (n 15), ch 2 for a detailed discussion of the issue.

ill people. 9.6 million people provided at least 35 hours of care a week. This estimate does not include young people with caring responsibilities, who may amount to some two to four million extra carers.[17] It should be emphasised, however, that many who give care themselves receive care from others. Carers of older people in Europe are predominantly (75 per cent) female, with an average age of 55. Around half are children of the person cared for. On average 45.6 hours of care are provided for each older person a week. Only two fifths of carers of older people are able to combine their care with any paid work.[18] The burden of this family care is heavily gendered.[19]

As is clear from the statistics, the gendered burden of care is significant. This means that the state response to care is especially important in the context of promoting gender fairness, as the EU has recognised:

> The objectives of equality between women and men and increased female labour market together with changes in family structures and demographic challenges, mean that this vision needs to be challenged and responsibilities for dependent persons need to be better shared with the rest of the community through public funded schemes. Families can no longer be left alone with the duty to care for their dependent relatives and special attention needs to be paid to families who face additional challenges such as lone parents and large families who are at a higher risk of poverty. Most families wish to take on their responsibilities, but they cannot fulfil that role alone. They need support from public solidarity through integrated, holistic and sustainable family policies based on the three main elements that all families need – resources, time, and services.[20]

Any policy concerning family care for older members requires an acknowledgement of the obligations that families have towards all their members, including children, youth, adults with needs and older people. Family members, especially women, who are expected to meet all these needs, risk social exclusion, poverty and health problems. A key feature of intimate care is that its nature and extent can be unpredictable. Planning one's time and one's life can be difficult. Ensuring a fair share

---

[17] C Glendinning, H Arksey, F Tjadens, M Moree, N Moran and H Nies, *Care Provision within Families and its Socio-Economic Impact on Care Providers across the European Union* (University of York 2009).

[18] Ibid.

[19] T Schmid, M Brandt and K Haberkern, 'Gendered Support to Older Parents: Do Welfare States Matter?' (2012) 9 *European Journal of Aging* 39.

[20] AGE, *Intergenerational Solidarity: The Way Forward* (AGE 2010).

of the burden of care work is a matter of justice within the family and across society.

The central need is to move to a system that acknowledges that care of older people is a collective responsibility and not simply an individual one. The costs of meeting these needs should be shared in a fair way across all members of society. That does not mean that everyone must receive care in the same way. It may well be that the way the needs are met will vary between individuals, communities and across boundaries. The needs may be met by family members, state institutions or state funded individualised care. Currently the needs of older people are primarily left to family members who are only just able to meet those needs, and the disadvantages flowing from those needs primarily affect middle-aged women.[21]

3.1 Why the State Should Care about Care

In this next section, the arguments as to why the state should be concerned about care for older people will be explored. There are three particular interests. First, it is essential to those needing care that this care is provided effectively. It cannot be assumed that individuals can meet their own needs. As Fernandez et al argue:

> The case for public sector intervention for long-term care funding is strong. The lifetime costs of long-term care services can be substantial and may deplete the assets of all but the richest service users. State supported collective funding solutions can make sure that enough protection is provided to those in greatest need, and/or with the least ability to pay, and help avoid catastrophic costs.[22]

Second, the state has significant interests. If family members fail to provide this and the burden of it fell on the state the financial loss could be huge. Third, it is important that those providing the care do not suffer a significant social and or economic cost from doing so. The failure of the law and society to properly value care in the past has been a significant contributor to the disadvantageous position of women in society. As has been argued:

> Families have long been held responsible for the care of children, grand-children, disabled, dependent and/or elderly relatives. However, this was very

---

[21] C Glendinning and D Bell, *Rethinking Social Care and Support: What can England Learn from other Countries*? (Joseph Rowntree Foundation 2008).

[22] Fernandez et al (n 14).

often at the expense of gender equality as women were expected to bear the sole responsibility for caring for their relatives, a contribution which is still undervalued and unrecognised.[23]

These issues need to be explored further. Assuming it is unacceptable for individuals to be left in great need without any help, if people stop caring, through choice or economic need, that burden would fall on the state. As an example of the potential costs to the state if care was not performed, Carers UK argues that performing the work of informal carers would cost £119 billion, if the state had to perform it, a sum that exceeds the £98.8 billion spent on the NHS.[24] If the state through a relatively low level of payment or support can ensure family carers keep caring and/or that people are not deterred from caring then such intervention can be said to make much economic sense.[25] By supplying sufficient economic and support services to maintain care levels, the government would in fact be saving significant sums of money.[26]

A central part of the justification for state involvement in care is that the state and the EU have an obligation to promote gender equality. The majority of care work is undertaken by women. As Susan Himmelweit and Hilary Land argue:

> The level of public expenditure on care is therefore a gender issue, since women have greater care needs than men and fewer resources to meet them. Inadequate funding also affects women in the paid care workforce and, when paid care is not forthcoming, as those more likely to end up providing unpaid care. Thus, inadequate spending on care is effectively a transfer of resources (unpaid labour) from women to relieve taxpayers, disproportionately men, of their responsibilities to provide for the most vulnerable citizens.[27]

If, therefore, it is accepted that the gender gap does need tackling, there are three key fronts to address: ensuring that the decision to care does not greatly penalise individuals; to encourage a fairer sharing of care labour between men and women; and to encourage equal access to paid employment for men and women. It is, perhaps, unsurprising that most European countries adopt some kind of a balance between these

---

23   AGE (n 20).

24   Carers UK, *Valuing Carers* (Carers UK 2011).

25   L Lloyd, 'Call Us Carers: Limitations and Risks in Campaigning for Recognition and Exclusivity' (2006) 26 *Critical Social Policy* 945.

26   S Himmelweit and H Land, *Reducing Gender Inequalities to Create a Sustainable Care* (Joseph Rowntree Foundation 2008).

27   Ibid.

approaches. At the same time the states can be seen to be providing for carers, while also supporting carers who seek to work and promoting a more equal sharing of care tasks.[28]

There seems in many European countries to be no clear vision of how the state would like to see the division of care between family members and state care.[29] That may well be entirely appropriate. It may be that it is not for the state to set down a single method of care provision. Creating options that allow individuals to fashion the appropriate response for them and their families may be the ideal. Janet Gornick and Macia Meyers argue for a range of solutions to deal with the problems:

> The role for public policy would be to encourage the dissolution of gender divisions in the home through the use of parental leave; to transform the workplace from its current androcentrism to reduce working hours and become more flexible to allow for better work/care balance; and to protect parents' rights for time to care and children's rights for quality care through provision of high-quality childcare provided by well-trained and well-paid care workers.[30]

3.2 Nature of Care

Here are some of the ways the state could seek to engage with the provision of care for older people by family members:

- The provision of state care, so that less is expected of family members. This could range from the provision of care services, to the provision of residential care. Currently, in many European countries there is widespread concern about care in nursing homes, ranging from lack of nutrition and lack of privacy to excessive restraint and the use of force. If this is to be offered as an option the standard of care must be such that it is a dignifying, realistic and attractive option.

- Providing payments and support for carers. This can be through benefits; provision of protection within labour law; or credits through a tax system. This approach would be designed to enable a

---

[28] T Warren, G Pascall and E Fox, 'Gender Equality in Time: Low-Paid Mothers' Paid and Unpaid Work in the UK' (2010) 16 *Feminist Economics* 193.

[29] R Mahon, 'Child Care: Towards what kind of Social Europe' (2002) 9 *Social Politics* 343.

[30] J Gornick and M Meyers, *Families That Work: Policies for Reconciling Parenthood and Employment* (Russell Sage Foundation 2003).

family member, where possible, to combine employment with their caring responsibilities.

● Encouraging the wider community to take on care of older people. In Denmark a Substitute Grandparent Scheme offers an older person as a volunteer to provide child care for parents who cannot take time off work to care for a sick child. This could be adapted to provide short term care need for older people who need a substitute grandchild to provide basic health care or social needs.

Traditionally where the state has sought to provide support in this area, the focus has been on meeting the needs of the person needing care. However, there is a growing acknowledgement of the need to support the person offering care. This raises the issue of whether the state should focus on supporting the person offering care or the person receiving care. This choice can be significant. Mary Daly and Jane Lewis explain:

> The choice has potentially deep ramifications because in the first instance – making the payment to the person requiring care – welfare states are in effect distancing themselves from how the care needs are actually satisfied, whereas making the payment to the carer is a trend in the opposite direction – drawing more people within the direct embrace of the welfare state. To the extent that welfare states follow the first model, we could be seeing the emergence of a new type of welfare citizenship. In this regard cash benefits and services have to be analysed closely together.[31]

Applying these in a practical context could lead to a range of ways of channelling benefits.[32] These could range from providing the individual needing care with a budget they could use to employ carers;[33] to giving the carer an allowance to spend on providing the care; to giving the carer a direct payment for support.

If financial support is to be offered to family carers, then a key issue is whether these are to be regarded as compensation for lost pay[34] or

---

[31]   M Daly and J Lewis, 'The Concept of Social Care and the Analysis of Contemporary Welfare' (2000) 51 *British Journal of Sociology* 51.

[32]   B Da Roit and B Le Bihan, 'Similar and yet so Different: Cash-For-Care in Six European Countries' Long-Term Care Policies' (2010) 88 *Millbank Quarterly* 286.

[33]   Ibid.

[34]   J Lewis, 'Gender and Welfare Regimes: Further Thoughts' (1997) 4 *Social Policy* 160.

providing the carer with a sufficient sum to live on.[35] The issues are not straightforward. As Janice Keefe, Caroline Glendinning and Pamela Fancey put it:

> On the one hand, cash payments for family carers do recognize and attempt to ameliorate the direct and opportunity costs associated with caregiving and provide some formal recognition of the caregiving role. On the other hand, these programs can entrap women into caregiving roles by offering financial support in place of other care options.[36]

This issue also reflects the relationship between the state and family members offering care. Caroline Glendinning and Hilary Arksey[37] have suggested four approaches that public bodies could take towards carers. These are:

- Carers as resource: carers are supported in order to maintain their care-giving role
- Carers as co-workers: carers are regarded as working with social services in order to provide services to those in need
- Carers as co-clients: carers are recognised as having needs in their own right and to be in need of services to maintain their well-being
- Superseded carer: services should be offered to the service-user to enable them to be independent and no longer need a carer.

There are, however, dangers in focussing just on the state provisions for carers. There is a risk that it will sideline those actually receiving care.[38] It overlooks the power that is exercised in care. The language of care itself implies vulnerability and reinforces the social construction of disability. It also portrays care as a uni-directional activity, which is an inaccurate portrayal of most caring relationships, which are marked by mutuality.[39] A better approach may be to focus on promoting caring

---

[35]   J.Keefe, C Glendinning and P Fancey, 'Financial Payments for Family Carers: Policy Approaches and Debates', in A Martin-Matthews and J Philips (eds), *Ageing at the Intersection of Work and Home Life: Blurring the Boundaries* (Lawrence Eribaum, 2008).

[36]   Ibid.

[37]   C Glendinning and H Arksey, 'Informal Care', in P Alcock, M May, and K Rowlingson (eds), *The Student's Companion to Social Policy* (Blackwell 2008) 219–25.

[38]   C Beckett, 'Women, Disability, Care: Good Neighbours or Uneasy Bedfellows' (2007) 27 *Critical Social Policy* 360.

[39]   See J Herring, *Caring and the Law* (n 15) for further discussion.

relationships, which are responsive to the needs of both parties. There are many shared interests between the 'carer' and the 'cared for'. Having a safe work environment is essential for all as is a good standard of housing and provision of equipment. A carer who is exhausted or dispirited is of little benefit to the person needing care.

As well as the nature of state support, there is a question of how it is to be funded. Fernández and colleagues[40] suggest that three primary models can be found across Europe:

(1)   Safety net system. This focuses the state intervention on those individuals who lack the ability to pay for services. Others are expected to buy in care for any unmet care needs. This is seen as reducing state expenditure, but leaves some needs unmet.
(2)   Universal system. This seeks to meet or support the care needs of the whole population. This can be a substantial burden on tax funded systems. This may be reduced by required co-payments for some systems.
(3)   A progressive universalism. This combines universal entitlement with a means tested system. As the system benefits a greater number of people less stigma is attached to claimants.

Most European countries have access to universal funded care. England is somewhat unusual in that public funding for social institutional care (for example, where a person is unable to live independently, but does not need hospital care) is subject to asset testing, including, importantly, their home. Due to property values only those at the bottom of the economic spectrum who have assets under £21,000 can access public funding. Around half of all social care spending comes from users themselves.[41]

3.3 Personal Budgets

An increasingly common form of assistance across Europe is offering the person needing care a personal budget, which can be used to purchase care. This can include care from a family member, although in many systems (including England) the budget cannot cover care from a person living with the person needing care. This exclusion is primarily influenced by pragmatic reasoning. If the aim of the payments is to encourage care then it may be assumed that payments will not influence the

---

[40]   Fernández et al (n 14).
[41]   Glendinning and Bell (n 21).

provision of care where the carer lives with the person needing care, but might where they are living separately.

The use of these personal budgets has become popular. Holland, Italy, Austria and England, for example, have developed them. Supporters of these budgets emphasise the choice this provides. It enables the person needing care to have control over who provides the care and what kind of care is used. One can find cheery examples of where an older person has preferred their carer to take them fishing, rather than to a drop in centre. They may prefer to be taken out to afternoon tea than to lunch. They also offer recognition for some family care that would previously have gone unrecognised. However, as mentioned earlier, where the carer is living with the person cared for in some countries the budget cannot be used for that, such that only some care is recognised.

Cynics see the personal budgets as an attempt to restrict public responsibility. If the care provided is not adequate, that can be dismissed as the fault of the person arranging the care, rather than the state. It also assumes too that the person needing care is in a position to organise it, whereas for many this will be an overwhelming and burdensome responsibility. Further, and importantly, giving the choice of state supported care provision to the person needing care does not recognise the need to support the family members providing care in addition. There is a concern that increasing levels of care can upset the balance between family and state care, although one survey found that use of state services had not impacted on levels of family care.[42] A comparative survey found that where legal obligations were imposed or cash payments were available care was even more unequally distributed between men and women.[43]

The use of personal budgets can be regarded as part of a wider picture of increased use of market-based models and the private sector (both for profit and not for profit organisation) in care provision.[44] These 'cash for care' schemes have been popular with more conservative welfare states as well as more liberal ones. For the conservative state it can be a vehicle of upholding family life and promoting independence, while liberal states might regard it as an efficient way of providing care, and one that

---

[42] S Olav Daatland and A Lowenstein, 'Intergenerational Solidarity and the Family–Welfare State Balance' (2005) 2 *European Journal of Ageing* 174–82.

[43] Schmid, Brandt and Haberkern (n 19).

[44] T Hervey, A Stark, A Dawson, J-L Fernández, T Matosevic and D McDaid, 'Long-Term Care for Older People and EU Law: The Position in England and Scotland' (2012) 34 *Journal of Social Welfare and Family Law* 105–24.

recognises the work of women.[45] They are seen as promoting choice, which is seen as a good in itself. It is in line with the general marketisation of public services. The payments have also been supported by some disabled people and older people as giving them greater control and power over how their care is delivered. There is some evidence that cash for care involves less bureaucracy for the state and lower transaction costs so that care is cheaper to provide,[46] although critics would say that these costs are transferred to those needing care and their families.

3.4 Defamilisation

For some commentators a central theme in relation to support for care is defamilisation. This is a claim that we are witnessing the transformation of care from being a private, familial practice into being a public one.[47] That is not necessarily to say it does not involve family members, but that their role is to act on behalf of society, rather than as family members. The use of budgets can be seen as recognition that family care can no longer be depended on and that families will become agents of the state and paid for their work, rather than the work falling under the auspices of family love. Some see another aspect of defamilisation, namely a change in expectations or perceptions of obligations about whether care for an older relative is expected and in particular how much care might be expected. Certainly there appear to be variations across Europe over the extent to which family care is provided, but it is unclear whether the cause is social, economic or cultural differences.[48]

There is no consistent picture of this in Europe. The way that different countries have responded has been well summarised by Rodrigues and Schmidt:

> Scandinavian countries (i.e., the so-called Social-Democratic welfare regimes) have aimed to improve gender equality through labor market participation by providing care services outside the family, hence enabling women to take up paid employment (often in the care sector). By contrast, Conservative welfare regimes (such as Germany and Austria) and countries from the 'Latin Rim' (such as Italy, Spain, Greece, and Portugal) have placed a higher weight on

---

[45] H Arksey and P Kemp, *Dimensions of Choice: A Narrative Review of Cash-for-Care Schemes* (University of York 2008).

[46] Ibid.

[47] R Rodrigues and A Schmidt, 'Expenditures for Long-Term Care: At the Crossroads between Family and State' (2010) 23 *Journal of Gerontopsychology and Geriatric Psychiatry* 189–93.

[48] Ibid.

maintaining the traditional role of the family in welfare provision as part of the principle of subsidiarity in shaping their policies (i.e., state intervention is limited to the cases where the families' ability to secure welfare for its members has been depleted). Finally, 'Liberal' welfare regimes (like the UK and Ireland) have sought mainly to confine the role of the state as well as its size, as measured by public expenditures.[49]

For many countries the primary move has been to encourage carers to combine their care with paid work. It is easy to be cynical about the government's attempts for carers to be self-financing. The double shift work pays taxes and meets the state's obligations. A less cynical approach might be that suggested by Maxine Eichner, who supports the model of the 'supportive state', a midway model. She explains, focusing on the example of children:

> It conceives of the state as serving an integral role in supporting families, not simply after they break down, but in the ordinary course of events. In this conception, the state possesses a duty to structure institutions to support children's welfare and development, a duty that exists simultaneously with parents' own responsibility for children. Yet the state's role is a limited one, which provides the institutional scaffolding to support caretaking, while also expecting family members to meet caretaking needs.[50]

She sees this as requiring the state 'to arrange societal institutions in such a way that family members can meet the basic physical, mental, and emotional needs of dependents without impoverishing or exhausting themselves or their financial resources'.[51]

There is another issue concerning the relationship between state support and those in a caring relationship. If the state is supporting caring relationships, it might be argued that as care requires considerable skill then the normal consequences of skilled work should apply: training, supervision and regulation. It may be noted that with increasingly sophisticated technologies, the skill required in caring for a disabled person is considerable. The more the emotional side of care is emphasised, the more the benefit of psychological training becomes apparent. Indeed the state could take the view more generally that if caring becomes a trained profession then the professional carer is better placed

---

[49]   Rodrigues and Schmidt (n 47) 193.
[50]   M Eichner, *The Supportive State* (Oxford University Press 2010) 70–2.
[51]   Ibid.

to undertake the work than a family member or friend.[52] Helen Reece has warned about the danger of calling for greater state support for carers: 'financial dependence on the State brings State and citizen into a relationship that the State will continue to exploit'.[53]

The response to these points is to emphasise the importance of the relationship in care. Although technique may be a part of the work, the relationship is central. Spontaneity, informality and fun may be important to care, and may be undermined by regulation. The skills acquired in a relationship are those that are personal to the relationship and cannot be taught or supervised, because they are unique to the two parties. I agree that we can set minimum levels of care and no doubt there are carers in some cases who cannot provide the required standard, but it must be recognised that the skill of the carer is often highly personalised. They know the person receiving care and the care is given in the context of their relationship.

4. POVERTY

The link between poverty and old age is well established and has a long history.[54] Women living on their own are particularly hard hit.[55] Nearly a quarter of all pensioners in the UK are living in poverty.[56] Not all European countries have such a strong link between old age and poverty. German pensioners are less likely than the average person to be affected by poverty. Across the EU-27 generally, 16 per cent of men compared to 23 per cent of women aged 65 and over faced a poverty risk.[57]

The primary response to the issues of poverty in old age within the EU has been to encourage older people to work longer.[58] Increasing employment and active participation of older people makes it more likely that they will be contributing to the economic well-being of society and less likely that they will require resources. These efforts are bolstered by

---

[52]   H Reece, 'Review: The Autonomy Myth: A Theory of Dependency' [2008] *Child and Family Law Quarterly* 109.

[53]   Ibid, 114.

[54]   A Hoff, *Tackling Poverty and Social Exclusion of Older People – Lessons from Europe* (Oxford Institute of Ageing 2008).

[55]   Ibid.

[56]   Ibid.

[57]   A Vlachantoni, 'Financial Inequality and Gender in Older People' (2012) 72 *Maturitas* 104–7.

[58]   T Maltby, 'Extending Working Lives? Employability, Workability and Better Quality Working Lives' (2011) 10 *Social Policy and Society* 1–10.

protection against age discrimination in employment.[59] An alternative is to improve state provision of benefits in old age, however given current economic problems that is an unrealistic option. Increasingly, insurance schemes are being investigated, with people being encouraged to insure against costs in old age. To be affordable such schemes typically require government assistance, for example by capping the cost of care that an individual may be expected to cover.[60]

4.1 Financial Order and Care Provision

Family law has to a limited extent recognised the costs of care of children through child support payments and payment of financial orders on divorce.[61] However, it has done relatively little to recognise the past and future costs of care of older people or vulnerable adults. Family law has used the law on child support and financial orders on divorce to ensure that where a relationship has led (or will lead) to unequal sharing of child care responsibilities, the financial burden of this is, at least to some extent, shared. However, it has done relatively little to take into account the burden of support for older relatives. Poverty in old age among women is particularly prevalent following divorce. The failure of courts or those negotiating on behalf of divorcing or separating couples to think about the consequences of the breakdown into retirement are significant contributors to this problem. While most jurisdictions have powers to require a sharing of pensions provisions or financial provision to cover old age, in practice, unless the couple is very wealthy or the pension is of considerable value, this is rarely used as an option.[62]

Another less popular response to poverty in old age is requiring adult children to support their aged parents if they are in need.[63] There is a widespread feeling that there is at least a moral obligation on adult children to provide some support for their infirm parents; however, it is hard to find a convincing basis for this sense of obligation. It could be

---

[59] J Herring, 'Age Discrimination and the Law: Forging the Way Ahead', in E Parry and S Tyson (eds), *Managing an Age Diverse Workforce* (Palgrave 2011).

[60] The issues are well discussed in A Dilnot, *Fairer Funding for All* (Department of Health 2011).

[61] J Herring, 'Why Financial Orders on Divorce should be Unfair' (2005) 19 *International Journal of Law Policy and the Family* 218.

[62] J Ginn and D Price, 'Do Divorced Women Catch Up in Pension Building?' (2002) 14 *Child and Family Law Quarterly* 157.

[63] See e.g. the discussion in J Herring, 'Together Forever? The Rights and Responsibilities of Adult Children and their Parents', in J Bridgeman, H Keating and C Lind (eds), *Responsibility, Law and the Family* (Ashgate 2008).

argued that there is a reciprocated obligation. Because parents provided for children in their vulnerability, children should support parents when parents become infirm. However, because care as a child is not accepted voluntarily by the child, it may be this argument is weaker. Another argument is that the obligation flows from the relationship that exists between the parties. That, however, would appear to suggest that where an adult has a poor relationship with a parent there is no obligation. There has even been a claim that there is an implied contract between children and parents that children will offer support in old age.

5. GRANDPARENTS

Grandparents are now the single most important source of pre-school child care after parents. One survey found that 44 per cent of children in the UK were receiving regular care from grandparents.[64] Over half of women in paid work with a child under five leave their child with the child's grandparents.[65] However, there is also evidence that older people, especially men, who divorce early on in life have weaker links with their families in old age.[66] Society has yet to see the full consequences of the increased rate of divorce.

It is not surprising that as the nature of families change this impacts on the role of grandparents.[67] The explanation for the increasing role of care by grandparents is a result of both rising levels of marital breakdown and, especially, increasing rates of employment among mothers. The expense, unreliability and guilt that can be associated with non-familial child care leads many mothers needing child care support to turn to their own mothers. This has led some commentators to suggest that the traditional nuclear family is being challenged by a three-generational model: child-mother-grandmother.[68]

---

[64] E Ferguson, B Maughan and J Golding, 'Which Children Receive Grandparental Care and what Effect does it Have?' (2008) 49 *Journal of Child Psychology and Psychiatry* 161.

[65] Social and Community Planning Research, *Women's Attitudes to Combining Paid Work with Family Life* (SCPR 2000).

[66] W Solomou, M Richards, F Huppert et al, 'Divorce, Current Marital Status and Well-being in an Elderly Population' (1998) 12 *International Journal of Law, Policy and the Family* 323.

[67] G Ochiltree, *The Changing Role of Grandparents* (Australian Family Relationships Clearing House 2006).

[68] G Dench and J Ogg, *Grandparenting in Britain: A Baseline Study* (Institute of Community Studies 2002).

As for the law of grandparents, the increasing role they are playing in children's lives has led to arguments that grandparents have rights. While some European countries have grandparents recognised as a legal category, their rights tend to be limited. In English law, for example, while grandparents are recognised as relatives[69] and thereby can make direct applications to courts for orders, they have no positive right to contact. Indeed, when it comes to an application for contact a grandparent is legally in the same position as any other adult in the country. Of course, where there is a close relationship between the child and grandparent, it will be the quality of the relationship, not the grandparent status, which will be key when the court comes to decide whether to make an order for contact.

Perhaps the strongest way of claiming that grandparents have rights of a grandparent would be by reference to article 8 of the ECHR, which protects the right to respect for family life.[70] In *Marckx v Belgium*[71] the European Court of Human Rights (ECtHR) confirmed that article 8 was not restricted to parents and children and 'includes at least the ties between near relatives, for instance those between grandparents and grandchildren, since such relatives may play a considerable part in family life'. For the tie to exist, there must be a fairly close relationship between the child and grandparent.[72] So doubtless there would be said to be family life if the child were living with her grandparents[73] or had regular contact with them.[74] In *L v Finland* the ECtHR stated:

> The Court recalls that the mutual enjoyment by parent and child, as well as by grandparent and child, of each other's company constitutes a fundamental element of family life.[75]

Of course, establishing the existence of family life will be only the first hurdle for any family life claim. Article 8(2) justifies an interference in the rights of grandparents where that is (inter alia) necessary in the interests of others. Kaganas and Piper argue that if the parents object to

---

[69]   Children Act 1989, s 105.
[70]   See the excellent discussion in F Kaganas and C Piper, 'Grandparents and Contact: *"Rights v Welfare"* Revisited' (2001) 15 *International Journal of Law Policy and the Family* 205.
[71]   13 June 1979, (App No. 6833/74).
[72]   *X, Y and Z v United Kingdom* [1997] 24 EHRR 143, para 52.
[73]   *X v Switzerland*, (1981) 24 DR 183, App No 8924/80 (10 March 1981).
[74]   *Price v United Kingdom* (1988) 55 DR 224. See also *Boyle v United Kingdom* (1994) 19 EHRR 179.
[75]   At para 101.

grandparental contact the case will be seen as involving a clash between the rights of grandparents and parents. They argue that in that event, the strong line of case law from the ECtHR on respecting parental authority[76] means that the rights of parents will win out. Harris et al agree, suggesting that in such a case the parents' 'right to control the personal relationships ... of their children' will win the day.[77] Despite the academic support for this view it is not beyond question. I have two reasons for suggesting that it is more difficult to predict how a human rights analysis would operate than academic commentators have suggested. First, in the analysis presented above the cases are treated as involving a clash between the rights of parents and grandparents. However, there are also the rights of the children to take into account. Indeed the ECtHR has held that the rights of children should be regarded as crucial. It may be argued that children, especially where they have a close relationship with their grandparents, have important rights that that relationship be retained, even if that is against the wishes of their parents.[78]

A major argument against explicitly granting grandparents more rights has been made by Gillian Douglas and Neil Ferguson.[79] They argue that in the clear majority of cases families are able to resolve appropriately issues surrounding relationships between grandparents and grandchildren following a separation. They are concerned that legal intervention is normally used not as a way of asserting grandparental rights, but rather as part of the battle between the mother and father. The general norm governing grandparent-grandchild relationships is that the grandparents respect the decisions of parents concerning the raising of children, including the issue of contact with grandparents. They are concerned that giving grandparents a more formal legal status will challenge that norm. They see no case for giving grandparents as a group special legal help in the process, over and above other people who may play a significant role in the child's life.

---

[76] E.g. *Nielsen v Denmark* (1989) 11 EHRR 175.

[77] D Harris, M O'Boyle and C Warbrick, *Law of the European Convention on Human Rights* (Butterworths 1995) 317.

[78] *Re B (A Child)* [2009] UKSC 5.

[79] G Douglas and N Ferguson 'The Role of Grandparents in Divorced Families' (2003) 17 *International Journal of Law Policy and the Family* 41.

6. ELDER ABUSE

Elder abuse has reached the position that domestic violence did several decades ago.[80] There is now an acceptance of the problem and that something needs to be done, but there is much dispute over what the correct response is. For too long it has been hidden and ignored.[81] Even now that it has been accepted as an issue requiring state attention, many European countries are still struggling to find the correct legal response.

In developing a legal response to elder abuse it will be argued that the starting point must be that older people have a fundamental human right to protection from abuse. That obliges the state to put in place legal and social structures to combat elder abuse, although as we will see there are dangers that the protective measures may themselves be abusive and may fail to give due weight to rights of autonomy.

Although this section will focus on the legal responses to elder abuse it must be recognised that the problem is caused by broader social attitudes towards older people and a range of societal practices. It is only in tackling these that elder abuse can be effectively challenged. As the Toronto Declaration on the Global Prevention of Elder Abuse puts it:

> Ultimately elder abuse will only be successfully prevented if a culture that nurtures intergenerational solidarity and rejects violence is developed.[82]

6.1 Definition

A whole chapter could be written on the correct definition of elder abuse. There is ample discussion elsewhere[83] and this section will be very brief. There is no standard definition of elder abuse.[84] The abuse of older people can take many forms. It can involve sexual abuse,[85] financial

---

[80] District Judge Marilyn Mornington, *Responding to Elder Abuse* (Age Concern 2004).

[81] House of Commons Health Committee, *Elder Abuse* (The Stationery Office, 2004) at 1.

[82] World Health Organisation, *The Toronto Declaration on the Prevention of Elder Abuse* (WHO 2002).

[83] See, for example, J Dixon, J Manthorpe, S Biggs, A Mowlam, R Tennant, A Tinker and C McCreadie, 'Defining Elder Mistreatment' (2010) 30 *Ageing and Society* 403.

[84] A Brammer and S Biggs, 'Defining Elder Abuse' (1998) 20 *Journal of Social Welfare and Family Law* 385.

[85] R Hawks, 'Grandparent Molesting: Sexual Abuse of Elderly Nursing Home Residents and its Prevention' (2006) 8 *Marquette Elder's Advisor* 159.

abuse, misuse of medication, physical abuse, neglect and humiliating behaviour.[86] It can be carried out by relatives, carers, friends or strangers.[87] As it covers such a wide range of behaviour it is unsurprising that a single definition cannot be agreed.[88] The World Health Organisation has adopted the following definition:[89]

> a single or repeated act or lack of appropriate action occurring within any relationship where there is an expectation of trust, which causes harm or distress to an older person.

A recent literature review looking at evidence of elder abuse around the world concluded that 6 per cent of older people had suffered significant abuse in the last month. 5.6 per cent of older couples had experienced physical violence in their relationships. 25 per cent of older people had suffered significant psychological abuse.[90] There can be no doubt that elder abuse is prevalent and a major blight on the lives of many older people.

6.2 ECHR Approach

I will use the rights as set out in the ECHR as the basis for my argument that elder abuse is a serious violation of a person's human rights.[91]

6.2.1 Article 2: The right of life

Article 2 not only prohibits the state from intentionally and unlawfully taking life, but also requires the state to take appropriate steps to safeguard the lives of people living within its jurisdiction.[92] This requires there to be effective criminal law to deter violent crimes and an effective mechanism for law enforcement. In some cases this extends to taking specific measures to protect individuals whose life is at risk at the hands

---

[86] House of Commons Health Committee, *Elder Abuse* (The Stationery Office 2004), at 1.

[87] C McCreadie, 'A Review of Research Outcomes in Elder Abuse' (2002) 4 *Journal of Adult Protection* 3.

[88] C McCreadie, *Elder Abuse: Update on Research* (Age Concern 1996).

[89] World Health Organisation, *The Toronto Declaration on the Prevention of Elder Abuse* (WHO 2002).

[90] C Cooper, A Selwood and G Livingston, 'Prevalence of Elder Abuse and Neglect: A Systematic Review' (2008) 37 *Age and Ageing* 151.

[91] S Choudhry and J Herring, 'Righting Domestic Violence' (2006) 20 *International Journal of Law, Policy and the Family* 95.

[92] *L.C.B. v the United Kingdom*, 9 June 1998, § 36, *Reports* 1998-III.

of another.[93] That obligation must be interpreted in such a way that the burden on the state is not disproportionate or impossible.[94]

6.2.2 Article 3: The right not to suffer torture and inhuman or degrading treatment

Serious elder abuse could constitute an infringement of the right to protection from inhuman or degrading treatment under article 3 of the ECHR:

> No one shall be subjected to torture or to inhuman or degrading treatment or punishment.

Of the three kinds of prohibited conduct torture is seen as worse than inhuman or degrading treatment.[95] The phrase 'inhuman treatment' in article 3 includes actual bodily harm or intense physical or mental suffering.[96] 'Degrading treatment' includes conduct that humiliates or debases an individual; or shows a lack of respect for, or diminishes, human dignity. It also includes conduct that arouses feelings of fear, anguish or inferiority capable of breaking an individual's moral and physical resistance.[97] Depression, learned helplessness and alienation, post-traumatic stress disorder, guilt and denial have been cited as resulting from elder abuse.[98] This suggests that an ongoing relationship in which the older person is subject to a series of incidents, which seen individually might appear minor, could amount to a breach of article 3. A lack of respect of a person's humanity can be included.[99]

Article 3 not only prohibits the state from inflicting torture or inhuman or degrading treatment on its citizens, but also requires the state to protect one citizen from torture or inhuman or degrading treatment at the hands of another.[100] A state will infringe an individual's rights under article 3 if it is aware that that person is suffering abuse at a sufficiently

---

[93] *Osman v the United Kingdom*, 28 October 1998, § 115, *Reports* 1998-VIII.

[94] *Opuz v Turkey* [2009] ECHR 33401/02.

[95] *Ilascu and others v Moldova and Russia* [GC], App No 48787/99 (8 July 2004), para 440.

[96] *Ireland v the United Kingdom* [1978] 2 EHRR 25.

[97] See *Valašinas v Lithuania* [2001] EHRR 479.

[98] R Wolf, 'Elder Abuse and Neglect: Causes and Consequences' (1997) 31 *Journal of Geriatric Psychiatry* 153.

[99] *Albert and Le Compte v. Belgium*, 10 February 1983, Series A, no. 58, para 22.

[100] *A v UK* [1998] 3 FCR 597.

high level at the hands of another and fails to take reasonable or adequate or effective steps to protect that individual.[101] There is a particular obligation on the state to protect the article 3 rights of vulnerable people, such as children.[102] The obligations imposed on the state include ensuring that there is an effective legal deterrent to protect victims from abuse; to ensure that there is proper legal investigation and prosecution of any infringement of individual rights; and where necessary to intervene and remove a victim from a position where she or he is experiencing conduct that is prohibited by article 3.[103] These obligations arise in cases of elder abuse, just as they do in cases of child abuse or domestic violence.

6.2.3   Article 8: The right to respect for private and family life

Included within the right to respect for private life, which is protected by article 8, is the right to bodily integrity. This in turn includes 'psychological integrity' and 'a right to personal development, and the right to establish and develop relationships with other human beings and the outside world'. Like article 3, article 8 has been interpreted to mean that not only must the state not infringe someone's bodily or psychological integrity, but also the state must ensure that one person's integrity is not interfered with at the hands of another. In other words it is not just a 'negative right' inhibiting state intrusion into citizen's private lives, it places 'positive obligations' on the state to intervene to protect individuals.[104] However, unlike article 3, this is a qualified right. It is permissible for the state to fail to respect an individual's right to respect for private life under article 8(1) if paragraph 2 is satisfied. So, if the level of abuse is not sufficient to engage article 3 but falls within article 8 then it is necessary to determine whether rights and interests of other parties justify an interference with the individual's article 8 rights. It would therefore be possible to make an argument that the rights of the abuser, or perhaps even the victim, justify the state in not intervening to prevent or remedy a breach of article 8.

There is a balance here between protecting the current autonomous wish of the victim, with the increase in autonomy they may experience if they were removed from the abuse. Many victims in these cases have

---

[101]   *E v UK* [2002] 3 FCR 700.

[102]   *A v UK* [1998] 3 FCR 597, para 20.

[103]   See S Choudhry and J Herring, *European Human Rights and Family Law* (Hart Publishing 2010), chs 8 and 9.

[104]   S Choudhry and J Herring, 'Domestic Violence and the Human Rights Act 1998: A New Means of Legal Intervention' [2007] *Public Law* 752.

conflicting wishes. They want to remain in the relationship, but they want the abuse to stop. In such a case it is not easy to determine what is promoting their autonomy. It is not possible to respect these two conflicting desires. I suggest that where the abuse is low-level, the infringement on autonomy in remaining in the relationship will be limited. John Williams[105] discusses a hypothetical case of a son stealing £10 from his mother now and then. There autonomy is only infringed in a small way by the abuse. If however the relationship consisted of persistent emotional abuse, the interference in her autonomy in removing her from the relationship may be less than allowing her to remain in it. It must be remembered that being in an abusive relationship is itself undermining of autonomy. Leaving a person who does not want to be protected to suffer abuse is not necessarily justified in the name of autonomy. Shortly I will set out a proposal as to how the law should balance the interests in well-being and autonomy.

6.2.4 Article 14: The right to protection from discrimination
Article 14 of the ECHR states:

> The enjoyment of the rights and freedoms set forth in this Convention shall be secured without discrimination on any ground such as sex, race, colour, language, religion, political or other opinion, national or social origin, association with a national minority, property, birth or other status.

Although age is not included in the list of prohibited grounds of discrimination, the words 'such as' indicates that this is not a closed list. Indeed, the ECtHR has shown itself willing to add to the list. It is generally accepted that age is included within the ambit of article 14.[106] The article is not a 'standalone' right and can only apply when one of the other rights in the convention is interfered with. In this context the argument can be made that a failure to provide an effective protection against elder abuse not only amounts to an interference in a person's article 3 or 8 rights, but does so in a way that also amounts to age discrimination. The argument would be that failure to have an effective legal response to elder abuse has a particular impact on older people and hence discriminates against them on the basis of age. The rights under

---

[105] J Williams, 'State Responsibility and the Abuse of Vulnerable Older People: Is there a Case for a Public Law to Protect Vulnerable Older People form Abuse', in J Bridgeman, H Keating and C Lind (eds) *Responsibility, Law and the Family* (Ashgate 2008).

[106] *Rutherford (No 2) v Secretary of State for Trade and Industry* [2006] UKHL 19.

article 14 are not absolute rights and interference with them can be justified if there are reasonable and objective grounds. However, the courts have been very reluctant to find a justification for discrimination.[107]

6.2.5 The implications of a rights-based approach

Adopting a rights-based approach will require the state to ensure that older people are protected from abuse.[108] This requires a clear set of duties on local authorities to investigate, intervene and protect older people who are being abused, or are at risk of abuse. This is reflected in the Council of Europe Convention on Preventing and Combating Violence against Women and Domestic Violence. For example, article 18 requires the parties to 'take the necessary legislative or other measures to protect all victims from any further acts of violence'. It is not enough simply to expect victims of elder abuse to apply for protection. Proactive responses are needed. Further, when considering how to respond to issues around elder abuse the court should put the rights to protection of elder abuse at the heart of their consideration.

7. CONCLUSION

The issues raised for older people in family law are significant. On the one hand older people can be sources of significant support, both practical and financial, in raising children. Their increasing role has led to calls that grandparents should be given a more official footing in family law, by being given grandparents' rights. On the other hand older family members can have complex financial, social and health needs. Traditionally the burden of caring for these has fallen on family members. This has caused significant disadvantage to women in particular and their work has gone unrecognised. This chapter has also considered the issue of elder abuse and argued that the European human rights framework requires an effective set of remedies to respond to this serious problem.

---

[107] For further discussion see Choudhry and Herring (n 103) ch 2.

[108] J Manthorpe, 'Local Responses to Elder Abuse: Building Effective Prevention Strategies', in A Wahidin and M Cain (eds), *Ageing, Crime and Society* (Willan 2006).

RECOMMENDATIONS FOR FURTHER READING

D Abrams, P Russell, C-M Vanclair and H Swift, *Ageism in Europe: Findings from the European Social Survey* (Age UK 2011).

S Choudhry and J Herring, 'Domestic Violence and the Human Rights Act 1998: A New Means of Legal Intervention' [2007] *Public Law* 752.

B Da Roit and B Le Bihan, 'Similar and yet so Different: Cash-For-Care in Six European Countries' Long-Term Care Policies' (2010) 88 *Millbank Quarterly* 286.

J-L Fernandez, J Forder, B Trukeschitz, M Rokosova and D McDaid, *How can European States Design Efficient, Equitable and Sustainable Funding Systems for Long-Term Care for Older People?* (WHO 2009).

C Glendinning, H Arksey, F.Tjadens, M Moree, N Moran, H Nies, *Care Provision within Families and its Socio-Economic Impact on Care Providers across the European Union* (University of York, 2009).

M Hartlapp, 'Deconstructing EU old age policy: Assessing the potential of soft OMCs and hard EU law' (2012) 16 *European Integration online Papers* 3.

J Herring, *Older People in Law and Society* (Oxford University Press 2010).

J Herring, *Caring and the Law* (Hart Publishing 2013).

R Rodrigues and A Schmidt, 'Expenditures for Long-Term Care At the Crossroads Between Family and State' (2010) 23 *Journal of Gerontopsychology and Geriatric Psychiatry* 189.

B Sloan, *Informal Carers and Private Law* (Hart Publishing 2012).

Index